RESILIENCE BEYOND REBELLION

RESILIENCE BEYOND REBELLION

How Today's Rebels Become
Tomorrow's Parties

Sherry Zaks

CORNELL UNIVERSITY PRESS **ITHACA AND LONDON**

Publication of this book was made possible with a grant from the University of Southern California.

First published 2025 by Cornell University Press

Library of Congress Cataloging-in-Publication Data

Names: Zaks, Sherry, 1984– author.
Title: Resilience beyond rebellion : how today's rebels become tomorrow's parties / Sherry Zaks.
Description: Ithaca : Cornell University Press, 2025. | Includes bibliographical references and index.
Identifiers: LCCN 2024045528 (print) | LCCN 2024045529 (ebook) | ISBN 9781501782473 (hardcover) | ISBN 9781501783357 (paperback) | ISBN 9781501782497 (epub) | ISBN 9781501782480 (pdf)
Subjects: LCSH: Frente Farabundo Martí para la Liberación Nacional. | Political leadership—El Salvador—History—20th century. | Organizational sociology. | El Salvador—Politics and government—1992– | El Salvador—History—Civil War, 1979–1992. | El Salvador—Politics and government—1979–1992.
Classification: LCC JL1579.A54 Z35 20 (print) | LCC JL1579.A54 (ebook) | DDC 302.3/50972840904—dc23/eng/20250225
LC record available at https://lccn.loc.gov/2024045528
LC ebook record available at https://lccn.loc.gov/2024045529

For Evan

Contents

Acknowledgments

In every way, this book is about traversing the delicate tightrope between change and continuity. But if there's one thing that never changes, it's my love of a good parallelism.

Change

This book is the culmination of a long and twisting journey. It has found a home at many institutions. It has found readers in people who study the same thing as me and people who have never studied political science a day in their lives. And it has changed for the better at every step along the way. My promise is to spend the rest of my career paying forward the generosity and engagement that so many have shown me.

To its core, this book is representative of my own academic transformation. I owe so much of that transformation to the people who knew just how to push me. At very different points, Rich Orgera and Helen Delfeld challenged me in a way that taught me how to expect—and get—more from myself. I am eternally grateful for their mentorship and lifelong friendship. In defiance of every progress report I received in grade school, I hope this book is evidence that I have finally worked to potential.

The project began at the University of California, Berkeley under the influence of a motley crew who, together, represent five of the best decisions I've made in my career thus far. David Collier and I met in 2010 when I baked a cake in the shape of one of his books. Emails about that cake turned into conversations about methods, meetings in Syracuse and Berkeley, and ultimately a push to leave my current institution. David set me on an intellectual path that changed my work and life for the better in more ways than I can count. I'm so excited to finally add this last student book to his shelf.

The first time I met Ron Hassner, our thirty-minute meeting lasted two and a half hours. Thirteen years later, we have still not managed to end meetings on time, and I hope we never do. In Ron, I found a mentor, an inspiration, and a friend. I never left Ron's office without new insights and a face sore from laughter. Ron pushed the hardest for a single and underrepresented standard: that my work never be boring. More than anything, I hope this book meets his exacting standards. If it doesn't, I hope it at least makes it down a Disneyland Log Flume ride.

Leo Arriola accidentally (and repeatedly) referred to this project as "your book" when it was in its earliest stages. Somehow both a ruthless and compassionate pragmatist, Leo always pushed my work to be analytically rigorous and clearly presented. His amazing support and feedback is a huge part of the reason why those earliest ideas are finally between covers.

Thirteen years ago, I walked into Heather Haveman's office and said, "I want to do a project using organizational theory to model rebel-to-party transformation, but I've never studied organizational sociology and I need a bullshit detector." Her full response was, "Sounds fun, I'm in." And she was. In June of 2017, she handed me a printed and line-edited copy of my first draft. Her comments, which are (still) sitting next to me as I write this in 2024, made this project a better book than it ever would have been.

Ruth Collier's instruction was likely the single most influential part of my training. A substantive chameleon, Ruth can bring the highest standards of conceptual, logical, and analytic rigor to every project that crosses her desk. My work and my writing are immeasurably better because of her. On this point, I would be remiss not to also extend my deepest gratitude to every member of every PS 290 seminar I attended.

After leaving Berkeley, this book first found a home at Dartmouth College's Dickey Center for International Understanding. Despite being rather far afield from the specialties represented among the faculty, I received invaluable feedback from Stephen Brooks, Nelson Kasfir, Jennifer Lind, Katy Powers, and William Wohlforth. Then in 2018 and again in 2024, this book—with me in tow—found a home at Stanford University's Center for International Security and Cooperation (CISAC). I am so grateful to Martha Crenshaw, Lynn Eden, Scott Sagan, Ken Schultz, and Harold Trinkunas for their mentorship over the years. My two CISAC cohorts represent the Platonic ideal of intellectual community. Fiona Cunningham, Erik Lin-Greenberg, Chantell Murphy, Rhiannon Neilsen, Caleb Pomeroy, and Lindsay Rand are amazing colleagues who have become lifelong friends. And, as promised, a special shout out to Maxime, who made me procrastinate writing this book to sew a button back on his shirt.

At the University of Southern California, when the book and I emerged from lockdown, the Center for International Studies coordinated a book workshop that remains one of the highlights of my career. My deepest gratitude goes to three academic role models—Anna Grzymala-Busse, Reyko Huang, and Paul Staniland—who flew out to L.A. armed with some of the most engaged and astute feedback I've ever received on any project. I am also so grateful to the many

USC colleagues who contributed to this book through participation in my workshop, research assistance, and the casual conversations that often make all the difference: Jeb Barnes, Chlöe Bernadaux, Laura Breen, Allison Hartnett, Gerry Munck, Jose Muzquiz, Tine Paulsen, Brian Rathbun, Stephen Schick, Jess Walker, and Carol Wise.

This book found a forever home at Cornell University Press with Jackie Teoh. Comparing my experience with Jackie to other publishing stories is like finding a Pixar movie stuffed in a collection of Grimm's fairy tales. She is somehow a jack of all trades and a master of them as well. Jackie is a brilliant editor, a nuanced marketer, and a deeply compassionate human with excellent taste in food. Somehow, even in this moment, I am excited to start on book 2 just to do it all over again.

Continuity

A core premise of the book is that without an anchor, change can be as damaging as it is refreshing. Anchoring the moves, the affiliations, the different job titles, and the endless drafts has been the most amazing community of people I could hope for. Adequately thanking everyone who has been there for me through this process is somehow more daunting than writing the book ever was. First and foremost, thanks to my family who has had to hear of nothing but book panic and LA traffic for the better (or worse) part of five years.

One morning in 2013, Sarah Parkinson sent me a link to a book with the following text: "Hey, I just finished this book. It's weird and technical; I think you'll love it." The book was John F. Padgett and Walter W. Powell's *The Emergence of Organizations and Markets*. It was my first exposure to organizational sociology. I do not know what book I would have written were it not for that moment, but it would have been less good and far less enjoyable. Like the book she handed me that day, my conversations with Sarah over the years changed the way I think about the political world for the better. I am profoundly grateful for every role she has played in my life—friend, colleague, coauthor, mentor, and the fiercest advocate—and especially grateful for her teaching me how important roles are in the first place.

I owe an immeasurable debt to all of my friends who, during every crisis, provided reassurance that I was, in fact, working to potential (or who made me laugh enough to forget to panic about it): Noam Bleiweiss, Jenn Cryer, Rex Douglass, Dani Gilbert, Laura Jakli, Billy Lezra, Seth Masket, Liz Ortiz, Libby & Pop Ortiz, Ali Puente-Douglass, Ian Smith (no, not that one), Kai Thaler, Nancy Wadsworth, Jack Wolflink, and the entire crew at Deadly Nerd Gym. Hilary

Matfess and Meg Guliford make me laugh as often as they make me think. I am so lucky to have them as colleagues and friends. Sarah Orsborn's comments made the book infinitely better and our absolutely ridiculous antics kept me going. Pogo, a true Swiss-army human, commented on my work with forensic precision, built me a desk to incorporate their comments, and helped plan a party to celebrate my sending it off.

As I was rounding the corner to the book's first submission, Alena Wolflink read and commented on the entire manuscript in seventy-two hours. While that stint of generosity was motivated in part by the promise of a homemade five-course Indian feast, she has since read every review and every new draft without commensurate bribery. Alena's capacity for intellectual engagement and her endless generosity with those skills are two of countless reasons I am so lucky to have her in my life. I cannot wait to make this book into a cake, but before that, I promise to finally bake one just for her.

Every word of this book (except for any time I use the word "upon," sorry) is dedicated to my wife, Evan Ramzipoor. If there is one relationship that embodies the tightrope between change and continuity, it is my marriage. For ten years—spanning five houses, four institutional affiliations, three states, two cross-country moves, and one tenure clock—Evan and I have woken up and written together side by side. In the easiest moments, I got to share the archival finds that made me yelp and the sentences that made me proud. In the hardest moments, I got to look over and know that the most brilliant person I have ever met chooses to be next to me. And regardless of which moments took up the most space on a given day, I would emerge from my book to find a story waiting for me. On many days, my only crumb of motivation was the promise of guiltlessly immersing myself in the adventures that press at Evan's mind until they are released onto paper.

In all the interstitial moments, we made our own stories: traveling, eating, climbing, punching, more eating, and hiding small animals around the house for the other to find. I could double the length of the manuscript and only scratch the surface of everything Evan has done for me to make this book possible. I'd have to double it again to catalog everything they've done to make me feel loved, worthy, and even remotely sane. Ev, it's not that I couldn't have done this without you; but as with most things in life, I wouldn't want to.

Abbreviations

ANDES	Asociación Nacional de Educadores Salvadorenos (National Association of Salvadoran Educators)
BPR	Bloque Popular Revolucionario (Popular Revolutionary Bloc)
CEB	*comunidades eclesiales de base* (Christian base communities)
CG	Comandancia General (General Command)
ERP	Ejercito Revolucionario del Pueblo (People's Revolutionary Army)
FARC	Fuerzas Armadas Revolucionarias de Colombia (Revolutionary Armed Forces of Colombia)
FDR	Frente Democratico Revolucionario (Revolutionary Democratic Front)
FMLN	Farabundo Martí Liberación Nacional (Farabundo Martí National Liberation Front)
FPL	Fuerzas Populares de Liberación (Popular Liberation Forces)
PCS	Partido Comunista de El Salvador (Communist Party of El Salvador)
PRTC	Partido Revolucionario de Trabajadores Centroamericanos (Central American Workers' Revolutionary Party)
RN	Resistencia Nacional (National Resistance)

RESILIENCE BEYOND REBELLION

TRADING BULLETS FOR BALLOTS

It is easier to start a war than to end it.

—Gabriel García Márquez, *One Hundred Years of Solitude*

Confronted with life's hardships, some people snap, and others snap back.

—Diane Coutu, 2002

In January 1992, after twelve years of fighting in the Salvadoran Civil War, the Farabundo Martí National Liberation Front (FMLN; Farabundo Martí Liberación Nacional) signed a ceasefire and power-sharing agreement with the country's central government. The Chapúltepec Peace Accords included a clause unorthodox for their time: if the FMLN demobilized its combatants, it could form a political party and run both legislative and presidential candidates in the 1994 elections. In spite of a few hitches, the FMLN was officially registered just months after the accords were signed. From the outside, the next eighteen months looked like a whirlwind as the FMLN morphed from a battle-hardened insurgency into a skilled political party. The group held rallies, ran campaigns, mobilized constituents, and won parliamentary seats under the same name—and the same flag—it used in the war. To date, the FMLN has persisted as one of the central parties in Salvadoran politics.

A very different story emerges, however, if we turn to militant organizations in Sierra Leone, Colombia, Turkey, and elsewhere. Groups like the Revolutionary United Front (RUF; Sierra Leone) and the Ejército Popular de Liberación (EPL; Colombia) were presented with nearly identical power-sharing opportunities, but their parties barely got off the ground. While the FMLN managed to secure votes from some of its wartime rivals, the RUF, for instance, could not even count on its own members to show up at the polls.[1]

In light of conventional understandings of rebellion, the failures should be the unsurprising cases. Yet, in the face of individual, organizational, and environmental obstacles to forging a political party out of an ebbing rebellion, nearly 50 percent of militant groups given the opportunity to transition at the end of war manage to do it successfully. The divergent trajectories of rebel successor parties raise the question at the heart of this book: Why are some militant organizations able to seamlessly transform into political parties on the heels of war while others die trying?

To explain how rebel groups survive the existential risks that accompany the electoral opportunities, this book offers a new theory of rebel-to-party transformation that places the militant organization at the center of the analysis. At its core, rebel-to-party transformation is an organizational phenomenon. It involves taking a militant organization—a group with a preexisting set of roles, relations between them, institutions governing their behavior, and goals[2]—and transforming it into an organization of a fundamentally different type, and then demanding that it function in a very different environment. Success and failure happen at the organizational level. Building a theory that explains both the process and prospects of successful transformation demands a dedicated organizational approach.

Drawing on insights from organizational sociology, I develop a new framework for modeling the inception, structure, and transformation of militant groups. I argue that the answer to the book's core question lies in the surprising diversity of noncombat structures built during conflict. Specifically, some rebel groups have what I call *proto-party structures*: wartime subdivisions staffed with experienced individuals who work together performing tasks relevant to electoral politics. Governance wings, social service wings, and political-messaging wings carry out sophisticated political tasks during war that mirror the core functions of party organizations. Beyond providing tangible skills that translate into the electoral arena, proto-party structures also provide a source of stability—anchoring rebel organizations during a period of intense disruption. Crucially, however, not all rebel groups have them. Leveraging qualitative evidence from El Salvador and a novel global dataset of rebel successor parties, I show that wartime organizational structures hold the key to rebel-to-party success.

Current Explanations, Continuing Puzzles

The end of the Cold War marked a watershed for domestic conflict resolution. As funding for proxy wars dried up overnight, provisions allowing rebel groups to participate in elections were a quick and reliable way to entice belligerents to the negotiating table. The stakes were clear. Countries recovering from civil conflict usually have a bleak prognosis. They face an uphill battle of healing from collective trauma, navigating the legal and interpersonal dynamics of reintegrating former combatants and wartime refugees, rebuilding damaged infrastructure, and, perhaps most pressingly, dealing with the risk of conflict resurgence.[3] Even in the presence of robust demobilization programs, ex-rebels not only retain close social ties but also frequently continue acting in an organizational capacity "outside the institutional channels of the state," thereby increasing the risk of remobilization.[4]

Rebel-to-party transition promises to mitigate these risks. The logic is straightforward: giving former rebels the opportunity to participate in electoral politics and voice dissent through *legal* channels should reduce the likelihood that they express dissent through violent ones. Scholars have demonstrated that completed rebel-to-party transitions are associated with postwar stability, development, and democratization.[5] The question is, how do the rebels do it?

Answering this question is difficult because it demands that we rethink what we're studying and how we're studying it. First, the rebel-to-party process is actually two outcomes rolled into one phenomenon.[6] On the one hand, rebel groups undergo an internal *transformation*: a set of structural and institutional changes needed to forge a party organization. On the other hand, rebel groups undergo an external *transition*: a shift toward operating in a new (electoral) environment. Building a party organization and participating in electoral politics are related, but they capture different processes, entail different challenges, and have different observable indicators. Understanding the formation and performance of rebel successor parties demands a thorough explanation of both outcomes. Yet, the balance of inquiry is tipped heavily toward explaining transition, while the process of organizational transformation remains elusive.

From descriptive accounts of the process to theories explaining electoral participation, existing research has made critical inroads into a multifaceted phenomenon. Taken together, descriptions of the rebel-to-party process make up an extensive end-of-war to-do list for militant groups to complete as they look ahead to electoral politics: (1) dismantle combat units, (2) reformulate decision-making structures, (3) restructure finances, (4) recruit "competent candidates for public office," (5) build party structures, and (6) adapt to the postconflict environment.[7] Accordingly, transformation unfolds by a process of structural replacement—building party structures to replace decommissioned combat units[8]—spearheaded by elites who are simultaneously renegotiating their command structure to more closely resemble that of a political party.

The intuitiveness of structural replacement masks the scope of its omissions. To build party structures, we must first ask, what are party structures? And, for that matter, what are rebel structures? Even a rudimentary description of organizational change demands an inventory of the new and discarded subdivisions of the group, yet the content of "party structures" remains unspecified. Without it, arguing that rebels transform by "building party structures" is tantamount to explaining that metamorphosis proceeds by "building butterfly structures." It may be technically true, but it is analytically unhelpful.

Even if we were to fully specify party structures, we would find that the structural replacement hypothesis buckles under scrutiny.[9] Changes to a group's structure are "rare and costly" and the more extensive the change, the more it "subjects the organization to a greatly increased risk of death."[10] According to organizational theorists, nearly every item on the to-do list—for example, "dismantling one structure and building another," replacing leadership from the outside, and "reformulating established power systems"—is a direct threat to both organizational stability and the capacity to adapt to changing environments.[11] Consequently, the first four items on the list are not only difficult on their own, but succeeding at them would make the fifth item even less attainable.

Lastly, existing descriptions place an undue emphasis on leaders' agency over the process. In some descriptions, leaders have the power not only to decide whether their organizations adapt but also to strategically time transformation to capitalize on recent military successes.[12] However, treating elites as the sole arbiters of transformation is problematic because it exclusively locates organizational challenges in the upper echelons of the rebellion without defining the scope of elites or the bounds of agency. While rebel leaders play important roles, reducing transformation to elite negotiations quickly falls into the trap of what Paul Staniland calls "unrealistic voluntarism": that leaders could effect change "if only they put enough thought or effort into it."[13] Broadly, we should be skeptical of emphasizing elite agency absent organizational constraints.[14]

In sum, existing accounts of the transformation process underestimate how brittle rebel groups can be. They assume too easily that rebel-to-party transformation can truly proceed—and succeed—by completely refashioning the organization in the interlude between the last bullet and the first ballot. By not acknowledging the existential risks of major organizational overhauls we are liable to overlook what organizations need to insulate themselves against collapse.

Moving beyond description, current approaches to explaining transformation and electoral participation can be disaggregated by the locus of their effects: institutional context, demand-side explanations, and supply-side explanations. The first branch of theories examines whether electoral participation provisions in negotiated settlements facilitate transition either by providing a smooth path to electoral politics or by incentivizing third parties to monitor elections.[15] Others draw on the party-systems literature arguing that different electoral institutions affect the barriers to entry for new parties.[16] The exogenous obstacles (and advantages) that rebels face are indispensable considerations as they attempt to transform and pivot into electoral politics. However, without considering the internal obstacles, these theories are unable to parse success from failure.

Demand-side explanations turn their attention to the factors driving voter mobilization. Some argue that popular support during the war means former rebels enter the electoral arena with a built-in constituency.[17] More recently, Sarah Daly paved a new path aimed at explaining why belligerents with violent wartime legacies are nonetheless able to secure an ample vote share on election day. She theorizes that voters are equally likely to mobilize out of fear of conflict resurgence as they are out of policy preferences.[18] Since the stakes of rebel-to-party transition hinge on the party's long-term political integration, explaining voter mobilization is a crucial piece of the puzzle. However, demand-side explanations ask a subtly different question that makes a large analytic difference. Asking what incentivizes people to vote for a rebel successor party assumes that party consolidation has already happened. Accounting for success and failure in party formation is analytically prior to demand-side explanations of electoral victories.

By specifying wartime organizational traits that affect postwar party success, supply-side theories should come the closest to getting traction on organizational dynamics. Scholars in this tradition posit five explanations: (1) prewar party experience, (2) centralization and cohesion in the organization, (3) the presence of "convertible capabilities," (4) wartime territorial control, and (5) resource endowments.[19] When scrutinized through an organizational lens, however, each trait raises questions that compromise its theoretical viability.

The prewar party hypothesis is intuitive: if you were a party before, all you have to do is do it again. But is party politics really just like riding a bicycle? If the average conflict lasts ten years, will prewar electoral skills be as sharp when the war ends as they were going in? Much like playing an instrument or writing in cursive, "organizations remember by doing," and the corollary (sadly for former parties and my jazz saxophone days) is that skills "decay with disuse."[20] This theory lacks a clear transmission mechanism whereby party-relevant skills are kept intact and deployable at a moment's notice.

Other hypotheses draw directly on organizational concepts, but they do so without acknowledging some sticky countervailing effects. Centralization, bureaucratization, and cohesion are great if the goal is to avoid fragmentation at all costs, yet they quickly become liabilities if the goal is to swiftly adapt to a changing environment. In practice, bureaucracy and centralization are a double-edged sword: what organizations gain in effective control, they sacrifice in flexibility.[21] Steven Levitsky drew attention to this apparent paradox in party dynamics when finding that, in Argentina, the Justicialist Party's capacity for adaptation was primarily attributable to its weak institutionalization and decentralized structure.[22]

Convertible capabilities, territorial control, and "bush bureaucracies" have distinct referents but operate through the same demand-side mechanism: each represents a capacity to mobilize wartime supporters into postwar voters.[23] This branch of theories further illuminates shortcomings of demand-side explanations. Though wartime support may well predict postwar willingness to vote for the rebel successor party, it does not explain their ability to cast votes come election day. Voter mobilization requires registration (which itself requires official identification and basic literacy), knowledge of election timing, transportation to the polls, and a measure of confidence in the safety of showing up and voting for the party they want in office. Without accounting for the nascent party's organizational capacity to assist in the logistical undertakings required to convert supporters into voters, demand-side theories will only ever explain voter *galvanization*, not voter *mobilization*.

Last, although access to sufficient resources is an incontrovertible factor in rebel-to-party success, the value of resources is presented as organizationally invariant. However, not all organizations have equal capacity to efficiently deploy resources or the desire to allocate them in the same way. Rather, as Michael T. Hannan and John Freeman observe, "the politics of resource allocation" prevent some organizations from quickly redirecting resources in response to upheavals.[24] As such, theorizing about resources in the absence of structural mediators will overlook this critical source of variation in whether more resources can make the rebel-to-party difference.[25] As with the other explanations, we can get more precise traction on the outcome when we consider explanations like resource endowments through an organizational lens.[26] Crucially, rebels understand the interplay between resources and organization. An FMLN analyst demonstrates this reasoning explicitly: "For some time, it has been possible to organize groups of military operatives in each base, but mostly in name only. Until today, these groups have not operated. The causes? Weakness in the organization, and lack of shoes."[27]

From the outside, electoral participation provisions seem like winning the postconflict jackpot: former rebels are not only granted amnesty but also given influence over the future of the country for which they ostensibly fought. From the inside, however, the end of war and demand for immediate restructuring is a massive shock to the organization.[28] Even for mature organizations with abundant resources, undergoing extensive internal changes while learning how to function in a new environment poses severe existential threats. Hannan and Freeman offer a quip that both encapsulates and complicates the phenomenon: "failing churches do not become retail stores."[29] But in the case of rebel-to-party transformation, they sort of do. What we need then is an approach suited to modeling both outcomes—and the actors at the heart of them.

Organizational Approach and Theory of Rebel Successor Party Formation

Angelo Panebianco began his treatise on political parties by noting that "most contemporary analyses resist studying parties for what they obviously are: organizations." Thirty years later, Sarah E. Parkinson and Sherry Zaks argued that the same is true for many of their precursors.[30] This is not to say that political scientists ignore organizations.[31] In recent years, conflict scholars have leveraged organizational traits to explain everything from patterns of violence and restraint to wartime resilience to fragmentation to conflict resurgence and even rebel-to-party transformation.[32] Yet, our existing toolkit is systematically incomplete. We have imported a limited vocabulary of traits capable of describing the shape of organizational structures (e.g., centralized, hierarchical, fragmented), but we lack the vocabulary to describe the content of those structures or trace the other implications of those traits. The result is a good intuition served by inadequate tools.

A central goal of this book is thus to offer a corrective and a path forward by building a theory of rebel-to-party transformation on organizational foundations. Doing so is not simply a matter of adding new concepts to the mix; rather, it entails recognizing that organizations behave in unique ways, are bound by unique constraints, and are vulnerable to unique risks—all of which must be baked into our theories. Building an organizational theory of the rebel-to-party process involves three conceptual and analytic moves: recasting the outcomes of interest in organizational terms, expanding our language for describing and theorizing about the organizational structures that affect the outcome, and examining the full scope of traits that affect the group's operations, dynamics, and potential.

First, consider the outcome. Rebel-to-party transformation involves taking an organization with a structure optimized to wage war and turning it into an organization capable of running campaigns, winning elections, and governing once in office. In organizational terms, this outcome is fundamentally a puzzle about how groups execute a massive organizational change. Providing a veritable blueprint for theory building and analysis, the organizational literature identifies four questions a comprehensive theory of change must answer: What changes?

How does the process of change unfold? What is the context of change? And what traits allow some organizations to survive the overhaul?[33]

The second step examines how structure affects the prospects for change. When it comes to surviving the risks of transformation, scholars agree that change is easier to the extent that groups have structures with "preexisting competencies" relevant to their post-transformation needs.[34] Put simply, rebel-to-party transformation will be less difficult if some parts of the organization are as useful for being parties as they were for being rebels. Assessing the variety of competencies demands an expanded understanding of rebel organizational structure. Namely, specifying the roles and subdivisions present in an organization tells us the variety of skills the group has at its disposal. From there, it is not a far leap to imagine the importance of a nuanced structural inventory when that same organization has to suddenly perform a different set of tasks.

The irony is that the necessary structural insights are prominent in the conflict literature, we just need an organizational lens to see them. Specifically, the literature on rebel governance is built on the observation that rebels engage in diverse behaviors beyond the combat realm. Rebels *govern* civilians; they *provide* social services; they *distribute* propaganda.[35] Undergirding these behaviors, however, are robust structures that make the governing, provisions, and distribution possible. Taking an organizational approach enables us to take critical insights about what rebels *do* and translate them into insights about what rebels *are*.

Finally, groups will be more likely to survive major overhauls if they have traits conducive to resilience. Resilience describes an organization's capacity to survive in the face of major shocks. Of course, militant groups operate in volatile environments, but the shocks of war are usually short-lived: lost battles or augmented counterinsurgency operations. Conflict scholars who have adopted resilience frameworks usually do so to explain rebels' capacity to weather these temporary shocks of war as they continue the fight.[36] In other words, the literature as it stands is well equipped to explain resilience *within* rebellion. Not all shocks, however, are temporary. An end to the conflict and the opportunity to transform into a political party permanently change the demands placed on the organization. As such, rebel groups must not only be able to weather the shock but also fundamentally alter their structure to function under the new order. The formidable tasks and risks associated with this disruption demand a theoretical framework capable of explaining resilience *beyond* rebellion—one that captures both the capacity for survival and the process of transformation.

The Content of Change: Rebel vs. Party Structures

The first part of the theory addresses the content of change: what about the organization changes and what traits make it possible? Taking an organizational approach allows me to specify what parties need, what rebels have, and why some rebel groups are better poised to close that gap than others. Some—though not all—rebel groups build structures during war that mirror the core structures of party organizations. These proto-party structures hold the key to successful transformation. Subdivisions dedicated to governance, political messaging, and social service provision imbue militant organizations with relevant skills, expertise, and organizational routines that meet the demands of electoral politics. When they exist alongside traits like self-reflection and flexibility, these structures enable rebel groups to more effectively pivot from the battlefield to the campaign trail than their more homogeneous counterparts. However, militant groups vary considerably in the number of proto-party structures they build. To foreshadow the dataset I constructed to test the theory statistically, figure 0.1 depicts the range of proto-party diversity across rebellions. Along with other wartime traits that facilitate adaptation and resilience, proto-party structures (or the absence thereof) form the foundation of my theory.

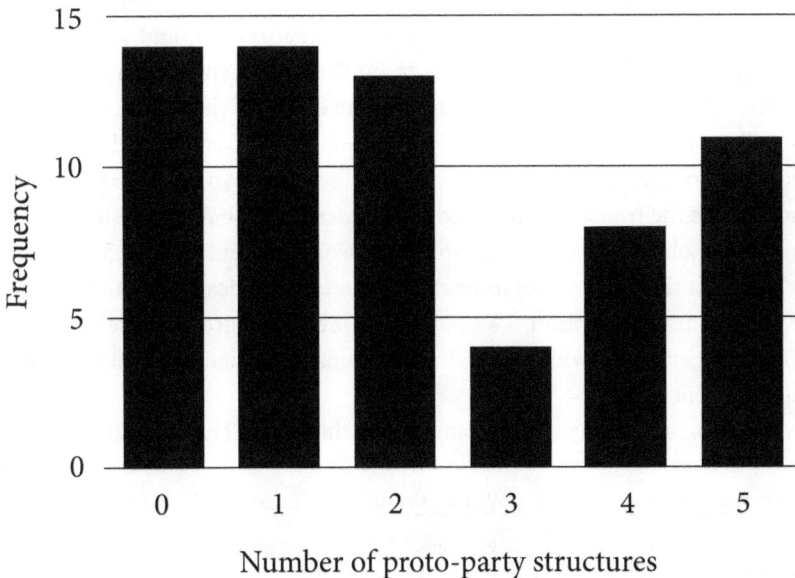

FIGURE 0.1. Distribution of proto-party structures across rebellions

The Process of Change: Reconstruction vs. Repurposing

Explaining organizational change demands more than just a more comprehensive inventory of rebel and party structures. How do you actually build a party out of the pieces of rebels? The answer is, it depends. Different structural legacies give rise to different processes of party formation. Crucially, however, they are not equally likely to work. Groups that end the war with relatively homogeneous organizations—comprising structures dedicated primarily to combat and logistics—will have no option but to build a party from scratch. Recall, however, that rebuilding an organization from the ground up is difficult and destabilizing.

By contrast, groups that end the war with proto-party structures intact face a much less treacherous path to change. Beyond accruing relevant experience throughout the war, rebel groups that include proto-party structures are able to transform by redirecting resources through established channels to augment existing subdivisions staffed with experienced personnel. For these groups, the transformation process unfolds by repurposing what they already have rather than building, staffing, and integrating new structures from the ground up. While organizational change is never simple, forging a party by repurposing existing resources is not only more efficient but also less destabilizing than gutting the organization and building a new one in its place.

These depictions, of course, represent the extremes in party building. Rarely will groups need to entirely gut the organization, and just as rarely will they have a built-in party ready to hit the campaign trail on day one. In reality, militant organizations will have some divisions that retain their utility as well as gaps that demand rapid construction. Thus, we should expect to see some combination, but the more a rebellion can lean on repurposing, the more stable the transformation and the greater the probability of success. The theoretical objective is not to simplify the world beyond realism, but instead to highlight that differences in wartime structures critically affect the process of postwar transformation. The extent to which rebel groups have embedded skills is the extent to which their organizations are structurally anchored during turbulent times.

Figure 0.2 summarizes the organizational theory of transformation.

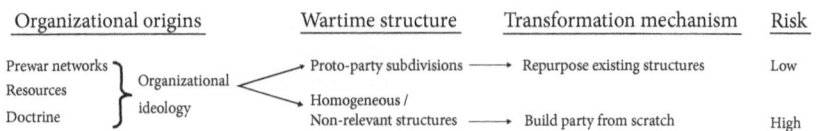

Organizational origins		Wartime structure	Transformation mechanism	Risk
Prewar networks	Organizational ideology	Proto-party subdivisions →	Repurpose existing structures	Low
Resources		Homogeneous /		
Doctrine		Non-relevant structures →	Build party from scratch	High

FIGURE 0.2. Overview of theory

The Context of Change: Transition to Electoral Politics

Organizational transformation is only half of the rebel-to-party battle. After surviving the end of war, the demobilization process, and the internal dynamics of party building, rebel successor parties still have a monstrous task ahead: convince people that they are worth voting for.[37] Since the stakes of transition hinge on political integration of the rebel successor party, a comprehensive theory must explain not just how parties form, but why some parties stick. The final part of the theory explains how wartime structures can—and do—translate into voter mobilization and long-term integration.

Taking an organizational lens to insights from the rebel governance literature is instructive here as well. Organizations with subdivisions dedicated to governance, local administration, and service provision enter the electoral arena having already forged the type of political linkages conducive to galvanizing potential voters.[38] Beyond currying favor with local populations during the war, these structures confer the skills and organizational capacity to convert wartime support into postwar votes. Specifically, civilian-facing structures built during war are prime candidates for repurposing to manage the heavy logistical lift of voter registration and mobilization.

Here I summarize the testable propositions from the theory:

- Rebel organizations articulate clear organizational ideologies, which reliably predict their wartime organizational structures and priorities.
- Groups whose organizational ideologies center on the importance of local engagement are more likely to build proto-party structures than those whose ideologies focus on battle readiness and militancy.
- Militant organizations that end the war with proto-party structures intact will transform by repurposing existing structures.
- Militant organizations that end the war with homogeneous organizations (or structures that do not bring "portable skills") will transform by building party structures anew.
- Militant groups with legacies of organizational flexibility and self-reflection will be more likely to survive transformation.
- Rebel groups with proto-party legacies are more likely to both successfully transform into parties and exhibit electoral longevity when they enter the party system.

Assumptions

The organizational theory of transformation accounts for each stage in the rebel-to-party process. As with any theory, it is built on a few core assumptions that must hold for it to accurately describe the formation, consolidation, and integration of rebel successor parties. First, I have to demonstrate that proto-party structures are not epiphenomenal to the outcome. In other words, if some prior (antecedent) condition shapes both the wartime structures and rebel-to-party success, then organizational structures may be incidentally correlated with the outcome, but not consequential. To address this issue, I precede the rebel-to-party theory by first accounting for the origins of wartime organizational structures. In addition to explaining the source of the theory's key explanatory variable, this analysis directly addresses whether the factors purported to influence structure—prewar networks, resources, ideology—also account for transformation.

Building on prior work, I argue that prewar networks, resources, and ideology play critical organizational roles, but only insofar as they are filtered through the organizational ideology of rebellion. Organizational ideology affords new insight into why groups that subscribe to identical doctrines nonetheless have distinct beliefs about what rebellion entails on the ground and exhibit different capacities to bring that rebellion to life. Through this lens, prewar networks, resources, and doctrine combine in predictable ways to shape the structures groups build in service of their goals, but they are inextricable from the organizational dynamics that mediate them. I test this theory (and the underlying assumption) in chapter 2 and demonstrate that no one factor is independently sufficient to explain wartime structure or postwar transformation.

Second, for proto-party structures to operate via the mechanism I propose, I must find evidence of dedicated structures—rather than just behaviors or individual skills. Otherwise, the specific utility of organizational subdivisions is less consequential than I anticipate. Moreover, groups must exhibit significant variation in proto-party structures from one insurgency to the next. If all groups (or no groups) invest resources into building robust noncombat subdivisions during conflict, then we must look elsewhere to get traction on how to parse rebel-to-party success from failure. In chapter 3, I elaborate on the logic of why dedicated subdivisions are necessary for the theory to hold, and throughout the book I provide both qualitative and quantitative evidence illustrating the extent and variation of these structures.

Third, not only must the relevant structures persist until the end of war, but groups must also exhibit plausible "transmission mechanism."[39] If, alternately, groups emerge with proto-party structures, but the structures wither as the war progresses, then these structures are not an enduring organizational legacy with the capacity to influence postconflict politics. Similarly, if, at the end of war, skilled rebels "jump ship" to find better jobs, then these structures are significantly less likely to be converted into competent subdivisions in the new party.

Fourth, and perhaps most importantly, rebels must understand the organizational value of proto-party structures. While the theory does not require that rebels intentionally build structures with future transformation in mind, it does demand evidence that the composition, diversity, and evolution of their organizations occupy a central role in wartime strategy. Subsequently, those leading the transformation must indicate that they understand the postwar utility of wartime structures. If, instead, rebels build partylike structures during war, but then scrap those wings to start anew in the electoral arena, then wartime features are likely playing less of a role in successful transformation than the theory predicts. In short, for this theory to hold water, we need evidence that rebels are good organizational theorists, too.

Scope Conditions

Broadly, the theory applies to nonstate armed groups engaged in a violent political conflict with an incumbent power, who have the opportunity and desire to compete in electoral politics. Groups must be engaged in a localized conflict, since becoming a party requires a target government in which to participate. Thus, the theory is only apposite to groups for whom a within-state political solution is conceivable. As such, transnational groups, such as al-Qaeda or Boko Haram, which seek to expand their influence over many states (rather than vie for political influence within a single state) are outside the scope of this theory.[40] After all, one must be able to specify where a group would become a party (or fail) to assess the legality of transitioning into politics.

Additionally, the theory only applies to groups that have the willingness and opportunity to participate in legal, competitive politics. While the desire to build a party is insufficient to account for organizational transformation, it is nonetheless necessary. If a central goal of this book is to parse why some groups succeed at party formation while others fail, we will only get meaningful answers by comparing groups that all tried, but had different results. Legal opportunity is the institutional complement to willingness. To assess the success or failure of a rebel-to-party transformation, the group must have attempted party formation in a place where party formation was legal.[41]

Here, I turn to a few key areas where my theory does not draw exclusionary lines. First, I make no distinction between groups involved in civil wars—particularly as the literature conventionally defines them—and groups involved in lower-level violent conflict. The theory explains how militant organizations transform into political parties. The severity of the conflict and number of battle deaths per year do not bear consequentially on this outcome.[42]

Second, the mode of conflict termination is inconsequential so long as the group has the legal opportunity to form a party. Whether party formation was a built-in condition of a negotiated settlement (e.g., Renamo or the FMLN) or it was a choice the organization made independent of conflict termination, the process of transformation and salience of organizational factors remains. Of course, if the group is defeated militarily, it is unlikely to have a legal path to politics or the organizational capacity to get there. More controversially, perhaps, conflict termination—or at least disarmament—is not a scope condition at all. Previously, disarmament has featured as a scope condition both for the range of groups considered in a given analysis and as a defining feature of rebel-to-party success.[43] As I have argued in previous work, retaining an armed wing does not inherently prevent the organization from functioning as a political party. To wit, treating "failure to disarm" as synonymous with "failure to transition" gives rise to ambiguous measurements and prevents scholars from asking important questions.[44] Many "former" rebel groups go on to have long-standing, electorally successful careers while maintaining an armed wing. Omitting these groups from analyses prevents us from asking important questions about whether and how political integration shapes patterns of violence.

Finally, while I do not draw a hard line on regime type, the theory works best in cases where rebel successor parties enter at least a semicompetitive electoral system. In contrast, some groups transitioned into one-party statehood after military defeats or deposing their colonial governments. Here, I anticipate that their organizational transformations likely unfold in similar ways to that of other groups, yet we will find less of a tie between the group's capacity for voter mobilization and its governmental staying power.[45]

Research Design and Data

The formation, consolidation, and integration of rebel successor parties is many outcomes rolled into one phenomenon. As such, my research design tracks with the disaggregated outcomes that structure my theory: the formation of the organization and then the content, process, and context of change. Broadly, I use a mixed-method approach combining intraorganizational process tracing in the FMLN with cross-national and subnational statistical tests on two original datasets.

Case Selection and Qualitative Data

The Farabundo Martí National Liberation Front is the empirical through line of the book. The unique circumstances under which the FMLN coalesced are important for understanding the analytic purchase of the case. Beginning in 1970, leftist revolutionary movements began to crop up across El Salvador. The FMLN originated as five different politico-military organizations (OP-Ms) with different structures, different views on rebellion, and different sources of funding. At the behest of their patron, they reluctantly came together under the same name, in the same country, to fight for the same outcome, drawing on (essentially) the same support system. The FMLN waged an eleven-year civil war against the government, which in 1992 culminated in a negotiated settlement providing a legal path for the organization to transition into party politics. Beginning with El Salvador's first truly democratic elections in 1994, the FMLN party has been consistently successful at both the local and national levels; since 2009, two FMLN candidates have held the presidency.

Two key details, however, make the FMLN an unparalleled opportunity for this analysis. First, due to the severity of internal rivalries and the haste to get a rebellion off the ground, the leaders allowed each of the five OP-Ms to retain its own organizational structure and routines. Crucially, the component OP-Ms differed considerably in whether and to what extent they valued and built proto-party structures. Second, after failing at their initial attempt to overthrow the Salvadoran government, each constituent OP-M retreated to a unique area of the country. As a result, local populations typically only interacted with one of the five groups throughout the war. Thus, the Salvadoran case exhibits a pronounced geographical phenomenon, the implications of which are analytically invaluable. Five militant organizations, with different levels of proto-party diversification, occupied different territory and interacted with different populations. As a result, this case holds constant every other factor purported to shape the emergence, structure, and behavior of militant groups.

To exploit the intraorganizational variation, I conduct comparative process tracing within a single organization. For the qualitative analysis, I draw on over three hundred archived documents from six archives in both El Salvador and the United States, dozens of recorded interviews and radio broadcasts from the war, and published individual histories. The wartime documents vary in type, though the most useful primarily fall into three categories: internal memoranda, diaries, and propaganda. Along with secondary sources, I use these documents to construct organizational biographies of the FMLN's constituent groups— tracing their structures, operations, and territorial occupations through space and time.[46] I rely primarily on archival data to test a core assumption underlying the theory: that rebels think about organizations about as much as I do. Again, while leaders need not have their organization's full trajectory planned out at the start of war, they cannot be ignorant of organizational dynamics either.

In contrast, asking former (let alone current) FMLN members about wartime organizational structures carries a few risks that could call into question whether the mechanisms I propose reflect reality. The most benign hitch is that people may simply have an inaccurate or incomplete memory about where they were situated in the organization and what the organization looked like beyond their rank. Second, and more problematically, asking directly about organizational structure risks imposing an abstract and post-hoc framework on actors whose dynamics and decision-making were driven by other considerations entirely. This concern mirrors what Sarah E. Parkinson calls "doctrinal bias." Doctrinal bias refers to the empirical blind spots that emerge when researchers' questions are shaped by their own (narrow) understanding of a phenomenon.[47] Even asking about organizational structures risks forcing my own theoretical lens on others' experiences and interpretation of their pasts.

Finally, since internal wartime documents serve strategic purposes, they are likely to give accurate representations of the organization's structure. Relying on archived documents from wartime prevents some (though not all) intentional misrepresentation of the organization. Specifically, since the FMLN is currently concerned with its political standing, members may be liable to portray the wartime organization through rose-colored glasses—playing up social services, downplaying violence. To be sure, I would expect this bias anywhere—post-hoc justifications of involvement with violent organizations are commonplace and do not always reflect the motivations to participate at the time of joining. Yet, I expect the bias to be more severe where individuals have a vested interest in their party's future success. As a result, this form of misrepresentation would bias results in favor of my theory, which I aim to avoid.

Of course, archival sources are not devoid of bias. My access to any information from the war demands that it was written down in the first place, preserved, curated, and made available. Each stage in that process brings a new risk of loss: sensitive information may be destroyed during the war, incriminating information may be destroyed after it, archivists may curate or avoid information that paints the group in one light or another. While these biases cannot be avoided entirely, triangulating across sources and document types can help counterbalance some of the effects. Moreover, many of the documents central to my analysis were captured and preserved in their entirety during the war. As such, the group did not have the opportunity to strategically edit or destroy sensitive information.

Quantitative Data

To complement the qualitative case work, I constructed two quantitative datasets to help get traction on my theory. The primary data contribution is a novel cross-national dataset that includes fine-grained data on rebels' wartime organizational structures and their postconflict electoral performances. The Insurgent Structures and Outcomes data comprise seventy-eight rebel groups that operated between 1974 and 2018. I draw on primary sources, secondary sources, and consultation with country- and group-level experts to code wartime organizational characteristics, including but not limited to proto-party structures, sources of finance, and the types of local security engagement groups exhibit.

I also bring quantitative data to bear on the Salvadoran case. I created a municipality-level dataset that exploits the geographic variation in the FMLN's wartime presence and the groups' differing commitments to building proto-party structures. Drawing on hundreds of primary source and secondary source documents, I code whether an OP-M (and which) occupied territory during the war. I then merge this dataset with municipal-level electoral results from El Salvador's 1994 elections to test whether proto-party structures built during war predict the FMLN's postwar electoral performance.

Empirical Tests

The first set of tests I devise aim to assess key features of organizational content. How do militant organizational structures originate? Do wartime structures develop (and diverge) in line with my expectations? To ensure that wartime organizational structures are not epiphenomenal, I employ process tracing to test my hypotheses about the organizational origins of the FMLN's different sects. The first analysis begins ten years before the war. I test the organizational ideology theory against alternative explanations of militant group structures from the literature using prewar documents and interviews and comparing those accounts to the FMLN's actual structure on the eve of the insurrection. Then, I trace the evolution of their structures and key traits throughout the conflict to ensure that proto-party structures (1) vary and (2) do not exist in name only.

Next, I test the theory's mechanism: the process of transformation. Specifically, given the divergent organizational development between FMLN subdivisions, I ask whether transformation proceeds as I expect. I use process tracing to map the parallel transformation processes across the FMLN's constituent groups. In line with my predictions, the organizations that developed robust proto-party structures during the conflict consciously repurposed those structures into comparable roles in the new party. Conversely, the more combat-centric group (the Ejército Revolucionario del Pueblo—ERP) was forced to build party structures from scratch and, as a result, was marginalized from the process.

The final set of empirical tests pivots from testing hypotheses about internal transformation to test whether organizational traits also predict rebels' successful transition into electoral politics (i.e., the context of change). Not only is political integration the more observable outcome (relative to transformation), but the stakes of allowing rebel groups to participate in politics also hinge on their integration into the electoral system. Alongside important contextual factors like the electoral system, I expect that proto-party structures provide distinct electoral advantages to groups that build them. To test this expectation, I construct an original cross-national dataset comprising detailed organizational information and rebel-to-party outcomes on seventy-eight militant organizations that had the legal opportunity to transition into politics. In addition to the cross-national test, I leverage the municipality-level dataset to test whether the FMLN received more votes in municipalities under the control of OP-Ms that built more robust proto-party structures during the conflict. This subnational test helps confirm that the aggregate proto-party measure in the previous test is not capturing a different dynamic entirely.

Contributions

In explaining the structure, evolution, and transformation of rebel organizations, this book contributes to several literatures in comparative politics and international relations. First and most directly, the insights that follow from the organizational approach advance the rebel-to-party literature by illuminating the scope of challenges militant groups face on the heels of war as well as the organizational traits enabling them to overcome those challenges. In short, this approach reveals both new questions and new answers that are central to this field. Moreover, armed with tools apposite to tracing the structural evolution of rebel groups, this framework allows us to test—and upend—the assumption that party building begins only once the war ends. In doing so, the book reveals a new mechanism of organizational transformation, the applications of which transcend rebel-to-party studies.

The second contribution is a set of powerful tools for modeling rebel organizations and their dynamics. By taking the consolidation and structure of rebel organizations as the analytic starting point, this book reveals new and critical dimensions along which militant organizations vary. Insights about structural variation and the organizational ideologies that shape those structures together lay the groundwork for conducting more incisive comparisons among rebel groups. In turn, these comparisons may help us get valuable traction and new perspectives on the dynamics central to conflict research, including rebel governance, patterns of violence and restraint, recruitment tactics, and conflict resurgence.

For example, scholarship examining the microdynamics of civil war has a distinct behavioral focus: we ask who joins rebellions and why, under what conditions groups forcibly recruit participants and from where, how and when rebels deploy different forms of violence, and, more recently, when and why rebels engage in behaviors beyond violence.[48]. To be sure, understanding the motivation, timing, and variation in these behaviors is critical. Organization, however, is what makes those behaviors possible and predictable. This study contributes the conceptual and theoretical foundations needed to model the organizational structures underlying the behaviors we observe. Layering an organizational approach onto the microdynamics of civil war sheds light on the institutions, structures, and constraints that govern coordinated behavior during conflict.

Zooming out from conflict research, this book addresses an apparent tension in the literature and provides a unified path forward. Despite studying an outcome that, at its core, concerns the process of changing institutions to respond to exogenous demands, rebel-to-party scholars rarely take historical institutionalist approaches. This apparent oversight is both shocking and understandable. On the one hand, the rebel-to-party literature is sidestepping a set of theoretical approaches aimed at explaining both change and stasis in the face of exogenous shocks (i.e., critical junctures). In short, the type of phenomenon at the heart of historical institutionalism describes the rebel-to-party trajectory to a T. On the other hand, these approaches primarily emphasize the difficulty of change. Noting that patterns of institutional reproduction give rise to path dependence (even in the face of inefficiency) and that change is risky, scholars in this tradition note that change is rare and (usually) incremental. As such, historical institutionalism seems like an odd choice to bring to a subfield where major changes are more the rule than the exception.

The organizational approach derived here works toward resolving this tension and putting scholars of change in productive conversation with one another. Bringing key organizational characteristics like role diversification and flexibility into the analysis allows us to see that the same *change* (here, rebel-to-party transformation) is not actually the same *challenge* from one group to the next. These concepts and the organizational framework that contextualizes them can help historical institutionalists account for—and even predict—the major changes that happen in the face of path dependence. Conversely, this framework also makes historical institutionalism more compatible with inquiries that deal in major transformations.

Road Map

The book proceeds in three parts. Part I (chapters 1 and 2) lays the conceptual and empirical foundation for building an organizational theory of rebel-to-party transformation. Chapter 1 takes a critical step back and develops a comprehensive organizational approach in service of modeling rebel-to-party transformation. While political scientists have often turned to organizational traits to help explain various important political dynamics, I demonstrate that when we hold our existing analytic toolkit up to the empirical reality of militant groups, even our capacity for accurate description falls short.[49] Developing an organizational theory of rebel-to-party transformation is impossible without a more complete understanding of the actors at the heart of this process. Drawing on organizational sociology and empirical evidence from rebel organizations, I expand our conceptual and theoretical toolkit, use it to model the origin of rebels' wartime organizational structures, and build an organizational theory of rebel-to-party transformation.

Chapter 2 uses intragroup comparative process tracing to follow the organizational development of the FMLN's five subgroups from 1970 to the onset of war. In so doing, this chapter serves a threefold purpose. Most broadly, it serves as a contextual introduction to the primary case of the book, the FMLN. It also tests the theory of organizational origins presented in chapter 1—thereby allowing me to test the assumption that organizational structures are epiphenomenal to the outcome. Finally, examining the FMLN through the lens of the new framework highlights the descriptive shortcomings of our existing organizational toolkit.

Part II, comprising chapters 3, 4, and 5, leverages the organizational approach and empirical insights laid out previously to build and test the organizational theory of rebel-to-party transformation. They proceed in lockstep with the theory—exploring the content, process, and context of transformation. The front end of each chapter develops the theoretical framework and the back end employs comparative process tracing to test each theoretical component. Focusing on the content of change, chapter 3 develops the framework mapping proto-party structures in rebel groups to the core structures of party organizations. It also specifies key wartime traits that facilitate adaptation: the ability to repurpose existing resources in response to shocks. Then, the empirical section traces differences in the formation and evolution of proto-party structures across different sects of the FMLN.

Chapter 4 then lays out the mechanism: the process of organizational transformation. Drawing on structural insights from chapter 3, I derive two pathways to party building. Which path they take is contingent on their organizational endowments at the end of conflict. Rebel groups with largely homogeneous, combat-centric structures will come to the negotiating table (mostly) empty handed. These groups will be forced to build party structures from scratch. However, militant organizations that developed robust proto-party structures during war have the option to repurpose and augment existing structures. To test this theory, I trace the FMLN's internal restructuring as it builds a party ahead of the 1994 elections. While the group's initial plans entailed giving the five component organizations an equal role in the nascent party, I demonstrate that the OP-Ms with the most developed proto-party structures wound up spearheading the transformation, while the more combat-centric group was marginalized, despite its preeminent role in the FMLN during the war.

Chapter 5 pivots to theorize and test the conditions under which rebel successor parties actually transition and integrate into electoral politics. I argue that the utility of proto-party structures transcends the organization's boundaries. Specifically, organizations with functioning proto-party structures are forging politically salient relationships with local populations and other organizations (e.g., unions, student groups, and professional associations) during war. Nascent rebel successor parties can then leverage these relationships when their priorities turn from war making to voter mobilization. I test this theory both cross-nationally and at the municipal level in the Salvadoran case. Proto-party structures far outperform alternative explanations of rebel-to-party transition from the literature when it comes to predicting long-term political integration.

Part III looks outward and ahead. Chapter 6 transports the theory beyond the borders of El Salvador. Here, I trace the organizational evolution and divergent rebel-to-party prospects of two organizations outside of Latin America: Renamo in Mozambique and the RUF in Sierra Leone. For different reasons, both cases constitute hard tests of the theory, which nevertheless explain the overall trajectories and the seemingly idiosyncratic counterexamples in each case. Finally, the conclusion summarizes the core findings, enumerates the book's contributions, outlines salient areas for future research on rebel-to-party transformation and militant organizations more broadly, and engages the central implications for counterinsurgency and postconflict policy.

Part I

REBEL ORGANIZATIONS AND THEIR ORIGINS

1

AN ORGANIZATIONAL THEORY OF TRANSFORMATION

This book is motivated by a single empirical fact: at its core, rebel-to-party transformation is an organizational phenomenon. It involves taking a militant organization—a group with a dedicated set of roles, relations between them, norms and institutions guiding behavior, and goals—and transforming it into an organization of a fundamentally different type.[1] Making the jump from rebel group to political party requires a different set of roles, different ways of relating, new (and discarded) behavioral norms, and very different goals. Success and failure in rebel-to-party transformation happen at the organizational level—and getting traction on this process requires a comprehensive organizational approach.

To be sure, conflict scholars often lean on organizational intuition to explain important outcomes—including this one. Consider this common and intuitive refrain from the rebel-to-party literature: To transform from a violent militant organization into a viable political party, rebels must "build party structures from scratch" on the heels of war.[2] On multiple dimensions, this proposition takes organization seriously. It locates the phenomenon at the organizational level of analysis, it captures the salience of organizational structures, and it implies that transformation—the change in the group's form—is the outcome in need of an explanation. The problem is not that we are ignoring organizations, it is that we are taking organizations as seriously as our existing toolkit allows.

Before I propose a corrective, an important and outstanding question remains: are rebels thinking about organization as much as I am? The answer is a resounding yes. Militant groups and their leaders are thinking about organizations broadly, deeply, and even humorously—and it would behoove us to follow suit. Indeed, my most unexpected archival find was reference to a running joke among Central American leftists in the 1970s: Q: *What do you get when five Salvadorans meet? A: Three organizations.*[3] The fact of the matter—albeit counterintuitive to some—is that writing a good joke about something demands taking it very seriously. True to form, the origin story of the Farabundo Martí National Liberation Front (FMLN) is one of coalition building, infighting, splintering, and endless negotiations about structure and organizational protocols.

The decade preceding the Salvadoran Civil War (1970–79) was punctuated by a variety of revolutionary leftist groups springing up and splitting off across El Salvador. The regime's blatant repression in this period exacerbated budding rifts in the underground Communist Party (PCS) over whether to take up arms.[4] No longer convinced that peaceful engagement was plausible, a contingent calling themselves the Fuerzas Populares de Liberación (FPL) split off in 1970 to wage a prolonged popular war in the countryside. Two years later, some members within the FPL became frustrated at the lack of military progress and split off to form the Ejército Revolucionario del Pueblo (ERP) and wage a massive, conventional war against the regime. Two years after that, some members within the ERP decried others for being too militant and they split off to form the Resistencia Nacional (RN). In 1976, yet another faction split from the ERP: a group of radicalized students and faculty calling themselves the Partido Revolucionario de los Trabajadores Centroamericanos (PRTC) sought a more politically-oriented revolution across Central America. Finally, in 1978, following a massive voter-intimidation campaign that culminated in a state-perpetrated massacre of civilians, the PCS had a change of heart and formed an armed wing.

Each group was vying for both popular and international support to get the one true revolution off the ground. Then, in 1979, the Sandinistas' victory against the Samoza regime in Nicaragua established precedent for a successful leftist insurrection while simultaneously creating an opportunity to exploit the military supply chain from Cuba to Central America. There was only one catch. While Fidel Castro indeed viewed the Nicaraguan victory as an opportunity to incite leftist revolutions throughout the region, he made Cuban support contingent on the five groups establishing a united front. Not without considerable drama, they agreed.

The five groups came together under the FMLN umbrella, yet each retained its own organizational structure, its own tactical approach, and its own finances.[5] The FMLN was complex and multifaceted: a conglomerate of armies, mass organizations, international and diplomatic wings, and countless alliances with professional associations. In a document recounting the FMLN's emergence, RN Secretary General Fermán Cienfuegos said the following of the organization: "The agencies we have abroad have correspondents, and the documentation centers have analysts in economics, financial affairs, the political situation in the U.S., as well as other groups of intellectuals and professionals who study other areas. *It is a structure that even we do not know, for this, we would have to sit down and study it for a month. At this time, the FMLN does not have an official organizational chart.*"[6]

To be fair, describing the organizational structure in the midst of war is perhaps a difficult and inappreciable task. The question is, how well equipped are we to do it now? The literature is replete with in-depth accounts of the FMLN and sophisticated analyses of the war it fought.[7] Moreover, scholars of the Salvadoran Civil War are, overall, quite a harmonious bunch. New research tends to focus more on revealing new dimensions of the conflict than overturning what came before. However, when it comes to the organization at the center of these analyses, researchers' descriptions of the FMLN sometimes diverge so sharply, one questions whether they are talking about the same group: The FMLN was "fragmented" with a "limited and decentralized structure."[8] Yet, it was "well organized [and] ideologically sophisticated."[9] It was an "unwieldy coalition of quarrelsome groups," which nevertheless "achieved some cohesion."[10] Tommie Sue Montgomery tells us that RN had "a more formal structure than the other [component groups]," yet, according to Leigh Binford, the ERP "is the best organized."[11] The FMLN was "the strongest guerrilla group to ever emerge in Latin America," and yet, according to one of its leaders, it was *pegada con saliva*—glued together with spit.[12]

The goal here is not to reveal which description is right and which is wrong. The spoiler is that they are all correct. Irrespective of whether they were all wrong, half wrong, or all right, their simultaneous existence points to the same problematic conclusion: political science lacks a systematic framework for describing and analyzing organizations. The problem is reminiscent of the blind men and the elephant: each description accurately portrays some aspects of the organization, but is incorrect or incomplete for others. The contradictions arise because our discipline has borrowed an incomplete handful of organizational concepts and we lack a framework for applying them. These shortcomings, in turn, compromise our ability to describe organizations fully or compare organizations to each other.

This chapter aims to remedy these shortcomings. By first specifying the conceptual and empirical boundary that rebels must traverse as they move from the battlefield to the campaign trail, I identify key gaps in our understanding of rebel and party organizations. Taking an organizational approach, I argue that when rebel groups diversify their wartime structures into domains like governance, political messaging, and social services, their organizational legacies set them up for a smoother and less-risky path into electoral politics than their more homogeneous counterparts.

Defining Rebels and Parties

To understand how rebel groups become functioning political parties on the heels of war—and why I approach this question in the way I do—we first need a clear picture of the actors and dynamics at the heart of this study: rebels, parties, and change. The rebel-to-party story is really about two types of change: an internal transformation in the form of the organization and an external shift in the environment in which it operates. Because the book engages two types of actors and the process of changing from one into the other, we need definitions of rebel groups and political parties general enough to obtain across contexts, yet specific enough to preserve the outcome. Some definitions of political parties, however—for example, "nongovernmental political institutions"—are so broad that they erase the conceptual line between rebels and parties entirely.[13] Drawing on my previous work, I propose taking a functionalist conceptual approach to defining the actors at the center of the phenomenon. Motivated by Panebianco's argument that political parties "can be distinguished [from other organizations] by referring to the specific environment in which they carry out a specific activity," I define rebels and parties in terms of their functions and their environments.[14] By centering (1) their internal functions and (2) their environments, this approach accounts for the start and end points of both types of change.

Rebel groups are armed organizations that operate outside the legal electoral environment by using violence as at least one strategy to influence the outcome of a political incompatibility within a given territory.[15] This definition imposes two critical scope conditions for the purposes of studying rebel successor parties. Viable rebel-to-party contenders cannot simultaneously operate as a political party during the conflict.[16] Broader understandings of militant organizations may well omit this scope condition, yet it is critical for preserving the outcome: transforming from one type of actor (and one environment) to the other.

In Giovanni Sartori's words, political parties refer to "any political [organization] identified by an official label that presents at elections (free or not free), and is capable of placing through elections, candidates for public office."[17]

This definition is optimal for a few reasons. It specifies the function and environment of party organizations, it takes a catholic approach to electoral openness (making it applicable to a wider range of regimes), and it engages the rebel-to-party literature on its own terms.[18] Furthermore, by making office holding a criterion of party status, this definition more closely comports with the agreed-upon stakes of rebel-to-party transition: the long-term integration into legal politics.[19]

The Limits of Our Organizational Toolkit

Political science is clear on the point that both rebel groups and parties are organizations and need to be studied as such.[20] Functionalist definitions provide important insight into the subdivisions undergirding rebels' and parties' defining activities; however, they are susceptible to a bias that is particularly consequential for this study. Since our goal in defining political organizations is to answer the question, what makes this type of organization distinct from others?, definitions will focus on what makes the actors unique, rather than what makes them *complete*. For example, defining rebellions as nonstate organizations that use violence to resolve political incompatibilities is both accurate and misleading. This definition may well cause us to—as Zachariah Mampilly warns against—"reduce militant organizations to their most gasp-inducing components."[21] Even describing rebel-to-party transformation means specifying the structures that change and the process by which change unfolds, yet we lack a consistent and complete set of tools for modeling rebel and party organizational structures beyond their defining features.

To illustrate precisely where current approaches fall short, I turn to Nidia Díaz. Díaz was a commander of the PRTC, one of the five politico-military organizations that make up the FMLN. Figure 1.1 is one of many illustrations of the PRTC's structure from the journal Díaz kept during the war.[22] This organizational chart is one quick sketch of one-fifth of one rebel organization. The question I pose here is, how well equipped are we in conflict studies—or political science, more broadly—to even describe this small slice of the group's structure?

The answer is, not much. Holding our existing toolkit up to the PRTC's structure is both bleak and illuminating. Table 1.1 lists the modal concepts used to describe organizations in both the rebellion and the political party literatures. These concepts allow scholars to get some traction on the arrangement of the organization (hierarchy, centralization), the direction and quality of channels through which orders travel (bureaucracy, cohesion, institutionalization), and the size and configuration of combat units (cell structure versus larger brigades).

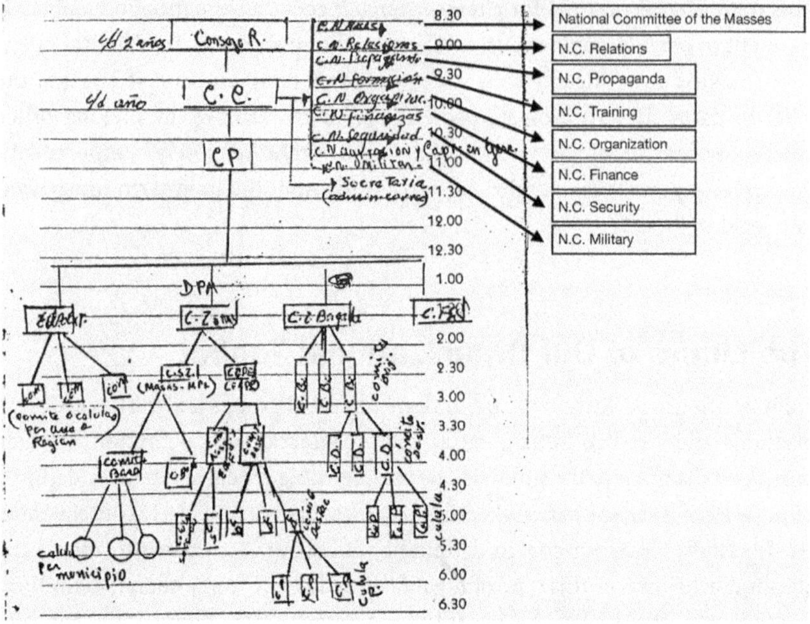

FIGURE 1.1. PRTC organization illustrated by Commander Nidia Díaz. Wartime Diary, Nidia Díaz Papers Collection, box 1, folder 6, Hoover Institution Library & Archives. Arrows, text boxes, and translations added by Sherry Zaks.

TABLE 1.1. Existing organizational toolkit

CONCEPT	DEFINITION/DEFINING FEATURES	CITATION
Formal structure	Command and control, cooperation, decision-making, resource allocation	Staniland (2014, 25)
	"Networks of military units" + Leaders	de Zeeuw (2008, 8)
Military units	Soldiers and their leaders	de Zeeuw (2008)
Membership profile	(Militant) recruitment tactics	Weinstein (2007)
Fragmentation	Number of organizations in a movement, institutionalization among organizations, distribution of power across them	Bakke et al. (2012, 266)
Cohesion	"Create & maintain cooperative effort toward attaining the organization's goals"	Kenny (2010, 533)
	Cooperation enabling unified action	Pearlman (2011)

(continued)

TABLE 1.1. (continued)

CONCEPT	DEFINITION/DEFINING FEATURES	CITATION
Bureaucracy	"Bureaucratic specialization"	Staniland (2014, 27)
	"Tightly controlled," "disciplined"	Kalyvas (2015, 126)
	Bureaucratic institutions implied to be nonpredatory	Reno (N.d., 267)
Capability/strength	Material resources, degree of complexity, and ability to communicate	Ishiyama and Widmeier (2019)
	Size of membership	Acosta and Rogers (2020)
Centralization	Command has a clear, hierarchical structure	Doctor and Willingham (2020)
Institutionalization	"Enduring collections of rules and organized practices embedded in structures of meaning and resources . . ."	Hoover Green (2018) Levitsky (2001)
Hierarchy	"Clearly defined . . . levels of authority and responsibility"	Álvarez (2010)
Leadership	Whether leadership (structure) is cohesive	Staniland (2014)
Organizational capacity	"Ability to recruit, retain, & mobilize"	Palmer-Rubin (2019)
	Establishment of governance or administrative structures	Ishiyama and Widmeier (2020)
	"Ability to maintain organizational integrity under stress, to mobilize people & material to fight, . . . and to direct resources toward their goals."	Cunningham, Huang, and Sawyer (2021)

Yet, examining these concepts alongside the organizational chart of the PRTC (figure 1.1) reveals a pronounced gap between the structure of the group and our ability to describe it.

Two shortcomings highlight the need for a more integrated organizational approach. First, our conceptual inventory is systematically incomplete: most of our concepts focus on the organization's *arrangement* to the exclusion of the organization's *content*. However, describing the shape of the organization's components without specifying the scope of tasks the group performs severely restricts how much we know about it. Again, consider figure 1.1: branching from the Central Committee (labeled "C.C." in the chart) are nine subdivisions of the organization, most of which are dedicated to noncombat tasks such as propaganda, education, and financing. Even at the level of the rank-and-file, only some cells are active combat while others are affiliates of political mass organizations. As an organization, the PRTC exhibits a wide diversity in its roles and subdivisions—and we lack the vocabulary to even acknowledge them, let alone analyze their effects on the organization as a whole. To illustrate this problem conceptually, imagine a hierarchical organization with an entrenched bureaucracy, high levels of cohesion, and a strong commitment among the rank-and-file to the institutions guiding its behavior. Without specifying the different roles within the organization, it is unclear whether I am describing the US military, the Catholic church, or Harvard.

The second issue concerns how we apply the concepts we have. Organizational attributes are generally treated as though they have a fixed valence. Fragmentation is bad for organizations; cohesion is good.[23] Bureaucratization confers strength and durability.[24] And the list goes on. Even when we acknowledge that a "negative" trait confers an organizational advantage, we are more likely to deem the case puzzling than to rethink how the concept works. For example, Paul Staniland notes that in some cases fragmented structures were crucial for organizational survival. Similarly, in the parties literature, Steven Levitsky observed—contrary to many expectations—that weak institutionalization enabled the Justicialist Party to succeed. What appears digressive, however, is actually quite predictable when we consider the traits in light of the outcome. Both authors were looking to explain organizational adaptation to environmental shifts. As an outcome, however, adaptation is more challenging in the presence of traits that give rise to rigidity.[25] The pervasiveness of this problem highlights the importance of casting our outcomes in organizational terms before searching for explanations.

This fixed-valence problem is compounded by a tendency to apply traits "to the organization as a whole, when they clearly apply only to parts."[26] Once again, we find assessments taking the following forms: organizations are fragmented or cohesive, centralized or diffuse, strong or weak.[27] This tendency reveals how scholars who study the same organization can alternately characterize it as both fragmented and cohesive, as we saw with the characterizations of the FMLN. We need an approach capable of parsing organizational structures in such a way that we can apply traits only to the pieces that comport with that description. In the FMLN's case, for example, fragmentation manifested almost exclusively within the General Command: each group (and thus, each leader) disagreed with the others over the best way to fight the war, leading to discord at the top. Yet, the different groups were remarkably cohesive in their own right. By contrast, Sierra Leone's Revolutionary United Front (RUF) exhibited pervasive fragmentation: it lacked central control, it lacked horizontal coordination, and loose collections of foot soldiers often made their own decisions. These two different manifestations of fragmentation likely have very different implications for a variety of organizational outcomes. However, existing approaches lack the descriptive nuance to capture this distinction.

What are the implications of these shortcomings? To illustrate the consequences of an incomplete approach to studying organizations, consider the human face as an analogy. A face is at once a collection of individual pieces, a composite of those pieces, and a thing that changes over time in a way that is driven by both its innate features and the environment. Now, imagine a colleague asked me to describe a guest speaker they were picking up from the airport, and I said, "She has brown eyes." This fact is not false, and it is not entirely useless, but it is incomplete. Eyes are an isolated feature, and color is only one trait of them. Alternately, if I were to just provide an aggregate trait and say, "Her face is very symmetrical," that would also not be especially helpful. Symmetry—like hierarchy—tells us some information about the arrangement of individual facial features, but not the content of those features: eye color, eye shape, skin tone, nose width, and so on.

Like the human face, organizations exhibit traits at multiple levels: their individual structural components (roles, subdivisions, internal networks; eyes, nose, hair texture), how those structural components aggregate to create holistic features (cohesive, fragmented, hierarchical; symmetrical, feminine, masculine), and how they evolve over time (how an organization adapts to new environments; how a face ages). Without a holistic understanding of how individual facial characteristics vary and interact to render how someone looks, those traits—on their own—lose much of their meaning.

By reducing the concept of organizational structure to the top-down flow of military orders, we restrict ourselves to only examining those traits that describe the path and efficiency with which orders and discipline move from commanders to foot soldiers. As such, many descriptions of rebel groups (and, likely, other organizations) are inadvertently one-dimensional. The limitations of our concepts, in turn, narrow the scope of inferences we can draw, acting essentially as analytic blinders. Scholars interested in describing or comparing militant organizations end up doing so along a limited number of dimensions—because those are the concepts we have. Moreover, an incomplete and imprecise understanding of organizational traits has led scholars to misfile important insights about rebel organizations into insights about rebel behavior.[28] Yet, "behaviors" like governance, civilian administration, and social service provision tell us as much about what rebel groups are (their structures, their priorities, their resource allocation) as they tell us about what rebel groups do.[29] The takeaway is that current organizational approaches have a wealth of descriptors, but imprecision in what they are describing. In short, we have adjectives in need of nouns.

Building a New Organizational Approach

Though I generally believe the devil is a suspect figure for whom to advocate, I take his side for a moment to address an important question: Why do organizations deserve such special treatment? At the risk of being fanciful, the answer is that once they coalesce, organizations take on a life of their own. With that life comes unique traits, dynamics, goals, and challenges that transcend the individuals who make up the group at any given time. Organizations are actors and collections of actors. They are agents and constraints on agency. Understanding organizational dynamics—how they form, function, transform, and fail—demands an integrated approach that accounts for these unique properties. This approach has three analytic pillars, which I detail in the following pages.

Specify the Outcome in Organizational Terms

Taking an organizational approach first entails specifying the outcome in organizational terms. Rebel-to-party transformation involves taking an organization with structure optimized to work during war and turning it into an organization capable of running campaigns, winning elections, and governing once in office. In organizational terms, this outcome is fundamentally a puzzle about how groups execute a massive organizational change.

Recasting rebel-to-party transformation in terms of organizational change provides a concrete path forward for theory building and analysis. It situates what may appear to be an idiosyncratic phenomenon within a familiar class of outcomes. While rebel-to-party transformations are relatively recent phenomena with a small—albeit growing—literature, organizational change is not. Exploring the process and prospects of change has been core to organizational sociology for decades. This step thus directs us to a vast and instructive literature that identifies the scope of questions a theory of organizational change must address as well as a set of possible answers. What changes? How does change unfold? How does the context factor into the process?[30] To explain why some rebel groups succeed while others fail, we must also ask what traits (or other factors) make survival more likely? What provides stability amid the upheaval?

The organizational change literature yields two key insights that help get traction on these questions. First, transformation is less destabilizing to the extent that organizations have preexisting skills that are relevant to their new (electoral) needs. Second, organizations will benefit from a legacy of flexibility enabling them to absorb shocks and quickly reorient these skills into the budding party. Put simply, rebel-to-party transformation will be easier if some parts of the organization are equally useful for being parties as they were for being rebels. Yet, those structures will only be useful if the organization has a history of self-reflection and adaptation.

Recasting rebel-to-party transformation in terms of organizational change proves to be both fruitful and thorny. On the one hand, taking a comprehensive organizational approach ensures that our theories are constructed to explain the full range of questions that the phenomenon raises. On the other hand, the literature points us toward answers that lie outside the scope of our existing organizational toolkit. Consequently, building an organizational theory of rebel-to-party transformation first demands that we take a step back and expand our conceptual vocabulary.

Identify Relevant Structures

Think back to the refrain that motivated this chapter: to become parties, militant groups must build party structures on the heels of war.[31] To be clear, I am not arguing that this transformation mechanism is entirely inaccurate. I am, however, arguing that to test whether it is, we need to know what rebel structures are, what party structures are, and what it takes to build, change, and destroy them. If we cannot describe a literal snapshot of an organization's structure, explaining rebel-to-party transformation—what those structures are and how they change over time—is unthinkable.

Henry Mintzberg begins his foundational text on organizational structure with one of the more intuitive definitions of organizations I've yet found: "Every organized human activity . . . gives rise to two fundamental requirements: the division of labor into various tasks . . . and the coordination of these tasks to accomplish the activity."[32] Thus, organizational structure refers to the collection of roles (the different types of labor) within an organization and the types of relations coordinating interaction among those roles. This insight throws the shortcomings of existing characterizations of militant groups into sharp relief: most address only a single type of relation (the downward flow of orders), and most omit discussions of roles entirely.[33] To boot, what few roles we regularly acknowledge—leaders, commanders, foot soldiers—paint a combat-centric picture of what rebellions are made of.

ROLES AND SUBDIVISIONS

When it comes to understanding rebel-to-party transformation, roles are the most critical, yet underspecified, component of structure. Roles, according to Parkinson and Zaks, are individual or collective "positions defined by the skills and practices used, the tasks assigned to them, the objectives associated with them, and their relationships to other roles."[34] Thus, roles like foot soldier, platoon leader, or smuggler are defined in part by what individuals in those roles do (fight, lead, smuggle) and in part by the relationships they have with other roles (e.g., a leader is not a leader unless they have people who report to them). Zooming out, individuals are often part of collective roles or subdivisions within the organization, like a platoon, a radio station, a press wing, or a hospital.[35] A subdivision refers to a group of people within an organization who consistently work together performing related tasks in service of a specific goal. As we will see later, the diversity of subdivisions holds the key to explaining successful transformation.

Regardless of whether rebels indeed build party structures from the ground up or come to the table with preexisting competencies, modeling rebel-to-party transformation requires a comprehensive description of the structures parties need and the skills (and structures) rebels have at their disposal. By delineating the various types and divisions of labor within organizations, subdivisions directly capture institutionalized skill sets. To foreshadow the theory, this inventory of rebel and party subdivisions will allow scholars to evaluate whether some wartime structures have postwar utility.

Before moving on to the analytic implications, I want to forestall an important question: Why are subdivisions uniquely valuable over individual skills? In other words, is there a meaningful difference between an organization with a dedicated press wing and an organization without a press wing, but whose membership counts a number of good writers among its ranks? The answer is yes, and it boils down to visibility and experience. On the first point, rebel leaders looking ahead to electoral politics must take stock of their organizational resources: What do they have at their disposal? What do they no longer need? Leaders, however, are not omniscient. Organizational subdivisions (say, a wartime press wing) are easily visible from the top; individual skills are not. Even if members in unrelated roles happen to be especially adept at a skill the new party needs, those skills are private information. In short, combatants who also have a way with words are at risk of being unwittingly demobilized.

The second advantage of subdivisions comes in the form of experience. Members of a political-messaging division have spent the war practicing and refining skills with direct application to party politics. As such, they aren't just good writers, they are good at communicating the group's message to the people they need to convert from supporters to voters. Extant wings also confer organizational experience: the structure is already integrated into the organization and its members have spent years working together and ironing out their division of labor and norms around communication.[36] Thus, membership in an electorally relevant subdivision provides as much experience with logistics and coordination as it does with the skills required to produce content communicating the party line.

RELATIONS

The second component of an organization's structure is its relations: the social linkages between roles. As "the backbone of organizational structure," relations specify how different roles and subdivisions interact and where roles are positioned within the organization.[37] Thus, relations determine the organization's shape and internal dynamics. If the key insight driving us to reconsider roles is that not all rebels carry guns, then the key insight driving us to reconsider relations is that not all interactions involve giving or receiving orders. Relations are both deeper and broader than previously acknowledged.[38] Most important for the present study, militant organizations exhibit a wide variety of extraorganizational relations. External relations take the form of alliances or rivalries between other militant groups; affiliations with other organizations such as political parties, nongovernmental organizations, or labor unions; and linkages with local populations. Again, with few exceptions, conventional portrayals of the interaction between rebels and "civilians" focus on the production and type of violence or the lack thereof.[39] On the ground, however, relations between rebels and local populations range from coercive to familial, from extractive to mutually supportive, from authoritarian to democratic. Since the long-term survival of rebel successor parties depends in part on their ability to mobilize voters, the variety and extent of external relations have critical implications for organizational functioning both during and after the conflict.

Turning to the analytic implications, scholars acknowledge that the skills acquired, practiced, and refined during wartime have consequences for how the war is fought and what rebel organizations do when the war is over.[40] A nuanced understanding of organizational structure provides a framework for specifying the scope of relations and skills different militant organizations have at their disposal and how the corresponding organizational differences affect a variety of outcomes. As a result, while we implicitly acknowledge that rebels do more than just kill—they govern, provide social services, write and distribute propaganda— this framework allows us to systematically translate observations of rebel *behavior* into insights about the group's *structure*.

Identify Relevant Organizational Traits

The previous section laid out the building blocks of organizational structure: roles, subdivisions, and relations. To explain how militant organizations survive the massive overhaul that rebel-to-party transformation entails, we need more than just an inventory of useful (and less useful) structures. The first thing we learned when viewing rebel-to-party transformation through an organizational lens was that we do not just have to explain how rebels do it, we have to explain how rebels survive it. What traits promote resilience beyond rebellion? The nature of the outcome requires both resilience (an organization's capacity to endure shocks and continue functioning in spite of them) and adaptability (an organization's capacity to function in a new way in response to new demands).[41] Once again, our existing toolkit is found wanting. Indeed, many of the traits we invoke most often (bureaucratization, centralization, hierarchy) tend to foster rigidity, inhibiting precisely the type of flexibility rebel-to-party transformation demands.

The organizational literature sheds light on problems, but it does not leave us in the lurch for solutions. In addition to preexisting competencies, organizations are more likely to survive major overhauls if they have traits and practices that confer flexibility: diversification, deference to expertise, and a culture of self-reflection. Stemming from the preceding structural insights, the first trait is diversification. Diversification asks a simple question: Does an organization specialize in one type of task or many? While massive change is always difficult, organizations with a wide scope of expertise on which to draw are more likely to find creative solutions quickly and from within.[42] To foreshadow the theory, all types of diversification are conducive to flexibility, but aspiring successor parties will likely benefit from diversification into some domains more than others.

The second trait that facilitates quick adaptation to a changing environment is a culture of deference to expertise. This trait works in tandem with preexisting competencies. Militant organizations may have the skills needed to pivot efficiently into electoral politics, but the leaders must be willing to tap into relevant expertise irrespective of where it falls in the wartime hierarchy. Finally, organizations that practice critical self-reflection (particularly if it is routinized) tend to be more resilient to shocks than their less mindful counterparts. Much like individuals, organizations that view failures as an opportunity for growth and keep close tabs on environmental risk will develop the skills to see and respond to threats quickly. When put into practice, this cycle of failure-reflection-adaptation creates what Debra Minkoff calls a "repertoire of prior flexibility," which matters because one of the best predictors of future resilience is past resilience.[43]

An Organizational Theory of Rebel-to-Party Transformation

In the preceding pages, I listed the key components of an organizational theory of change and the two traits that make change easier for some groups than others. Explaining any organizational transformation means accounting for what changes, how change unfolds, and whether the environment shifts alongside the organization. Surviving even the smallest change is more likely when groups have preexisting competencies and a legacy of flexibility. The problem (and reason for the interlude between that paragraph and this one) was that our existing tools were inadequate to even list the structural differences between rebels and parties—let alone to systematically identify the structures and traits that would make transformation possible. Expanding our conceptual toolkit allows us to bridge the disjuncture between the intuition that rebels must build party structures and our inability to specify what those structures are and what structures rebels had to work with. Here, I build a three-part organizational theory of rebel successor party formation, which corresponds to the driving questions in the organizational change literature: What changes? How does change unfold? How does context factor into the process?

The Content of Change

The most basic account of organizational change must specify how the group differs between the beginning and the end of the transformation. What about the structure is altered? What remains the same? According to conventional accounts of building rebel successor parties, the answer to "what changes?" is "everything." Taking an organizational approach to the question reveals two facts that disrupt this assertion: (1) rebel groups are often much more structurally diverse than previous depictions imply, and (2) change is easier when groups have preexisting competencies. The first part of the organizational theory of transformation synthesizes these two insights. After disaggregating political party organizations into their core subdivisions, I use this blueprint of what parties need to evaluate the postwar utility of the different structures rebels have.

In an investigation of the changing strength of parties, Richard S. Katz and Peter Mair lay out a framework that sheds light on parties' organizational diversity. They identify—albeit without organizational parlance—three core subdivisions of the party: the party in public office, the party on the ground, and the party in central office.[44] The party in public office refers to the governing apparatus.[45] The party on the ground refers to the subdivision that forges linkages with society, including party congresses and ancillary organizations (e.g., youth wings, women's wings, and student organizations). Finally, the party in central office refers to the subdivision that coordinates campaigns, oversees media and press, and acts as a conduit between the other two wings. Of course, party organizations will vary in the composition of and diversification beyond these structures. The goal here is not to suggest that political parties are uniform, but to identify the structures that support their most central needs. In doing so, this framework strikes an important balance: it is specific enough to identify the tasks associated with each major subdivision of the party, but general enough to obtain widely across party organizations.

This blueprint of party organizations allows us to specify the types of structures that rebels need in order to function as a political party. Thus, at the very least, we can more concretely specify what "party structures" refers to when we are told that rebels must build them on the heels of war. Notwithstanding the value of this newfound clarity, the organizational framework allows us to take the analysis a step further. Rather than simply asking what types of structures rebels need to build when war ends, this insight into party organizations raises a more important question: are there some rebel groups that don't need to build much at all?

Looking beyond combat and logistics wings, I identify a collection of wartime subdivisions that functionally mirror the core elements of party organizations. Wings dedicated to governance, social service provision, and political messaging imbue rebel groups with structures, routines, and skills that are critical for functioning in electoral politics. Since—in addition to their wartime utility—these subdivisions have direct electoral utility, I refer to them as proto-party structures (irrespective of whether future party building was part of the organizational plan). Proto-party structures play a critical role in the formation and performance of rebel successor parties. Because organizations specialize in "doing the same things in the same way, over and over," rebel groups with party-relevant structures will have less to learn and less to disrupt as they pivot from the battlefield to the campaign trail.[46] As such, these proto-party structures represent the preexisting competencies that facilitate smoother transformations.

The Process of Change

Since—as the empirical record suggests—wartime organizational structures vary dramatically in their postwar relevance, the next logical question is how different organizational legacies affect the process of party building. As such, the second part of my theory unpacks the mechanism of transformation. Following a postwar audit in which leaders assess the gap between what they need and what they have, the process of building a rebel successor party will effectively unfold in one of two ways: reconstruction or repurposing. If the audit reveals a sizable gap between the organizational needs of a party and the organizational resources of the rebellion, then the party-building process will unfold as the conventional wisdom suggests. Groups that end the war with more homogeneous, combat-centric organizations will have no choice but to dismantle their militias and build the governing, messaging, and outreach subdivisions from the ground up. This process will often involve recruiting specialized talent from outside the organization to staff new wings while simultaneously integrating the new subdivisions into the organization. Consequently, the literature is not incorrect in identifying reconstruction as a path to party formation; the problem is that this transformation mechanism is inherently unstable. Building even a single wing from scratch means hiring skilled personnel, sorting the division of labor, and establishing new routines for both working together and performing whatever task they were hired for (be it writing or governing or community organizing). This process is not impossible, but it is inefficient, it compromises organizational legitimacy, and it leaves a lot of room for error.

If, alternately, the postwar audit turns up a collection of subdivisions whose skills and functions match the needs of the party, then the transformation process can unfold by repurposing existing wings and only dismantling what is no longer needed. Herein lies the value of proto-party structures. In the first place, repurposing wings staffed with members who were part of the armed struggle helps preserve organizational legitimacy. When familiar pieces of the organization remain intact during change, organizations reduce the likelihood of internal conflicts that arise when longtime loyalists are passed over in favor of outside talent. Second, repurposing existing subdivisions is a more efficient and less risky party-building mechanism.[47] When the process of change unfolds by building on what is already there, resources and information can flow through existing channels to an existing subdivision to be managed by people who have experience working together. Thus, the extent to which rebel groups can repurpose existing subdivisions whole cloth into the new party is the extent to which the organization benefits from the skills, relations, and routines that come with it.

The reality of postwar party building lies somewhere between these two extremes. Rarely will a group need to build absolutely everything from the ground up and just as rarely will they have a fully functional inbuilt party ready to hit the campaign trail. Yet, the more proto-party structures the rebel organization has, the less risky transformation will be. Each structure acts as an anchor point, stabilizing the organization amid an otherwise turbulent time.

The Context of Change

One question remains: if it looks like a party and it quacks like a party, can it win like one? If the stakes of rebel successor party formation hinge on whether former belligerents have access to legal (and peaceful) channels for dissent, then the final part of the theory must address whether becoming a party in form actually affects whether groups become parties in function as well. This step in the theory shifts focus from transformation (the internal organizational changes required to build a party out of the pieces of rebels) to transition (the external pivot from operating on the battlefield to operating in electoral politics). What affects whether successor parties can mobilize voters, win seats, and hold onto those seats once they've won them?

Whether rebel successor parties adapt to electoral politics is a function of three factors: their capacity to perform electoral and governing tasks, their capacity to mobilize voters, and the institutional constraints of the new party system. The party's wartime organizational legacy shapes the first two factors in crucial ways. Performing electorally relevant tasks is the most straightforward application of proto-party structures. Groups with experience in governing and political communication with the masses will hit the campaign trail with at least some of the necessary skills built in.

The real question, however, is how one-time rebels go from winning hearts and minds to winning votes and seats. When it comes to electoral performance, voter mobilization is so important that it borders on obvious. As such, the literature is rich with explanations: territorial control, administrative capacity, populist ideology, political wings, and networks of ethnic support all operate through this mechanism. The resources associated with these wartime experiences should translate into an ability to convert wartime supporters into postwar voters.[48] To be sure, popular support during the war is likely a good predictor of whether citizens will want to vote for the rebel successor party. Wartime support, however, does not explain the long path from political alignment to casting a ballot. Voter mobilization requires registration (which itself requires official forms of identification and basic literacy), advance knowledge of when the election is, transportation to the polls, and a belief in the baseline safety of showing up and voting for the party you want in office. Without explaining how the party acquires the capacity to assist in the logistical undertakings required to turn supporters into voters, demand-side theories that focus on wartime support will only get as far as explaining voter galvanization, but not mobilization. Truly explaining the latter means accounting for the new party's organizational capacity to channel excitement into action.

Once again, taking an organizational approach reveals the otherwise elusive mechanism connecting wartime support to postwar votes. Beyond the advantages they bring to organizational change, many proto-party structures maintain consistent relations with locals as well as other organizations (such as trade unions, religious institutions, and student groups). Crucially, these relations transcend violence and extraction. By regularly interacting with citizens in administrative and, indeed, mobilizational capacities, groups with proto-party legacies can leverage existing relations and experience to help manage the logistics of voter mobilization.

Where Do Organizational Structures Come From?

The book's original (and considerably duller) subtitle was "How Wartime Organizational Structures Affect Rebel-to-Party Transformation." While the new one is a fair bit catchier, it also obscures the heart of the theory: that variation in wartime structures influences postwar party success. To wit, structure is so integral to the theory that we required a new vocabulary for describing the many ways it varies. Yet, the centrality of rebels' wartime structures—to say nothing of the ink spilled on a framework for describing them—raises an important question: where do these structures come from?[49] Why do some groups diversify into a host of sociopolitical domains like governance and mass mobilization while others remain more homogeneous and combat-centric? More consequentially still, how do we know whether organizational structures are independently salient or whether they are by-products of an antecedent (and simpler) cause that also predicts rebel-to-party success?

These questions are not trivial. From a practical standpoint, if a simpler explanation accounts for both organizational structure and successful transformations, then it obviates the approach laid out earlier and the theory that follows. And the implications of that finding would not be limited to this study. Any evidence that structures are epiphenomenal to organizational change would disrupt a decades-old literature in sociology. What would this evidence look like? For one, we would need to identify a variable that could reasonable determine both organizational form and rebel-to-party success. Then, we would need evidence that groups with comparable prewar traits built comparable organizations and experienced similar outcomes. Finally, we would need evidence that the mechanism of transformation is not a function of organizational form, but of the initial trait that also happens to shape structure.

I turn to the rebellion literature to identify the factors most likely to account for wartime organizations (and, potentially, postconflict outcomes). Although few scholars examine wartime structure as their main outcome of interest, and fewer still theorize the origins of noncombat subdivisions, the literature reveals four explanations of how rebel organizations coalesce and why they take the forms they do.[50] Broadly, existing explanations attribute variation in militant structure to one of four factors: ideology, state context, resource endowments, and prewar social networks.[51] These factors, though important, lack a direct mechanism by which they translate into a consistent organizational form (let alone the successful postwar transformation of that form into a political party). Take ideology, for example. Though ideology has been shown to affect patterns of violence, recruitment practices, quotidian interactions and socialization, claim making, and the institutions the group adopts, groups with similar ideological stances often build very different organizations.[52] In other words, the process by which ideology translates from the red (or green or any other color) book into the organization's form remains elusive. As I demonstrate in the following chapter, even rebel groups that emerge within the same ideological, social, environmental, and resource contexts exhibit fundamental differences in their structures.

Existing explanations nevertheless provide a useful starting point for theorizing structural origins. Moving beyond this starting point demands a deeper understanding of the unique features of the early organizational context and an explication of how each variable works in an organizational medium. In their embryonic stages, organizations lack the inertia and institutional constraints we normally associate with them. As such, this context is akin to a critical juncture, except rather than deviating from an existing path, leaders are forging a path for the first time. Absent these constraints, leaders will have considerably more agency over major organizational decisions as the group coalesces.[53] Of course, agency is not without limits. As Staniland rightly notes, leaders "do not have the freedom to make whatever kind of organization they want."[54] What, therefore, shapes and constrains their decisions about the kind of organization to build?

I argue that the nature and extent of structural diversification in militant groups is a function of the group's organizational ideology, which, in turn, mediates how they use their resource endowments and the prewar social networks from which the group emerges. This explanation builds on insights from the literature by accounting for how these variables operate in an organizational context, which is where existing explanations fall short. In reality, ideologies need actors to harbor them. Resources need actors to wield them. Social networks need actors to comprise and reproduce them. And the properties of those actors matter.[55]

Organizational Ideology

Organizational ideology refers to the principles and priorities that emerge when a broad ideological or military doctrine (like Maoism or Conservatism) is filtered through a decision-making body in a specific context.[56] Thus, for rebel groups, organizational ideology will define how the struggle should look on the ground: what type of war they fight (e.g., conventional war, prolonged popular war, acts of terrorism and sabotage), what tasks are part of the struggle (e.g., violence against the government, education of the people, international messaging), and what their objectives are (e.g., regime change, Communist revolution, power sharing). The implications for structure are straightforward. Leaders who espouse ideologies emphasizing the importance of political education and mass mobilization will likely aim to build an organization with diverse and specialized subdivisions capable of performing these tasks. Thus, where ideology generally refers to an established political doctrine that exists independently of the actors who espouse it and the context in which they operate, organizational ideology captures the context-sensitive interpretation of that doctrine and its corresponding implications for rebel group structures and institutions.

In this sense, we can think of organizational ideology as the rebel group equivalent of denominationalism. For example, Christianity, writ large, is a religion founded on the teachings of Jesus Christ and the core beliefs that he (1) is the son of God and the messiah, (2) died for our sins, and (3) will return. Within Christianity, however, are a variety of denominations with logically consistent practices. Different churches cleave to (and reject) different principles, organize and worship differently, and embrace distinct ways of engaging both their congregants and the masses beyond them. As such, there are some instances where saying "Bob is a Christian" can tell us a lot of information (say, on the question of polytheism). Yet, there are other instances where saying "Bob is a Christian" tells us very little (say, on the question of same-sex marriage). If we want a distinctly Christian heuristic for the latter, we would make much more reliable guesses about Bob's politics if we knew whether he belonged to an Evangelical church or a Unitarian one. Such is the utility of organizational ideology. Though—for now, at least—we lack such clean denominational labels in rebellion, organizational ideology captures the logically consistent differences even between groups espousing the same dogmas.

Crucially, organizational ideology can also help get analytic traction on groups whose political ideologies are elusive. After all, some leaders' preferences are shaped by factors other than "published ideological doctrine."[57] Nevertheless, these preferences are often as consistent as they are observable. For example, while exiled intellectuals formed the initial core of Sierra Leone's RUF—setting the stage for a robust political education apparatus grounded in a clear ideology—the leadership was distrustful of the intellectual elite and made early efforts to marginalize their role in the organization.[58] As a former combatant recalled: "[Leader] Foday Sankoh promoted the semi-literate because they were more loyal to him and were less likely to take over the movement. He did not like the educated ones."[59]

Members of the elite core were barred from promotions within the organization and many were exiled entirely. Thus, in a sharp departure from their roots, the RUF was notoriously considered ideologically bereft and its organization comprised almost exclusively combat units and networks dedicated to illicit mining.[60] However, the absence of political doctrine does not mean the absence of a cohesive set of ideas dictating the organization's structure and objectives. Organizational ideology allows us to capture the organizing principles of war irrespective of whether they are attached to a theoretical doctrine. Without it, analysts can easily fall into the trap of characterizing organizations as ideologically bereft even though they operate according to consistent organizing principles.

Organizational ideologies, in turn, shape how groups will use and allocate resources and how they leverage the social bases from which they emerged. Both additional factors represent key opportunities and constraints for the nascent rebellion's structure. Yet, they do not constrain or endow all rebellions equally. If organizational ideology allows us to infer the type of organization rebels want to build, the resources and personnel to which they have access will determine just how close they can get. By shedding light on the group's wartime priorities, organizational ideology can reveal not only what types of resources rebel groups will seek, but also how resources will be allocated within the organization once they are acquired. This frame can thus provide insight into the types of structures that may emerge during war if and when resource endowments allow for it. Prewar social networks, likewise, affect wartime structures in more ways than we have previously documented. Beyond assisting in recruitment and contributing to group cohesion, prewar and wartime networks affect structures by determining the range of skills emerging organizations have at their disposal.[61] However, whether and how those skills will translate into corresponding subdivisions is also a function of organizational ideology. Thus, two groups that emerge with strong links to teachers unions, say, may still build very different organizations depending on whether their leadership espouses an ideology that views political education as central to the struggle.

Rebels' wartime organizations are irreducible to a single prewar trait or condition, but that does not mean they are unpredictable. Rebel leaders spill a great deal of ink adapting their political ideologies to their organizational contexts.

Taking this more granular approach to ideology allows us to trace how these views give rise to distinct organizational forms. In the following chapter, I delve into more detail about how to identify organizational ideology and I test whether this approach adequately predicts the organizational development of the FMLN.

Bringing an Organizational Approach to the Micropolitics of Rebellion

In Jeremy Weinstein's foundational book on insurgent organizations, he argues that "a clear understanding of the micropolitics of rebellion is achieved by focusing on how groups organize violence."[62] Of course, studying how groups organize violence—their strategies for combatant recruitment and training, their technologies of war, and their pattern of violence against civilians—is a crucial area of conflict research. How groups organize and produce violence is an important dimension along which rebel organizations vary. However, it is only one dimension. The exclusive focus on the production of violence deceptively casts rebel groups in a unidimensional light. As a result, many analyses of militant group dynamics are built on untested assumptions about the actors at the center of their theories. Rebel organizational structure refers to more than just the arrangement of combat units or the chain of command that connects them. Moreover, as Mampilly, Parkinson, and others have observed, even understanding how rebels produce violence is better achieved by acknowledging the myriad wings of the organization that do not brandish guns.[63]

Doing so, however, required taking a step back and reexamining the very nature of organizations in the first place. Insights from organizational sociology, when synthesized into a cohesive approach, help open the black box of intraorganizational phenomena: how organizations emerge, how structural components and ideologies combine to imbue organizations with different traits, and how they change over time. Taking a more comprehensive approach to the study of rebel-to-party transformation—and militant groups more broadly—has three central implications, which together facilitate new avenues for research within and beyond the scope of this book. In short, a clear understanding of the micropolitics of rebellion is best achieved by focusing on how groups organize.

ORGANIZATIONAL ORIGINS
OF THE FMLN

If we take a bird's eye view of the FMLN on the eve of war, we find a complex, multifaceted organization. Figure 2.1 presents a simplified depiction of the FMLN (and its affiliated mass organization, the Democratic Revolutionary Front [FDR]) in the lead-up to the 1981 insurrection.[1] Shorthand descriptions will note their umbrella structure: five politico-military organizations (OP-Ms) begrudgingly came together under a single banner to secure Cuban support. More detailed accounts will include their ties to mass organizations and the fact that the OP-Ms operated differently from one another.[2] Zoom in to any one cell, however, and we find that the differences are more than just operational. The organizational chart is like a fractal; magnifying any one part reveals ever more complexity. Indeed, it takes very little digging to find that the OP-Ms comprised different levels and different configurations of military units, finance divisions, media wings, education wings, international diplomacy divisions, radio stations, journalists, writers, technicians, and near-countless structures bridging their affiliation with agricultural cooperatives, trade unions, and political parties. Each OP-M was distinct from the others, both in structure and in culture. Members were loyal and disciplined within their ranks, yet they were prone to quarreling when two OP-Ms crossed paths.[3] Nevertheless, they all fought under the same name—quite successfully—for the same outcome.

How did the FMLN organization come to be this way? Were the respective structures inevitable consequences of the resources or the prewar networks that fed into each group? Or is the story multifactorial? This chapter evaluates both

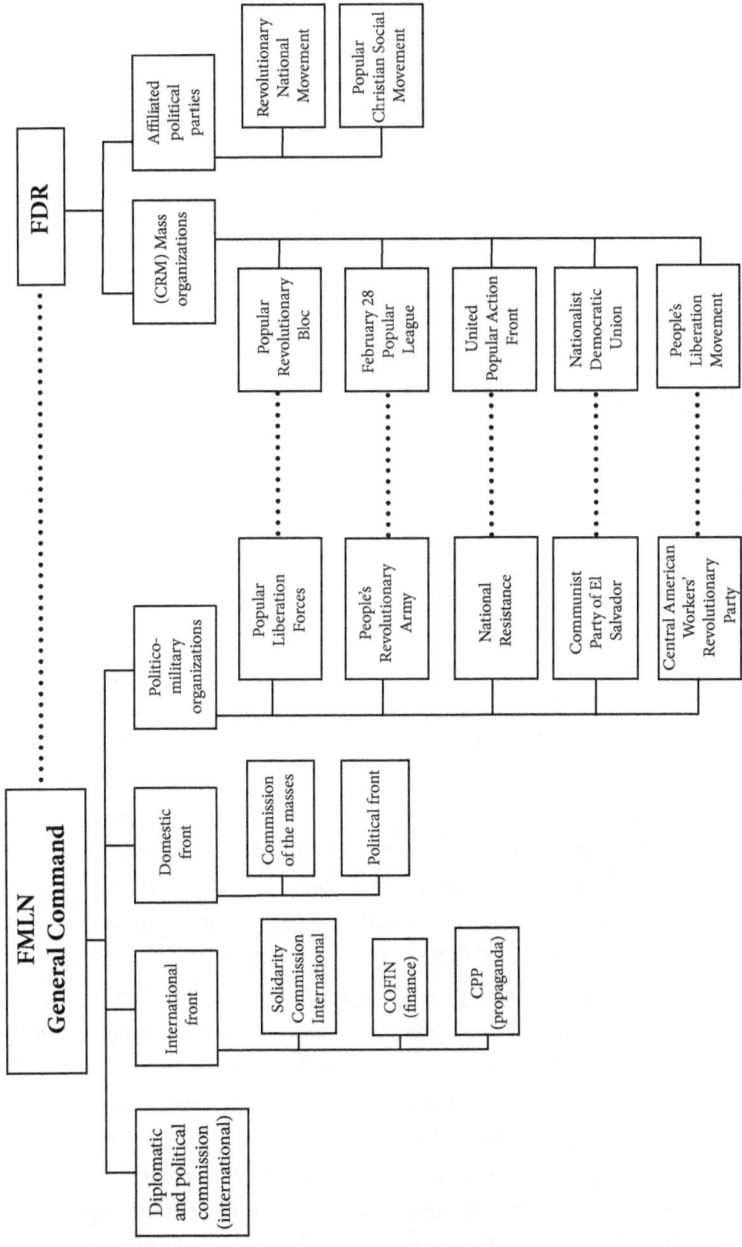

FIGURE 2.1. FMLN-FDR structure (1981)

the new and conventional organizational approaches by testing their respective abilities to explain the emergence and early structure of the FMLN. Using both descriptive and deductive process tracing, I trace the FMLN's evolution from the founding of the Partido Comunista de El Salvador (PCS; the Communist Party of El Salvador) in 1930 up through the early years of the war. Tracing the FMLN's structure through an organizational lens allows me to test the conceptual adequacy of our existing toolkit, demonstrate the analytic purchase of the new approach, and resolve the descriptive contradictions that motivated chapter 1. Finally, it sets the stage for the question that motivates the remainder of the book: How do the respective structures within the FMLN affect its prospects for rebel-to-party transformation?

Why Focus on the FMLN?

As a case, the FMLN strikes a remarkable analytic balance between uniqueness and generalizability. On the one hand, the OP-Ms' organizational and operational autonomy, their geographical separation, and the similarities and differences in the social networks from which they emerged make for an uncommon organization. Though umbrella organizations are widespread among rebel groups, the "seed groups" tend to (at least partially) dissolve into the central structure within a few years, thereby muddying the rigor of intragroup comparisons. The FMLN is distinct in this regard: the OP-Ms retained their own organizational structures until party formation began in earnest.

On the other hand, the groups that make up the FMLN represent variation on important dimensions that allow the insights from this chapter to travel well beyond El Salvador's borders. Some were based in urban centers, others in the hinterlands. Some emerged among the intelligentsia, others among a mostly illiterate peasant class. Some forged politically and administratively diverse organizations, others were considerably more homogeneous. Analytically, the unique features of the FMLN case provide both variation and control where they are most needed. As such, the FMLN represents a rare opportunity to conduct comparative process tracing within a single organization.

To situate the analysis, the next section provides the historical and social backdrops to the war (see figure 2.2 for a map of El Salvador's departments). The historical discussion recounts the increasingly repressive tactics adopted by the Salvadoran state between 1930 and 1980, which provides both the motivation for and obstacles to fomenting a revolution. The social discussion portrays the existing networks and levels of politicization within Salvadoran society. Together, these discussions provide needed context for tracing the social roots of the rebellion and testing theories about how state tactics, resource availability, and prewar networks shape insurgent structures. Leveraging dozens of early internal documents, memoirs, and press releases, I use process tracing to track development of the respective groups comprising the FMLN. I demonstrate both the descriptive and predictive value of the new organizational approach developed in chapter 1.

Backdrop to the Salvadoran Civil War

The dire sociopolitical conditions that eventually culminated in the Salvadoran Civil War have their roots firmly planted in the economy. Throughout its colonial and independent history, El Salvador's economy has been fueled by a single agricultural export—first it was cocoa, then indigo, then coffee. With the switch to coffee—a much more labor-intensive crop than the others—came a massive demand for agricultural workers. Power was increasingly consolidated in the hands of coffee oligarchs and the government—the Venn diagram of which was essentially a circle. In turn, the elite leveraged draconian land reform policies to restructure Salvadoran society in service of a single goal: maximize coffee production.[4] Peasants were bound to coffee plantations through feudal labor institutions and Indigenous communities were broken up and dispersed both to meet labor needs and to forestall the risks of a coordinated uprising.

By the 1920s, the picture of Salvadoran politics was already grim, yet a cascade of events set off by the Great Depression culminated in a military dictatorship that would ultimately set the stage for civil war fifty years down the line. The already radicalizing labor movement became even more militant when the Great Depression cut coffee harvesters' wages in half.[5] Contemporaneously, El Salvador's first freely elected president quickly garnered resentment on both sides: the labor movement resented the lack of meaningful agricultural reforms; the coffee oligarchs resented his refusal to pander to purveyors of the sole product driving the economy.

As disenfranchised workers began threatening violent insurrection, the military staged a coup—ousting President Arturo Araujo, installing a military government, and cracking down on labor organizations with mass arrests. Undeterred, Farabundo Martí—one of the radical leaders of the Communist Party and the eponym of the FMLN—called for mass uprisings of workers and students across the country on January 22, 1932. Authorities did not merely stamp out the insurrection. The army, the National Guard, and other security forces around the country engaged in a coordinated retaliation so severe that it earned the name La Matanza—the slaughter. Within a few weeks of the uprising, between ten thousand and forty thousand peasants were murdered.[6] Indeed, Elisabeth Jean Wood argues that the army only stopped killing at the behest of landlords who "complained that there would be no labor left."[7]

Three short years from 1929 to 1932 shaped the country for the next five decades. In the wake of La Matanza, the military dictatorship further consolidated the repressive labor institutions that had emerged prior to the Depression. The state engaged in a rapid expansion of military and paramilitary organizations with the express purpose of "policing the labor forces."[8] To prevent future rebellion, the Communist Party was banned, labor unions were "officially discouraged," and all peasant organization was outlawed with the sole exception of church gatherings.[9]

Notwithstanding the relative economic success throughout the 1950s and '60s, the confluence of multiple events beginning with the 1972 elections contributed to an unprecedented level of unrest in the 1970s that culminated in the creation of the FMLN. At the time, the National Conciliation Party (PCN) dominated politics, but the Christian Democrats had been gaining momentum since the late 1960s. El Salvador's facade of progressive reforms was abruptly torn down when, after the news media announced José Napoleon Duarte of the Christian Democrats the winner of the presidential election, the military forcibly suspended all press coverage, causing a three-day news blackout. On the fourth day, the media were coerced into broadcasting fabricated election results, which handed the victory to the PCN's candidate, Arturo Armando Molina. The clear election rigging and cooptation of the news media fed into the stirring urban and rural unrest.

FIGURE 2.2. El Salvador map with departments

The Social Roots of Rebellion

In the aftermath of La Matanza, the Communist Party went underground and maintained a small membership committed to peaceful engagement with Salvadoran politics.[10] Beyond that, there were few explicitly political organizations of which to speak. If indeed prewar social networks are the bedrock of rebellion, the government's proscription of political organizing should have set the stage for failure.[11] However, two contemporaneous trends—one urban and one rural—gave rise to a few social bases on which rebellion could flourish. In the cities, professional organizing was occasionally tolerated. Though professional organizations still needed to maintain low profiles, student organizations, labor associations, and teachers' unions became hotbeds of radicalization throughout the 1960s and '70s.

Christian Base Communities: Liberation Theology, Literacy, and Campesino Mobilization

In the countryside, radicalization came from an unexpected source. Inspired by the progressive reforms of Vatican II, radical catechists brought liberation theology to the rural masses across Latin America. Both the ideological content and the social implementation of liberation theology laid the foundation for political revolution. In a drastic break from conventional biblical interpretation—namely, that any suffering was the will of God—liberation theology called for the poor to reflect on their situation, study the Bible, and use the Word as the basis for political action to improve their lot.[12]

This goal was achieved through the construction of Christian base communities (*comunidades eclesiales de base*, or CEBs). Priests would travel through rural areas and establish communities of between ten and thirty members who would meet for Bible study. Although ordained priests would lead the initial classes, these groups were "encouraged to develop [their] own leadership" by electing lay teachers and lay preachers.[13] In the early 1970s, the church set up training centers for the leaders of CEBs in which the newly elected "delegates of the Word" learned skills that would prove vital far beyond the realm of religious life. According to John Hammond, the training program was built around three pillars: (1) biblical study; (2) "national reality," which examined social and economic structures of El Salvador through a Marxist lens; and (3) "techniques of popular organization," which focused on how to plan meetings and manage group dynamics.[14] In just under a decade, more than fifteen thousand campesinos were trained as community leaders through church programs.[15]

Yet, as Hammond notes, the emphasis on active participation in studying not only the Bible but also the political and social structures of El Salvador cast a harsh light on the state of literacy in rural areas.[16] With literacy rates hovering around 50 percent, teaching the population to read was an essential first step.[17] In response to this crisis of literacy, public education became the liturgy of these communities. Both the training of leaders and the public education that took place in the communities was firmly rooted in the Freirean pedagogical tradition, in which learning is achieved through political engagement. Literacy was taught by choosing a variety of words—one for each letter of the alphabet—that had religious, social, or political meaning to the campesinos. While simultaneously learning the letters that composed the word, students were encouraged to reflect on the concept as it pertained to their lives.[18] As such, religious activities transformed from a respite from the people's suffering to a solution for it.

As the social backdrop of the nascent rebellion, it is difficult to overstate the political implications of Christian base communities. For the first time in half a century, CEBs provided a quasi-legal context and a set of strategies for rural political organization. The pedagogical approach employed in the communities aroused a newfound political consciousness among the peasant class centering on education, social justice, and overcoming oppression. Moreover, the process of training "delegates of the Word" gave rise to a contingent of grassroots leaders throughout the country.[19] As such, when the FMLN later encountered these communities, the rebels did not have to struggle against a population complacent with the status quo.

The Rise of the Politico-Military Organizations

By 1970, the PCS was experiencing deepening rifts between those committed to reforming Salvadoran politics exclusively through legal, peaceful channels and those who felt the time had come to take up arms against the regime. The decade preceding the war was punctuated by splinter groups fracturing and coalescing across the country, each vying for primacy. The former Communist leader Salvador Cayetano "Marcial" Carpio was the first to go. In 1970, Carpio and a handful of followers broke away to form the Fuerzas Populares de Liberación (FPL). They began clandestinely organizing militias in preparation for waging a prolonged popular war—a strategy imported from the Vietnam model.[20] Carpio dubbed the FPL a politico-military organization.[21] In an interview with the journalist Marta Harnecker, he elaborated on the concept and how it captures the critical balance between peaceful political work and militarization:

> HARNECKER: What do you mean when you say "politico-military organization"?
>
> MARCIAL: [Politico-military means] combining all the means of struggle in which the political work must be complemented by the army. . . .

When we proclaimed the organization as "politico-military," we did
so in response to a real need, because there were organizations that
refused the military route. . . . [However] by considering ourselves as a
politico-military organization, we tried to avoid falling into pure militarism. . . . From the beginning we were clear that the political side is
fundamental, it has to lead the war, and the military is subordinate.[22]

Notwithstanding Carpio's push to strike political-military balance, which the
PCS refused to engage, it was only two years before divisions emerged in the FPL
leadership over how best to mount an insurrection against the state. Led by Sebas-
tián Urquilla and Joaquín Villalobos, a growing contingent believed the FPL was
focused excessively on political training and mass organization at the expense of
what was really needed: militarization. Believing that the state was too weak to
require prolonged warfare, this contingent split from the FPL to form the Ejército
Revolucionario del Pueblo (ERP) in 1972.[23] This split was far from the last. The ERP
fractured in 1974, giving rise to the Resistencia Nacional (RN), and then again in
1976, resulting in the Partido Revolucionario de Trabajadores Centroamericanos
(PRTC). Finally, in 1977, the PCS rethought its peaceful stance following the state's
massive voter-intimidation campaign, which culminated in a public massacre of
civilians. In response, the PCS leader Schafik Hándal concluded that armed struggle
was a necessity and the group began assembling militias.[24] While "OP-M" derives
largely from the FPL's specific approach, it quickly became the standard term used
to refer to the five constituent organizations that would make up the FMLN.

Though each group had a clear (and unique) vision of how the insurrection
should go, executing any one of their plans in practice—whether rural or urban,
quick or prolonged—demanded extensive military training and adequate supplies. The groups spent years competing unsuccessfully for Cuba's support. Then
in 1979, the Sandinistas' victory against the Samoza regime in Nicaragua simultaneously established precedent for a successful leftist insurrection in Central
America and created an opportunity to exploit the supply chain from Cuba to
Nicaragua. There was only one problem. While Fidel Castro viewed the Nicaraguan victory as a favorable moment to incite leftist revolutions throughout the
region, he insisted that the left in El Salvador would only receive support on the
condition that the revolutionary groups form a united front. Not without considerable drama, they agreed. Following a year of fraught negotiations, the five
leaders came together in October of 1980 to form an umbrella organization they
called the Farabundo Martí National Liberation Front in honor of the leader and
martyr of the 1932 peasant uprising against the government.

Despite pushback from the ERP—whose leaders argued that the FMLN
should be a truly unified front—the composite organizations each retained

their own ideology, structure, and tactical approach throughout the war.[25] Thus, the leaders from each constituent organization together composed the General Command, which in theory (if not always in practice) operated via democratic centralism; and the OP-Ms on the ground continued operating as they had prior to unification.[26]

Explaining the FMLN's Structure

How did the FMLN come to be structured the way it did? What accounts for the stark variation across the OP-Ms, and what are the implications within and beyond the war? Drawing on conventional theories of militant groups' structures and the integrated explanation I lay out in chapter 1, I derive a series of organizational predictions. Though most conventional explanations of rebel group emergence describe the organization as a whole, where possible, I extrapolate to make more nuanced predictions about suborganizational variation in accordance with the new approach and, more importantly, to suit the specifics of this case. For each explanation, I identify the type of evidence needed to support a given account of structure.

Doctrinal Ideology

The broad principles of ideological doctrine seldom translate into clear organizational blueprints. As such, deriving a coherent (let alone complete) argument about how a given ideology dictates a corresponding organizational structure can be a mystifying task. However, if there were ever a situation where the ideology argument should work, Marxist-Leninist organizations would be it. Leninist thought establishes an inextricable link between ideology and organization, citing a vanguard party, propaganda and political education, and peripheral organizations in service of recruitment and mobilization as core organizational priorities.[27] Since organization itself is central to Marxist-Leninist doctrine, deriving a set of structural predictions is more straightforward here than for groups espousing other ideologies.[28]

If ideology is the core determinant of organizational form, groups should build structures to support behaviors advocated by Marxist doctrine: civilian governance, political education, and propaganda. Crucially, given that all the OP-Ms (i.e., the five subgroups composing the FMLN) subscribe to the same overarching doctrine, conventional ideological explanations would lead us to expect structural similarities across the FMLN's component organizations. Their structures should differ only insofar as the respective OP-Ms have access to different resources (thereby making some subdivisions more difficult to support) or draw on different social networks to feed into the organization (thereby making some subdivisions more difficult to staff). Most broadly, if ideology is driving organizational structure, we should also expect the FMLN's structure to mirror that of other Marxist-Leninist organizations worldwide.

Structural (State-centric) Explanations

Structural theories attribute militant organizational form to leaders either exploiting or being constrained by the broader context in which they operate.[29] Given that each component of the FMLN emerged in the context of the same repressive state apparatus and under similar (if not identical) structural conditions, these accounts of organizational structure suggest the OP-Ms should be organizationally comparable as well. By their nature, structural explanations of militant organizational form will not be especially conducive to explaining why organizations emerging in the same context differ considerably from one another. Nevertheless, the logic can be extended to make some predictions.[30]

To the extent that the FMLN's composite groups exhibit differences, they should be functions of emerging in different structural conditions. For example, the FPL and ERP emerged and operated primarily in rural areas, where the state's reach was considerably weaker than in cities like San Salvador, where the PCS was headquartered. Additionally, differences in terrain, state reach, and even the social networks surrounding the nascent rebellion may likely account for different organizations. However, absent from the literature are fine-grained predictions about how these divergent structural conditions might translate into predictable organizational variation. This omission is reminiscent of the problem with ideology. Namely, it is easy to imagine that different structural conditions might give rise to different organizational forms; it is considerably harder to specify logically (let alone empirically) which organizational dimensions (roles, relations, institutions, or traits) these structural features would affect and how. Michael Horowitz, Evan Perkoski, and Philip B.K. Potter's theory yields a specific, albeit narrow, prediction. According to their structural theory, we should expect tactical diversification when militant groups face state repression and competition from rival groups.[31] Thus, since each OP-M faced competition from four rivals, we should expect tactical diversification across all of the groups.

Resource Endowments

While the resource explanation is not often used to explain suborganizational variation, it too can be amended to make more granular predictions. If resource endowments contribute to opportunistic recruitment profiles and indiscipline, then we should expect these outcomes to manifest in the ERP and the PCS.[32] Though the ERP lacked a wealthy social base, Cuba's preference for the ERP's strategy and the ERP's control of supply lines meant that it often had the most resources and the best weapons.[33] On the financial front, the PCS led the pack. It had a robust network of international support predating the war—and this wealth was not a secret.[34] As Ralph Sprenkels observed, "interviewees often joked that, in lean times, everyone wanted to defect from their own factions and join [the PCS] because [they] were never short of food, medicine, weapons, or ammunition."[35] In contrast, Amelia Hoover Green describes the FPL as "largely bereft of both arms and money [in the early years of the war]."[36] Consequently, it should boast more ideologically committed recruits, and thus, greater discipline than the other two factions.

Conventional resource endowment theories focus primarily on material resources and only account for variation in the recruitment profile of militant groups and not the specific structures they build. One could reasonably extend resource explanations to account for the type of structural diversification relevant to the rebel-to-party theory advanced here. Specifically, if building wartime structures dedicated to social service provision, political messaging, and governance better positions rebel groups to take on party-relevant tasks once the war ends, one might expect that the operation and maintenance of these wings is entirely a function of whether groups have the resources available to construct them in the first place. If this hypothesis holds, we should then expect the most pronounced organizational diversification to occur in the OP-Ms with the greatest access to resources, the ERP and the PCS. In contrast, we should expect the FPL and the PRTC to exhibit a sort of organizational sparseness, at least relatively speaking.

Prewar Networks

Finally, if prewar networks explain organizational structure, we should expect structural parallels between OP-Ms cut from the same social cloth. The FPL and ERP are the most obvious contenders to test the full breadth of this theory. Both groups emerged in poor, rural areas of El Salvador: Chalatenango and Morazán, respectively.[37] Both coalesced among the CEBs established in the 1960s and '70s. And for both groups, these communities were not just backdrops to a burgeoning rebellion; rather, they were integral parts of the FPL's and ERP's organizational development.[38] According to Staniland's framework, we should expect the FPL and the ERP to exhibit the following structural similarities by virtue of being rooted in similar networks: bureaucratic specialization, standard operating procedures, and coherent ideology.[39]

Staniland goes on to predict that strong vertical ties with locals will also give rise to an "organizational backbone to govern, provide services, and control the population."[40] In organizational terms, this hypothesis implies that strong (or comparably strong) vertical relations will result in organizations developing similar roles or subdivisions to manage those relations. In other words, this theory posits that the strength of ties can predict organizational content. Since the FPL, ERP, and PRTC emerged with strong ties to local communities, we should observe structures that support governance, social service provision, and local administration.

Integrated Theory of Organizational Emergence

Each factor previously enumerated matters. Even through the lens of the new organizational approach, existing theories are not supplanted; they are made more complete. Rather than dismiss them or even frame them as "rival explanations," I demonstrate that previous explanations are on the right track with a rickety vehicle.[41] The theory I propose in chapter 1 integrates these factors and relates them more directly to the scope of organizational structures relevant to rebel-to-party transformation. Specifically, to understand how organizations change, we must first understand what structures they start with and how they came to be that way.

The outcome I seek to explain is the FMLN's organizational structure at the point of emergence—with particular attention paid to the diversity and type of noncombat subdivisions.[42] As noted in the previous chapter, leaders have more room to make consequential organizational decisions at the nascent stages of rebellion than at later stages when organizations fall into patterns of inertia. Whether they are following an established blueprint for insurgency or formulating a structure from the ground up, the question is the same: what drives and constrains their choices?

Organizational ideology is likely to play two key roles in the FMLN's organizational genesis. First, splits will fall along organizational-ideological lines; groups will fracture and coalesce around different views of "how to get the job done." Second, organizational ideology, in turn, will shape structures both directly, as leaders rely on those principles to determine what form their organization should take, and indirectly, by conditioning how resources and social networks are incorporated into the organization as it coalesces. Groups whose foundational principles emphasize political work and mass engagement will likely construct more numerous—and more extensive—political and administrative wings outside of the combat domain. In contrast, groups that coalesced around principles emphasizing the central role of militancy will likely build noncombat structures only to the extent that they directly serve the combat apparatus.

Confirming this mechanism is not without challenges. In the first place, attributing any organizational outcome to this concept demands evidence that organizational ideology is conceptually valid. In practice, this means finding evidence that leaders are intentionally adapting doctrine into organizational guidelines and then finding evidence that they are making organizational decisions in accordance with those principles. Otherwise, wartime structures may still be incidental outcomes of some antecedent condition that better explains both structure and, eventually, transformation. Table 2.1 summarizes the organizational predictions for the FMLN's structure, disaggregated by theory.

TABLE 2.1.   FMLN organizational expectations by theory

THEORY	MECHANISM	FMLN PREDICTIONS
Ideology	Doctrine prescribes structure	All OP-Ms should have comparable structures; extant differences must be attributable to other factors.
Structural	State and regime factors	OP-Ms should have comparable structures.
	Urban vs. rural emergence	The FPL and ERP (rural) will be organizationally similar to each other and different from the PCS and RN (urban).
	Competition	All OP-Ms should exhibit tactical diversification because they emerged in competition with one another.
Resources	Recruitment profile	The ERP and PCS will attract opportunistic, less ideologically committed recruits while the FPL attracts more ideologically committed recruits.
	Capacity	The ERP and PCS will have the resources to diversify most extensively; the FPL and PRTC should exhibit the least structural diversification.
Prewar networks	Comparable and cohesive networks	The ERP and FPL should exhibit structural and relational similarities to each other and distinctions from each other OP-M.
Organizational	Organizational ideology and resources	The FPL, PCS, PRTC, and RN will diversify into more party-relevant domains than the ERP.

Organizational Analysis of the FMLN

Using comparative process tracing, we can now track the FMLN's organizational evolution from its initial fractures to its postinsurrection structure(s). The objective is twofold: to test the predictions derived from the various theories of organizational emergence and to acquaint the reader with the structural nuances across the FMLN's constituent parts. While I touch on all five OP-Ms, the analysis focuses most extensively on the FPL, the ERP, and the PRTC to optimize across meaningful variation and tractability. The FPL and ERP were the two largest organizations composing the FMLN. They split and armed earlier than the others and, as a result, they were central players in the negotiations to unify. Moreover, they stemmed from similar—if not identical—social bases, held comparable territories throughout the war, and faced similar amounts of state violence. At the outset, their only detectable difference was in how they wanted to get the job done. The PRTC, in contrast, was the smallest of the OP-Ms. It formed late and joined the negotiations even later—so much so that it cost the PRTC any real say in the future of the revolutionary left.[43] To situate the analysis, the section begins by elaborating on the organizational ideologies, structural context, prewar networks, and resources of each group.

Since the core of the argument hinges on whether organizational ideology is conceptually (and empirically) valid, let us begin there. Evidence from the ground is conclusive. Marxist-Leninist doctrine guided the rebellion, yet each OP-M articulated a different interpretation and cleaved to (and rejected) different principles. The salience of organizational-ideological distinctions is evident even in how leaders discuss their organizations. One of the few areas in which Carpio (FPL) and Villalobos (ERP) agree is in their outright rejection of the idea that a doctrine as broad as Marxism-Leninism is sufficient to determine the organization's approach or structure. Indeed, Carpio even calls Marxism-Leninism the "common trunk" from which the PCS and the FPL emerged—careful to note that where they differ is in how they "interpret and apply it to the Salvadoran condition."[44] Similarly, when asked how the FMLN defined its core ideology, Villalobos responded, "Within the FMLN and the FDR, *there are many different doctrines.*"[45] In a written account of the FPL's origins, the Central Command makes a nearly watertight case against equating broad dogma with specific outcomes.[46] "Dogmatism is a false application of Marxism-Leninism, with static, dead, mechanistic methods that kill its creative spirit, turning it not into a guide to action, but a vast repetition of formulas that try to be applied to a reality."[47]

Even Carpio, the most ardent Marxist, rejects the notion that Marxism can be adopted whole cloth:[48]

"[We are] clear that Marxism is . . . a scientific instrument for the interpretation of reality that permits us to find the most correct solutions and proposals for each situation."[49]

The PRTC commander "Roberto Roca" further reifies organizational ideology when he speaks of the movement as a whole: "We want democracy and stability and we'll want help from abroad. We're an expression of . . . pluralism [the broad spectrum of Marxist and democratic views represented in the opposition]. Our new society cannot be built under the domination of one political force."[50]

At one point or another, each group stresses that Marxist doctrine works only when it is adapted to the Salvadoran context. Each organizational ideology, in turn, has clear structural implications.

Through the FPL's lens, Marxist-Leninist ideology clearly points to a prolonged popular war firmly rooted in the masses. The FPL sought to "establish the infrastructure of resistance" among the population, which Carpio viewed as essential to waging a successful revolution.[51] Crucially, this argument is not merely rhetorical; FPL leaders argued explicitly that the organization must reflect this priority: "No revolutionary movement seeking the liberation of the people can do so without developing an adequate structure that allows the widest participation of the masses in the war."[52]

Of course, seeking mass support is not unique. Local support is regarded as indispensable to any successful rebellion for everything from material provisions to recruitment to discretion.[53] Beyond these critical roles, the FPL regarded the masses as "much more than just logistical support."[54] They were considered extensions of the movement—players whose organization, education, and politicization was a defining feature of the struggle. FPL leaders spoke early and often of this priority.[55]

Finally, the FPL's organizational ideology casts the revolution as a multidimensional fight: they consistently emphasized the importance of "incorporating the people into *the diverse tasks of the war*: education, ideological training, political messaging, diplomacy."[56] This call is as much a prescription for organizational structure as it is an articulation of the group's priorities. Carrying out any of these tasks in practice demands an organizational structure that reflects its ideals.

The founding documents of the ERP tell a very different story. Crucially, the ERP's leaders were also staunch adherents of Marxist-Leninist thought.[57] Despite their comparable commitment to a socialist revolution, the group's organizational ideology differed markedly from its counterparts and had direct implications for its structure. In a stark contrast to the FPL's stance that militarism should be subordinate to political work, the ERP wrote that "the seizure of power through arms, the resolution of the problem through war . . . is the highest expression of the revolution."[58] Indeed, the front cover of the ERP's first printed call to action features Mao Zedong's slogan: Power is born of the rifle.

The primacy placed on military action abounds in the ERP's writing: "Freedom is not requested, it is conquered with weapons in hand," "without a revolutionary army, the people will have nothing," and "only with the power of arms can the working class defeat the armed bourgeoisie."[59] However, it would be wrong to assume that the ERP was a hypermilitant force devoid of principles. The ERP was built on a cohesive set of principles encompassed by the foquismo theory of revolution, and the organization was structured accordingly.[60] The principles shaping its organizational and strategic approach were based on two core beliefs. First, the ERP leaders believed the people were sufficiently aggrieved that as long as they knew of revolutionary action, they would join it.[61] Second, the leaders were convinced that the state was too weak to defend itself. As such, the ERP leaders felt that time spent organizing the masses was wasteful; to them, popular uprising was an inevitability. To the extent that they viewed mass organizing as a good use of time and resources, it was only "as a means of gaining new recruits."[62] As Hugh Byrne notes, the ERP "put less emphasis on developing an independent peasant movement and more upon harnessing the grievances of the peasantry into military action."[63] This view of revolution paves the way for a more homogeneous organizational structure that prioritizes expansion of the armed forces.

The PRTC's organizational ideology is evident from the moment it broke with the ERP. In a document recounting the origins and history of the PRTC, Nidia Díaz (one of the group's founders) attributes the split directly to disagreements over how the war should be fought and how the organization should be structured to reflect its ideological orientation.[64] The PRTC's approach was much closer to that of the FPL: its members, too, expressed frustration with the ERP's sole focus on militancy.[65] They viewed the armed struggle as necessary, but not primary. Echoing Carl von Clausewitz, Díaz writes, "The point is that armed struggle is a way to carry out the political struggle. It is to do politics through weapons because you were excluded from engaging in an unarmed political fight."[66]

The PRTC heavily emphasized the importance of coordinating and interfacing with the masses. To achieve this goal, the group placed organization and political education front and center—both within and beyond its ranks. The primacy of political, educational, and mass work permeates its writing and is evident in how PRTC members think and talk about the organization.[67] The notable distinction in the PRTC's interpretation of the struggle was its commitment to a pan–Central American revolution, which had distinct organizational implications down the line.

Before examining how the groups' respective ideological tendencies shape their organizations, we must first consider their contexts and the social bases in which they emerge. Following Staniland's logic, I account for the nucleus of each OP-M as well as the local social base in which each is embedded.[68] Similarly, I expect that an organization's underlying social networks will shape the efficacy of command-and-control structures (e.g., communication, discipline, and hierarchy). Illuminated by the new organizational approach, however, I also expect that social networks—filtered through a group's organizational ideology—will shape the content of the organization: the roles and subdivisions within the group and the type and extent of interactions beyond the group's bounds.

At the top, the FPL, ERP, and PRTC had similar origins. The FPL's leadership primarily comprised activists from the labor movement and educational sectors. Many professors rose to prominence within the movement, including one of the founders of ANDES—a radical teachers union that maintained close ties with (and often fed into) the FPL and the PRTC throughout the war.[69] The PRTC, likewise, originated among radical teacher and student unions. Perhaps surprisingly, the initial nucleus of the ERP looked quite similar. The ERP's core was also deeply rooted in revolutionary teacher and student organizations, the labor movement, and peasant cooperatives as well as artists and poets.

The social bases of the FPL and ERP were even more similar—differing most notably in their locations.[70] The FPL was primarily based among the campesinos of rural Chalatenango, a department in northern El Salvador. The ERP was headquartered in rural Morazán, a department in the east. Both departments were among the poorest in the country; both are quite rural and were populated largely by agricultural workers and their families. Both departments also suffered tremendous violence at the hands of the state.[71] As such, the broader structural conditions of their organizations were similar as well. Furthermore, in spite of the strict proscriptions on public organizing, CEBs flourished in both areas.[72] Thus, both the FPL and ERP were forged among politicized social bases with some experience in leadership and popular organization. And CEBs would come to play integral roles in both organizations.[73]

Before moving on, a brief detour is in order. Specifically, the incorporation of these networks occupies an interesting place at the intersection of organizational ideology and social networks that should not be taken as given. CEBs pose a notable explanatory challenge as the social foundation of a Marxist rebellion.[74] If, indeed, a strict adherence to doctrine were the guiding force in determining organizational structure, then we should expect staunch Marxists to balk at the incorporation of religious networks. Alternately, if the organizations' ideological principles trump their guiding doctrine, then both the FPL and the ERP should embrace these networks, but they should do so in very different ways. The FPL takes up this question explicitly in a document articulating how its organizational ideology shapes it structure:

Our revolutionary work is directed against the enemy of the people, it is not aimed at undermining religion. [Our] experience in this area indicates that religious activity and revolutionary activity *can be fruitfully combined* in the interests of the people. . . . The FPL accepts in its ranks every honest revolutionary who consciously subscribes to our strategy and politics as well as our organizational and disciplinary guidelines, provided their religious practices do not pose an obstacle.[75]

Where the groups did ultimately diverge was in their resource access—both in material goods and manpower. In terms of size, all estimates place the FPL and ERP at relative parity. Each had somewhere between three thousand and four thousand armed members during the war.[76] The PRTC, in contrast, was the smallest OP-M, with an armed membership hovering between five hundred and seven hundred.[77] The groups split differently on the material front. While the FPL, ERP, and PRTC emerged as relatively resource poor, Cuba's (eventual) decision to favor the ERP's strategic approach resulted in a notable resource disparity between the ERP and the others throughout the war. Recall that the FPL was notoriously resource-poor.[78] And as the PRTC glibly noted of themselves, their early cadres were "lacking shoes, but had great morale."[79] The disparities were sufficiently severe that the ERP allegedly exploited them to try to recruit members from other OP-Ms with the promise of more goods and better weapons.[80]

Similar Origins, Divergent Paths: The FPL and the ERP

The FPL and ERP exhibit notable parallels in their prewar networks and the populations among which they emerged. According to some theories, these parallels would lead us to expect similarly structured organizations—at least on the dimensions we are equipped to evaluate.[81] We should expect effective command-and-control structures, high levels of discipline, cohesion among the leadership as well as the rank-and-file, and strong vertical ties to local populations.[82] Even their membership profiles should look similar, given the tools we have to describe them: since neither group was especially well endowed (at least until Cuba came into the picture) we should expect early members to be ideologues rather than opportunists.[83] Conventional organizational tools point only to two areas in which we might observe differences: (1) in the size and tactics of their military units, and (2) in their combat resources, since the ERP eventually came to occupy a privileged role vis-à-vis Cuba's supply lines. To be sure, this is exactly what we find. By the late 1970s, the FPL and ERP are cohesive and disciplined, and both have forged strong ties to populations in their respective areas.[84]

However, these traits paint a picture that is both accurate and misleading. While the FPL and ERP were similar on these dimensions, they diverged sharply on others. If my theory holds, their distinct organizational ideologies should lead the FPL and the ERP to use the same resources to build very different organizations. Given the value that the FPL placed on "the political side of the fight" combined with its prewar roots in the education and union sectors, I expect this group to build robust subdivisions dedicated to political education and political messaging. Moreover, the members' staunch commitment to grounding the revolution in mass organization suggests that we should observe a deeply embedded organization with social outreach structures and high overlap between the networks composing its social base and the (related) subdivisions of the organization. In contrast, the primacy placed on spectacular displays of military force should lead the ERP to forge a much more homogeneous structure with more utilitarian relations between the organization and its surrounding communities. The divergence tracks in lockstep with my expectations.

If organizational ideology shapes role diversification the way I anticipate, the leaders' heavy emphasis on diverse political and mass work should be reflected in the FPL's structures. Far from just talking the talk, the FPL's internal documents are filled with concrete organizational tasks to this end, all of which (eventually) came to fruition on the ground. FPL leaders immediately documented the need to create the internal structures necessary to coordinate what they call "the diverse tasks of war," including "the [urgent] need for propaganda, finances, and education."[85] "The organizational structure was being created from the top down because the base was not yet defined. We saw the need for [our] Central Committee to create national commissions and rely on them to coordinate the different aspects of work: a Mass Commission, Military, Relations, Organization, Propaganda, Education, Finance, etc."[86]

To wit, they emphasized seven organizational tasks that had to come before fighting: "organizing the workers, creating unity among labor unions, organizing the peasantry, creating a peasant-worker alliance, organizing different popular sectors, creating the necessary political vehicles to incorporate the popular sectors, and strengthening clandestine organizing."[87] Indeed, the process of constructing the FPL followed this directive so closely that it actually caused rifts severe enough that dissenters eventually split off to form the ERP.

The process of building up the organizational base followed suit. This trend is evident in both the FPL's recruitment strategies and the brokerage structures it built to link the rebellion with popular organizations. Even from the beginning, recruitment efforts prioritized skilled personnel who could be promoted to political and organizational work. This emphasis is explicitly laid out in documents recounting the FPL's organizational formation, as the following quote illustrates:

"Each of the five members of the Central Command was forced to find 15 collaborators as a cover to be able to eat, sleep, etc. Among these 75 collaborators, the most advanced would be promoted to do political work. So the command grew, and we gave them the name 'Support Groups.' Their role was to take charge of the political work[;] . . . they were not just logistical support."[88] Beyond the top-down recruitment tactics, even the FPL's intake forms illustrate the extent to which political aptitude was prized above almost all else. Following basic demographic questions, the next section was titled "Political, Ideological, and Military Level," in which recruits were asked to explain their knowledge of the FPL's political-military line and their knowledge of Marxism-Leninism.[89] They inquired about recruits' prior military experience as well, but the emphasis on vetting recruits based on their education levels, political knowledge, and skill sets provides clear evidence that the FPL was looking to staff subdivisions beyond its combat wings.

To broker relationships beyond the FPL's membership, leaders built "political structures of the masses" to coordinate, provide services to, and conduct political-ideological training among the local population, even prior to the war.[90] They also constructed a mass organization, the Popular Revolutionary Bloc (BPR), which helped coordinate action between their affiliated student and labor groups and the clandestine side of the rebellion.[91] The composition of the BPR mirrored that of its leadership: labor unions, revolutionary teacher and student organizations, as well as agricultural cooperatives and a popular culture group.

Finally, the FPL's value of organizational diversification is evident even in how the group sees its armed forces, as the FPL leader Leonel González illustrates. In discussing the importance of mass mobilization, González says, "[Our plan is to] . . . make each one of our combatants an organizer of the people."[92] They also built structures dedicated to political education within the organization to promote discipline and ensure members understood their role. Consider, for example, how Carpio characterized a military cell—the unit that we would assume would have the most clear task and narrow scope:

"What role does a cell have? To study and control militancy. But this is only part of their work. If a cell does not enhance the political-ideological knowledge of its members, then it has no purpose. The cells exist fundamentally to carry the Party line to the masses, to organize and guide them."[93] As Jenny Pearce notes, they viewed their territory within the same framework:

> The FPL had never seen the zones of control as mere military rear-guards. Rather they saw them within a broader framework of political mobilization, and as a means by which the civilian population could guarantee their needs and organize their society independent of the military command of the FPL. . . . They contrasted their view with the

situation in territory controlled by the ERP, where the [local popular organizing] tended to be a means of mobilizing people for the war effort rather than for political preparation.[94]

Thus, in the run-up to the insurrection, the FPL built an organization that reflected its view of what revolution is. It is, of course, worth noting that many of the organizational structures the FPL planned prior to the war were not fully developed until shortly after the 1981 insurrection. For example, the group's early attempts to create mass literacy and educational structures were ad hoc and inefficient—though eventually the FPL would go on to build a robust educational apparatus and local governance structures.[95] Nevertheless, its codified plans to diversify into a wide scope of social, political, and administrative domains give rise to clear organizational predictions that manifest in its wartime structure.

The ERP's ideology yields a very different set of organizational expectations. Two priorities suffuse the group's writing: militancy and communication, where the latter exists primarily in service of the former.[96] Thus, we should expect a strong and expansive combat division, and any structural diversification beyond that should focus on logistics and communication. Unsurprisingly, the ERP dedicated most of its resources to building and training its army. As James Dunkerley notes, the ERP limited its work throughout the 1970s to perfecting its military capacity, "in which it far outstripped the other groups."[97]

Notwithstanding their laser focus on militancy, ERP leaders understood that recruits are won rather than born. They just thought winning would be easy. A guiding premise of ERP operations was that the public was sufficiently aggrieved that merely learning about antigovernment action would be enough to galvanize them. All they needed was information. ERP graffiti from the era neatly captures this sentiment: *Estar desinformado es como estar desarmado* (to be uninformed is to be unarmed).[98] Thus, complementing the ERP's emphasis on assembling combat units was an explicit call for a robust communications apparatus to coordinate action.[99] There was just one hitch: the rebels had no way to get the word out. The media blackout following the 1972 elections culminated in lasting and rigid control over all media outlets.[100] El Salvador had no free press to speak of, journalists were routinely targeted by the regime, and the penalty for distributing antigovernment literature was often death on the spot.[101]

Two external challenges shaped the form a communication wing would take: First, the regime's draconian control over print media meant that even if they could efficiently produce written material, the people would be unlikely to take it. Second, even if they could print and distribute their message, nearly half of the population couldn't read.[102] Their solution was beyond ambitious: to create a mobile radio station in under a month with the broadcast strength to reach the capital. What followed is a prime example of how state-centric (structural) features shape organizational structures in critical ways beyond what Horowitz, Perkoski and Potter predict.[103] José López Vigil's memoirs speaks directly to the interplay between repression and organizational composition:

"The repression was brutal. Print media was no longer effective. If you had a leaflet in your bag, it could cost you your life. Was it worth risking the lives of those handing leaflets out, to say nothing of those accepting them? Maybe that's why the idea of a radio station took root—*they can't frisk you for a voice.*"[104]

From both an organizational and logistical standpoint, any one component of this plan was quixotic: Only shortwave radios were legal, which meant they needed to find one, find a technician capable of converting it into an AM transmitter, hire the staff to run and maintain the station, and make the whole operation mobile. Nevertheless, in just thirteen days, ERP members stole a sixty-pound shortwave radio; recruited Toño, an electrical engineer who managed to convert "The Viking" into an AM transmitter; and found Carlos Henríque Consalvi (a.k.a. "Santiago"), a journalist who would host the radio's programming and eventually become "the most recognizable voice in El Salvador."[105]

Thus was born ¡Radio Venceremos!—not just a radio station, but a subdivision of the ERP that managed to broadcast twice a day for the entire twelve years of the civil war. Furthermore, the ¡Radio Venceremos! subdivision would eventually expand to include a host of publications, including books, newspapers, and pamphlets.[106] The logistics of maintaining this operation were enormous: they needed staff, writers, technicians, and, crucially, protection, as they were one of the most sought-after targets of the Salvadoran army.[107]

Beyond (and even including) the organizational and operational feat that was ¡Radio Venceremos!, diversification outside the combat realm was always subordinate to the ERP's army. Even ¡Radio Venceremos! was viewed primarily as a logistical tool. It was a way to convey information (rather than ideology) and to coordinate action among the movement and the masses. As Villalobos notes in an interview, "The role of ¡Radio Venceremos! is precisely to break the [state's] information blockade, to allow other information to be available."[108] Further, the one-time ERP member Francisco Jovel recalled how the leadership eschewed ideological discussion: "People [inside the ERP] really looked down on those who were interested in the theoretical and intellectual training of guerrillas."[109] Beyond core logistical tasks like financing and distribution, ¡Radio Venceremos! was the ERP's most extensive diversification move.

Zooming out, the origin story of ¡Radio Venceremos! highlights how macrostructural features (like state repression) are filtered through organizational ideology (the critical role of communication) to shape the group's decisions. As López

Vigil's evocative quote illustrates, the regime's particular brand of repression and El Salvador's systemic illiteracy together explain why the ERP opted to build a radio station over other, simpler forms of communication. The takeaway is that structural and contextual idiosyncrasies can incite different types of diversification— but to find them, we need a model of organizations that acknowledges variation beyond the combat realm.

Turning back to the ERP's organizational trajectory, I examine how its prewar connections to CEBs figured into the group. In contrast to vast governance structures the FPL planned and (eventually) built to interface with local populations, the ERP took a staunchly utilitarian approach to the masses.[110] Despite being similarly situated among CEBs, the ERP leadership saw these networks as important, but only as a pool of viable resources. When asked why having influence over the masses was necessary, Villalobos replied predictably: "Because we depend on them. Without the masses, we in the rearguard would not have had the greatest opportunity— lacking both human reserves and supplies."[111] Those who would later leave the organization characterized the ERP's view of the masses in an even grimmer light, arguing that the ERP was "building an armed apparatus detached from the mass struggle," which was "an erroneous position" that made it possible to cultivate not only "sensationalist actions" but also "contempt for the masses, the mass struggle, and political work."[112] The extent to which the ERP did build administrative structures to coordinate local populations was to form People's Military Committees, which functioned exclusively as a training and recruitment apparatus.[113]

Finally, unlike the other OP-Ms, each of which were quick to build an affiliated popular organization, the ERP remained indifferent to mass political mobilization. Though initially it affiliated with the United Popular Action Front (FAPU), the ERP's militaristic approach "lost peasant support" and FAPU eventually broke ties with it.[114] Unsurprisingly, given its priorities, the ERP remained reluctant to build another mass front for some years.[115] As Tommie Sue Montgomery notes, when the ERP finally did build one in 1978 (the Ligas-Populares 28 de Febrero, or LP-28), it was "the result of a belated recognition by the ERP that if it did not, it was going to be left in the dust by the FPL and the RN."[116] Predictably, and despite primarily comprising faculty and students from the University of El Salvador, the LP-28 had the "least developed political program."[117] It was used to "capitalize on the social influence developed by the guerrillas [throughout their strongholds]" through militia teams, which eventually "fused with the ERP" to establish its stronghold in Morazán.[118]

Reminiscent of adages about hammers and nails, the ERP-FPL comparison illustrates how organizational-ideological differences shape how leaders view local communities, resources, and the state context in which they emerge. Organizational ideology is a frame, a lens through which leaders see the world. While frames can complement and call attention to important features of a picture, they are also borders—forcing other features out of bounds. Leaders will see the world through the tints and distortions of their principles. In practice, this means two leaders can look at the same world, see very different opportunities, and, in turn, build very different organizations—which is exactly what we find.

As the smallest of the OP-Ms, the PRTC is a useful counterpoint to test the other side of the organizational resources hypothesis.[119] Namely, one might reasonably assume that structural diversification is a by-product of size.[120] After all—just statistically—the more people you have, the more skills you likely have access to. In turn, once these skills exist within the organization, corresponding subdivisions may coalesce organically around them. Were that the case, however, we would expect very different trajectories from both the ERP and the PRTC: of all the organizations, the ERP should be the most organizationally diverse, the PRTC should be the least so. Additionally, the PRTC lacked the territorial stronghold of its larger counterparts. The absence of a rearguard matters because many scholars view rebel-held territory as a necessary condition for activities like rebel governance (and thus, the building of governance and administrative structures).[121]

Yet the PRTC, despite being poorer and less than one-fifth the size of the ERP, boasted a highly diverse structure across what will prove to be some of the most salient organizational domains for this study.[122] In spite of the factors stacked against them, members of the PRTC built an organization that clearly reflected the organizational ideology articulated previously. Initially, their international organization spanned Costa Rica, Honduras, and El Salvador with Zonal Directorates in each of the countries.[123] By 1980 their Salvadoran contingent also comprised the Adan Diaz political-ideological school and the Humberto Mendoza military school to train new recruits.[124] The primacy of political, educational, and mass work permeates the PRTC's writing and is evident in how PRTC members think and talk about the organization—in addition to how they built it.[125] Throughout Díaz's field diaries, for example, the cadres and subdivisions dedicated to peaceful political work take clear primacy over the military when she depicts the organization's structure (see figure 2.3).[126]

The PRTC's priorities are as evident in the structures they built as they are in the recruitment strategies they employed to fill those structures. Figure 2.4 depicts a redacted control sheet for people enlisting in the PRTC.[127] Reminiscent of the FPL's intake forms, the content and order of the questions is revealing. Following basic demographic data, the forms immediately ask whether a candidate can read and write and what grade of school they completed. They ask for express justification for joining the PRTC (and what, if anything, prompted the recruit

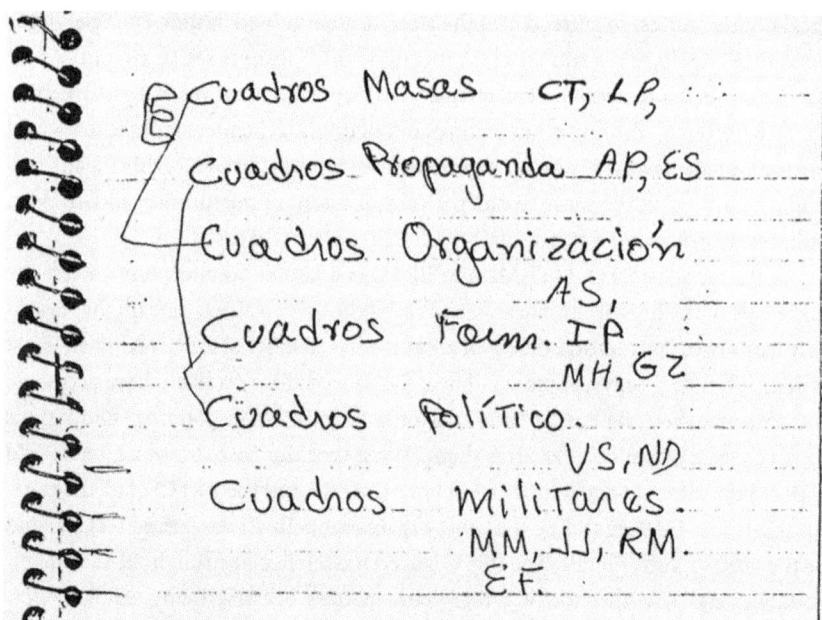

FIGURE 2.3. PRTC organizational documents. Wartime Diary, Nidia Díaz Papers, box 1, folder 6, Hoover Institution Library & Archives.

to leave a different OP-M). Finally, they ask whether the recruit has undergone political or military training. These questions demonstrate a clear interest in the scope of skills potential members bring to the table. And the leaders confirm this inference from the top. In a document outlining the plan for political expansion of the PRTC, Díaz expressly calls for the organization to "prioritize those with skills as propagandists and political organizers."[128]

Ultimately, if wartime organizational structures were governed solely by resources or the structural conditions under which the group operates, we would not find this level of diversification among the group with fewest resources. Yet, the PRTC eventually built a mass organization, it set up administrative councils to interface with and govern local populations, and it built and ran schools during the war.

The Remaining OP-Ms

The FPL, ERP, and PRTC were just three of the five politico-military organizations that made up the FMLN. Beyond them, the RN and the PCS also boast unique organizational ideologies and distinct social bases, and they built corresponding structures and affiliated mass organizations. Here, I briefly recount

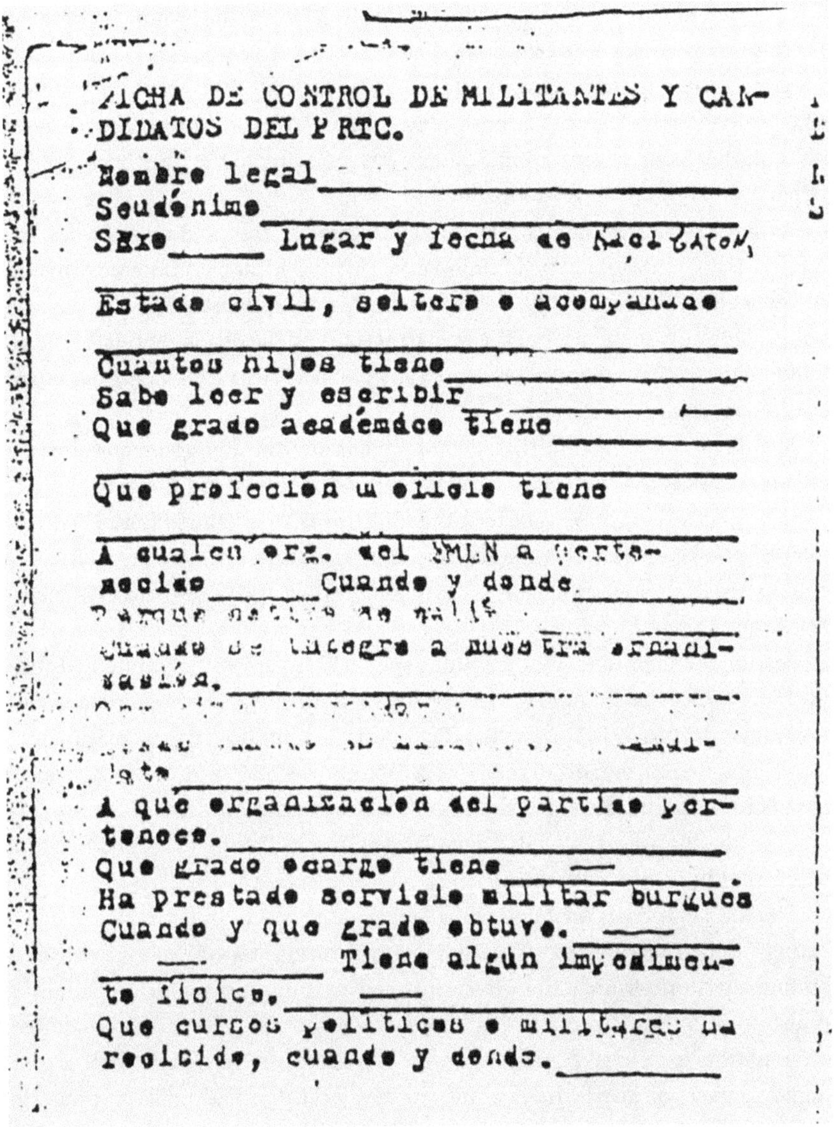

FICHA DE CONTROL DE MILITANTES Y CAN-
DIDATOS DEL PRTC.
Nombre legal
Seudónimo
Sexo_____ Lugar y fecha de Nacimiento
Estado civil, soltero o acompañado
Cuantos hijos tiene
Sabe leer y escribir
Que grado académico tiene
Que profesión u oficio tiene
A cuales org. del FMLN a perte-
neciдo_____ Cuando y donde
Porque nació de nulis
Cuando se integra a nuestra organi-
zación.
...
la to
A que organización del partido per-
tenece.
Que grado ecargo tiene
Ha prestado servicio militar burgues
Cuando y que grado obtuvo.
_____ Tiene algún impedimen-
to físico.
Que cursos políticos o militares ha
recibido, cuando y donde.

FIGURE 2.4. PRTC organizational documents. PRTC Recruitment Cards, Nidia
Díaz Papers, box 1, folder 2, Hoover Institution Library & Archives.

the emergence of the other two groups and the process of building the FMLN to
contextualize the case.

Like the PRTC, the Resistencia Nacional also originated as a faction within
the ERP. At the top, the ERP's founding nucleus was quite diverse, comprising
individuals from the educational sector, organized labor, and the arts. While this

diversity could have evolved into an organizational asset, the group was beset by the same brand of ideological fissures that characterized earlier splits. Hardliners were committed to prioritizing military action above all else; others felt political engagement should occupy a more central role.[129] Worse yet, these ideological divisions fell along organizational faults corresponding to the lines between different groups composing their core.

As former ERP members recounted, "In light of the predominance of the militaristic organizational bent, finding the right political path became difficult. At the level of the leadership, there was a concern for mass work and internal political life only in theory, but the very structure and the organizational focus on building the armed apparatus prevented any practical steps from being dedicated to this concern."[130]

Members of the faction that eventually became the RN consistently wrote of "impasses" at the leadership level and "clashes between the theoretical level" (which acknowledged the salience of political work) and "the practical" (which focused almost exclusively on building "militaristic cliques").[131] These divisions culminated in the entrapment and murder of the poet and prominent ERP member Roque Dalton.[132]

Fearing for their lives after Dalton's assassination and still discontented with the narrow focus on grandiose military action, the more politically-oriented faction broke away in 1974 to form the RN. The RN emphasized a mass orientation, which manifested organizationally as structures dedicated to organizing local populations, forging strong alliances with labor associations, and of course, formally affiliating with the United Popular Action Front—the mass organization that earlier broke ties with the ERP.[133]

The RN's emphasis on a political-ideological orientation in service of combating fascism manifested in predictable organizational ways. It emphasized bottom-up work, which the group fostered by building political schools.[134] It also built a robust propaganda wing, which Montgomery notes, "acquired a reputation for incisive analysis of the Salvadoran reality" and "had a profound impact" on the FMLN's ability to develop a "unified political program by 1980."[135]

Finally, the government's ever-growing corruption and militarization ramped up to the point that the PCS, the Communist Party, could no longer ignore it. The ruling party enlisted the help of the Democratic Nationalist Organization (ORDEN) (a state-controlled paramilitary organization) to engage in a massive voter-intimidation campaign ahead of the 1977 elections. When people gathered in San Salvador to protest the fraudulent elections, ORDEN alongside state security forces indiscriminately opened fire on the crowd. In response to the massacre, the PCS concluded that armed struggle was a necessity.[136] It began assembling militias, which eventually coalesced into an armed wing, the Forces Armadas de Liberación (FAL).[137]

Given their established dedication to peaceful political engagement, the PCS formed and maintained robust subdivisions dedicated to political messaging and international diplomacy. It viewed both the military and sociopolitical sides of the struggle as crucial and interdependent. As the PCS leader Schafik Jorge Hándal noted in an interview, "Of course, the armed path to revolution does not exclude the struggle to implement socioeconomic reforms. This fight plays an important role both in the political education of the masses and in the effort to broaden the range of allies in the democratic anti-imperialist struggle."[138]

The long-standing PCS presence in San Salvador meant that its inclusion in the FMLN brought a wealth of urban support networks built around the Communist Party. Crucially, since the PCS has been in existence since the 1930s, these networks were well established. Yet, the most important support networks that the PCS contributed to the FMLN were not those at home, but abroad. The PCS had a catalog of international contacts that exceeded those of the Salvadoran state, which proved crucial to the FMLN's ability to secure funding and resources throughout the war.[139] It was through the PCS's contacts with the socialist world that the soon-to-be Political-Diplomatic Commission (CPD) would be able to travel to and station official representatives in nearly three dozen countries.

A More Comprehensive Model of Rebel Organizations

Absent the organizational approach derived in chapter 1, the FMLN's structure would remain analytically intractable. The analysis in this chapter reveals that conventional approaches are problematic on two dimensions. First, alternative theories of militant group structures rarely yield predictions that pan out on the ground. Ideological, structural, and prewar network theories all lead us to expect structural similarities where instead we find difference. And on the flip side, resource-based explanations predict differences where instead we find similarities.

Second, these explanations were not developed in the context of a comprehensive organizational approach. As such, each factor is tied only to some features of organizational structure, but not others—and never the same parts. While certain variables may explain the strength of disciplinary institutions, the strength of ties to local populations, or differences in tactical approaches, none can (nor do any purport to) explain the content and diversification of militant organizational structures.[140] Examined through a more complete organizational lens, it is clear that attributing wartime structure to any single antecedent condition is naive, if not impossible.

As it is conventionally understood, ideology performs poorly in accounting for many aspects of rebel groups' structures. To be sure, we find some structural similarities between the FMLN and other Marxist-Leninist organizations, such as a Vanguard Party (i.e., a mass political front) and comparable bureaucratic structures promoting democratic centralism. However, these similarities mask an even greater wealth of differences. Even if we were to only stick with the structures ideology purports to explain, the five OP-Ms vary considerably in their respective emphases on building mass fronts. So, even the theoretical commitment to Vanguardism is not uniform.[141] More broadly, the FMLN's structure was unique from other Marxist-Leninist rebels in ways for which ideology cannot account. A core problem is that ideological explanations do not account for the full scope of organizational features—nor do they account for the most important, at least for this study.[142]

The groups vary widely in their levels of diversification, their engagement with the masses, and the extent to which they prioritize noncombat work as part of the struggle. Even where ideological predictions appear to map onto structure—giving rise to structural similarities between the groups—the respective internal narratives suggest an alternate mechanism is in play. While both the FPL and the ERP established radio stations, which grew into broader propaganda wings, the FPL viewed its propaganda apparatus as a tool of political education and liberation, whereas ERP leaders saw ¡Radio Venceremos! primarily as a tool of mobilization and strategic communication in service of the fight. Ultimately, organizational ideology (as it is conceptualized here) accounts for the salient differences across the groups.

Structural explanations alone also fall short of accounting for organizational nuance. In this chapter, I enumerated three theories that make organizational predictions based on structural or state-level features. Attributes of the state or regime cannot account for any differences across OP-Ms, since they emerged in the same context. Alternately, theories attributing differences to urban versus rural emergence would lead us to expect the most similarities among the groups with the most stark differences: the FPL and the ERP. Finally, I find some support for the last structural explanation—that intergroup competition will incentivize diversification—but not where the authors would expect (namely, in military tactics). Specifically, we observe an important extension of this logic in the ERP's acquiescence to building a mass front. Thus, rather than intergroup competition leading to tactical diversification, the same logic plays out in a different domain. Acknowledging that the other OP-Ms were at an advantage—if only in their pools of viable recruits—the ERP built the LP-28 to keep up.[143] While this theory does not account for the full scope of organizational differences, evaluating it through an organizational approach demonstrates that it has more explanatory power than even the original authors may conclude. Critical to arriving at that insight, however, is a more comprehensive model of rebel organizations.

Organizational theories about resource endowments use groups' wealth to make predictions about their recruitment profiles, which in turn are posited to shape patterns of violence.[144] Since the FMLN allowed each group to maintain its own funding structures (as well as its own recruitment tactics) and wealth varied considerably from one OP-M to the next, this case again presents an ideal opportunity to test this theory.[145] However, I find no convincing evidence in support of this explanation. As Hoover Green observes, the groups composing the FMLN were highly disciplined across the board.[146] Moreover, Wood argues that the most salient material resource that could be provided during the war—land—was not a selective benefit.[147] As such, one only had to provide "minimum support" to the rebellion to make free riding an option.[148] This insight cuts off resource endowment theories at the source: material benefits are not even sufficient to explain participation in rebellion, let alone the organizational features purported to follow later.

Finally, evidence from the rebellion supports some of the predictions deriving from prewar network theories. Groups that emerged among similar social bases do exhibit similarities in their levels of cohesion, their articulation of a coherent ideology, their ties to local communities, and many of their bureaucratic procedures.[149] However, the logic does not reliably extend to predicting other parts of organizational structure. If, as Staniland argues, robust ties to local communities "make it possible to quickly establish institutions for local control" and "make it possible for leaders to share their ideology . . . [by] facilitating political education," we should have observed similarities in organizational form among groups with similar goals embedded in similar networks.[150]

The FPL and ERP were the ideal test cases. Since they were cut from essentially the same cloth and deeply embedded among the same types of communities, we should have found the most structural similarities in popular organizing, local administration, and political education. The evidence, however, reveals a sharp divergence even in their initial structures on these dimensions. From early in their organizational life, the FPL built precisely the types of structures we would expect from this hypothesis. The ERP, in contrast, eschewed them. Thus, while I do find support for the hypothesis that prewar networks influence organizational structure, the new framework provides the analytic nuance to specify with greater precision the traits that social networks can and can't shape.

The deep dive into the formation of the FPL, ERP, and PRTC reveals how much variation we overlook when our understanding of militant organizations is limited to the arrangement and composition of their combat units and the tactical approaches they use. This comparison also reveals why "political wing" is a blunt conceptual tool. By definition, each of the politico-military organizations had political wings (a term they themselves used); however, the content, breadth, and prioritization of those political wings differed considerably from one OP-M to the next. The new organizational framework allows us to make more accurate predictions about the FMLN's emergence and more nuanced descriptions of its structure and traits in the run-up to the civil war.

Epilogue: The Run-Up to War

From December of 1979 to May of 1980, leaders from the five organizations met in Havana to negotiate the terms of unification. Notwithstanding various walkouts and noticeable absences (usually by one of the RN or the ERP), the meetings led to a successful unification on May 22, 1980.[151] They formed a five-man General Command, comprising the leader from each of the OP-Ms, and each group came together under the umbrella they called the Farabundo Martí National Liberation Front to honor Farabundo Martí, the leader and martyr of the 1931 peasant uprising. Crucially, however, the OP-Ms did not dissolve into a united front. Each retained its own organizational structure, its own tactical approach, and its own finances.[152] Additionally, as the OP-Ms came together under the FMLN umbrella, their affiliated mass fronts united as the Coordinadora Revolucionaria de Masas (CRM). The CRM then formed alliances with marginalized political parties to form the Democratic Revolutionary Front (FDR). Of the five component groups, the ERP's strategic approach happened to be most similar to that of the (recently successful) Sandinistas in Nicaragua.[153] Accordingly, the Cuban sponsors insisted—much to the dismay of everyone else—that the Salvadorans adopt the ERP's military-first approach to revolution. The plan was to mount a single violent insurrection on January 10, 1981, which would coincide with a nationwide strike and a mass defection from the armed forces. This meant the FMLN had only three months to arm, train, and mobilize the population for the optimistically titled "Final Offensive."

At the risk of inciting even more animosity among the groups, Cuba and the FMLN leadership agreed that the best course of action was to allow each OP-M to retain its own organizational structure. This directive, however, came with a rather large asterisk: Because the run-up to the incursion was so short, the fastest way for each group to build a large standing army was to strip its political cadres of members and repurpose them into the armed forces.[154]

FMLN leaders planned a three-part insurrection to maximize both the military and psychological impact on the government. The first component was a nationwide military offensive in which the five OP-Ms would simultaneously attack bases of the Salvadoran Armed Forces (FAES). The second component entailed calling for a nationwide worker's strike—in part to demonstrate support for the movement, and in part to create mass chaos. The commotion would force FAES troops to spread their manpower too thin to get control of the country. The third component of the Final Offensive was to encourage a mass defection from the armed forces.[155] Over the course of the previous year, numerous lower-level members (mostly affiliated with the ERP) had been infiltrating the armed forces with a two-part goal: gather intelligence on the state of the armed forces and incite unrest within the FAES ranks.

On January 10, 1981, strategic guerrilla attacks enabled FMLN forces to commandeer a state-owned radio station to inform the people of the rebellion and call for the mass strikes.[156] According to many accounts, the first few hours of the insurrection played out in the FMLN's favor: popular organizations mobilized supporters to go out into the streets and in some places the Salvadoran army seemed to be on the defensive.[157] However, the leaders' sanguine hopes of a single insurrection that would hand power back to the people were soon dashed. Unable to secure the radio station for long enough, Carpio was able to tell people to "prepare for a general strike," but not when the strike would be. Defections from the army were far below FMLN estimates, and state forces were soon able to regain control of military barracks and public spaces. Within a few days, FMLN leaders reluctantly announced "the end of the first phase of the general offensive" and withdrew from the cities to regroup in the hinterlands in the north and east of the country. By all scholarly, military, and internal accounts, the Final Offensive was a complete failure. Unlike other military debacles, however, the Final Offensive was not simply a matter of being overpowered by a well-equipped military. On the contrary, the FAES fared little better than the nascent insurgency and they exhausted many of their resources in the process.[158]

The immediate aftermath of the Final Offensive was a critical juncture for the FMLN as its members retreated, regrouped, and moved forward with the rebellion. The question is, where did the organizations go from there? While the account of their development illustrates the sheer diversity of organizations that can arise under the same context, the rapid shift to a military-first directive meant some of the structures most central to rebel-to-party transformation were decimated. However, whether and to what extent the groups stuck to the ERP strategy or repopulated their messaging, administrative, and outreach subdivisions will have major implications for how the group evolved and adapted as the war went on.

Part II

THE CONTENT, PROCESS, AND CONTEXT OF CHANGE

WARTIME ORGANIZATIONAL LEGACIES
Building Proto-Party Structures

In mid-1983, the FMLN commander Nidia Díaz scribbled *"¿Qué falta?"*—or, "What's missing?"—into her field diary. While we might expect rebel leaders to ponder their shortcomings during war, this question becomes puzzling when we consider the context: in 1983, when she asked what the organization was missing, the FMLN was at the top of its game. On the battlefield, it had the upper hand against the regime. Off the battlefield, it was steadily gaining both local and international support. If rebels' concerns about their wartime organizations were limited to their capacity to wage war, Díaz's diary would have been blank that day. Instead, it is littered with bullet points, enumerating the future political, educational, and organizational directions of the PRTC and the FMLN more broadly.

Conventional portrayals of rebel organizations do little to help us make sense of Díaz's musing. As I demonstrated in chapter 1, many, if not most, models of rebel organizations focus on the effectiveness with which they produce violence—and the structures responsible for it.[1] To be sure, a focus on the militant aspects of rebellion is crucial for getting traction on conflict strategies and variations in patterns of violence during civil war.[2] However, this analytic focus on the militant subdivisions of rebel groups has inadvertently been interpreted as a holistic portrayal, rather than a scope condition. As a result, militant organizations are often treated as unitary, homogeneous actors comprising "armed fighters and the commanders who lead them."[3] This assumption predisposes scholars to characterize the line between war and peace as more of a discontinuity than it is in reality. Indeed, we are told rebel groups need to build party structures from scratch "because electoral politics require a different set of skills than those demanded in wartime."[4]

By these accounts, rebel groups should not make particularly good political parties. They have spent years, if not decades, engaging their opposition on the battlefields. Many (though not all) have committed heinous acts of violence against not just their opponents but noncombatants as well. Thus, while we may not expect a rebel commander to pose this question at the height of their military success, it seems considerably more warranted as they grapple with party transformation. This stage is often characterized by endless and tenuous ceasefires, frustrating rounds of negotiations, and an uncertain opportunity to participate in legal politics. In light of the very different road ahead, we find again the same refrain: that rebel groups must suddenly build party structures "from scratch" and "learn the art of non-violent politics."[5] If these refrains hold, we should expect groups attempting to make the jump into the legal political sphere to have to (and want to) break from their wartime legacies as swiftly and emphatically as possible. In other words, on the cusp of party formation, the answer to *"¿qué falta?"* should be "everything."

Even nominally, however, the empirical record suggests otherwise. At the most superficial level, most rebel successor parties keep their name when they decide how to present themselves on the ballot.[6] Beneath the surface, many wartime organizational legacies persist as well. Yet, rather than being detractors to transformation—bygone vestiges of conflict that obstruct peacetime politics—I argue that many of the structures built during war are essential for it.

Too often, wartime organizational legacies are bracketed in favor of explanations that lie outside the rebellion or outside the conflict theater entirely. For example, consider the prewar-party hypothesis: the argument that having once operated as a political party makes rebel-to-party transformation more likely.[7] In short, *prewar* performance is the key to *postwar* performance. But what do we make of everything that happened in between? Of course, from a practical vantage, some bracketing is understandable. There are important questions to be asked about the extent to which wartime structures are *knowable* for clandestine groups—and some structures are harder to gauge than others. However, every scholar of organizational change highlights the importance considering the organization's recent past to explain success or failure in the organization's new future.[8]

This chapter tackles Díaz's question and the other questions that arise when we hold the empirical record up to the conventional wisdom. *¿Qué falta?* is fundamentally a question about the structure, content, and evolution of the wartime organization. To fully account for the structural aspect of rebel-to-party transformation, we have to know what rebels are starting with and what they are working toward. What structures do rebels have? What structures do parties need? Which structures make transformation into successor parties easier, and which obstruct it? What traits allow some rebel groups to exploit or shed their legacies? What's missing—and, perhaps more importantly, *what isn't*—as rebel groups look ahead to a new battle on the campaign trail?

I argue that the capacity for successful rebel-to-party transformation lies in rebels' wartime organizational legacies. Organizations need two things to insure themselves against the volatility of change: relevant skills and the ability to exploit them. Thus, one part of transformation is a function of the diversity and type of organizational subdivisions built during wartime. Moving beyond unitary, combat-centric models of rebel groups, I identify a variety of subdivisions commonly—though not universally—built during conflict, which mirror the functions and goals of structures in party organizations. Where present, these proto-party structures provide decisive advantages when rebel groups face the pressure of postconflict transformation. Specifically, wartime subdivisions dedicated to governance, political messaging, social outreach, and other noncombat tasks imbue the organization with personnel, skills, and routines that retain their value in the electoral arena. As a result, some rebellions come to the negotiating table equipped with the structural building blocks of political parties. In sum, party building often starts when the first bullet is fired, not the last.

An equally important part of transformation is rebels' capacity to exploit these structures under pressure. Militant organizations must display a capacity for critical self-reflection and flexibility—traits upheld as paramount in explanations of organizational change, yet infrequently found in political science.[9] The sanguine focus on wartime bureaucracies and institutionalization masks their pitfalls: entrenched bureaucratic procedures are the enemy of flexibility. I identify traits critical to overcoming these issues: rebels' ability to identify shortcomings and their willingness to change paths.

This chapter develops the first piece of my three-part theory of transformation—accounting for the *content* of change. Using the framework outlined in chapter 1, I map the core structures and variation among both militant and party organizations. The newfound conceptual precision from taking an explicitly organizational approach allows me to specify what parties need, what rebels have, and how the gap between the two varies from one militant group to the next. More specifically, I show that the gap between rebel structures and party structures is a variable, not a constant. To test whether this conceptual break from the literature holds in practice, I trace the parallel organizational evolutions of wartime structures within the subgroups of the FMLN.

Armed with a more thorough understanding of the composition and constraints on organizations, I motivate this theory by revisiting the outcome through an organizational lens. Rebel-to-party transformation is fundamentally a puzzle about executing and surviving a massive organizational change. The difficulties of transformation occupy two sides of the same coin. Throwing out existing routines and personnel destabilizes the organization, and the complementary challenge is the difficulty of learning new skills while also adapting to a new environment.[10] Accordingly, transformation is easier to the extent that groups have "preexisting competencies"—established skill sets embedded in the organization that perform similar functions to those needed in the new environment.[11] Thus, it is less risky when an organization can just do an old thing in a new way. In other words, although change is inherently difficult, it is not uniformly so.[12]

Rebel-to-party transformation is, however, a unique type of organizational change because we have a built-in template for the outcome: political parties. This is not to say that all parties look the same. Nevertheless, we know what types of tasks parties perform and the environments in which they function, which together provide broad insight into the internal structures parties need to support their activities.

The Content of Transformation: Rebel and Party Structures

Explaining how party organizations are forged out of rebellions demands an explicitly organizational approach—one that can account for both the content of the transformation (i.e., the specific structures that form the old and new organizations) and the process of transformation (i.e., how subdivisions and decision-making structures are altered and what obstacles they encounter along the way).[13] This chapter deals specifically with the former. To explain how one builds a party out of the pieces of rebels, I start by specifying the building blocks of each.

Unfortunately, the rebellion scholarship and party scholarship exhibit a parallel oversight: despite a broad agreement that it is valuable to conceive of rebels and parties in organizational terms, there is much less consensus on what that entails analytically.[14] I use the framework from chapter 1 to bring to light the (often) implicit organizational insights from both literatures. To assess which wartime legacies set rebels up for success—and which do not—as they reconfigure to function in the electoral arena, I first examine party structures.

Mapping Party Organizations

To shed light on which wartime structures affect party building, let us take a step back to examine what we know about parties as organizations: how they are structured, what skills they need in order to function, and the variety of functions they perform. Political parties—like rebel groups—are multifaceted organizations. They are irreducible to a single goal (winning elections—or winning wars). To paint them as unitary actors is to overlook the variety of activities, tensions, structures, and objectives within the organization, which can simultaneously work toward and detract from these broader goals.[15] Though most studies of the organizational features of political parties focus on aggregated traits (e.g., institutionalization, bureaucratization, centralization), the literature is punctuated by a few crucial works that help unpack the diversity and type of roles that make parties what they are.[16]

In a long, if sporadic, tradition, party scholars like V. O. Key, Samuel Huntington, Kenneth Janda, and William Schonfeld laid a critical analytic foundation for disaggregating political parties beyond their parliamentary-extraparliamentary distinction.[17] A common thread runs through their work: each scholar independently notes that parties must be understood as "working coalitions" of separate organizations.[18] "Variety," Key argues, "is the reality of party organization."[19] To specify what structures parties need in order to function, I start by asking, what is the nature of this variety?

Drawing on this legacy, Richard S. Katz and Peter Mair synthesize organizational insights into a useful framework for disaggregating the party organization into three core structural components: the party in public office, the party on the ground, and the party in central office.[20] While they refer to these branches as the three "faces" of the party, in organizational terms, these components represent broad subdivisions of the party organization. Each demands different types of personnel, with different skills, to carry out different tasks, in service of different objectives.[21] Reducing the party to any one element masks the variety of tasks and dynamics that undergird party functioning. Thus, the subdivisions Katz and Mair identify shed light on what "party structures" actually refer to.

Since the objective here is to identify the types of tasks parties must be able to perform—and, by extension, the types of structures they need to support those activities—I briefly outline how each subdivision functions and fits into the organization. The party in public office refers to the governing apparatus of the party.[22] It comprises the members who run in elections and eventually occupy seats in government. This wing has the most direct control over creating and enacting policy. They also interface and negotiate with other political actors both inside and outside of government.[23]

The party on the ground refers to the subdivision responsible for forging linkages with society. The objectives associated with this wing include managing and maintaining external relations with those needed to keep the party in office. In short, they are responsible for building a loyal constituency. The structures that compose the party on the ground are the party congresses and committees that exist at various levels of the state, as well as the ancillary membership organizations (e.g., youth wings, women's wings, and student organizations).[24]

The third party structure is the party in central office. This wing comprises the national executive committee and the central party staff.[25] Functionally, the party in central office coordinates campaigns, oversees media and press, and acts as a conduit between the party on the ground and the party in public office. It is largely responsible for building the party platform and deciding how the core tenets of the party will be communicated to the grassroots and represented in policy. Broadly, the formation and communication of party identity lie with the party in central office

Of course, party organizations differ in terms of the priorities, overlap, and strategies they employ across these fronts. Moreover, they differ in the extent to which they emphasize (via dedicated personnel and resources) these subdivisions at all.[26] This framework is especially useful because it optimizes between nuanced and flexible insights into the types of structures and skills party organizations require. At the most general level, political party organizations will always require a governing sect, a national committee to coordinate elections and party messaging, and a division that forges linkages with society. Each subdivision allows for a variety of different structural elements depending on the party, its approach, its objectives, and its environment.[27]

These insights help flesh out the otherwise-vague concept of party structures. They equip scholars with the analytic and conceptual precision needed to specify what party organizations need in order to function in a competitive electoral environment. Armed with a nuanced conception of what parties do and how they are structured to do it, this framework allows me to move beyond abstract questions like "how do rebel groups transform into political parties?" and toward a set of more nuanced questions like "which wartime activities are best suited to pivoting toward these tasks?" and "which structures best prepare militants to operate in these political domains?"

Mapping Rebel Organizations

To motivate this section I revisit the hummable tune of the rebel-to-party literature: to successfully transform, rebel groups must build party structures from scratch once the war ends because "electoral politics require a different set of skills than those demanded during wartime."[28] The purpose of this chapter and the next is to treat this refrain as a set of questions rather than a set of facts. What skills—and corresponding structures—do parties need? What skills—and corresponding structures—do militants build during conflict? Armed with a more nuanced conception of what parties do and how they are structured to do it, this section asks whether the organizational legacies of war can ever work in service of the party.

It is now widely acknowledged that rebels do more than just fight battles. They govern; they provide social services; they extract, process, and sell natural resources; they provide political education, both externally and internally; and the list goes on.[29] With few exceptions, however, these critical insights about what rebels *do* during war are seldom interpreted as insights about what rebels *are* during war. In other words, while these observations are treated as *behavioral* insights, they are also *structural* ones.

Any routinized (as opposed to ad hoc) task—whether it's providing governance or selling diamonds—requires a dedicated role or subdivision to coordinate, execute, and support it. Thus, routinized behaviors reflect the structures that produce them. Take, for example, creating propaganda. To perform this task regularly, the group needs a dedicated wing of personnel who coordinate the content, writing, printing, and distribution of the group's message. If, alternately, routinized behaviors were not direct evidence of underlying organizational structures, wartime propaganda would be generated by a different set of combatants who spontaneously perform "political-messaging duties" each day or week. It quickly becomes clear that the alternate story would be inefficient and unsustainable, if not outright ridiculous. As such, rebels' wartime behaviors provide critical information about the skills, priorities, and personnel embedded in the organization.

Taking an organizational approach to transformation reveals that one key to succeeding lies in the diversity and type of noncombat structures rebels build during war. In a departure from most analyses of militant organizations, I look beyond combat units and identify a set of wartime subdivisions that mirror the core structures of party organizations: governance and administration, political messaging, social service provision, and citizen education and outreach. These proto-party structures imbue the organization with the relevant skills, institutions, and personnel required to operate in an electoral and governing capacity once the conflict ends. While all militant organizations have combat units, rebel groups vary considerably in the scope and development of structures dedicated to noncombat tasks.

Proto-Party Structures: The Currency of Transformation

In a departure from nebulous concepts like "political wings" and "organizational resources," I identify specific organizational structures that map directly onto the core structures of party organizations in terms of the functions they perform and the personnel that compose them. These wartime proto-party structures can be sorted to roughly correspond to the party structures in Katz and Mair's framework (see figure 3.1). Conceptualizing militant organizations in these terms illustrates the range of partylike activities in which rebel groups have developed competencies.

The first set of wartime structures with postconflict utility are the wings in charge of governance and administration of local populations. In terms of Katz and Mair's framework, governance divisions broadly mirror the party in public office in that they form the public face of the nascent party and confer legitimacy on the organization. Adapting Ana Arjona, Nelson Kasfir, and Zachariah Mampilly's definition of rebel governance to reflect the organization, governance structures refer to the subdivisions that facilitate militants' "regulation of the social, political, and economic life of non-combatants during war."[30] Specifically, these structures carry out tasks like taxation and market regulation, land and resource allocation, building infrastructure, social service provision, and dispute resolution.[31]

Rebel governance tasks vary widely, but none can be accomplished without dedicated resources, established routines, and skilled personnel. Hezbollah, for example, had an extensive service sector bureaucracy, which managed everything from building and staffing schools to providing potable drinking water to running medical clinics to collecting garbage in the areas it administered.[32] In El Salvador, one of the FMLN's sects (the FPL) established local governance structures known as Poderes Populares Locales (Local Popular Power, or PPLs), in which rebels created extensive zones of democratic political control. PPLs

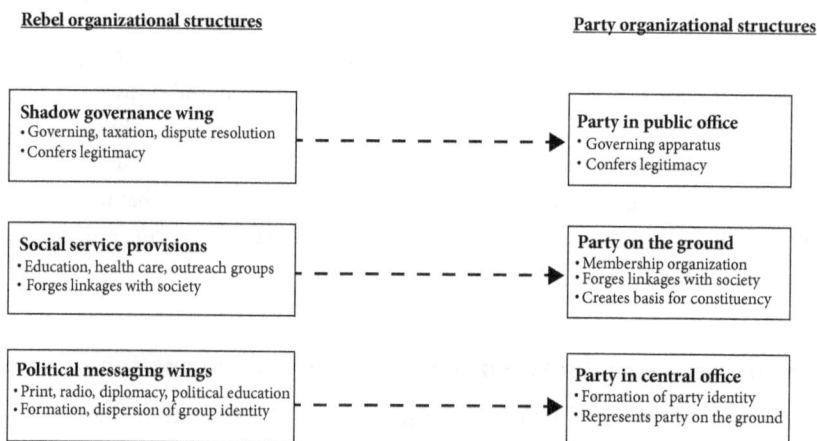

Rebel organizational structures   **Party organizational structures**

| **Shadow governance wing**
• Governing, taxation, dispute resolution
• Confers legitimacy | - - - - - - - - - -▶ | **Party in public office**
• Governing apparatus
• Confers legitimacy |

| **Social service provisions**
• Education, health care, outreach groups
• Forges linkages with society | - - - - - - - - - -▶ | **Party on the ground**
• Membership organization
• Forges linkages with society
• Creates basis for constituency |

| **Political messaging wings**
• Print, radio, diplomacy, political education
• Formation, dispersion of group identity | - - - - - - - - - -▶ | **Party in central office**
• Formation of party identity
• Represents party on the ground |

FIGURE 3.1.   Mapping wartime structures to party structures

integrated local populations into administrative structures via extralegal elections and managed dispute resolution, economic regulation, security, education, agricultural production, and a variety of other governance activities.[33]

To be sure, many governance tasks actually transcend the responsibilities of political parties. For example, providing security and local judiciary systems are—as Mampilly notes—more reflective of the state apparatus than a party.[34] As such, every governance division may not have a clear political-party counterpart. Nevertheless, rebel organizations with governance subdivisions accrue a variety of organizational benefits relevant to postconflict transformation. First, these structures often require personnel with specialized administrative skills, whose experience in the organization with relevant political tasks provides leaders with an internal pool of viable party members. Second, a wartime legacy of governance structures imbues the organization with the personnel, skills, and experience to engage in nonviolent political coordination with local populations. Third, the challenges of coordinating among different sectors (both internally and externally) means the organization has learned at least some of the crucial skills required for political coordination in government.[35] Finally and most broadly, governance structures enhance both the legitimacy and political credibility of the rebels.[36]

The second set of wartime structures that mirror core party structures are the subdivisions dedicated to social and political outreach (e.g., providing social services or political education) and managing ancillary organizations (e.g., youth wings, student unions, women's wings, and trade associations). Broadly corresponding to what Katz and Mair call the party on the ground, these outreach structures forge politically salient linkages with the community on which they rely for political and logistical support. Ancillary organizations, in particular, have clear counterparts in party organizations and, as such, can form the basis of a politically mobilized and loyal constituency after the war ends without much change to the structures or relations that they comprise.

An alternative—though not entirely unwarranted—perspective views youth and student organizations (as well as social service provision) as little more than thinly veiled pools for semicoercive combatant recruitment.[37] Of course, this interpretation may be true in some cases, or recruitment may be one of many functions these ancillary organizations serve. As a generalization, however, this view conflates "participation" with "fighting," thereby reifying the assumption that combat is the only activity for which rebels recruit. After all, if all rebels do is fight, then recruitment is all about finding fighters.[38] Sometimes, this characterization is accurate. As a generalization, however, it obscures the complexity and variation in recruitment tactics and rebel-citizen dynamics. Participation in rebellion takes many forms—varying both within and between conflicts.[39]

The final class of wartime structures with clear postconflict relevance are what I broadly refer to as political-messaging wings. Mirroring—at least in part—the party in central office, these structures manage the articulation, refinement, creation, and distribution of media conveying the group's political message. As such, political-messaging wings are responsible for taking the group's core ideology and translating it into a cohesive, digestible, and transmissible narrative—to members and outsiders alike.

Much as parties do, many rebel groups produce tailored narratives for multiple audiences simultaneously. Some of the messaging is intended for local populations, some is intended for internal distribution, some is directed at the opposition (e.g., trying to encourage defection), and some is directed at foreign sponsors or the diaspora.[40] The FMLN, for example, ran two radio stations and published multiple newspapers and magazines—and those cover just the domestic messaging wings. Furthermore, one of its five leaders published in *Foreign Policy* (in English) during the war, gracing the magazine with what might be the most compelling, if not intimidating, corresponding author footnote: "Joaquín Villalobos is a member of the directorate with the rank of commander of the Farabundo Martí National Liberation Front." The takeaway is that political messaging is not an ad-hoc activity—particularly in the preinternet days. Even written media requires teams of (often multilingual) writers, photographers and developers, designers and illustrators, printers, and distributors.

It is worth noting that political-messaging wings as formal structures have retained their salience over time, despite the accessibility of social media and online publishing. Notwithstanding what cute epithets like "the Twitter Revolution" would have us believe, rebel groups have not interpreted the shift in the medium of publication as an easy way out. Though they may no longer need access to photographic processing or printing presses, these roles are being replaced by digital artists, graphic designers, and software engineers. Contemporary political messaging like *Dabiq* (an English-language publication distributed by the Islamic State of Iraq and the Levant) or Special Force 1 and 2 (Hezbollah's video game series) require a lot more than 240 characters to get off the ground. The production quality and consistency of this propaganda speaks to the organizational diversity of the respective groups involved.

Beyond the clear applicability of skills, I expect militant organizations with well-developed messaging wings to have three advantages over their less vocal counterparts. First, these structures create and reify a core political identity, which contributes to a more cohesive organizational culture and mitigates the risk of change.[41] Second, the opportunity to develop their messaging strategy over the course of the conflict gives these groups a sort of trial-and-error period. They can test what resonates and what needs refinement before their political platform has to (legally) "go live" when campaigning begins.[42] Third, when campaigning starts, groups with preexisting messaging wings already have at least the skeleton of a platform on which to run. Rebel-to-party scholars often allude to the process of building a cohesive political platform as one of the primary challenges of making the jump into the political arena.[43] Wartime political-messaging wings should thus provide rebels with a considerable head start on this crucial asset.

For rebel groups seeking to reinvent themselves as political parties, proto-party structures confer four advantages to the organizations that build them. First, since the organization has skilled personnel and existing routines, proto-party structures narrow the presumed gap between the skills needed during war and the skills needed to function in electoral politics.[44] In organizational parlance, these "preexisting competencies" will make transformation less taxing because the group will not have to suddenly "learn the art of nonviolent politics," or at least, the learning curve should be considerably less steep.[45] The second and third advantages concern the process of transformation—how the organization undergoes and survives a massive overhaul in its structures, its objectives, and its environment. I address these advantages in greater detail in chapter 4, but briefly, proto-party structures contribute to organizational diversity (which broadly enhances groups' resilience to shocks) and provide a less disruptive path to party building, enabling groups to repurpose existing structures rather than starting from a blank slate.

The fourth benefit is less intuitive, but equally crucial. Proto-party structures benefit the organization by forcing groups to confront relevant challenges. Returning to Katz and Mair's framework, the authors note two challenges associated with the party in public office: (1) they must be attentive to the electorate, and (2) they face a set of constraints from needing to work collectively with "coalition partners, civil servants, [and] officials at other levels of government."[46] In the wartime context, rebels with governance structures will face similar challenges. On the one hand, of course, these challenges are organizationally taxing—which is in part why we find rebel governance a puzzle worth investigating.[47] On the other hand, facing these challenges during wartime represents an early opportunity for organizational learning, thereby attenuating the gap in knowledge as they pivot to campaigning and mobilization.

Facilitating Change: Self-Reflection and Flexibility

To explain how militant organizations survive the massive change that rebel-to-party transformation entails, we need to account for more than just useful structures. As with elite athletes and musicians, talent can only take organizations so far. At a certain point, the capacity to execute a risky move is more about whether they have the traits to absorb shocks and continue functioning at a high level under pressure. Here, I identify the organizational traits most likely to facilitate rebel-to-party transformation. Two undertheorized organizational traits put some groups in a better position than others to quickly exploit their varied skill sets when the time is right. The first is the capacity for critical assessment and self-reflection; the second is what Debra Minkoff calls a "repertoire of prior flexibility."[48] Self-reflection is about consistently seeking information with an eye toward improving performance.[49] From an organizational standpoint, this trait is present to the extent that leaders have institutionalized mechanisms for seeking and incorporating feedback. In other words, the group needs a culture of self-reflection.

This trait not a given. Organizations, like individuals, can tend toward openness or stubbornness. On the battlefield, stubbornness can almost be forgiven. The problem, as Vaughn Tan deftly observes, is our tendency to conflate uncertainty with risk.[50] As such, the openness required for innovation can easily feel like risk acceptance, especially in unsafe environments. In turn, organizations are liable to stick with what they know, even when those strategies are no longer working. While major organizational changes will be unavoidable once the group has to pivot to electoral politics, making these changes will be easier to the extent that they know how to evaluate their shortcomings and the skills at their disposal.[51]

Critical self-reflection is the theoretical side of change; to actually enact it, organizations must be flexible in practice. Flexibility describes an organization's ability to adapt under duress. While militant groups are no strangers to adversity, developing a repertoire of flexibility is less about surviving a constant threat of death (e.g., fighting consistent battles in the same way) than it is about facing new threats to their survival or operating in new conditions. For example, insurgencies often encounter boosts or tactical changes in counterinsurgency strategy to which they must respond. Or they suffer a particularly deadly incursion—perhaps one that took out a leader or a critical logistical subdivision. In these cases, flexibility means using existing organizational resources in different or innovative ways.[52]

The extent to which rebel groups have undergone substantial organizational changes in the past is the extent to which they are better poised to adapt and survive major changes in the future. This cycle is what Minkoff means by "developing a repertoire of prior flexibility."[53] Before party transformation, many rebellions undergo significant internal shifts (either by force or by strategic choice). These changes may arise from a variety of circumstances: shifts in sponsorship or funding, upticks in counterinsurgency efforts, the decision to build new wings of the organization to cope with new obstacles or exploit new opportunities, leadership turnover, and a variety of others. For example, following a surge in US military aide to the Salvadoran regime, the FMLN's use of conventional warfare was no longer sufficient to keep government forces at bay. In response, the group adopted the war-of-attrition approach of one of its subdivisions and subsequently reorganized its military units across the organization to wage a guerrilla insurgency. This change was made easier because the FMLN had one subdivision already employing this tactic, and undergoing this change made the organization more open to organizational innovation in the future.

A reasonable question to ask at this point is whether organizational flexibility is realistic for a hierarchical military organization, or merely aspirational. Scholars come down quite hard on both sides. David Close and Gary Prevost explicitly argue that "political-military fronts cannot have flexible structures [because] they are command organizations."[54] They maintain that malleability is incompatible with hierarchy. Others, however, have unearthed evidence of flexibility in places we might not expect it. Sarah Parkinson's analysis of the Palestine Liberation Organization mobilization following the 1982 Israeli invasion of Lebanon expressly contradicts Close and Prevost's assertion. She demonstrates that clandestine and flexible structures "emerge *from formal militant hierarchies.*"[55] Thus, rather than being antithetical to military hierarchy, organizational flexibility can be a *consequence* of it.

Moving off the battlefield, Anna Grzymała-Busse observes the presence and implications of flexibility in an equally surprising place: pre-1989 communist parties.[56] While acknowledging that many communist parties of the era "lacked incentives" to devise flexible policy strategies and "became the stereotype of unchanging behemoths," she observed that not all exhibited the same stubbornness. Grzymała-Busse not only demonstrates variation in flexibility, but also that the parties displaying policy responsiveness had more favorable outcomes than their rigid counterparts as they sought to reinvent themselves in the wake of 1989: "The more a party promoted policy innovation prior to 1989, the more it fostered pragmatism and flexibility in policy making. The more it had subsequently implemented these innovations, the more experience the party elites received in overcoming administrative reluctance, organizational entrenchment, and other . . . barriers to party regeneration."[57] Crucially, these traits go hand in hand: together, self-reflection and flexibility mean the organization has a culture of continuous innovation. The leaders accept the possibility of wrongdoing, search for new ways of operating, and enact changes accordingly. In short, these traits combat organizational rigidity, which is anathema to successful transformation.

Empirical Analysis: Tracing Wartime Legacies

The central argument of the book is that the organizational legacies of war shape rebels' prospects for and path to party formation at the war's end. This chapter develops the first part of the theory: explicating the organizational content that facilitates change. I argue that proto-party structures and institutionalized flexibility together facilitate postwar transformation by imbuing rebel groups with relevant skill sets and the capacity to leverage them into the electoral arena.

The next logical question is whether and to what extent rebels actually build these proto-party structures and adopt a culture of flexibility in practice. Crucially, it is worth noting that phantom structures do exist. As William Reno documents in the National Patriotic Front of Liberia (NPFL), leaders constructed "the veneer of a government administration, legislature, and courts . . . primarily . . . to gain international recognition and for additional opportunities to collect bribes."[58] Since many proto-party structures concern the nature of interactions with local populations, it would be reasonable to expect leaders to exaggerate the extent to which those interactions are characterized by service and downplay the extent to which those interactions are characterized by violence.

Thus, before I test their relevance to party transformation, I first ask, what do rebels' wartime organizations look like on the ground? In this section, I conduct process tracing using a wide variety of primary source material from across the FMLN's subgroups. To make the argument that wartime organizational legacies are central to postwar party formation, I must be able to demonstrate the following: First, rebel groups must build functioning proto-party structures that operate according to the theory. In short, at least some militant organizations must build structures that actually function—in contrast to the "phantom structures" Reno documents in the NPFL. Moreover, these structures must vary from one group to the next. If everyone builds them, then they will not account for variation in rebel-to-party outcomes. Second, these structures must persist until the end of war. If instead proto-party structures exist for a short while, but are dismantled long before the end of the conflict, this discontinuity would call into question the mechanism of my argument.

Beyond the structural considerations, substantiating this theory requires evidence that groups undergo organizational changes in the way that I expect. Are leaders thinking about organizational dynamics and flexibility? Or are their decisions ad hoc or based on some other calculus entirely? If we consider the business world, we know that C-level executives think deeply about their organizations in the face of change: they are considering growth dynamics; they are bringing in organizational consultants; they are talking about resilience to economic downturns. Do these conversations happen as much on the battlefield as they do in the boardroom? To assess the FMLN's capacity for flexibility, I look for evidence of how leaders respond to failure: Do they admit it? Do they attribute failures to organizational shortcomings or external shocks? How do they respond?

Recall that at this point in the war, the strategic directive from the FMLN General Command still de-emphasized local political engagement in favor of military recruitment. Obviously, this directive has clear organizational implications accompanying the behavioral ones: if the emphasis is exclusively on fighting, organizational resources should be dedicated to combat divisions and logistical support. Yet, I expect that the extent to which this decree played out *in practice* will vary considerably as a function of the groups' respective organizational ideologies of war. In light of their founding principles and the unique geographical dispersion that occurred in the wake of the failed insurrection, I expect that the groups' initial ideological and structural disparities will be further entrenched in this period.

The FMLN on the Heels of Failure

By all scholarly, military, and internal accounts, the Final Offensive was an abject failure. Some of the problems were attributable to logistical blunders (e.g., the FMLN broadcasted information about the insurrection but the state cut them off before they could give a date or time).[59] Some were due to naive miscalculation—the ERP vastly overestimated the number of people who would defect from the army; others overestimated how many would turn out for the general strike.[60] Yet, the lion's share of the failure was organizational. Despite agreement among *some* FMLN commanders and their patrons about the plan, top leaders remained divided over the appropriate military strategy. Neither the FPL nor the RN favored a violent insurrection, and many cadres from these OP-Ms neglected to participate in what was supposed to be coordinated military action.[61] Indeed, scholars have argued explicitly that were it not for the vitriolic relations between leaders, the FMLN would likely have achieved a swift victory during that period.[62]

Infighting, however, was not the group's only organizational gaffe. After nearly a decade spent prioritizing mass mobilization and political cadres (with the exception of the ERP)—the FMLN had only a few months to build up and train a standing army.[63] Even the ERP, which favored violent insurrection from the start, lacked the tactical and strategic training needed to mount an insurrection at the scale they had planned. At this point, the FMLN faced a major organizational dilemma. The most readily available source of military recruits was its affiliated mass organizations, yet, as Bracamonte and Spencer note, "stripping the political wing of its key cadres meant that there was no guarantee that the organizations would come out into the streets for the insurrection."[64] Nevertheless, they took the risk. On the advice of the Sandinistas, FMLN leaders opted to repurpose key cadres from its mass organizations into combat units ahead of the insurrection.[65]

Seventy-two hours after the Final Offensive, FMLN combatants withdrew to their respective bases to regroup, rebuild, and try again. While the General Command held firm to its military-first strategy, the prolongation of the war (beyond a single insurrection) meant that each group was to focus on building up a strategic rearguard. This directive had important implications both for the organization and the analytic purchase of studying it. Recall that, from the beginning, each OP-M retained its own organizational structure. Thus, the diversity and nature of subdivisions, activities, institutions, and external relations were still under the jurisdiction of the OP-Ms' respective leaders. This organizational decision in conjunction with their postfailure retreat created a unique geographical phenomenon that persisted throughout the war: five groups, with five different structures, and five different interpretations of revolution settled in distinct regions of the country. As a result, the war is characterized by geopolitical conditions in which each OP-M receives the same directives, but functions (largely) autonomously.

Although the January offensive was a failure any way you turn it, the manner in which the FMLN leadership reacted to the blow had beneficial organizational repercussions that shaped its evolution. In the aftermath of the insurrection, the General Command held numerous meetings to debrief, reflect, and identify tactical errors in its approach.[66] By and large, the leaders converged on what went wrong;[67] the strategic approach was a good one, but the organization lacked the training, cohesion, and communication to execute it. Eager to take advantage of a good revolutionary moment, they sacrificed preparedness for enthusiasm. The PCS leader Schafik Hándal reflected on this failure in an interview: "The delay in unifying the revolutionary organizations did not allow us to take advantage of the . . . situation of 1980. Unity should have been consummated a year earlier, but analysis is slower than objective reality."[68] Joaquín Villalobos (ERP) corroborated this point, attributing the failure to take power at that time to "the lack of unification upon a strategic line within the revolutionary movement."[69]

Though the FMLN was still growing, the failed offensive paved the way for the organization to consolidate around a core principle that shaped its trajectory: espíritu autocrítico—literally, the spirit of self-critique. In essence, autocrítico is the organizational equivalent of the "growth mindset": an approach to problem solving in which individuals view failure as a learning opportunity rather than evidence of deficiency.[70] To be sure, this concept was not new. Each of the OP-Ms boasted an explicit commitment to autocrítico in their formative years.[71] And they embraced it both privately—as in the case of Nidia Díaz scribbling "¡que *falta?"* in her field diary—and publicly—as in the many cases of leaders writing openly about this approach in popular publications during the war.[72]

The pernicious effects of rivalry dealt a sobering blow to the leadership. But even this awareness was no guarantee of future harmony. In the wake of such a profound failure to execute a plan only one of the five groups truly endorsed, the General Command could have gone one of two ways. One option was that all of the members bring to the table their commitment to *autocrítico*, and ask, in good faith, what went wrong? In an equally plausible world, however, egos could easily trump principles. Even one or two people doubling down on avoiding blame could prevent a culture of self-reflection from sticking. From an organizational standpoint, having a consensus-based leadership structure was likely quite helpful in preventing the latter.[73] Requiring consensus meant that accountability for the failure was dispersed across many people rather than concentrated in a single individual. Psychologically, this dispersal of responsibility made it easier for leaders to ask what went wrong without needing to point (only) to themselves.

While consensus is not a necessary condition for critical self-evaluation, it was helpful for institutionalizing the practice during the organization's rocky adolescence. Moving forward, the General Command more explicitly incorporated the OP-Ms' varied strategic approaches into a holistic arsenal. As Bracamonte and Spencer argue, this intellectual shift allowed the FMLN to "change the priority depending on the current strategic situation."[74] The question, of course, is whether this commitment bore fruit in practice.

Organizational Evolution, 1981–1984

In the run-up to the first incursion, the OP-Ms had neither the time nor the resources to see their organizational plans to fruition. For all except the ERP, the combat-centric directive pushed them even farther afield as they were forced to temporarily repurpose political cadres into military roles.[75] In the wake of the retreat, however, the OP-Ms had the time to regroup and rebuild their organizations in accordance with their founding principles. As the FMLN entered the new strategic phase in preparation for the "Second Offensive," their geopolitical dispersion affords a unique opportunity to trace how organizational structures evolve during war. The ERP leader Villalobos recounts the circumstances leading up to the rematch:

> This offensive put the army on the defensive by concentrating it in its own strategic areas. That gave us a few months of peace of mind and allowed us to create the seven strategic fronts, the seven concentrations

of forces and the existence of that rearguard that gave us the possibility of preparing people. . . . Even the enemy's own offensives became a preparation school combative. All those months, the months in which we resisted in those positions forced us to learn. Not only did we have the terrain to prepare the men, but we were also forced to solve the problem of military tactical learning in the concrete, facing the enemy.

It was not a school in which we graduated people and then took them to a theater of operations, but rather we were with the rearguard and the theater of operations intermingled there, because sometimes the enemy took us out of certain areas and then we returned to retake ground control. This also implies that people learned engineering work to protect themselves from artillery bombardments, from aviation, on the basis that this was the order of the day and happened on a daily basis. In other words, what made good military contingents form in Morazán, in Chalatenango, in Guazapa was the fact that for many months in those areas they had to fight almost daily against the enemy's effort to annihilate us.[76]

The groups' physical and ideological isolation from one another were compounding forces, allowing five different groups to evolve according to their own visions, without interference from the others. I trace whether and how those principles translated into measurable organizational outcomes.

The ERP: Militancy in Morazán

After the January offensive failed to overthrow the government, the ERP retreated to its base in Morazán department in eastern El Salvador. To the ERP, retreat meant an opportunity to build and train its armed forces and prepare for another shot at overthrowing the regime through violent insurrection. Thus, their goals upon returning to Morazán were to liberate the northern half of the department by wiping out any government and paramilitary presence, and to establish a rearguard dedicated to military training.[77] To be sure, the ERP did not take a completely maladaptive approach. In responding to a question about how the ERP pivoted to build a popular army in the wake of the January failure, the leader Villalobos explicitly identified where adjustment was needed: "Our current conditions [in the wake of the retreat] mean having to build an army. Once the door is closed on the possibility of an insurrection, we face the need to achieve greater attrition of the army, which in turn forces us to fine-tune our military structures."[78]

In line with my expectations, the ERP's organization evolved in lockstep with its organizational ideology of war. It focused almost exclusively on building a standing army, which it rapidly achieved.[79] Despite near-constant incursions from the government and paramilitary forces, the rebel army managed to gain the upper hand. By 1983, northern Morazán was decisively under the control of the ERP.[80] While Villalobos was hesitant to denote Morazán as a fully liberated zone, this region was by far the most autonomous rearguard the FMLN had in the early stages of the war.[81] To the extent that the ERP diversified, its focus was on building logistical subdivisions in support of the war effort: "establishing hospitals, production brigades, and training camps."[82]

What were the organizational implications beyond the battlefield? The level of autonomy the ERP exercised in the region would lead some to expect governance structures and mass political mobilization to follow in turn.[83] As Reyko Huang argues, "Where rebels tap into civilians as a significant war-making resource,"—which the ERP did—"the latter become politically mobilized"—which locals did not.[84] In reality, the militarization of Morazán was as evident in the ERP's relationship with the masses as it was in its internal dealings.

It is here where opening the black box of rebel organizational structures really matters. To be fair, assuming that political mobilization follows necessarily from territorial control is easy because the organizational structures rebels (often) build are so robust that mobilization *appears* seamless. In reality, political engagement is effortful and the variation across cases is salient and systematic. Consider the account of Miguel Ventura, a local priest who worked closely with the ERP in Morazán throughout the war. He writes the following about the population living in ERP-controlled territory in the first phase of the war: "Some of the people [in northern Morazán] had been involved in the liberation process during the 1970s, while others had lived under the control of the military and did not have a clear vision of the revolutionary process. . . . There was little sense of community" among civilians living in the area.[85]

While the ERP was not isolated from the masses, its engagement was unidimensional. The people existed to support the war effort, not the other way around.[86] For example, when asked why the army must move with the masses, Villalobos responds predictably: "[We move with the masses] because we depended on them. In other words, we in that rearguard, without the masses, would not have had the best chance, neither of having human reserves nor of having supplies. This forces us to depend on the masses in order to survive. We had to protect the masses and take it into consideration for any plans for military maneuvers."[87]

Crucially, relegating the masses to a support role was a choice rather than an inevitability. Recall that, like the FPL, the ERP was built in the context of the Christian base communities (CEBs) of the 1960s and '70s. As such, it drew its support from a well-politicized social infrastructure—it just chose not to use it as such. Binford's research further corroborates this argument, noting that "between 1981 and 1983 even the church was subordinated to the revolutionary process and assigned the task of preparing the population for the insurrection that the ERP believed was imminent."[88]

Diversification, like most things, is a dilemma rather than an unencumbered virtue. Rebels face a trade-off between putting all their eggs in one basket and being jacks of all trades and masters of none. In the first phase of the war, the ERP came down hard on the former. The decision stemmed from two beliefs: First, that a second offensive executed with a better army and more extensive communication system would level the regime. Second, that political mobilization would follow necessarily from a successful insurrection.[89] The decision to continually shirk the political side of the fight had problematic consequences, however, which the ERP was starting to feel. As Binford notes, the ERP's military emphasis turned it into "the best-organized and most formidable military force of the guerrilla groups," but it "lacked a mass political base."[90] Moreover, as 1983 progressed, the ERP faced an intensifying counterinsurgency strategy from the government. It was losing personnel faster than it could recruit and train replacements, at which point the group briefly turned to forced conscription.[91] While it abandoned the practice after only a few months in response to criticism, ideological support for the ERP dropped precipitously in this period.[92]

The FPL: Diversification in Chalatenango

The progress of the war and development of the ERP in Morazán were largely representative of the FMLN more broadly during this phase; yet if we turn to Chalatenango, a very different story emerges. In the aftermath of the failed insurrection, the FPL retreated to Chalatenango where—much like the ERP in Morazán—it had originated out of the CEBs of the 1970s. Yet, the similarities between OP-Ms stop here. In contrast with many operations elsewhere, FPL insurgents in Chalatenango "placed great emphasis" on developing grassroots governance structures in cooperation with locals.[93] Rather than simply controlling territory, the FPL's priority was to "establish the infrastructure of resistance" among the peasantry.[94] This approach to territorial administration followed from the FPL's ideological orientation emphasizing "social and community organizations" in service of a prolonged popular war.[95] Here, I detail the social and political structures that the FPL built during this time and their implications for both the FPL and the future of the broader movement.

Before I begin, however, it is worth addressing a potential misinterpretation of the FPL's activities during this period. Keeping in mind that the General Command's directive was to build up large battalions for engaging the armed forces in conventional warfare, one might interpret the FPL's political activities as insubordination, and thus, not worthy of comparison. I argue, however, that the FPL's approach represents not insubordination, but a logical interpretation of orders filtered through the FPL's organizational ideology. The FPL emphasized a revolution through a popular war achieved by politicizing and mobilizing peasants in the countryside.[96] In essence, FPL ideology does not understand an insurrection as something that can be divorced from political mobilization. According to Jenny Pearce, the FPL interpreted the concept of "rearguards" (which OP-Ms were instructed to establish in the countryside) as something more than a military designation. She argues that FPL leaders viewed rearguards and liberated territory "within a broader framework of political mobilization."[97]

Moreover, while the FPL dedicated significant organizational resources to bolstering its administrative, social service, and press divisions, it did not neglect its army. Recovered documents from the FPL's armed forces reveal concrete plans to augment its battalions. The plans lay out broad military objectives (e.g., sabotaging strategic highways and communication lines, setting fire to oligarchs' properties), detail various workshops on how to make weapons, and even assign teachers to the different workshops.[98] Yet, even in its military plans, the FPL's political through line is clearly embedded. Figure 3.2 depicts a section of a document in preparation for what the authors called the Second Offensive.[99] While the majority of the content concerns armed operations, the two lines with arrows

```
ORDEN # 3

COMANDANCIA D R U.

Orden de preparar Segunda Ofensiva:
 1o. Reorganizar, reagrupar, reabastecer fuerzas para futuras misiones;
 2o. Emboscar a enemigo en movimiento para recuperar armas;
 3o. Jefes deben planificar nuevas operaciones;
 4o. Consolidar y organizar los mandos conjuntos, asegurar estrecha
     coordinación de todas las organizaciones;
 5o. Repliegues ofensivos, no caer en pasividad;
 6o. Cada tiro un enemigo nuestro y un fusil más.

Realizar las siguientes tareas:
 1o. Abastecerse, preparen puestos recepción y_____.
 2o. Estructurar comunicación;
 3o. Organizar unidades estratégicas móviles;
 4o. Ampliar y limpiar zona retaguardia;
 5o. Consolidar políticamente nuestras fuerzas;

Indicaciones:
 1o. Todas las Organizaciones deben recibir armas.
 2o. Armar a las fuerzas más fogueadas de cada Organización de acuerdo
     a las misiones; plnificar estrategia C.O.
 3o. Construir trincheras, túneles, refugios,
 4o. Hacer bastante armamento casero;
 5o. Crear poderío local farabundista
                    (-Servicios al pueblo 1o.)
```

FIGURE 3.2. Political priorities in military plans (FPL 1981). Orden de Preparar Segunda Ofensiva, David Spencer Collection, box 5, folder 4.5, Hoover Institution Library & Archives.

indicate plans to "politically consolidate our forces," and to "create local popular power structures (to provide services to the people)."

Even in the early stages of the war, FPL diversified into numerous proto-party domains. The scope and content of the FPL's structural diversification adheres closely to the organizational ideology the group articulated—but could not fully realize—before the war. Indeed, the breadth and depth of organizational development it achieved was no small feat given both its dearth of resources and the fact that it never managed to secure a fully autonomous rear-guard in Chalatenango comparable to the ERP's territory in Morazán. Here, I focus on three initiatives and corresponding subdivisions that together illustrate the FPL's organizational development in this period: the creation of local governance structures (PPLs), its education and mass literacy programs, and its press and propaganda wing.

PODERES POPULARES LOCALES

Recall that the FPL organized around the principle that mass participation in a prolonged popular war was the only tenable path to revolution. In stark contrast to the ERP, "the FPL never saw the zones of control as mere military rearguards[;] . . . rather, they saw them within a broader framework of political mobilization."[100] Thus, immediately following their retreat to Chalatenango, the FPL conducted an extensive analysis of the masses vis-à-vis the war.[101] The authors of the report concluded that "any revolutionary movement seeking the definitive liberation of the people must develop an adequate structure allowing for the broadest participation of the masses in the war."[102] To achieve this goal, the masses needed to be organized, ideologically cohesive, and self-governing.

In the rural areas the FPL controlled, this directive took the form of what the group called Poderes Populares Locales. PPLs were grassroots structures through which locals could organize, determine the needs of the community, and devise plans for attending to those needs.[103] While PPLs are "democratically elected . . . by the [local] population from their own ranks, the FPL had a heavy hand in coordinating and managing the structures."[104] Leaders across various PPLs formed the Boards of Sub-Regional Popular Power and Boards of Local Popular Power, both of which also included members of the FPL's mass organization and the chief of the local popular militias, and they had regular meetings with subdivisions of the FPL coordinating local administration.[105] The organizational complexity of the PPLs can hardly be understated, as illustrated in figure 3.3.[106]

The PPLs were central to the FPL's vision of how a prolonged popular war would integrate the masses to slowly remake the country in its vision. The PPLs were explicitly forged, as one former FPL member put it, "to create real

Structure of the PPLs

```
                    ┌─────────────────────┐
                    │  GENERAL ASSEMBLY   │
                    │     OF 'BASES'      │
                    └─────────────────────┘
                              │
                  ┌───────────────────────────┐ ─ ─ ─ ─ ─ ┐
                  │  Local Government         │           │
                  │  'Junta' or Council       │           │
                  │                           │           │
                  │  Council (Consejo) of     │           │
                  │      Popular Power        │           │
                  └───────────────────────────┘ ──────────┘
```

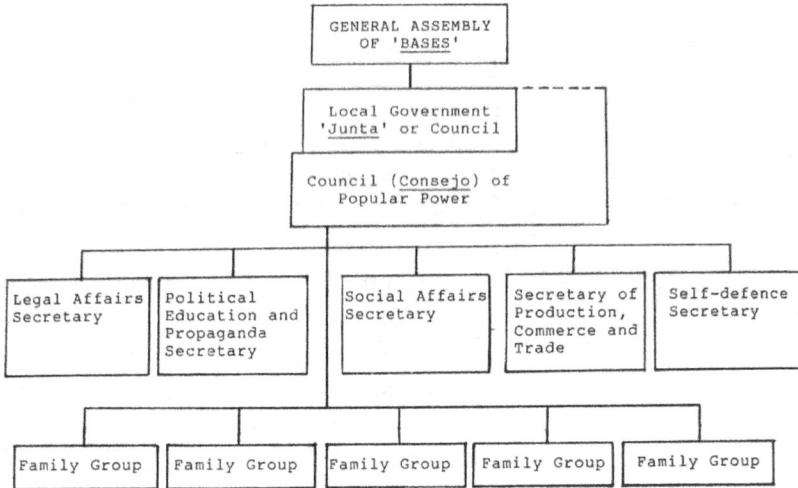

FIGURE 3.3. Organizational structure of PPLs illustrated in Pearce (1986). Copyright © Latin America Bureau.

links between our zones and the rest of society."[107] As such, these local governance structures differed markedly from what minimal local organizing arose in Morazán under the ERP.[108] The central role of the PPLs was not lost on the people participating, the rebels coordinating the them, or even the other OP-Ms. In what would prove to be a prescient analysis, Pearce notes that "many peasants, like the revolutionary organizations, see the PPLs as *the embryo of future forms of popular local government in a liberated El Salvador*, not simply as a means of solving the material problems that arise from war."[109] Fermán Cienfuegos—one of the leaders of the RN—later reflected on the importance of the PPLs and other comparable structures built during the conflict. At the midpoint of the war he referred to the FMLN as having "dispersed territorial power." The problem, he noted, was that the breadth and quality of power they had was inconsistent, even across territories they technically controlled: "To structure this power it is necessary to create new forms of organization that reflect our true capacity, because I can have 100 people organized in a hamlet but if there is no organizational form that reflects that power objectively, then it is not real, they are just scattered masses without links or permanent contacts."[110]

In other words, organized masses were of little use unless the FMLN built dedicated structures to coordinate and integrate them into the movement. Thus, the PPLs not only occupied the critical nexus between the FPL's organizational development and the relations they forged with the masses, but the leaders in charge of them understood their organizational and mobilizational value.

It is crucial, however, not to underestimate the challenge of creating participatory democratic institutions in a place with no legacy of political organization and a mostly illiterate population. To deal with the fist obstacle, the FPL leveraged its prewar social networks in CEBs. By fostering community, leadership, and political consciousness among campesinos, the CEBs provided an ideal medium for transferring the roles and skills from religious communities into an explicitly political sphere. In the search of PPL leaders, the rebels turned to catechists—the unordained "lay preachers," who had received political training in the previous decade. Rather than merely recruiting from among a known network (as the ERP did in Morazán), PPLs were constructed by taking collections of individuals with relevant skill sets and transferring them into new but related roles.

> You would think it was difficult to understand the tasks of administration of a place, especially for the peasants, many of them illiterate. But it really wasn't because the people knew what the needs were. We really know the function of each secretary. For the secretary of production and popular economy, we look for and elect a *compañero* who knows about farming, who himself uses a machete, a plough, who understands commerce. The *compañeros* involved in health need preparatory courses; the auxiliary health workers know how to manage a pharmacy and give talks on health. In education, there's usually a *compa* who can read, who has been to school until fifth or sixth grade and has shown willingness to teach those who don't know.[111]

Indeed, the way in which the FPL leveraged extant roles and relevant skill sets from church networks to construct local political organizations unfolded in lockstep with my theoretical expectations about how proto-party structures facilitate party transformation after war.

M IS FOR ~~MANZANA~~ MATANZA: FPL LITERACY PROGRAMS

Existing church networks helped the FPL overcome obstacles to mobilizing an otherwise politically inexperienced community. Yet, it still had to contend with the fact that more than half of rural Salvadorans were fully illiterate.[112] Given the FPL's objective of building a highly diversified organization capable of administering territory, mobilizing the masses, and, ultimately, taking over in a governing capacity, literacy was crucial.[113] In response to the inundating demand for literacy (from the organization and the people alike), the FPL forged one if its most robust social service divisions to provide literacy classes to local populations.[114]

Prior to the insurrection (and, thus, prior to the existence of PPLs), the FPL attempted to set up literacy programs in Chalatenango.[115] These early programs were ad hoc, lacking consistency in both scheduling and curriculum. By late 1981, however, the FPL was able to leverage three organizational resources in service of creating more widespread literacy programs in Chalatenango: (1) its affiliation with ANDES (a progressive teachers association), which provided access to experienced educators, (2) the PPLs, which provided an ideal organizational medium for administering literacy programs, and (3) its international networks, which provided educational resources.[116]

Once literacy programs were organized and routinized, they gave rise to a positive-feedback loop between education and political mobilization in the region. A community organizer in Chalatenango recounts this process:

> At first, there was an emphasis on the children . . . but many others said they wanted to learn too and the PPLs put literacy into their programmes as a fundamental element. We saw that literacy had a great deal to do with the organization of the people. . . . For the first time, there was popular government with a minimum programme which gained legitimacy as schools began to function. . . . The programme contributed to the development of the PPLs because, through literacy, people could be brought into more tasks; it mobilizes the population.[117]

Thus, the PPL structures not only acted as an organizational medium through which the FPL could provide education, but the education they provided strengthened the administrative wings by bringing more advanced and diverse skills. To be clear, the education-mobilization feedback loop was by design. The literacy curriculum drew on Paolo Freire's approach, using economically and politically salient concepts to first teach the basic tenets of literacy (writing, syllables, conjugation) and then to foster conversation about the concept itself.[118]

PRESS AND PROPAGANDA

Beyond its administrative and social service divisions, the FPL dedicated substantial organizational resources to building a robust political-messaging wing. Even in the early years of the war, the FPL's political messaging was not only extensive but also highly specialized. Both internal directives and the messaging that ultimately went to press suggest that the organization customized its messages and delivery to attend to the various groups of people it sought to influence. the following propaganda directive from an internal memorandum is one example:

> "It is necessary to increase our propaganda, but it must be propaganda that really touches the feelings of the people, their needs and interests. . . . [We must] direct propaganda to each level: to the popular masses (the different sectors in general) and to the puppets of the regime (the leaders and authorities). . . . We must focus and concretize the content of propaganda: differentiate the treatment of each sector."[119]

Crucially, this directive was not just wishful thinking. The FPL's press division was multimedia and multifaceted, comprising a radio station (Radio Farabundo Martí), a domestic press wing (The Salvadoran Press Agency, or SalPress), the Revolutionary Cinematographic Institute, and numerous divisions dedicated to internal messaging (e.g., the Farabundo Martí Documentation Center).[120]

Moreover, in the spirit of *autocrítico*, the FPL's internal memoranda consistently pushed to evaluate and improve its political-messaging operations. In a document titled "Assessment of the Politico-Military Work in the Disputed Zones," two pages out of six are dedicated expressly to plans for improving propaganda, political education, and political work among the masses.[121] Plans for improvement range from the organizational ("we've had improvement in the propaganda infrastructure . . . but we still have organizational difficulties . . . in the propaganda teams that prevent us from maximizing exploitation of [the infrastructure]") to the logistical ("we are lacking in typewriters . . . [and] we need to expedite the plans to obtain mimeographs") to the content itself ("there's been an improvement in the presentation and content, but we need more concrete and updated content . . . as well as clear follow-up").[122]

During the first few years of its life, the FMLN was a chimera—some parts of it bore so little resemblance to other parts that one would hardly recognize them as coming from the same animal. The early organizational trajectory of different OP-Ms sheds new light on the scope and implications of suborganizational variation. This analysis focused on the FPL and ERP, but the structural divergence was by no means unique to these two groups. Rather, the FPL and ERP are analytically instructive because they exhibited negligible differences in their origins: both groups emerged in rural areas among poor campesinos, both had strong ties to CEBs, and both had well-educated leadership. It is precisely the extent of their similarities that throws their differences into even sharper relief.

This analysis of the FMLN's postinsurrection trajectory has a few important takeaways. First, this section provides concrete empirical evidence that rebel groups build functioning (rather than nominal) proto-party structures and that their leaders approach organizational development with clear intentions. Second, the divergent trajectories of the ERP and FPL provide strong evidence that the *process* of organizational development proceeds in a manner consistent with my theoretical framework. Even in similar contexts, different leaders will exploit the same types of networks to very different organizational ends, which we observed in the differential use of CEBs in Morazán and Chalatenango. The third and broadest implication of this analysis is that it highlights the importance of expanding our analytic vocabulary to get traction on consequential differences both within and between organizations. Limiting ourselves to conventional organizational descriptors like command-and-control relations and cohesion, would erroneously lead us to conclude that the ERP and FPL are considerably more similar than they are. In reality, the two have wildly different organizational resources, advantages, and weaknesses as they head into the second phase of the war.

Organizational Adaptation (1984–1989)

In the first phase of the war, the FMLN made considerable military gains against the Salvadoran armed forces. Initially, its steadfast military focus paid off, and by 1983, the army was on the defensive. As a result, the insurgents had vastly expanded the territory under their control.[123] Heading into 1984, however, two related shocks to the wartime environment posed severe threats to the rebellion. Beginning in the mid-1980s, the United States underwrote a massive counterinsurgency campaign on behalf of the Salvadoran government. The influx of material support and training resulted in the government gaining the upper hand on the battlefield. To boot, US support came at a cost to the Salvadoran regime: Reagan put pressure on the Salvadorans to open the political sphere and curtail (or at least hide) human rights abuses.[124] The government complied, albeit begrudgingly. Forced disappearances declined tenfold and the 1984 elections were the most competitive in over fifty years.[125] In their wake, José Napoleón Duarte—the new president—reinstated the right to organize opposition groups, which had been illegal since 1931. Significant military, political, and social shocks followed, and, as we'll see, the FMLN was forced to adapt in the face of adversity.

The augmented counterinsurgency strategies and Duarte's political reforms posed three challenges to different dimensions of the FMLN's power: one military, one political, one social. From a combat standpoint, the FMLN found itself on the defensive for the first time in two years. Given the military's sudden capacity to wage a high-technology war, the FMLN's large, stationary battalions left them vulnerable to massive losses from a single strike. Even OP-Ms with popular support could not recruit fast enough to replace the fallen, and recruitment was even harder in Morazán where the ERP's ties to local populations had atrophied substantially.

On the political side, the most consequential shock was the newfound right to organize political opposition groups.[126] Of course, the FMLN's expansive political roots may cast the political opening in an auspicious light. However, it would be a mistake to assume that legal protections for political organizing were a foregone benefit to the rebels. In reality, thawing political rights could easily go one of two ways. On the one hand, of course, the FMLN could try to adopt a new strategy emphasizing political engagement and taking advantage of a newfound ability to mobilize supporters. On the other hand, the opportunity to organize *legally* meant that leftists could view the political opening as a reason to shy away from supporting a violent revolution, and opt instead to work toward gaining representation through legal channels.

Finally, on the social front, subsiding government violence resulted in an influx of former refugees returning to their homes. Individuals in the refugee camps had experienced their own organizational renaissance—spearheading literacy programs, popular education, self-governance (*autogestación*)—and they maintained close ties to the FMLN.[127] Moreover, they harbored fairly strong antigovernment sentiments. Still, their return was not a boon by necessity. In many cases, former refugees were returning to territory now under FMLN control, which meant that the social and administrative tasks of repatriation fell to the OP-M in charge. If managed well, returnees brought with them a host of "advanced technical skills" that the FMLN desperately needed as it sought new recruits.[128] Yet, the complications were not merely logistical. Research at the forefront of refugee studies suggests that repatriation often gives rise to local conflict between those who left and those who stayed, which places additional demand on the repatriating communities to mitigate potential conflict.[129]

This period was a multidimensional stress test for an organization that had only recently found its footing. While the FMLN successfully reinvented itself after the failed insurrection in 1981, this situation was different. Rather than facing one immediate and profound failure head on, it now confronted a series of disparate challenges (and opportunities), any one of which could easily fly under the radar. Without radical change, the FMLN was, as Bracamonte and Spencer described it, on "a collision course with disaster."[130]

THE SHIFT TO "A PEOPLE'S WAR"

Depending on their capacity to assess and adapt to this new environment, the sociopolitical changes the rebels faced could either be an asset to or the Achilles heel of the revolution. Whether the FMLN could exploit the opportunities was a matter of their ability to see what they needed and their ability to see what they had. The question is, how fine-tuned was their practice of self-reflection? I argue that two organizational features paved the way for the FMLN's successful navigation of Duarte's rise to power (and everything that came with it). First, their long-standing commitment to *autocrítico* created an institutionalized practice of searching for ways to perform better. Second, notwithstanding the official orders to focus on conventional military engagement, the FMLN comprised groups with diverse tactical, political, and social approaches to conflict. As a result, quickly changing its strategy meant it had the organizational resources to pivot to a different yet *existing* approach, rather than designing a new one from scratch.[131]

In keeping with the culture of *autocrítico*, the General Command quickly acknowledged the need to change strategies. It concluded that in spite of the rebels' territorial gains, the directive guiding the first phase came at substantial political costs. Realizing that they had focused too heavily on combat to the exclusion of mass mobilization, the new strategic directive took the FPL's approach as a blueprint for the second phase of war.[132] In an internal memorandum describing their new approach, FMLN leaders describe their shortcomings with astonishing clarity:

> Accepting the illegality of the masses was always a wrong criterion [on which to base our fight]. At the time, our approach was successful . . . but thousands of people were left without real perspective of the fight, many of whom remained with the FMLN only out of fear of repression or because they were forced by their circumstances. . . . Fundamentally, they have not had a concrete political practice to raise their levels of consciousness—they have only known a life of hiding and flight.[133]

Of course, recognizing their weaknesses was only half the battle. What remained was the Herculean task of overhauling the organization in the midst of war. The directive was twofold: restructure the military to fight a war of attrition and bolster political subdivisions to foster more informed political engagement from both members and the masses.

On the battlefield, zonal leaders were ordered to break up large battalions into small cells in service of implementing the FPL's prolonged popular war strategy.[134] The changes that the FMLN made to its military apparatus were substantial and the results were even more so. Not only were large battalions broken into smaller units, but the shifting emphasis from the battlefield to the political sphere meant that the FMLN drastically reduced its armed wing from around twelve thousand members at its peak in 1983 to only six thousand by 1987.[135] Despite halving their forces, the FMLN's reach was far greater in this period. With smaller, more mobile units, the group was able to infiltrate (to some degree) every department of El Salvador including the capital and other major cities.[136]

The most profound shift during this period was the FMLN's pivot toward local political engagement, which itself entailed multiple organizational changes.[137] The new phase of the war was characterized by a massive uptick in the FMLN's investment in its political subdivisions. Their goals were twofold: bolster political education within their own ranks, and use these new structures to forge links with and mobilize civilian populations. Implementing this plan entailed building structures dedicated to expanded political messaging, political education, and administration and governance. Yet, these structures were not born overnight. To varying degrees, the FPL, the PRTC, the RN, and PCS had spent the last decade building up politically relevant subdivisions, thereby laying a crucial foundation for the new directive.[138] Confirming the mechanism of organizational change, Wood explicitly argues that the FMLN's capacity to pivot toward political engagement was "the diversity of relations between the FMLN and various organizations."[139]

The FMLN's approach to mobilizing the Salvadoran population in this period was expertly crafted to exploit the new political freedoms accompanying Duarte's inauguration. The General Command displayed a keen awareness of the potential ramifications that followed from legalizing opposition groups. As they saw it, the only way out was through: "Legality then becomes the fundamental weapon of the masses."[140] Rather than passively allow competing opposition groups to spring up and distract from the revolution, the plan was to create those groups themselves. Across the country, the FMLN enacted a strategy called *poder de doble cara* (literally, "two-faced power"). It encouraged the masses to organize around locally salient issues—unions and workplace associations in the cities and agricultural cooperatives in the countryside. Then, the organizations would present the neutral, legal face of the organization to the state while maintaining clandestine ties to the FMLN.[141]

The organizational demands of this new approach cannot be understated. Across the FMLN, the OP-Ms had to build structures dedicated to providing internal political education, mass political education, and enhanced propaganda, as well as administration and coordination of the new mass organizations. Evidence of this structural augmentation abounds.[142] Figure 3.4 illustrates expansion plans for the PRTC. They address education, propaganda, further integration with the University of El Salvador, mass organization, and reintegration plans for returning refugees. Moreover, despite building myriad structures with fairly specialized tasks, we observe explicit care to avoid organizational rigidity—a known impediment to future changes. In her diaries, Díaz writes that the goal is to build structures that are *flexible pero solidas*—flexible, but solid.[143] A later, more formal memorandum from the PRTC echoes this sentiment:

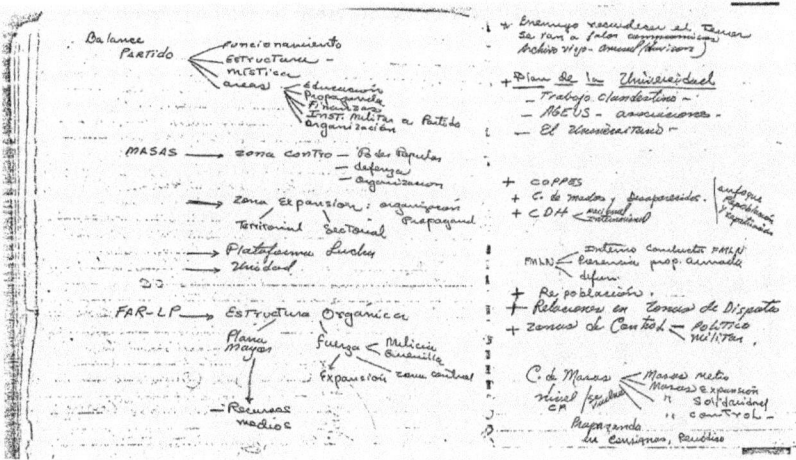

FIGURE 3.4. PRTC organizational evaluation and plans (Díaz, 1982–1984). Wartime Notebook, Nidia Díaz Papers, box 1, folder 8, Hoover Institution Library & Archives.

"These organizational forms will have to be flexible. We must seek to insert them into the state structures of the regime and take advantage of that infrastructure to bolster the security of our cadres and the masses. From there, we can exercise judicial and political control, not as an end, but as a means to facilitate and open more space in service of the organizational political work of the masses."[144]

In addition to catalyzing and incorporating new forms of mass organization, the General Command and the individual OP-Ms were quick to address the organizational challenge of repatriation.[145] As early as mid-1983, the FPL had already developed an elaborate plan addressing the relocation and reintegration of refugees.[146] Figure 3.5 suggests that the PRTC had as well. These plans had social, political, military, and economic components—ensuring that the repatriated families had appropriate provisions (e.g., clothing and shoes), were integrated into the PPL structures, and were integrated into and under the protection of the popular militias.

Poder de doble cara had two important implications for the organization's trajectory. First, the directive meant that building proto-party structures was now a matter of compliance—rather than defiance. To implement *doble cara* properly, the OP-Ms had to "create wings" to "integrate and mobilize the masses" and to build "schools for political instruction."[147] Implementing these structures in practice meant that the organizations also had to focus recruitment efforts on targeting high-skilled individuals, which the PRTC documents directly.[148] Thus, by expressly seeking to staff technical subdivisions of the organization, the FMLN's recruitment profile in the second phase of the war departs sharply from our conventional understanding of who insurgents target.

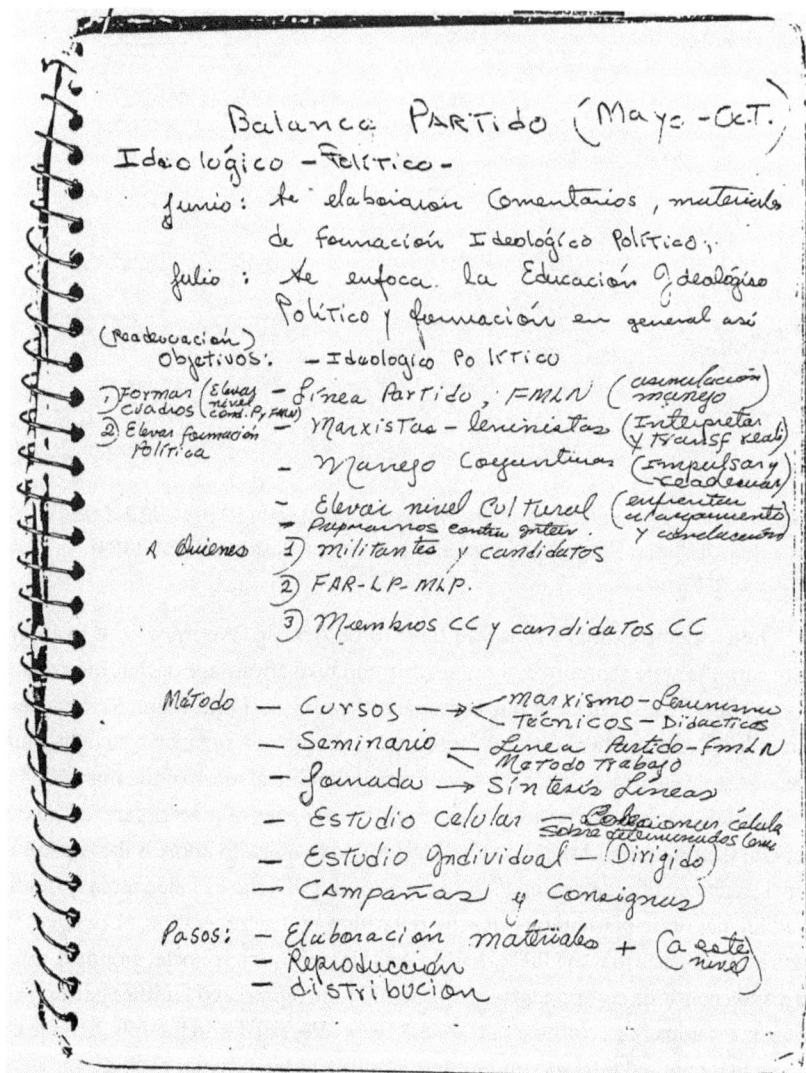

FIGURE 3.5. PRTC organizational evaluation and plans (Díaz, 1982–1984). Wartime Notebook, Nidia Díaz Papers, box 1, folder 8, Hoover Institution Library & Archives.

A Glimpse Back at Morazán

The political focus of the FMLN's new strategy (to say nothing of its explicit pivot toward the FPL's approach) raises an important question about the extent to which it was evenly implemented across OP-Ms. While cohesion among the groups increased in this period, differences on the ground persisted. Given the

ERP's continued reluctance to engage in substantial political work on top of its atrophied ties with local populations in its rearguard, I anticipate that its organizational development will not follow the same trajectory as the others. Evidence suggests that while the ERP ramped up political *activity*, it exhibits far less evidence of substantial *organizational* changes than the other OP-Ms.

Keeping in line with the *doble cara* directive, the ERP strategically exploited land reform measures and encouraged campesinos to form agricultural cooperatives, which ultimately resulted in some of the most influential peasant cooperative organizations in the country.[149] However, as Binford and others suggest, the ERP's relationship with these organizations was more hegemonic than in other regions.[150] For example, Wood observes that many peasant cooperatives were run by "strategically placed ERP political officers" and, at least initially, were fronts to "expand ERP influence."[151] Binford even goes as far as to argue that the "authoritarianism practiced by the ERP . . . restricted the political space within which relatively autonomous organizations might have proliferated," thereby suggesting that Morazán's newfound level of community organization occurred despite, not because of, the ERP's involvement.[152] Moreover, the ERP was more reactionary and opportunistic than other OP-Ms: community programs would emerge independently of the ERP (e.g., literacy programs or the Pan y Leche program aimed at feeding schoolchildren), and only "once programs demonstrated tangible benefits" would the ERP "defend them from assaults by the state."[153] Thus, while the ERP's implementation of *doble cara* and its broader move to embrace political action succeeded in forging ties to political organizations, the nature of those ties is better characterized in terms of exerting local control than integrated participation.

Tracing the FMLN's wartime evolution reveals a host of unforeseen nuance in its organizational composition. The divergent trajectories of the OP-Ms in the first phase of the war illustrates how and where proto-party structures took root. In this era, the insurgency's diversification into political domains was present, but uneven. Every OP-M under the FMLN umbrella built robust press and propaganda wings.[154] The FPL as well as the PRTC built subdivisions dedicated to mass mobilization, governance, and social service provision (especially education and health care).[155] The ERP, however, focused mainly on building out combat units and logistical subdivisions to support the fight. As such, this analysis shows that rebel organizations invest heavily in building structures that mirror the content of party organizations, but not uniformly so.

The FMLN's pivot in the second phase demonstrates the continuity and expansion of proto-party structures across the organization, as well as its capacity for flexibility and adaptation under duress. Many groups expanded their political influence in this era, laying the groundwork for future party capacity and voter mobilization. Additionally, the high command's institutionalized willingness to critique its performance and seek alternative paths to success not only served the organization well during the war, but I argue it also sets it up for success beyond the battlefield. Reflecting on the FMLN's performance at the five-year mark, the ERP leader Villalobos remarked, "We have been able to learn from every error . . . based on a serious self-critical spirit."[156] In the face of three major shocks to their environment, a set of disparate organizations—purportedly *pegada con saliva*—were nonetheless able to identify their shortcomings and devise a series of plans to combat them. The FMLN's deft reaction to facing a radically altered environment demonstrates not only its flexibility, but also what we might call its organizational proprioception: Leaders consistently demonstrate a keen awareness of what their organizations have, what they lack, and where their different "limbs" exist in the spaces they occupy.

Finally, this analysis of the FMLN's parallel organizational trajectories yields a set of clear predictions about which groups will be most equipped to pivot from the battlefield to the ballot box, which I explore in the following chapter. Given that organizational change is easier to the extent that rebel groups have preexisting competencies, OP-Ms with robust proto-party structures should be the ones spearheading the transformation. Specifically, I expect to see the FPL, PRTC, and PCS come out on top, while the ERP—despite its auspicious beginnings—is more likely to be marginalized in the party-formation process.

Tracing the Development of Proto-Party Structures

Understanding rebel-to-party transformation first requires moving away from the tendency to bracket the organizational legacies of war. Features of rebels' wartime organizations not only facilitate party building, but also may well endure beyond the conflict theater. Taking a more comprehensive approach to modeling the wartime evolution of rebel organizations reveals unforeseen variation on two important dimensions, which, together, will explain the rebel-to-party process in the following chapter. First, many rebel groups build structures that mirror the form and function of those in political parties. Second, some organizations exhibit and institutionalize flexibility, which makes adaptation to shocks more efficient and less risky.

Beyond elaborating the explanatory variables of the theory, the framework and analysis in this chapter highlight the importance of expanding our organizational vocabulary. Critically examining the content of rebels' noncombat structures reveals stark and systematic variation in how rebels organize, operate, and evolve. These insights put flesh on the bones of existing explanations of militant group structure and civilian mobilization. Absent the nuance the new organizational approach affords, even scholars with extensive case knowledge are liable to draw incomplete or misleading conclusions. For example, in describing the FMLN's organizational structure, Jocelyn Viterna reports the following: "The FMLN guerrilla army was exceedingly hierarchical. At its apex was the 'General Command,' comprising the top commander from each of the five component groups. . . . Although each branch raised its own money, secured its own weaponry, and structured its own forces, *they appear to have developed very similar organizational structures.*"[157]

Again, Viterna is not wrong, per se. The FMLN's subdivisions do exhibit structural similarities on a number of core dimensions: their hierarchical arrangement; the division of OP-Ms into political, military, and mass organizations; their disciplinary institutions. What this chapter reveals, however, is that on many other dimensions, those similarities are nowhere to be found.

Similarly, tracing the development of proto-party structures in Chalatenango, for example, elucidates one path by which the mechanism of Huang's civilian mobilization argument may play out on the ground. Yet the parallel trajectories of the FPL and ERP reveal a source of systematic variation in where that mechanism plays out—as local mobilization was considerably more robust under FPL rule. She argues, "Where rebels tap into civilians as a significant war-making resource, the latter become politically mobilized."[158] The framework developed here demonstrates that civilian mobilization is likely achieved through the structures rebels build to interface with local populations. Where those structures are less developed (let alone exploitative), civilian mobilization likely wanes as well.

The framework developed here sheds light on why Díaz scribbled *"¿Que falta?"* at the peak of the FMLN's military success. In contrast, existing conceptions of rebel organizations are not equipped to answer "What's missing?" and even more importantly, they are not equipped to shed light on *what's not* as militant groups stand on the line between military campaigns and political ones. The central takeaway from this chapter is not that not all rebels suddenly need to "learn the art of non-violent politics," as Close and Prevost suggest. Rather, it is that they often learn the art of nonviolent politics while simultaneously practicing the art of war.

PATHWAY(S) TO POLITICS

The Transformation Mechanisms

From the outside—and to many people on the inside—the end of conflict is an overdue respite from violence and turmoil. Yet, for rebel groups, the end of war is a major shock to both their organization and the environment in which they operate. The simultaneous end to conflict and demand to reinvent themselves as a political party fundamentally alters the group's needs, opportunities, constraints, and goals—all of which leaders must navigate while also preparing for elections and preventing spoilers. Thus, even if the ceasefire sticks, survival and stability are not foregone outcomes for all involved. While the opportunity to pivot from battlefield to ballot box may seem like a clear way to sidestep this existential threat, the reality is much more complex.

The wartime development of proto-party structures provides new insight into how rebel groups acquire skills with utility that transcends the battlefield. However, *useful* histories do not guarantee transferable histories—and they certainly do not translate directly into electoral success. Even the most politically diverse insurgency must undergo a massive organizational transformation at the end of the conflict, and wartime structures alone are insufficient to explain that process, for two reasons. First, successful transformation requires the ability to exploit those structures at a moment's notice. Second, and more important, it requires the ability to survive the organizational upheaval.

Conventional accounts of rebel-to-party transformation are framed as straightforward—if extensive—efforts in hiring and firing with an eye toward running for office in the upcoming elections.[1] Legislative seats, however, are not the only thing at stake. When it comes to massive structural overhauls, organizations are gambling with their lives.

To get traction on the causes and consequences of rebel-to-party outcomes, we must first understand rebel-to-party transformation as a process—specifically, a process of organizational change.[2] While the outcome refers to the point at which a militant organization takes on the form and functions of a legal political party, the process refers to the internal structural overhauls that get it there. Transformation as a process is underexplored largely because, once again, political science lacks tools for modeling these types of changes. As a result, even where scholars do address it, the process is not fully explicated. Different scholars have alternately characterized the transformation process as an "ongoing socialization with democratic behaviors," a series of attitudinal and organizational changes, and a series of internal elite negotiations alongside a robust outside hiring process.[3] The problems are twofold. First, not all of these processes are necessary. Second, even where they do exist, each of these factors is only a small part of the story; from an organizational vantage, there is much more to explain.

Internal transformations come with a host of risks and challenges.[4] After all, organizations specialize in "doing the same things in the same way, over and over."[5] Typical organizational changes involve one of two scenarios: (1) the organization does the same thing in a new way (e.g., the *New York Times* adapting to digital markets), or (2) the organization does a new thing in the same way (e.g., Tito's Vodka producing hand sanitizer at the beginning of the COVID-19 pandemic). These types of pivots are difficult enough. Rebel-to-party transformation, however, seems to demand both: that the organization perform a new set of tasks, using different methods, while also adjusting to a different environment. Moreover, the pressures of change become more numerous and more severe as the scale of the transformation grows. And as far as scale is concerned, the transformation from militant group to political party is as large as it gets. Thus, it also demands an explanation for how groups are surviving those changes, let alone thriving at their culmination.

The goal of this chapter is to dig into and resolve the paradox that comes into view when we hold accounts of the transformation process up to an organizational light. On the one hand, rebel-to-party scholars tell us the transformation process involves "build[ing] party structures from scratch" once the war ends, "finding people with appropriate skill sets to fill political and administrative positions," and "learn[ing] the art of nonviolent politics."[6] On the other hand, scholars who study organizational change tell us that "sharp breaks are seldom observed" and "[major] changes in organizational strategy and structure are likely to have negative consequences."[7]

If we take each literature at face value—the deeper we dig, the less we know. The tension between these two accounts is made even more taut when we consider that organizational sociologists largely focus on firms: legal businesses that operate (almost) exclusively aboveground. By their nature, firms comprise skilled and trained personnel; they have considerable and (usually) legally acquired capital on hand and a sizable pool of talent from which to recruit. But if organizational change is *difficult* at Apple Inc. or Ben and Jerry's ice cream company, then rebel-to-party transformation is nothing short of miraculous.[8] In short, to return to the quip that motivated this book in the first place, we are told that "failing churches do not become retail stores."[9] But in this case, they certainly seem to. The question then is, *which is it?*

The answer—albeit unsatisfying—is, a little of both, and a little of neither. The most optimistic models of rebel-to-party transformation do not account for the existential risks accompanying substantial organizational transformations. On the flip side, the most pessimistic models of organizational change too readily gloss over the fact that massive changes do happen—and that the organizations poised to survive these massive overhauls exhibit similar traits that contribute to both the change itself and their resilience to the process.

This chapter develops a theory of the rebel-to-party transformation process that accounts for the risks of organizational change and the traits that allow some militant groups to overcome them. I argue that groups' capacity to undertake and survive transformation is a function of key traits associated with organizational resilience (which are either incentivized or discouraged): structural diversity, deference to expertise, and routinized flexibility. Then, I demonstrate that the specific structures built (or not) during war give rise to different pathways by which transformation unfolds: reprioritization or reconstruction. Crucially, the former attenuates the risks of transformation while the latter exacerbates them.

An Organizational Approach to Transformation

When analyzed through an organizational lens, conventional explanations for how a rebel group becomes a party leave many key questions unanswered. But organizational theory is not just a bearer of bad news. While this approach reveals that rebel-to-party transformation is laden with unforeseen obstacles, it also sheds light on the traits that allow many groups to overcome those challenges. By examining the prospects of transformation from the rebels' vantage, we can more clearly see the scope of tasks that lie ahead as well as the threats to achieving them.

What is it like for a militant organization to stand in the liminal space between war and peace? As I alluded earlier, this period looks very different to (soon-to-be ex) militants than it does to outsiders. Since the move to electoral politics often implies an end to war, it is easy to downplay—or even to overlook entirely—the volatility of this period. Such sanguine views of conflict termination are evident throughout the literature on postwar democratization. For instance, Leonard Wantchekon and Zvika Neeman expressly set out to model "the transition from a *chaotic* status quo to a *more orderly* political regime."[10] This characterization, however, obscures the very real turmoil militant organizations face as they stand on the precipice of massive organizational overhaul and a markedly different future.[11]

Major organizational change is never easy, but transforming in the context of a volatile environment means rebels are adjusting to a moving target.[12] Indeed, in the related context of party adaptation, Angelo Panebianco explicitly argues that environmental turbulence destabilizes the party and its structures. Here, it is worth remembering that Panebianco is highlighting the risk for groups that are *already* parties.[13] The implications for transformation and how we study it are serious: rebel-to-party transformation isn't just something rebels need to do; it's a challenge rebels need to *overcome*. However, rebels not only risk failing at the ballot box; the very act of organizational change is risky, costly, and sometimes deadly.[14] As such, the capacity to transform into a political party on the heels of war requires more than resources. Rebel groups must also demonstrate a capacity for resilience and adaptation as they absorb the shock of the war's end and reconfigure to meet the demands of electoral politics.

To explain rebel groups' varying abilities to transform into political parties, I turn to two traits introduced in chapter 1—resilience and adaptability—and the factors that shape them. Organizations differ considerably in their ability to absorb shocks and adapt to new environments.[15] The first step in a theory of rebel-to-party transformation is to account for how the organization hangs together through the end of war and the transformation process. However, since the endgame is about more than just "bouncing back" to its original form, a comprehensive theory requires more than just resilience.[16] The second theoretical step requires accounting for the group's *adaptation* into a political party: the specific organizational changes enabling the group to perform key party functions in the new electoral environment.[17]

Broadly, both resilience and adaptation are about flexibility:[18] How much of a shock can the group absorb? How easily can the organization be reshaped? While the salience of these traits may seem intuitive or even obvious, it is worth noting the inherent paradox in the literature. Many traits scholars associate with successful transformation—centralization, bureaucracy, institutionalization—actually promote organizational *rigidity*.[19] To be sure, these theories are not entirely mis-guided. The organizational strength conferred by a centralized bureaucracy is often conducive to survival on the battlefield. Think of a phalanx: rigid strength is a perk when the organization faces a consistent type of existential threat.

However, when the threat fundamentally changes—and the organization must change with it—anything that promotes rigidness becomes a liability. To transform successfully, militant organizations must exhibit traits that temper the destabilizing effects of organizational change. Explaining the outcome, then, requires turning to new and sometimes counterintuitive places to account for rebel-to-party success.[20] In this section, I identify three core traits that facilitate resilience and adaptation: structural diversification (resources), deference to expertise (willingness), and repertoires of prior flexibility (experience).

Diversification

Diversification refers to the variety of roles or subdivisions within the organization that perform distinct tasks. It captures the range of skill sets an organization has at its disposal, defining not only "what an organization can do, but also what the organization *knows*."[21] Greater diversification enhances resilience by imbuing rebellions with a wide variety of skill sets and knowledge on which to draw as they navigate organizational change.[22] Even the most fervent pessimists concede this point.[23] As Gary Hamel and Liisa Välikangas poetically quip, "Variety is nature's insurance policy against the unexpected."[24]

Diversification is organizationally beneficial on two dimensions. Broadly, diversification of any sort will enhance resilience by imbuing the organization with a wide range of expertise and perspectives. More specifically, diversifying into relevant activities enables more seamless transformation into a political party. The fact of the matter is that organizational change is difficult, but it is not uniformly so. Transformation is both easier and less risky to the extent that organizations have experience with their future priorities. In organizational parlance, proto-party structures imbue the rebellion with "established competencies": preexisting structures dedicated to performing relevant tasks.[25] As such, rebel groups that diversified into proto-party domains in the midst of war should exhibit the greatest capacity for adaptation when the war ends.

This same intuition is present in the rebel-to-party scholarship. Many argue transformation should be easier for groups that operated as parties before the war broke out. Carrie Manning and Ian Smith, for example, argue that we should be more likely to observe successful transformations from groups with "experience in political organizing." To capture this skill, the authors assess whether groups operated as political parties prior to the outbreak of war.[26]

While this approach captures the intuition that institutionalized skills matter, I argue that it looks too far in the past to find party-relevant competencies. Bracketing the war further reifies the homogeneity assumption—that all rebels do during war is fight. Additionally, having once operated as a party does not account for whether or how the organization *retained* those party-relevant skills throughout the war.

By focusing on a wide range of party-relevant structures built during war, the theory developed here identifies a clearer mechanism by which experience affects future performance. Two expectations follow. First, militant organizations with greater diversification should be more likely to survive major shocks than their more homogeneous counterparts. Second, militant organizations that diversify by building proto-party structures during war will have an easier time transforming into political parties than those lacking political competencies. Diversification captures the organizational resources needed to survive and transform. In essence, it represents latent flexibility, because, as with any resources, having access to them does not guarantee their optimal use. The question is whether organizations are not just able, but *willing* to "divert resources from yesterday's programs to tomorrow's."[27]

Deference to Expertise

In the previous chapter, I argued that institutionalized flexibility was a critical wartime trait for surviving postwar transformation. Here, I elaborate on the mechanism by which it helps rebel groups become parties. An organization's willingness to be flexible requires a lot more than putting good intentions on paper. Resilience and adaptation under duress demand that organizational leaders prioritize relevant expertise—regardless of where the expertise lies in the organization. On this score, problems arise because hierarchy can be as much an analytic blinder on the ground as it is in scholarship. In both contexts, people equate hierarchy with a clear chain of command, definitive routines, cohesion, and, indeed, with organization itself.[28] As Luther Gerlach and Virginia Hine astutely observe, "in the minds of many, the only alternative to a bureaucracy or a leader-centered organization is no organization at all."[29] Part of this oversight is based on the assumption that hierarchy is incompatible with flexibility.

The problems with hierarchy run as deep as the word itself: if we trace *hierarchy* back to its root, it literally translates to "sacred rules." And sacrament is hardly conducive to flexibility. For any organization, a dogmatic commitment to hierarchy may also result in falsely equating rank with expertise. This blind spot can easily prevent leaders from seeing solutions that do not comport with the existing command structure. To overcome these problems and exploit the latent potential of proto-party structures developed during war, militant groups must exhibit a willingness to search for solutions that prioritize the quality of the solution over the rank of the solver.

If this prescription seems idealistic or even antithetical to military structures, the US Navy has a surprise in store. Consider the operational risks and procedures of manning an aircraft carrier. Aircraft carrier operations have almost no margin for error. The runway is 150 meters long, and slick with salt water and oil. Planes are taking off and landing contemporaneously, and they are fueled with the engines still running. If a landing jet overshoots the arresting wires, it cannot come to a stop on its own on the short (and busy) runway; if it undershoots the arresting wires, it can crash into the ship's stern. For an added level of chaos, the deck rocks with the ocean and is largely crewed by "20-year olds, half of whom have never seen an airplane up close."[30] Things can—and do—go wrong.

The deck has a mix of ranks standing in different physical positions and performing different duties at all times. As a result, just standing in one physical position may incidentally afford someone the perspective to see a problem that their superior cannot. Unsurprisingly, as Gene Rochlin and his colleagues observe, "events on the flight deck . . . can happen too quickly to allow for appeals through a chain of command."[31] If flexibility and deference are integral to resilience, how does the navy reconcile the high-risk, high-stakes chaos of daily operations with the "formal organization, steep hierarchy by rank, and clear chains of command"?[32] The answer is both simple and mind-boggling: they ignore it entirely. Every individual on the flight deck has "not only the authority, but the obligation to suspend flight operations immediately" and without penalty (even for being wrong).[33]

To be sure, the formal hierarchy still matters. But priorities shift when the stakes are high and expertise (or even just the right visual perspective) is diffused across ranks. Organizations can retain formality and centralization and simultaneously embrace flexibility when leaders acknowledge that temporary "flattening" is conducive to survival. Resilience is fostered when "individuals who are the most likely to have the relevant knowledge to . . . resolve a problem are given decision-making authority."[34] In other words, hierarchy is fine as long as it is more about the shape than the sacrament.

Deference to expertise is crucial in the rebel-to-party context because maximally exploiting preexisting competencies often means passing over high-ranking wartime commanders in favor of those involved in proto-party domains. Thus, we can expect to see smoother and more successful transformations among organizations with a legacy of prioritizing relevant expertise during the reorganization process, irrespective of the individuals' wartime rank.

Repertoires of Prior Flexibility

Finally, as I alluded to in the previous chapter, the more a group adapts in the past, the better it will be at adapting in the future. Surviving previous organizational transformations—or, in Debra Minkoff's words, developing a "repertoire of prior flexibility"— confers two notable advantages on rebel groups facing an additional major change in the future. First, organizations with a history of change and resilience are better able to seek creative solutions to novel problems. In essence, while deference to expertise combats *structural* rigidity, routinized flexibility combats *intellectual* rigidity. Although singular changes increase uncertainty and do pose risks to the organization, once a group has survived change, future transformations become less risky and less difficult. Second, groups that have successfully changed in the past tend to be more open to identifying shortcomings that need fixing. Once change becomes routinized, flexibility becomes part of the group's identity, rather than a threat to it. Thus, rebel groups that embrace an organizational culture of feedback and self-reflection will be more resilient to future changes.

The traits contributing to organizational resilience and adaptability work best in conjunction with one another. Preexisting competencies are of little use if, at critical junctures, leaders are not willing to defer to the expertise of others. Similarly, developing a repertoire of adaptability is more difficult for relatively homogeneous organizations, which lack diverse approaches to problem solving. Crucially, rebels' structural diversity—or lack thereof—lies at the root of resilience.

Before moving onto the final theoretical section, let us first take stock of what we know and what questions remain. Chapter 1 laid the foundation for taking an organizational approach to political phenomena. Chapter 3 built on that framework, demonstrating that proto-party subdivisions built during war provide rebel groups with both relevant and structured skill sets that translate to postwar politics. To be sure, the fact that proto-party structures are apposite to postconflict electoral strategy is fairly intuitive. Yet, as the conflict subsides and elections draw nearer, the group's continued survival hinges on whether it can quickly adapt and exploit those skills.

The preceding section derived one of the three unforeseen benefits of proto-party structures: by enhancing organizational diversity and relevant competencies, these structures make rebel organizations more resilient to change than their homogeneous counterparts. Having addressed the nature of wartime organizational structures, whether and to what extent they overlap with party structures, and the traits that enable rebel groups to survive and adapt at the end of war, two key questions remain. First, how does the transformation process actually unfold? Second, what do structures buy us analytically that we cannot just explain with an organization that employs politically savvy individuals?

Mechanism(s) of Change: Two Paths to Transformation

This section combines the structural insights from chapter 3 with the organizational traits detailed earlier to answer the book's core questions: How do you build a party out of the pieces of rebels? And why does it work sometimes and not others? I construct a theory elaborating the process(es) of rebel-to-party transformation: the sequence, nature, and challenges of organizational change on the heels of war. Drawing on the insights about rebels' varied organizational legacies, I develop a two-path model of transformation that sheds new light on the divergent prospects for success. Crucially, the path articulated in the literature (building party structures from scratch) is not wrong, it just applies to a narrower range of rebellions than was previously thought. The core takeaway is that transformation unfolds in different ways depending on the structures rebel groups build and refine over the course of the conflict.

While the opportunity to transition into party politics can arise in different ways, the organization's decision to exploit that opportunity is the analytic starting point of this framework.[35] At that point, the group must first engage in an organizational audit: an iterative process of self-reflection in which it evaluates the difference between what it currently has and what it needs in order to function as a political party. Then, depending on whether the audit reveals structures with postconflict utility, militant organizations face one of two paths to party formation: constructing a party organization from the ground up or repurposing existing wartime structures into party roles.

The literature's common refrain is that rebels must "build party structures from scratch," "learn the art of non-violent politics," and acquire the organizational and material resources to facilitate party transformation.[36] Regardless of whether transformation always unfolds this way on the ground, this adage raises an important question that is analytically prior to party building: How do rebels know exactly what they need? Before groups can even attempt party formation, leaders must conduct a thorough organizational audit to plan the transformation period.[37] On the one hand, they must ask, what has to go? Which structures are unlawful or unnecessary? On the other hand, leaders will ask, what can stay? Does the organization contain subdivisions or personnel whose continued involvement would benefit the new party? The rebellion must take stock of what it has, what it lacks, and what it no longer needs as it attempts to consolidate a party organization while simultaneously trying to survive the end of war.[38]

Although no one would deny that end-of-war audits happen, neither the nature nor the scope of the audit receives much scholarly attention.[39] From a practical standpoint, scholars exhibit a reasonable preference for observable outcomes: splintering factions, electoral participation, postconflict democratization, full demobilization. However, critically engaging the logistics of this phase is instructive, particularly for this theory. The audit process reveals the specific relevance of proto-party structures over politically relevant skills, and the audit's results determine how the transformation unfolds.

By focusing on full wings (i.e., subdivisions), my theory rests on the assumption that proto-party structures are uniquely valuable over individuals with what we might call proto-party skills (e.g., a combatant who is also skilled in political writing or union organizing). Thinking through the practical logistics of organizational audits substantiates this assumption and reveals why structures hold a privileged role over individuals. The logic underlying this assumption is simple: organizational structures will be easily visible from the top; individual skills won't. Consider figure 4.1. In the run-up to elections, the budding party needs—among other things—individuals skilled in political messaging. For the sake of simplicity, figure 4.1 represents an individual with the relevant skill set.

Let's consider the writers in a (stylized) organizational context, in which a given symbol represents an individual's skill and role within the group. For the

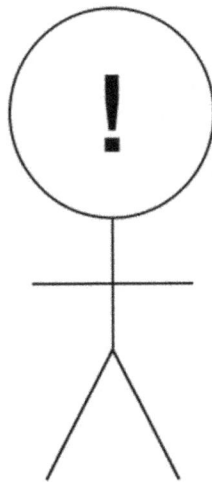

FIGURE 4.1.   Individual with messaging skills

sake of simplicity, assume rebel groups can exhibit one of three structures. In the first option, depicted in figure 4.2, the skilled individuals are nowhere to be found. This organization is relatively homogeneous: the majority of structures are constructed to perform the same task (say, combat), and the additional structures are small and likely work in service of combat (a financing wing and a logistical wing, perhaps). In the second option, figure 4.3, the organizational structure mirrors that in figure 4.2, yet some of the individual members in unrelated roles also possess the writing skills necessary for successful campaigning. Finally, figure 4.4 depicts a structurally diverse rebellion, which boasts an entire wing dedicated to political messaging and propaganda.

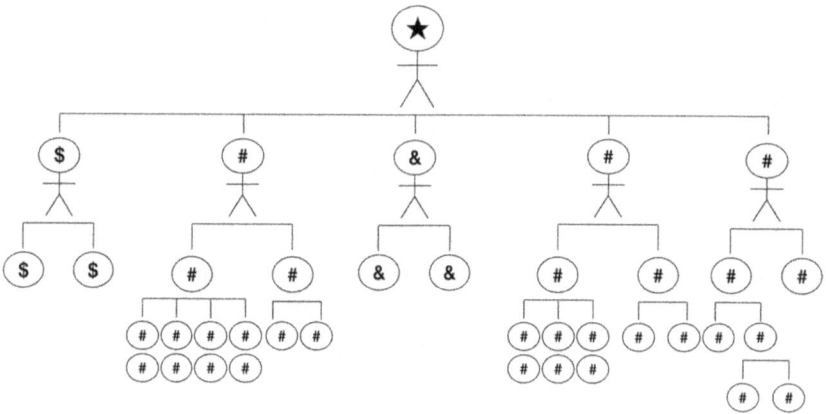

FIGURE 4.2.   Relatively homogeneous structure

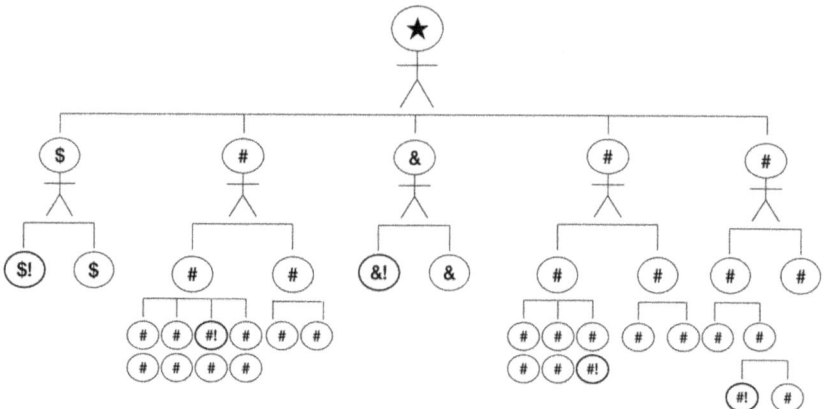

FIGURE 4.3.   Homogeneous structure with individual messaging skills

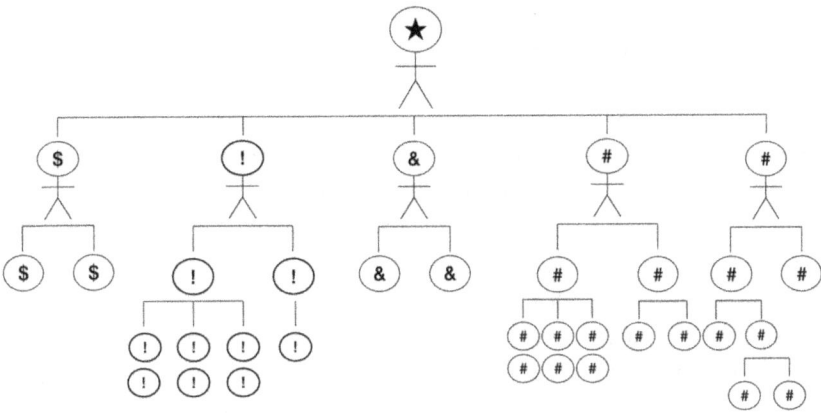

FIGURE 4.4.   Diverse structure with integrated messaging division

Given these three different structures, what will audits reveal? And what are the implications for transformation? The first and third structures have straightforward implications. Leaders of the first structure (figure 4.2) will come up empty-handed, leaving them no choice but to recruit writing skills from the outside. In contrast, leaders of the third structure (figure 4.4) will find a clear wing of personnel with both skills and experience relevant to the new party's needs.

The second structure, however, demonstrates why skilled *individuals* are not as valuable as dedicated *structures*. Keeping in mind that insurgencies often contain thousands of people, an audit of the structure in figure 4.3 will likely (albeit mistakenly) produce the same conclusions as an audit of the first structure (figure 4.2). The problem is straightforward: in most cases, individual skills are private information. Without dedicated subdivisions and bottom-up communication, leaders have no way to detect diverse skills among homogeneous structures. Taking the audit process into consideration reveals that even where "proto-party skills" are peppered throughout the armed forces, we lack a viable mechanism for explaining how leaders would identify them in the first place, let alone an efficient mechanism for combining them into a functioning unit. As Anna Grzymała-Busse observes in the formation of communist successor parties, any "structural, individual, or ideational [legacy] must be discernible . . . to affect the [new] party directly."[40]

Leaders are not omniscient and audits do not yield objective or holistic truths. For rebellions laden with "hidden talents," audits only turn up what leaders can see given the constraints of the organization's structure, operations, and channels of communication—to say nothing of time. Assessing two organizations with the same number of writers, say, can yield very different results if the writers are structured in one organization, yet dispersed (and in unrelated roles) in the other. Moreover, even if skilled writers manage to come forward and be hired into a new wing as the party coalesces, these individuals have no experience working together and the organization has little to no experience in that domain. This divergence is why individual skills are less likely to translate into efficient and effective transformation than integrated structures.

Beyond highlighting the logistical importance of proto-party structures, the results of organizational audits have pivotal implications for the transformation process. Depending on what the audit reveals, militant groups face two different transformation processes with two very different prospects for success. If a rebel group has a largely homogeneous and combat-centric structure, the process of rebel-to-party transformation will unfold in much the way conventional accounts assume. Namely, the organization will have no choice but to recruit new personnel and build party structures from the ground up. However, for rebel groups endowed with proto-party structures, the transformation process can work through reprioritization—an augmentation and promotion of existing wings—rather than constructing the organization from scratch.[41] Reconstruction and reprioritization are different mechanisms of transformation with fundamentally different risks of survival and prospects for success. The following sections trace the respective processes and their accompanying challenges, risks, and benefits.

Reconstruction: Building a Party from Scratch

The core descriptive insight of this book is that rebel organizational structures are more diverse than we currently account for, but not uniformly so. Thus, for some insurgencies, leaders will come away empty-handed—the audit having revealed a large gap between what the group has and what it needs. In the cases where leaders built and perpetuated relatively homogeneous, combat-centric organizations, the transformation process will unfold in much the way the literature portrays it. Leaders spearheading the transformation will have no choice but to build party structures from the ground up: recruiting experts from outside the organization, determining how the new party structures will be situated within the organization, and attempting to mitigate rivalries between longtime loyalists and new talent.

From an organizational frame of reference, rebel groups lacking proto-party structures exhibit four organizational deficiencies, only one of which is acknowledged in the current literature. Compensating for these deficiencies puts intense strain on organizational cohesion and resources, which in turn enhances the costs and compounds the risks of transformation.

The first (and only acknowledged) deficiency is that the nascent party lacks the personnel and corresponding skill sets needed for political domains in which the group must now operate. Thus, the leadership needs to find skilled individuals to take on the variety of administrative tasks needed to build and support a party organization. However, the process of organizational transformation is more intensive than just hiring qualified personnel to fill political positions, and it is riskier than just finishing the hiring process in time to campaign ahead of the elections. The second and related deficiency is the lack of corresponding structures: the relational protocols that determine how a given unit of individuals works together and how the unit is situated within the organization. Building a structure from scratch—say, a political-messaging wing—involves a variety of logistical considerations: establishing the roles within the unit (who writes what, who has veto power), deciding who reports to whom, and figuring out how resources are allocated and received. To boot, these decisions are more difficult to make when the people making them lack the necessary expertise or experience managing this kind of wing.

The third impediment to smooth transformation is the requisite trial-and-error period that accompanies expanding into a new domain.[42] Insurgencies with a well-developed political-messaging wing during wartime likely did not get it right on the first try; rather, they tried, failed, updated, and learned over time. They figured out early on which messages resonate and which fall flat. Furthermore, in the context of political messaging, groups with preexisting wings also had established channels of civilian engagement. In contrast, new messaging structures cobbled together in the aftermath of conflict face the added pressure of developing a cohesive political message and testing it through nascent channels during a period of marked instability for the organization.

Finally, the process of building and prioritizing new structures coupled with a dismantling of old (typically combat) structures threatens the stability of the organization.[43] According to Michael T. Hannan and John Freeman, major organizational change is destabilizing to the extent that it disrupts any of the four core aspects of the organization: (1) goals, (2) authority structures, (3) core technology (i.e., infrastructure and members' skills), and (4) strategies.[44] Building a party from scratch while dismantling combat units threatens the legitimacy of every core aspect of the organization as it existed during the conflict. Goals are shifted toward electoral and legal political engagement. Authority structures are disrupted as new hires in the party-building stage come to occupy high-ranking positions in the party to the exclusion of veterans of the insurgency.[45] Further, the set of skills and strategies on which the nascent party must rely depart markedly from their previous operations. Such disruptions can result in internecine conflict, mass defection, and/or splinter groups (which, in the case of insurgent organizations, would likely take the form of spoilers who choose to continue fighting even in the wake of peace agreements).

Notwithstanding an abundance of cheery idioms about "new beginnings," as an organizational strategy, "starting fresh" leaves much to be desired. One key expectation follows from this discussion: the extent to which a nascent party has to build political structures from scratch is the extent to which the party is unlikely to succeed in the long run. It faces greater costs, more challenges, and thus, more risks than its proto-party counterparts. This is not to say that successful parties have never trod this path. Yet, the inherent difficulty of party building in the wake of a settlement calls into question the assumption that all rebel-to-party transformations proceed (and succeed) through this route.

Reprioritization: Building a Party from Scraps

Although no organizational research is sanguine about the ease of major structural overhauls, even the most pessimistic theorists acknowledge that change is not uniformly difficult. Rather, the path to and prospects for successful transformation are a function of the group's organizational legacies. When postconflict audits reveal a variety of proto-party structures, the transformation process deviates from conventional models. Proto-party structures allow rebel groups to transform into parties by redirecting resources through established channels to prioritize existing subdivisions staffed with experienced personnel.

Proto-party structures offer numerous advantages throughout the transformation process. On the one hand, they increase the efficiency of transformation; on the other hand, they mitigate its risks. The most intuitive advantage is that the group contains personnel with experience performing a relevant task. The salience of relevant experience has not escaped the rebel-to-party scholarship: Jennifer Dresden writes on the role of "convertible capabilities," Ishiyama and Widmeier argue that establishing control zones during conflict allows the organization to acquire administrative skills that "assist in transformation," and, fundamentally, the logic of relevant experience underlies Manning and Smith's prewar party hypothesis.[46] Experience in a given domain is unquestionably important, as it reduces start-up costs and shortens the trial-and-error period as the group pivots toward party politics.

The benefits of proto-party structures, however, are as much about the structure itself as the experience with party-relevant skills. Three related advantages compound, giving rise to a more efficient and less risky transformation process. First, an established structure means rebels on the cusp of party formation not only have access to skilled individuals, but those individuals also have long-standing experience working together. Members of a civilian administration division, say, have established roles, an agreed-upon division of labor, and existing protocols for important actions (e.g., recruiting and training new members, resolving internal conflicts, and executing projects). As a result, proto-party structures can vastly reduce an unacknowledged cost of transformation: the social start-up costs, or what Arthur Stinchcombe refers to as the "liability of newness."[47] Expanding an organization into a new domain entails more than just hiring skilled personnel. The new hires must work out their collective approach to a new task and navigate working together for the first time all while working amidst a changing organization. Even for highly skilled individuals, this type of social learning under pressure is a heavy burden on organizational efficiency.[48] In short, the accrued experience of working *together* adds as much value as experience with the task on which they work.

The second and related benefit is that proto-party structures are already integrated into the organization. Thus, affiliated members not only have established relations among each other, but they also have established relations within the organization. Communication protocols between politically relevant units and the leadership already exist, as do channels through which resources can flow. As a result, the people most likely to remain in the organization throughout the rebel-to-party transformation process (the upper echelons of rebel leaders and the leaders of proto-party subdivisions) know how the organization operates, have a clearer sense of how to get (or even ask for) what they need, and potentially have an established rapport. Resources and information flow more efficiently through existing networks, which at such a critical time can be the difference between survival and death.[49]

Building on structural experience and organizational integration, the third boon to efficiency follows naturally: it is easier to repurpose and augment an existing wing than to build a new one.[50] This advantage is crucial because even understaffed and underfunded proto-party wings will make transformation smoother and faster. If augmentation is an option, it contributes to the efficiency of transformation at three different stages. First, leaders can directly consult proto-party staff during the assessment phase—this advantage goes beyond mere visibility of the structure. Experienced personnel will know with greater specificity what they need to operate at new levels as the rebel group reorients to election season. In contrast, military commanders building a party from scratch may have a sense that they need skilled messaging staff, but will likely be hazy on the details or scope of what they need.

Then, since the wing is already integrated, proto-party staff can more efficiently exploit existing channels to make those requests and employ any additional resources sent their way. Relatedly, no group will entirely escape needing to hire from outside the organization. Yet, people skilled in a given task are more likely to know others on the outside with similar skills. As such, even where hiring is needed, it will be more efficient than it would be otherwise.

In sum, proto-party structures pave the way for a new and more efficient transformation process from start to finish, while also mitigating the accompanying risks. Keeping existing structures intact anchors the transformation process. Promoting from within decreases the likelihood of sowing resentment by passing over individuals who were there in the thick of war in favor of new hires. For example, while the Mozambican resistance movement, RENAMO, had political-messaging structures in place during the war, its administrative capacity was sorely lacking, and its rank-and-file members had less than a second-grade education on average. Consequently, the leadership had to look outside the organization to fill positions as it grew its political structure. The ensuing rivalries between the "bush-based core" of the organization and the urban intellectual outsiders who were quickly promoted to high-ranking positions is well documented.[51] The inherent difficulty of transformation was exacerbated by mass defections from soldiers who felt slighted by the outsider promotions.

If indeed transformation occurs by reprioritization, case evidence should reveal a pattern of structural preservation. The "rebel" careers of five school-teachers in Mozambique illustrate this process well. In 1984—a full ten years before RENAMO ever appeared on a ballot—the leadership created a wing of politico-military commissars. Five schoolteachers were forcibly recruited to create a wing responsible for articulating a coherent political message to other soldiers. Later, in 1988, the same unit was augmented and dispatched in a campaign to provide political education to civilians. As the war came to a close, this group was again called on to aid in the negotiations process, and then promoted to high-ranking offices within the party.

It is worth noting, of course, that the two respective mechanisms represent more of a continuum than a fork in the road. Rarely will a militant organization come to the table completely empty-handed; rarely will it have a fully formed party in its back pocket. As I mention at the beginning of this section, while I present this theory as a two-path model of transformation, it is just a model. At the risk of besmirching the good name of Mr. Frost, the reality for militant organizations is that two roads rarely diverge in a yellow wood. Rather, for every organization, the transformation process will be some mixture of using what you have and filling in the gaps (albeit in different proportions). The takeaway is that every additional subdivision with postwar utility will make the transformation as a whole less taxing on the organization.

Transformation of the FMLN

The case narrative in chapter 3 left off at an optimistic point. By the late 1980s, FMLN forces had regained their military footing and vastly expanded their political influence both domestically and internationally. Internally, the organization was thriving as well: it experienced greater cohesion in this period, its combatants had better training, and its logistical and governance divisions were operating at a fuller capacity than had been possible in the early years of the war.[52] While the FMLN had in place many of the structures and traits conducive to successful transformation, those structures alone do not guarantee rebel-to-party success—nor is their wartime presence sufficient to infer their postwar legacy.

This analysis tests whether the process of transformation unfolds as my theory predicts. Specifically, the FMLN's proto-party structures should facilitate transformation by providing a more efficient path to party building, and their legacy of adaptation should enhance their resilience, by making change more routine and therefore less risky. Testing whether rebel-to-party transformation occurs by repurposing the organizational legacies of war demands very specific evidence. Beyond showing that rebel groups build partylike structures during war, I must show that they persist. In short, substantiating this argument requires evidence that rebel leaders are not just throwing the baby out with the bathwater. And this is not a given. Faced with a new opportunity in a new environment, leaders may have the impulse to start fresh. Thus, I must show that the leaders managing the transformation know the postconflict value of wartime structures and that they capitalize on it. In service of this task, I will also show that previous organizational changes in the FMLN occurred via the same path.

On the flip side, if rebel-to-party transformation adheres to the process articulated in the literature, attention to party formation should only be evident as the war comes to a close. Evidence of any of the following actions would call into question the role of proto-party structures and the mechanism of my theory. First, any indication that leaders are prioritizing outside hiring would suggest the organization lacks personnel with transferable skills (or, alternately, that leaders are unaware of the skills within the organization). Second, evidence of (successfully) building party structures from scratch would undermine both the mechanism and the motivating premise of the theory. After all, if rebels can *easily* construct party organizations in the interim between settlements and elections, then we have little to explain beyond their hiring capacity, which is likely driven by different factors entirely.[53] More specific to the FMLN, if the ERP succeeded in rapidly building party structures that performed at the same level as the legacy structures from the other groups, then structural repurposing may still be a path to transformation, but its benefits are likely less salient.

I retrace the FMLN's organizational steps in light of the hypothesized mechanism and then trace the process of rebel-to-party transformation. To substantiate the mechanism, I provide evidence of the three dimensions of this theory: the organization's legacy of resilience to major change, leaders' wartime valuation of their proto-party structures, and the postwar repurposing of these structures both within and beyond the new party.

Between 1984 and 1989 the FMLN continued to hold the Salvadoran armed forces at bay. While the total number of combatants was half of what it was at the FMLN's peak in 1983, the pivot to a war of attrition worked very much in the group's favor. Nevertheless, neither side was ever able to maintain the upper hand on the battlefield for long. Aware that it was facing a likely stalemate, the FMLN consistently tried to entice the government to come to the negotiating table, but the government always refused. See, for example, the cover of a 1986 pamphlet depicting the government's unwillingness to join the FMLN at the table.

By 1989, both the FMLN and the Salvadoran government were fighting as much against the clock as they were against each other. Funding for proxy wars was drying up quickly as tensions thawed between the USSR and the West. After the fall of the Berlin wall, both parties knew the war was as good as over. From an analytic standpoint, one could easily look at the timing of the transformation and tell a Cold War story about the war's end. To do so, however, would both obscure and oversimplify the dynamics in play. Notwithstanding the role glasnost played in putting financial and temporal pressure on both sides, it was ultimately the FMLN's international political-messaging division that forced the government's hand into negotiations.

When Duarte's government again denied the FMLN's request for a peaceful and democratic solution to the war, the rebels responded with force. During the fighting, members of the Salvadoran Army murdered six unarmed Jesuit priests. The government tried to claim the priests were orchestrating the offensive, but the FMLN immediately leaned on its international press wing. At this point in the war, it had the infrastructure to ensure the atrocity was covered in mainstream international news, and it used this power to pressure the government into negotiations. According to Bracamonte and Spencer, the event led to a "total loss of credibility in the eyes of the international community."[54] Facing both a loss of funding and massive international condemnation, the government was forced to enter negotiations in late 1989.

The FMLN exploited the state's decimated credibility to gain a considerable advantage at the negotiating table.[55] Yet, defections and ceasefire breaches on both sides made for a bumpy and protracted process. The Salvadoran government and the international community made disarmament and demobilization of FMLN combatants a requirement before proceeding with its legal transition into a political party. For its part, the FMLN feared that the government would renege once the rebels handed over their weapons. As such, the negotiation process extended over a two-year period that was punctuated by skirmishes as well as an embarrassing discovery of cached FMLN weapons after the group claimed to have fully demobilized. This event did cost the FMLN some of its international credibility, though not enough to jeopardize the negotiations.

The war ended on January 16, 1992, when both sides traveled to Mexico City and, under the supervision of the United Nations, signed the Chapúltepec Peace Accords. In addition to allowing for the "full exercise of [the FMLN's] civil and political rights," the Chapúltepec Accords included a variety of clauses for which the FMLN pushed during the negotiation process, including electoral reforms, the creation of an independent judiciary, the disbanding of paramilitary bodies, land reform, and a restructuring and reduction of the armed forces.[56]

Resilience within Rebellion

The first part of this analysis situates the FMLN's prior organizational changes vis-à-vis the theory of resilience and transformation. The purpose is twofold. Examining the organization's attitudes toward and execution of past change establishes its legacy of adaptation and resilience. Whether change was met with openness or resistance, whether it was approached in a methodical or ad hoc manner, whether its scope was ambitious or circumspect provides critical insight into how the FMLN will approach change in the future. Moreover, examining past changes in light of the mechanism I propose enables me to test whether previous transformations unfolded by the same repurposing mechanism.

Looking back over the FMLN's history reveals that prior changes were successful to the extent that the organization could repurpose existing structures to related ends—and the converse is true as well. The earliest evidence of structural repurposing came in Chalatenango. On the heels of the failed insurrection and equipped with few resources, the FPL nevertheless managed to build a robust network of local governance and education structures. This organizational expansion unfolds in lockstep with my theoretical expectations. Rather than building structures from scratch, the FPL leveraged the networks and leadership skills developed in Christian base communities to catalyze building new but related structures. As Pearce and others note, may of the early leaders in the PPL structures were the catechists (i.e., lay preachers), who had received training in leadership and oration in the previous decade.[57] Other PPLs repurposed leaders and structures from the Union of Rural Workers (which itself "had its origins in . . . the popular church").[58] In both cases, those involved explicitly noted the importance of exploiting existing structures and repurposing skilled individuals.[59]

Moving ahead, we observe similar dynamics in the aftermath of the 1984 elections. Facing a new sociopolitical reality, in which opposition groups were legalized and refugees were returning home en masse, the FMLN changed both its strategies and its organizational composition. Once again, success (and failure) was conditioned on whether groups could repurpose existing structures into related roles. The FPL and PRTC were able to build on existing messaging and educational structures to develop robust internal and external political training programs. In contrast, the combat-focused ERP struggled in this period. The political reorientation of the group required it to build comparable structures from scratch, which "posed a particular challenge to the ERP," according to Wood.[60] The exception that proves the rule was the FMLN-wide distribution of a training pamphlet commonly referred to as *The 15 Principles* (*Los 15 Principios del Combatiente Guerrillero*).[61] As Hoover Green observes, this manual is one of the most consistently cited sources of internal political education.[62] To achieve dispersion that wide, the FMLN leveraged the ERP-affiliated Radio Venceremos Press System to print and distribute the pamphlet. Here was a structure that already existed and operated in political, noncombat domains. While the group had difficulty building *new* structures, Venceremos was quickly mobilized to take on a large-scale task in the vein of its typical operations.

To assess the counterfactual, consider the FMLN's imprudent choice to "strip the political wings of their key cadres" to quickly build up understaffed combat units ahead of the Final Offensive in 1981.[63] The organizational and operational consequences were vast and bleak. Ahead of what was supposed to be a nationwide strike, the organization had in essence severed its structural ties to what few unions and professional organizations still existed in the country. Additionally, it had constructed a military out of people with no military experience and too little time to train them. And we now know how the insurrection played out: undertrained combatants were unable to stave off the Salvadoran military and without links to the labor force, the national strike was a failure.[64] This organizational misstep represents a complementary example of the risks of repurposing structures from one subdivision into an *unrelated* domain.

Notwithstanding the setbacks, the FMLN established legacy of adaptation in response to external shocks. More importantly, this resilience was not latent. Throughout the war, leaders reflected on these traits, which in turn, laid a stable foundation for future changes. As Villalobos once remarked, "We have been able to learn from every error . . . based on a serious self-critical spirit."[65]

In response to this organizational learning, leaders implemented intentional structural changes: "In short, the Party again underwent a new readjustment of its structures, its thinking, its guidelines, and its strategy and tactics to face the new challenges."[66]

THE LEGACY OF ORGANIZATIONAL AUDITS

Evidence of a postwar organizational assessment is a minimum requirement for my theory to hold. After all, if leaders are not critically examining the organization's advantages, resources, and deficiencies as they stand on the cusp of party formation, then organizational traits are likely subordinate to other factors affecting transformation. This view is reflected in the literature as well. Jeroen de Zeeuw, for example, argues that rebel-to-party transformation entails the "postwar challenge" of reorienting the organization and developing new tactics, strategies, and structures.[67] The question, however, is whether the auditing starts only when the war ends. I demonstrated in chapter 3 that organizational assessments were commonplace—one of the few institutions on which the OP-Ms agreed was the value of organizational learning and updating (*autocrítico*). Here, I examine the content of those audits. If wartime legacies play the central role in party formation that my theory proposes, I expect to find evidence that organizational assessments in direct service of political development happen early and often.

Internal documents, memos, and diaries reveal that organizational assessments were explicit and routine. In fact, rather than waiting for shocks, leaders were actually scheduling "*autocrítico* meetings."[68] Outlining the need for routinized assessments, FMLN leaders documented the imperative to "develop and maintain periodical evaluations that cover all the levels of the party to assess the necessary adjustments."[69]

More important, however, not only did the FMLN conduct detailed audits in the run-up to the major organizational changes delineated earlier, but I also find clear and consistent evidence that many organizational assessments were conducted expressly with party formation in mind. For an early example, consider this excerpt from an FPL document aimed at formalizing the strategic relations between FPL structures, the PPL structures, and ANDES (the teachers' union):

> The construction of the party is an urgent priority . . . it is necessary to have a *specialized party structure* up to the levels of the departmental teams.
>
> Tasks: *Form cadres with specialized party objectives, so that their (eventual) promotion organically strengthens the party because we have the core elements already in place.*[70]

The implications could hardly be more clear—and this level of foresight was not limited to the FPL. In a document outlining future organizational tasks, PRTC authors explicitly list among their objectives "*to create* in the process of the struggle, *organizational structures that are guaranteed to continue their work after the conflict*."[71]

Displaying a remarkable command of organizational dynamics, leaders' assessments also evince shortcomings that support my theory. In a document containing plans to augment the political cadres within the FPL, the authors note the following problem: "*Some of the limitations are* a function of staff shortages and *organizational issues*, such as *having to relocate [skilled cadres and individuals] to new positions* and therefore *wasting their time and expertise*."[72] Here, we find direct evidence that leaders not only made decisions based on expertise, but also that the failure to do so resulted in inefficiency, which they sought to correct.[73]

These assessments and the corresponding plans are nearly impossible to misinterpret. The FMLN's wartime legacy of continued self-assessment, critique, and adaptation meant that the audit following the ceasefire was just one more instance of an ongoing routine. Leaders display—if not exceed—the organizational awareness and acumen this theory demands and their decisions to augment and repurpose structures in the face of major changes tracks with the predictions laid out earlier in the chapter.

Resilience beyond Rebellion

The question now is, did the FMLN's wartime legacies bear fruit? In this analysis, I look for explicit evidence that personnel and subdivisions with relevant political experience are retained and prioritized as the FMLN gears up to operate as a party. So far, the evidence paints a picture of a structurally diverse organization, bound by flexible institutions, and run by leaders who routinely displayed the acumen to use these structures in service of their goals. Of course, these assets were not distributed uniformly. I expect to find that the balance of power in the new party is skewed in favor of the FPL, PRTC, and PCS—the OP-Ms that constructed the most robust proto-party divisions throughout the war.

On one side of the transformation were the OP-Ms who, throughout the war, had dedicated substantial resources to developing proto-party structures. The leadership and the individual OP-Ms immediately identified these structures as a viable foundation for the nascent party, as the following excerpts illustrate. For ease of reference, each quote is preceded by the corresponding OP-M or body:

FMLN General Command: We are in the period in which *we must have the capacity to translate our political capital developed during wartime* to the moment when there is peace in El Salvador, and the way we will do it is *through elections.*[74]

FPL: [Winning the '94 elections will ensure] *we can reorient local popular power structures* and control mayorships.[75]

PCS: *We enter 1991 with an accumulation of democratic and revolutionary cadres with strategic value.* They have been developed under the conditions of dual political-military power, *which puts us in a very good position to succeed.* We will promote a sustained policy that includes all existing sectors . . . to decisively influence the advancement and success of our political strategy.[76]

PRTC: *There are still five different organizational realities.* They exhibit different levels of development, different levels of force, we have worked in different areas and different sectors. Some have the means of communication and others do not. *The challenge now is to know how to manage all those differences while trying not to erase them with the stroke of a pen.*[77]

On the other side of the transformation, we find the ERP. The content of the ERP's organizational assessment strikes a very different tone from the documents and interviews quoted here. The following quotes are excerpts from an internal memorandum addressing the ERP's organizational strategy for party formation. In line with my expectations—and contrary to the audits depicted previously—its postconflict assessment revealed a dearth of structures with postwar utility; most of the tasks it outlines focus on what to build, rather than what to keep.

[W]e need to discuss . . . *how we are going to shape political structures.*

We need to discuss the principles of political party organization in general and *create the functional structure* that binds the union, social, judicial, and electoral struggles into a single effort.

Until now . . . we have fundamentally been a military and peasant force.

We need to . . . redesign the political forces in service of two grand objectives: fulfillment of the accords and to win the national government in the '94 elections.

We recognize that many of the organizational lines we have promoted have been in service of the war.[78]

The ERP has established that it is being reimagined in light of the new struggle. . . . *We humbly recognize that we need other capacities for the new challenges.*[79]

The single most notable thing about this document is that it tracks perfectly with expectations from the literature. At the end of the war, ERP leaders assembled, assessed what they had and what they needed, identified that they were lacking in party-relevant structures, and made a plan to build them now that the war was over. ERP leaders noted that in addition to building these structures they had to "relate more with the masses," "integrate ERP cadres into the unions," and "get grassroots leaders to convert to leaders of the party."[80] In short, after building the structures, they needed staff and votes. The ERP's party-building strategy is quite literally a good idea on paper. The problem is that it proved to be too little, too late.

THE TRANSFORMATION

Starting at the top, the five-member General Command was expanded into a fifteen-member Political Commission.[81] With an eye toward promoting unity and reducing conflict, the initial plan gave each OP-M equal representation across the party, irrespective of its size. Yet, when it came time to appoint personnel to specific tasks and nominate candidates for office, a different dynamic emerged. In line with the theory's predictions, the organization quickly moved away from what Luciak describes as the "artificial balance" in representation. Instead "other factors, such as a potential candidate's political experience, began to take precedence."[82] Spence's account elaborates: "Candidates were selected by departmental committees of the party where historical roles were debated against current performance in new kinds of tasks. Thus, being a good guerrilla or underground operative did not guarantee selection."[83] The new balance of power in the nascent party thus came to reflect wartime political legacies. As Tommie Sue Montgomery recounts, "The FPL emerged in 1992 as the largest and best organized politically. Of the five [OP-Ms], the FPL and the PCS made the quickest and most effective transition to electoral politics, the FPL because it could draw on years of political organizing and because it began transforming itself before the peace accords were signed. . . . In contrast, the ERP . . . was slow to organize politically."

Ralph Sprenkels later confirmed this dynamic, noting that the specific "political accommodations" in the settlement "resulted in former FPL and PCS cadres becoming the FMLN's backbone." Moreover, evidence from the inside strongly suggests that organizational repurposing was as intentional as it was common. "In the context of transitioning to legality, the [PCS] Central Committee made a marked effort to regularize its operation, giving continuity to a process that had already begun even under the precarious conditions of illegality."[84] The balance of power that emerged in the wake of the settlement strongly supports the mechanism driving the theory.

Below the leadership level, the same dynamics play out. Individuals and sub-divisions that took on proto-party roles during wartime persisted through the transformation. Leaders who managed governance projects during the war were tapped to take on formal governance and administrative roles in the new party.[85] At the subdivision level, the FMLN's press and propaganda divisions exhibit some of the clearest evidence of repurposing. As they looked ahead to the campaign trail, the burgeoning party had nearly twenty years of experience communicating with the people. In an internal memorandum addressing the organizational tasks ahead of the 1994 elections, FMLN leaders dedicated a section to the role of propaganda structures in the postwar environment, and Sprenkels reveals a similar process in recounting his work with the FPL during the transformation period:

> The communication capacity of the revolutionary movement is one of the key elements for its development [into a party]. During the first years of the dictatorship and the later years of the war, the popular forms of propaganda—the mural and the flyer—had a profound impact because they were new methods of breaking the censorship and defying the military. Now, it is important that we design new forms of propaganda that are in tune with the conditions of the new period.[86]

> Together with a comrade . . . we had to collect the different materials (paper, ink, typewriters, stencil machines) leftover from the wartime propaganda units active in Chalatenango and bring these to the new office of the FMLN to be opened in the city. At the same time, we were charged with designing a new propaganda strategy for the FPL around the FMLN's new image as a soon-to-be-legal political party.[87]

Note that in the first excerpt, Oscar Miranda (one of the directors of the PRTC's Political Commission during the war) not only speaks to the wing's critical role in the transformation process, but also addresses how only the *form* of the message must change (as does Sprenkels).[88] In doing so, both accounts lend strong support to the repurposing mechanism underlying the theory. The leadership further confirms the intentionality driving the reorganization: "*It is essential that each commission dedicates their efforts to their specific expertise.* [We must] avoid the dispersion and disintegration of these skills in order to achieve the most optimal results for each cadre."[89]

Similar examples of repurposing come to light across the FMLN. Community organizations and insurgent cooperatives that coalesced under *Poder de Doble Cara* during the war went on to form affiliated NGOs.[90] They took on governance and development projects in service of both the nascent party and the communities from which they came, forming what Wood characterizes as "a dense [FMLN] network of civil society organizations."[91] Miranda of the PRTC explicitly confirms this mechanism:

> Everyone is going to be left with something in their hands. All our structures and our men will follow three paths. The fighters . . . will go to agricultural production on the lands we have left.[92] A percentage of the structures will go to the National Civil Police, and another [percentage of the structures] will go to the political party organization into which we are going to transform.[93]

Crucially, organizational repurposing is not just an exercise in vanity—living on for the sake of living on. Instead, relevant structures are allocated to address real needs. The Salvadoran Association for Local Development and Democracy (ASPAD) is a prime example. Ahead of the 1994 elections, voter registration was one of the primary obstacles the FMLN faced—especially in rural areas (i.e., where most of its supporters and ex-combatants resided). Over one-third of the voting-age population was unregistered and lacked sufficient identification to register in the first place.[94] While the settlement created a tribunal dedicated to election oversight (TSE), according to Montgomery its members proved both unwilling and unable to "handle the logistics of a massive registration process."[95] The problem, of course, was that the TSE was a government agency, and the incumbent government (which was also up for reelection in 1994) had few incentives to ensure people who had lived under the FMLN for the past twelve years could now vote.

To fill in the logistical gaps, the FMLN spearheaded a massive repurposing of wartime municipal community organizations to form ASPAD.[96] This NGO not only facilitated a massive voter registration campaign but also conducted in-depth analyses on the process and problems with voter registration more broadly. Even here, the same suborganizational dynamics are present. As Rachel A. May, Alejandro Schneider, and Roberto González Arana argue, "The different factions of the FMLN varied in experience and success in organizing voters. The PCS, as the most established politically . . . was the most successful, and the ERP was the least [politically] experienced and . . . the least successful electoral faction of the FMLN."[97]

The same transformation mechanism also shaped postwar life beyond the party. Although the firsthand accounts of the organization's diversity are critical, the content of the negotiations is equally telling. Beginning with the counterfactual, if the organization itself were as homogeneous as rebellions are portrayed, we would expect the rebels' demands to center primarily on amnesty for ex-combatants; resources, both for demobilization and party formation; and context-specific concessions (e.g., land reform). The FMLN, however, came to the table with demands that laid bare its organizational diversity: reintegration scholarships and teaching certifications for "popular teachers," and legalization of its press divisions, including ¡Radio Venceremos!.[98] Figure 4.5 is an excerpt from an FMLN-affiliated newspaper, *Equipo Maiz,* outlining the tenets of the peace accords.[99]

FIGURE 4.5. Excerpt from *Equipo Maiz*'s popular edition explaining the terms of the settlement. *Los Acuerdos de Paz: Cuaderno No. 5*, David Spencer Collection, box 7, folder 7.15, Hoover Institution Library & Archives.

Wartime subdivisions that did not qualify for demobilization, yet did not *directly* serve a party function, transformed into postwar roles, fully intact. In the social-service sector, the FPL's medical wing was converted into PRO-VIDA (the Salvadoran Association of Humanitarian Assistance), an NGO dedicated to health care.[100] FMLN cadres in charge of territorial administration during the war were tapped to facilitate the land transfer program during the demobilization and transition process.[101] Finally, the postwar trajectories of ¡Radio Venceremos! and the FPL's *Radio Farabundo Martí* are worth elaboration. While the OP-Ms kept many of their press wings intact, radio stations did not fill the bill for party operations. Yet the thought of disbanding them was anathema to the FMLN. The Venceremos member José Ignacio López Vigil details the station's plans in his 1991 memoir: "Venceremos is on the agenda in the negotiations. They want us to return to civilian life, do they? Gladly, but we're taking our equipment with us, because that's how we'll take part in public debate. . . . It's time we dealt with all the interference by getting our broadcast license instead of using barbed wire."[102]

Both wartime radio stations successfully negotiated licenses. Sprenkels describes the sanguine "descent" of the stations "from the mountains to new out-fits in the capital city," where the goal was to continue their political role.[103] In light of their prestige and a newfound international patron, the other OP-Ms sought to get radio stations off the ground as well. In line with the predictions from my theory, these attempts at building new organizations from scratch failed.[104]

1994 AND BEYOND

Objectively, the FMLN made an impressive showing in the 1994 elections. Despite running against eight other parties, the FMLN took over a quarter of seats in the legislature and won thirteen mayorships, making them the second-largest party in the country.[105] Unsurprisingly, the party was disappointed with the results, and attributed what it considered a modest performance to systematic voter disenfran-chisement and intimidation. Nevertheless, from an electoral standpoint, the FMLN transformed its organization and made a successful transition into the electoral arena, where it remains a persistent contender in Salvadoran politics.

With the benefit of time and some existential security following its relative elec-toral success, the FMLN spent the following years working to create a more unified and effective party. FMLN leaders decided the best way to forge a unified path forward was to dissolve the remaining lines between the OP-Ms. While this deci-sion was likely beneficial for party cohesion, the obstacles to unification track with the theory's predictions. Consider Nidia Díaz's 2006 account of the PRTC's history:

> When the PRTC was dissolved, I appointed a team for the transition which did not work efficiently. When dissolving our structure, FMLN

institutions lacked the specificity and scope needed to properly engage with the politics and ideology of the PRTC's historical bases.

There has been a lack of attention to political training and organization. Each of the organizations that dissolved have faced this problem: FMLN institutions were insufficient to replace the specific focus that derived from each group.[106]

As these quotes illustrate, attempts to erase lines between the groups came with the added pressure of creating new subdivisions and new institutions while simultaneously trying to achieve new goals. Díaz articulates the organizational inefficiencies with textbook acuity. While these new structures did not result in the party's demise, the fact that they were inefficient to a level worthy of documentation hints at the problems with building an entire party this way.

Notwithstanding the OP-Ms plans for total dissolution, their organizational legacies persisted.[107] Press wings that originated in Chalatenango under the FPL continued to print FPL-branded messaging more than ten years after the FPL "dissolved."[108] More broadly, Carlos Guillermo Ramos, Roberto Oswaldo López, and Aída Carolina Quinteros are unequivocal in their characterization of the party, even twenty years on:

> In is . . . interesting to observe that the FMLN as a political party has not managed to establish any clear processes aimed at generational renewal. The leaders of the Front are basically the same political and military leaders of the war period. Indeed, the Vice-President for the 2009–2014 term and President elected for the 2014–2019 period was one of the principal members of the Front's General Command during the war and a signatory of the Peace Accords. The same is true for the deputies and internal party authorities.[109]

This excerpt speaks directly to the assumption at the heart of the rebel-to-party literature. Scholars and analysts find the FMLN's lack of an organizational upheaval remarkable. Rather than remarking on the fact that some rebel groups don't establish processes of renewal, what we should remark on instead is how any group survives them and why some rebel groups don't need them. The fact is, for many groups, operating as a political party is often not the sharp discontinuity it is so often framed to be.

Partido Democratica: A Shadow Case in the FMLN's Shadow

The FMLN's general success in electoral politics is not the end of its rebel-to-party story. Shortly following the 1994 elections, enduring rivalries led to a split in the FMLN in which the ERP and the RN broke off to form a party of their own, the Partido Democratica (PD). The ERP was by far the dominant force in the PD. Thus, from an analytic standpoint, the splinter presents an opportunity to test alternative explanations for and mechanisms of rebel-to-party transformation within the same case. The ERP's dominance means the PD is an example of attempted party formation by the most homogeneous of the FMLN's organizations. Alternative explanations of the outcome would predict likely rebel-to-party success. The ERP consistently held the most territory, it established the clearest rearguard, and it had no profound dearth of material resources.[110] It leaned heavily on local populations to support the war effort—a dynamic purported to translate into postwar political capital.[111]

From an organizational standpoint, however, the PD was lacking. This party was forged out of players who were marginalized during the FMLN's transformation in part because they lacked relevant political experience.[112] While the ERP emerged from war with a critical organizational resource—the voice of the resistance—it no longer had the control over ¡Radio Venceremos! that it once did. At this point in El Salvador's history, Venceremos was already set up in the capital broadcasting an unobjectionable mix of revolutionary songs, news, and Madonna. The ERP and the RN had distanced themselves from their other proto-party structures as well. Even after the FMLN's 1984 shift toward a political strategy, the ERP often used its affiliated political organizations as sources of military recruits.[113] While these allied organizations worked to boost their political influence throughout the war, their success came in spite, rather than because of, their ERP ties.

In the case of the RN, the group's wartime political resources would have been ripe for postwar repurposing into party structures. The problem was a lack of foresight. Consider FENASTRAS, the Salvadoran Federation for Union Workers. FENASTRAS, according to Sprenkels, was the "crown jewel in the RN's civil-political front" during the war, supplying funding, recruits, and spearheading political initiatives in concert with the RN's views.[114] Yet, as the war came to a close, RN leaders "had little clarity" on whether and how to continue their relationship with the union, and in the throes of indecision, they quietly went their separate ways.[115]

The ERP's hegemonic control over its political affiliates gave rise to severe tensions in its areas of control. Thus, in spite of the rich civil society that emerged among the population in Morazán and Usulatán, the ERP was largely unable to benefit from it. While the PD made it as far as the ballot, the party never garnered enough votes to win any seats. After its failure, the organization quietly disbanded and many members sheepishly returned to the FMLN.

Building on Wartime Legacies

The ERP did not harbor different goals from the other OP-Ms. Each group initially sought to overthrow the government and each intended to take power after the revolution. They had comparable prewar experience and comparable material resources. Although occupying the same ballot as the incumbent government was not always part of the plan, politics was in everyone's future from the outset. What differed across the OP-Ms were their paths and their success. Successful postwar parties are often built on wartime legacies—and when the wartime legacies are absent, so too are their electoral prospects.

The mechanism by which rebels transform into political parties is elusive when we analytically bracket the organization during war. This is not to say that researchers are not acknowledging that war happens, but existing approaches provide only a narrow view of what wartime organization entails. The result is a set of technically true, but holistically misleading conclusions: "It is not easy to transfer the skills from organizing a war to organizing a political campaign" and its corollary, any rebel group that wants to form a political party "must learn the art of non-violent politics."[116] Neither my theory nor the empirics dispute this premise; instead, they account for the pivotal fact that some groups learn it earlier than others. The next chapter addresses the final theoretical question: are wartime organizational legacies as compelling to voters as they are to scholars?

"FROM A THOUSAND EYES TO A THOUSAND VOTES"

Transitioning into Politics

The previous chapter demonstrated that the organization rebels build directly shapes the organization rebels can become. However, organizational transformation is only half of the rebel-to-party battle. After surviving the end of war, the demobilization process, and the internal dynamics of party building, rebel successor parties still have a monstrous task ahead: convince people that they are worth voting for. Thus, while chapter 4 explained how militant organizations become parties in form, the final question I address is whether they can become parties in function as well. In other words, if it looks like a party and it's registered as a party, can it win like a party?

Halfway through the war, the ERP leader Joaquín Villalobos was asked whether the organization was in a position to mobilize voters with the same success it had in mobilizing recruits. He responded optimistically, arguing that the people who supported the FMLN during the war—providing information, supplies, and sanctuary—would show up in equal numbers if the rebellion transitioned to electoral politics. *"Desde mil ojos a mil de votas"* (From a thousand eyes to a thousand votes), he said.[1] The question I ask here is, did Villalobos get it right? Does logistical support during the war translate into inevitable voter mobilization when the struggle moves from the battlefield to the ballot?

Wartime organization clearly matters for a rebel group's capacity to forge a party organization on the heels of conflict. But when the time comes to mobilize the thousand eyes on which they relied during war into the votes they need on election day, are those same structures up to the task? When it comes to explaining rebels' electoral prospects, proto-party structures have benefits that transcend the organization's boundaries. Organizational subdivisions dedicated to governance, social service provision, and political messaging not only imbue the rebels with skill sets needed to create a party organization, but also establish the type of political linkages needed for the successor party to act (and win) like one.

Chapter 4 focused on explaining transformation: the structural changes needed to forge a party organization.[2] But transformation does not capture the stakes of building integrated rebel successor parties. *Transition* is the shift toward operating in a new environment.[3] Organizational transformations and environmental transitions are related, yet they capture different processes, entail different challenges, and have different observable indicators.[4] As I note in previous work, this distinction gives rise to a conceptual hitch in the literature.[5] Although scholars occasionally allude to different processes, the conceptual line demarcating transition and transformation is never directly engaged.[6] More often than not, the concepts and their indicators are used interchangeably, which undermines clarity, concept validity, and the scope of questions we can even ask.[7] This chapter pivots from the internal transformation to examine how rebels make the outward transition into the electoral arena.

Parsing Transformation and Transition

To motivate the distinction in rebel-to-party outcomes, it helps to revisit the stakes.[8] In scholarship and policy making alike, rebel-to-party provisions are justified by a single argument: giving former belligerents access to legal avenues for dissent will prevent them from using violent ones. In so doing, postconflict integration reduces the likelihood of conflict recurrence and paves a smoother path for stability, development, and democratization.[9] The stakes involve some of the most central dynamics to our discipline. If indeed these benefits derive from the formation and inclusion of rebel successor parties, then we need to know both how these parties form and how they function.

Drawing on the organizational change literature, we can distinguish rebels' internal, organizational transformations from their external, environmental transitions.[10] Organizational transformation and environmental transition are related but distinct outcomes, which come with distinct challenges. In the postwar context, it is possible to have one without the other. For example, a militant group may reorganize in a way that mirrors a party organization's structure, but simply remain a local political actor without participating in electoral politics (e.g., the Zapatistas). A transformation without transition will likely have different implications for both the group and the political system than a transformation accompanied by a successful move into legal politics. Conversely, registering as a party without the organizational changes required to successful campaign, mobilize, and govern is considerably less likely to result in the long-term stability and democratization that rebel-to-party scholars tout as the benefits of postwar electoral inclusion. Many groups survive beyond the war's end, but some get much further in the electoral arena than others.

While the outcomes are related, parsing transformation and transition is crucial for two reasons. On the one hand, transformation does not happen in a vacuum; a changing organization both affects and responds to its environment—especially when the environment is changing as well. Beyond overcoming internal dynamics, rebel successor parties must operate under new rules, with new competition, by performing new tasks, in service of new goals (which themselves feed back into how they navigate reorganizing). On the other hand, the transition to a new environment is actor dependent: some organizations will be poised to confront these new challenges and perform these new tasks better than others. As such, the process of organizational transformation is considerably less salient if it doesn't translate into competent functioning.

This distinction is mirrored in the parties literature, where the analogue is party *formation* versus party *consolidation*.[11] Distinguishing transition from transformation enables future analyses to more directly speak to the parties literature, allowing scholars to examine the interaction between the functional move into politics and the organizational changes that promote (or inhibit) it.

While a distinct logic of transition and transformation is not explicated in the literature, most scholars define rebel-to-party outcomes in terms of electoral participation, which aligns with a transition into the political environment.[12] But this tack raises an important question: How much participation is enough for a transition to count? If the stakes outlined earlier guide conceptual evaluation—as they should—then the trade-offs of different approaches are highly consequential.[13] Existing approaches have laid an important theoretical and methodological foundation—paving the way for rich analyses and prodigious data-collection efforts. However, they exhibit a few unresolved conceptual issues.

First, scholars often demarcate successful rebel-to-party transition according to minimalist benchmarks of participation, such as party registration or ballot appearance.[14] While these indicators have the benefit of parsimony and observability across cases, neither fully captures political integration or the full scope of Sartori's criteria for qualifying as a party in the first place. Yet, the problem goes beyond concept validity. Beyond inadequately capturing what Robert Adcock and David Collier call the "background concept," minimalist indicators introduce problematic heterogeneity into the set of positive cases (particularly if the outcome is dichotomized, which it most often is).[15] On the flip side, overly strict criteria for successful transition—for example, achieving blackmail or veto power in government—needlessly excludes parties that nonetheless have access to government and can meaningfully contribute to policy making.[16]

The second conceptual issue concerns how or whether scholars define rebel-to-party failure. Although definitions of transition are fairly common, codified definitions of failure are considerably less so. Yet, defining failure is crucial for any comparative analysis.[17] After all, if we want to understand why some rebel successor parties succeed in the electoral arena while others fail, how we define the others is going to affect the answers we get. One tack—increasingly common among those using multipurpose datasets to conduct large-N analyses—involves borrowing the dataset's (broad) inclusion criteria to serve as the de facto scope conditions for the transition variable.[18] Researchers score transitions (however conceived) as a 1, then fill in 0s for all remaining observations in the dataset. Thus, for Benjamin Acosta and Aila Matanock, the implied definition of "failure" is "any militant group that did *not* participate in electoral politics." This approach, however, sometimes results in comparing successes to nonviable contenders: groups lacking the intent or even the legal opportunity to transition. For example, organizations like the Legion of Doom or the Animal Liberation Front are likely systematically different from those that tried and succeeded at party formation *and* those that tried and failed.[19] Consequently, this conceptual decision may produce empirical selection effects.

The third and related issue concerns the role of disarmament. While some distinguish "disarmament" from "party formation" to explore their relationship as a salient line of inquiry, one sect of the literature identifies "disarmament" as a necessary condition for both transformation and transition.[20] As such, any group that has failed to disarm entirely is deemed a failed transition, irrespective of its electoral outcomes. The logic is straightforward: hybrid militant-party organizations can use violence to influence or circumvent the political process. The "transition to peaceful politics" is, thus, incomplete.[21] To be sure, this hypothesis is compelling and important. However, translating this hypothesis into a conceptual *rule* prevents us from actually testing whether and to what extent it holds. Embedding disarmament as a defining feature of transition gives rise to three problems.

For one, this approach conflates an organizational outcome with a functional and environmental one. Whether the group demobilizes its armed wing is distinct from its electoral standing.[22] If an organization runs in elections and places candidates in office through those elections, it does not behoove us as analysts to say "that doesn't count" because something about the organization is off-kilter.[23] More broadly, engaging in activities in addition to the pursuit of

goals through policy channels does not inherently compromise the organization's status as a party unless these other channels are supplanting the political
process. Hezbollah, for example, owns and operates restaurants, cafés, and a
museum in addition to its political party and its armed wing. Do those activities make it less of a party? During the war, did those activities make it less of
a rebel group?

Conceptualizing successful transition in terms of disarmament also forces
scholars to conflate political party formation with cessation of violence, which
are two empirically (and conceptually) distinct outcomes.[24] This conflation not
only distorts the mechanisms at work but also limits the scope of questions we
can ask. If we are interested in rebel-to-party transitions because we want to
know whether incorporating rebel successor parties into the political process
affects the recurrence of violence or civil war, then whether the party chooses
to retain an armed wing is likely an important variable to consider in addition
to party formation. If instead we are interested in what prompts rebel groups to
disarm—and becoming a political party is just one of many possible routes to
disarming—then party formation and disarmament are distinct concepts on different sides of the equation. Disaggregating party transition from disarmament
opens up many lines of inquiry that are closed off when the former is defined in
terms of the latter.

Moreover, the disarmament criterion is not applied equally across all actors
in the conflict. After all, many office-holding parties maintain control over paramilitary organizations—that is, extrajudicial armed wings that function in service of the party—yet these parties are not deemed "incomplete." For example,
during the first half of the Salvadoran Civil War, the ruling party relied heavily
on the paramilitary group ORDEN to exercise control over rural areas.[25] While
the government's use of ORDEN was criticized, it was not deemed a nonparty
because it had an armed wing. As a result, this conceptual requirement creates
a double standard for militant groups on the one hand and incumbent parties
on the other without justifying how or whether these two actors truly represent
differences in kind.

Conceptualizing Rebel-to-Party Transition

Broadly, rebel-to-party transition occurs when a militant organization qualifies
as a legal, functioning political party. As such, the definition must parse groups
that are functioning as parties from those that are not. At a minimum, the benchmarks for successful transition must align with the benchmarks of how scholars
define political parties. On this point, the rebel-to-party scholarship is virtually
unanimous. Nearly every analysis that provides an explicit definition of *party*

relies on Sartori's definition:[26] "any political group identified by an official label that presents at elections, free or unfree, and is capable of placing through elections candidates for public office."[27] However, for analyses to test what we want to test, positive instances of transition must also capture the outcome undergirding the stakes: the political integration of rebel successor parties. This is not just an exercise in mincing words. If integration into the political system is the true source of rebel-to-party benefits, then the stakes of adequately capturing this outcome are pivotal to both analysis and security.

Drawing on Zaks 2022, I propose a conceptual framework that captures the full scope of political integration and lays the foundation for a viable measurement strategy. Keeping in mind Sartori's instruction that concepts are not just theoretical components but "data containers," conceptual frameworks are only valuable insofar as they inform inclusion criteria (who we should sort) and measurement (how we should sort them).[28] In accordance with principles of conceptualization explicated by Giovanni Sartori, Robert Adcock and David Collier, and Gary Goertz, I define the scope conditions on "failed transition" and the criteria for two further conceptual categories that capture different levels of political integration.[29]

FAILED TRANSITION

Since a core goal of conceptualization is to facilitate meaningful comparisons, the first conceptual category explicitly defines failed transitions or nontransitions.[30] Rebel-to-party failure occurs when a militant group engaged in a political conflict against a target government had the desire and legal opportunity to enter electoral politics but did not achieve even minimal benchmarks of party status.[31] As such, it must not register or appear on a ballot—even for a single election. In the empirical section that follows, I use this definition to specify key conditions that guide data collection and measurement.

NOMINAL PARTICIPATION

The next conceptual distinction captures minimal benchmarks for party status, which I call *nominal participation*. Groups in this category formally register as parties and sometimes appear on a ballot, but fail to win any seats. Thus, they transition into the electoral environment but fall short of political integration (functioning in a governing environment). The distinction is especially salient when groups run in only one or two elections before dropping out. Following the literature, I agree that taking logistical steps toward integration sets nominal participants apart from those that never even register. Yet, the factors associated with running are likely different from those associated with winning, and their implications for postconflict dynamics may be different as well. Accounting for the heterogeneity in rebel-to-party outcomes requires conceptual differentiation at consequential junctures.

SEATED PARTICIPATION

The final conceptual category distinguishes groups that have won at least some seats in postconflict elections. *Seated participation* captures a more comprehensive scope of functions that accompany political integration, maps more thoroughly to Sartori's definition of parties, and facilitates testing the mechanism by which rebel integration facilitates peace. Specifically, if peace hinges on the group's access to legal channels for dissent, our conceptualization should differentiate among groups with qualitatively different levels of access (those who pursue office versus those who take office). Though winning seats is not a requirement of party status, it is a salient conceptual category for theorizing the causes, implications, and mechanisms of rebel-to-party transition.

What Affects Transition?

Since transition is fundamentally about performing new functions in a new environment, explaining it means accounting for what rebel successor parties must do and the opportunities and constraints they face in the process. Rebels' transition into electoral politics is shaped by their capacity to perform preelection functions (campaigning, party rallies, fundraising), their ability to mobilize voters on election day, and the institutional context in which they operate.

Scholars diverge on the source of rebels' capacity for political mobilization. Some contend that the extent to which voter mobilization has its roots in war is largely a function of whether ex-combatants get out the vote for their former commanders.[32] Others argue that "reliance on civilian aid" in territorial strongholds forces militant organizations to establish a social contract, which can then be leveraged into election-day support.[33] Finally, for others still, rebels' capacity for campaigning and voter mobilization originates before the war began. According to Manning and Smith, groups that began as political parties *before* the war broke out can leverage their historical political experience into campaign success.[34] In sum, political mobilization is currently attributed to in-group loyalty, territorial control, and prewar experience.

Each of these arguments identifies a constituency (i.e., a set of potential voters) and establishes a link between the constituents and the new party (former membership, a wartime social contract, or territorial administration). To be sure, these conditions are critical for the party to function. However, the relations they describe are insufficient alone to account for mobilization, and the proposed mechanisms by which militant histories are connected to electoral successes overlook potential variation in their efficacy. The problem, I argue, is that we are not accounting for systematic differences in the types of relations or links that rebels forge with the communities they encounter. As such, these arguments are built on the assumption that one type of linkage (e.g., wartime support) can be easily translated into another (e.g., postwar votes). This assumption, however, does not find support in theory or on the ground.[35] Rather, in the same way that only certain structures are useful for party transformation, only certain types of relations are conducive to political mobilization. After all, we would not expect groups to be able to easily leverage coercive or extractive relationships into electoral support—which is largely why we find rebel-to-party transition puzzling in the first place.

The parties literature is instructive here. Scholars have developed a rich typology of the linkages political parties forge with their constituents because they understand that mobilization is contingent on the nature and trade-offs of different linkage strategies.[36] In the context of explaining rebel successor parties, however, it becomes clear that both literatures are incomplete. The parties literature presumes the relations between citizens and parties have always (and only) been peaceful; the postconflict literature does not specify the nature of relations at all.[37]

Proto-party structures bridge this theoretical gap by accounting for the variation in wartime relations. Broadly, organizations with functioning proto-party structures are less bounded than their combat-centric counterparts. Their day-to-day operations require interacting with the local population on dimensions beyond security and extraction, thereby thinning the border between who's in and who's out and creating opportunities for more diverse linkages. Specifically, governance and social service provision structures as well as affiliations with cooperatives and professional associations forge political links with local populations during wartime. Unlike relations characterized by violence and extraction, these relations characterized by political, ideological, material, and educational exchange are more easily (and intuitively) convertible into electoral support. The book's main hypothesis follows accordingly:

> H1: Groups that build more extensive proto-party structures during war will be more successful in electoral politics than those that do not.

Zooming out, this explanation once again highlights the utility of taking an explicitly organizational approach—even when we move beyond the organization's boundaries. Disaggregating the types of roles and subdivisions present in militant organizations allows us to more precisely characterize the types of relations those structures forge with people outside or on the margins of the organization. In contrast, if we model rebel organizations only in terms of their capacity for producing violence and the logistical divisions needed to support the armed apparatus, then our characterization of relations between rebels and local populations will be limited. As Mampilly argues, reducing complex militant organizations "to their most gasp-inducing components" obstructs the "broader set of interactions that [rebel groups] constantly engage in with local communities."[38]

The reality of electoral politics is that no one running for office comes with a built-in constituency, much less a loyal and mobilized one. Even popular, incumbent politicians in functioning democracies spend inordinate amounts of time and money on constituent outreach, campaigning, voter-registration efforts, and get-out-the-vote initiatives. And these candidates are not operating in a new system or facing an electorate that has never before seen a ballot. In the context of postconflict elections, mobilizing voters on election day requires more than just physical presence and political experience.

Finally, while organizations matter, so too does the institutional environment in which they operate. As rebel successor parties gear up to compete in elections, they face new rules of engagement, as it were. Specifically, the electoral institutions present will shape the nature and severity of obstacles to entering the political market. Since proportional representation (PR) systems allocate seats in proportion to the percentage of votes cast for each party, these institutions are more conducive to the inclusion of multiple parties, facilitate the emergence of smaller parties, and lower barriers to entry.[39] All else equal, I anticipate that rebel successor parties are more likely to experience *initial* levels of electoral success under PR systems. Crucially, however, while electoral institutions are likely to affect entry at early stages of transition, I do not expect them to have an effect on longevity. In other words, these institutions allow rebel successor parties to get their foot in the door, but they do little to determine whether they can stay. The second hypothesis follows:

> H2: Groups that emerge in proportional representation systems will be more likely to gain seats in immediate postconflict elections.

Insurgent Structures and Outcomes (ISO) Dataset

The end of the Cold War brought with it a boon in electoral opportunities for former rebels.[40] More and more, civil conflicts were ending through negotiated settlements rather than one-sided victory. With those settlements came provisions for electoral participation and other power-sharing arrangements. Scholars have seized on the increasing frequency of rebel-to-party opportunities to either create or expand cross-national datasets with variables suited to testing the causes and consequences of transition.[41] These data-collection efforts and the analyses based on them have laid a crucial analytic foundation in a high-stakes field. As I have noted in previous work, however, existing rebel-to-party datasets exhibit inconsistencies in both the universe of cases deemed relevant for comparative analysis and the coding of the outcome variable—even when they define *transition* the same way.[42] The overinclusion of nonviable contenders (e.g., the Animal Liberation Front) and the omission of groups that ultimately transitioned (e.g., Hezbollah in Lebanon) create samples that suffer from selection bias, which quickly finds its way into the results.[43]

I have constructed the Insurgent Structures and Outcomes (ISO) Dataset to build on these foundations while overcoming the pitfalls. The dataset collects empirically and conceptually informed data on rebels' wartime organizational structures and a nuanced scope of rebel-to-party outcomes. ISO seeks to identify the universe of potential and successful rebel-to-party transitions. I compiled the sample of cases by first collecting the full set of observations across existing datasets and omitting those that violated the inclusion criteria outlined later in this chapter. Then, drawing on primary sources, secondary sources, and consultation with country or group experts, I collected data on the wartime organizational characteristics of the remaining groups. The resulting ISO dataset is composed of seventy-eight rebel groups that operated between 1974 and 2018.

Keeping in mind Sartori's instruction that concepts are "data containers" as much as they are theoretical components, I draw on the conceptual framework laid out earlier to inform the inclusion criteria (who we should sort) and measurement (how we should sort them).

Inclusion Criteria and Scope Conditions

In light of the established selection bias present in previous analyses, the inclusion criteria for this dataset warrant special attention. Although there is room for expansion—since rebel organizational structures have analytic utility beyond understanding the outcome of this study—the scope of the ISO Dataset is currently limited to the set of potential transitions. The reasoning for this is purely pragmatic: collecting data on the internal structures of clandestine organizations is difficult and time intensive. As such, the current inclusion criteria of the ISO data align with the minimum conditions for rebel-to-party failure.

In a departure from some approaches, which rely on civil war termination or peace agreements to define the universe of cases, ISO compiles observations based on characteristics of the group rather than characteristics of the conflict.[44] As a phenomenon, rebel-to-party transition is not bound by the standard operational definition of civil war, nor is it limited to conflicts that have ended in peace agreements.[45] Thus, limiting the scope of observations to cases that satisfy tangentially related inclusion criteria risks omitting viable or even important cases from the analysis. Since the analytic objective is to use information about the group during conflict to predict the group's political trajectory, I derived inclusion criteria with two goals in mind: including the full scope of positive cases and defining the boundaries of an appropriate comparison set.

The inclusion criteria are twofold: First, the group must have made political claims on a government—either calls for expanded rights for a marginalized group, democratic reforms, revolution, or territorial secession.[46] This criterion does double duty. To count among potential transitions militant organizations must have expressed the desire to govern in one capacity or another. As such, it omits groups with objectives that are either too broad (e.g., establishing a regional caliphate), too narrow (e.g., animal liberation), or too unrealistic (e.g., anarchists) that party formation around those goals is unlikely or untenable.[47] Moreover, becoming a party requires a target government in which to participate. Specifying *where* groups would become parties is crucial to assessing the legality of and obstacles to transition. Including only groups that make political claims against a target government filters out groups with transnational objectives such as al-Qaeda or Boko Haram (both of which have appeared as failures in rebel-to-party analyses).[48] For these groups, a within-state political solution is either unlikely or undefined. To assess whether the outcome is even legal, we must be able to identify the specific government into which a group would transition. Unless a transnational group expresses interest in transitioning within a single state, it should not be compared to groups that do.

The second criterion is much more straightforward: rebels must have a legal path to party formation. This path can take a few forms. One route is through explicit electoral participation provisions codified in a negotiated settlement. As Matanock observes, nearly half of "conflict-ending settlements" since 1990 contain provisions allowing ex-rebels to participate in elections.[49] Unfortunately, while provisions for electoral participation are a convenient scope condition, not all rebel successor parties emerge through this path. In other cases, state institutions may simply allow for party formation, and militant organizations proceed accordingly. Hezbollah in Lebanon, for example, transitioned into politics without any explicit provision enabling it to do so. Legality as a condition may seem obvious, but some existing rebel-to-party datasets include among the failures groups that operate in states in which party formation is prohibited.[50] To truly fail, the group must have attempted transition in a place where party formation was possible. After all, one cannot treat rebel-to-party status as a variable if the outcome cannot vary.

Before moving onto coding, I address an implicit counterpoint. The inclusion criterion of Acosta's Revolutionary and Militant Organizations Dataset (REVMOD) and Matanock's Militant Group Electoral Participation (MGEP) dataset is *all militant groups*, defined as "nongovernmental entities using extra-legal violence to achieve political aims."[51] According to Matanock, broad inclusion criteria are important because "any of these groups may participate in elections."[52] Of course, the accidental omission of viable contenders is not ideal. However, their inclusion is not without costs. The trade-off takes the following form: collect data that (1) compare groups that succeeded to a narrower sample of groups whose desire for power-sharing was clear, yet unrequited, or (2) compare groups that succeeded to a much wider sample of groups that tried but failed *and* groups that never tried in the first place.

Ultimately, even an incomplete universe based on conceptually informed sampling is preferable for a few reasons. First, overly broad inclusion criteria will almost inevitably include organizations that are unlikely, unwilling, or unable to attempt transition. When the zeroes are made up of two systematically different populations, any analysis based on that sample is liable to suffer from selection bias.[53] Second, because the scope conditions on ISO are explicit, the range of groups to which inferences apply is similarly well defined. Thus, even if one finds a transition outside ISO's current scope, the condition that needs alteration will also be clear.

Variables, Measurement, and Data Collection

ISO contains a host of variables relevant to conflict and postconflict dynamics, but here I focus on outlining the variables relevant to my theory and the alternative explanations I test from the literature. For each variable, I discuss the measurement strategy, approach to data collection, and potential limitations or challenges.

REBEL-TO-PARTY TRANSITION

The core benefit of the conceptual framework is that it is theoretically bounded, yet operationally flexible. This discussion draws heavily on the measurement strategy I lay out in my 2024 article. I propose two measurement strategies for the outcome—one four-stage measure and one dichotomous measure—not only to test whether the theory is robust (or sensitive) to different coding schemes, but also to assess whether proto-party structures (and other variables) affect some steps in the transition process more than others. To briefly situate this discussion in the literature, all previous rebel-to-party analyses employ a dichotomous measure of transition coded according to different benchmarks of electoral participation. The coding schemes and dataset summaries are given in table 5.1.

TABLE 5.1. Overview of existing measures of rebel-to-party (RtP) transition[1]

DATA AND SCOPE	SUCCESS CRITERIA	RTP TRANSITIONS	RTP FAILURES	INCLUSION CRITERIA
SK&H (1975–2011)[2]	Electoral participation and disarmament	33	60	Peace agreements
MGEP (1980–2010)[3]	Electoral participation	91	660	All militant groups
M&S (1990–2009)[4]	Party registration	73	60	Civil war terminations
REVMOD (1940–2014)[5]	Party registration	69	388	All militant groups

[1] This table is reproduced from Zaks 2024.
[2] Söderberg Kovacs and Hatz's (2016) expansion of the Uppsala Conflict Data Program (UCDP) Peace Agreement Data.
[3] Matanock's (2016) Militant Group Electoral Participation.
[4] Manning and Smith's (2016) expansion of the UCDP Conflict Termination Data.
[5] Acosta's (2019) Revolutionary and Militant Organizations Dataset.

I propose a disaggregated measure of transition to reduce the heterogeneity evident in binary measures of the outcome. The four-stage measure synthesizes conceptual and empirical insights to justify adding nuance on two dimensions. Drawing on the conceptual framework, I first distinguish nominal participation (party registration or ballot appearance) from seated participation (groups that garner enough votes to take office). Then, upon examining postconflict elections, the data reveal that while many rebel successor parties become persistent seat holders in their respective governments, a significant number lack that same staying power. In this second group, successor parties win some seats in the first post-conflict election, but ultimately fail to pass muster in the long term. By the second or third election, their vote share drops below the threshold to take office and never recovers. To capture this empirical trend, I disaggregate seat winners into short-term participants and persistent contenders.[54] Placing these "one-hit wonders" in a distinct category enables scholars to test whether they exhibit systematic differences from groups that never make it beyond the ballot as well as groups that exhibit electoral persistence.[55] The measurement strategy is enumerated here:

- (0) Failures: groups with the opportunity to transition and desire for political participation, but that fail to register.
- (1) Nominal Participants: groups that registered as parties and/or appeared on a ballot but failed to win seats.
- (2) Short-Term Participants: groups that won seats, yet dropped out within three election cycles.[56]
- (3) Persistent Contenders: groups that won seats in three or more elections.

Due in part to the scarcity of cases and in part to the desire for parsimony, I also propose a dichotomous measure of rebel-to-party transition. Moreover, as table 5.1 illustrates, all previous analyses employ a dichotomized measure as well, thereby establishing a demand for a clean demarcation between "success" and "failure." Given that any binary measure of a complex variable will exhibit heterogeneity within categories, the challenge is to identify a cut point at which the heterogeneity is least problematic. The measure I propose departs from previous approaches, yet aligns with the underlying conceptual motivations in the literature: capturing rebels' integration into legal politics. While this approach departs from the rebel-to-party literature, Adrienne LeBas contends that holding seats after elections is a reliable indicator to capture both party status and political integration.[57] As such, I propose grouping nominal participants and nonparticipants together as failures and coding all seat winners as successes:

- (0) Failures: nonparticipants and nominal participants in the electoral system
- (1) Successes: rebel successor parties that won seats in at least one election

Collecting data on party registration and electoral outcomes was relatively straightforward. Much of the data were available from election databases, news sources, and databases of registered political parties worldwide. I also crosschecked my coding against all other rebel-to-party datasets.

Nevertheless, this approach is not without limitations. The most pressing issue with this measure (and the underlying conceptual framework) is its election-centric view of political parties. However, parties routinely perform important off-the-ballot functions like rallies, local organizing, and advocacy, which this framework does not capture. As a result, rebel groups that become active political organizations outside of the electoral arena are liable to fall between the conceptual cracks.

I argue, however, that the trade-off is worthwhile for a couple of reasons. First, holding seats after elections is a reliable way to capture both party status and political integration.[58] More important, capturing only groups that function in a governing capacity (or fail to) allows us to more directly test the mechanism underlying the stakes: that access to legal channels for dissent will prevent groups from seeking violent ones. While off-the-ballot parties perform important tasks, they do not as reliably have access to these channels as those integrated in government. Second, from both a practical and conceptual standpoint, functioning as a party in government is more easily standardized and operationalized in a way that implies similar outcomes across cases. Although it is an imperfect proxy, data collection is considerably more straightforward, reliable, and comparable using election-centric indicators.

PROTO-PARTY STRUCTURES

The book's core argument is that rebel groups with proto-party structures will have a decisive advantage as they both transform into political parties and transition into electoral politics. Chapter 3 identified three broad domains that correspond to the key roles of party organizations: governance, social services, and political messaging. To operationalize this concept I identify five distinct types of subdivisions, each of which falls under one of the categories: administration and governance, health services, educational provisions, affiliated community groups (e.g., a youth organization or a women's organization), and political messaging.

- *Governance and Administration:* This variable is coded 1 if I find evidence of routine governance in either controlled or contested territory, and 0 if I did not. Indicators of administrative capacity include resolving disputes; allocating resources (e.g., food, money, or basic goods); or building and managing public infrastructure (e.g., roads, electricity, waste removal).
- *Health Services:* This variable is coded 1 if the organization set up medical services accessible to local populations, and 0 otherwise. The extent of health provisions ranges from providing basic medical treatment to sick or injured civilians (as in the case of the National Council for the Defense of Democracy-Forces for the Defense of Democracy [CNDD-FDD] in Burundi) to constructing full-service hospitals (as in the case of Hezbollah in Lebanon).[59]
- *Community Groups:* This variable is coded 1 if the movement had an explicit youth, women's, and/or student organization during wartime, and 0 if they did not. Community groups capture both embeddedness among local populations and political education of those either outside or at the fringes of the movement. Because I want to capture long-term embeddedness, the community groups had to exist at least one year before the end of the war and they had to either have their own name or evidence of repeated meetings.[60]
- *Educational Provisions:* This variable is coded 1 if the rebel group provided basic educational services to local populations such as literacy programs or an equivalent to primary schooling, and 0 otherwise. To be

sure, most, if not all, educational services included some political component, but for this variable to get a 1, I required evidence that a curriculum existed outside of the organization's message. Where I found evidence only of "political education," this variable is coded 0, and directed education about the movement counts instead toward political messaging.

- *Political Messaging*: This variable is coded 1 if the group provides a regular source of news or propaganda. I do not elevate one medium over another, so I take any of the following as an indicator of a political-messaging wing: dissemination of written work (e.g., newspapers, flyers, pamphlets), creation of a radio or television station, or holding regular political education groups with local populations.

Using these indicators, I created a composite index of proto-party structures. The index is additive and unweighted since no theoretical reasons point to the relative importance of one domain over the other.[61] The proto-party structures variable thus captures the extent to which a given militant organization has diversified into salient political domains. Thus, a higher value on proto-party structures indicates greater political diversification. This variable will be used to test the book's core hypothesis:

> H1: A greater diversity of proto-party structures increases the likelihood that groups will achieve more advanced levels of rebel-to-party success.

POLICING AND SECURITY

I also collected data on whether rebel groups provided policing and security services to local populations during the conflict. This variable is also dichotomous and is coded a 1 if I found evidence that the group took over policing activities in an area. Examples of security services include civilians calling on the organization in the event of a robbery or harassment or rebels pointedly protecting civilians from attacks (either from the government or from other rebel groups). Policing captures the enforcement side of administration, but itself does not translate into a specific party feature. As such, I do not include it as part of the proto-party structure index.

I include this variable in the dataset because the goal is to have as thorough of an account of rebel organizational structures as possible. I have no theoretical reason to believe that policing has any specific effect on rebel-to-party transformations. I did, however, rerun the models with policing added as an additional control variable to test whether *any* diversification is good for rebel-to-party transition. The coefficient estimate is consistently small (typically around 0.1) and the standard error hovers around 0.7, suggesting that not just any diversification, but rather, proto-party diversification is the driver of rebel-to-party success.

Data Collection

The organization-level data derives from a variety of primary and secondary sources. These sources include firsthand accounts; archived communiques, pamphlets, and newspapers from within the rebel organization; state and NGO reports from conflict zones; scholarly works from individual conflicts; and media coverage of the war. I consulted a minimum of two different types of sources per case to minimize source-centric biases. As I discuss in the next section, accounts from rebel organizations, governments, and media outlets are each likely to exhibit different types of bias for different reasons.

Challenges, Limitations, and Trade-offs

While the outcome variable is clearly a contested concept, the most pressing empirical challenge is collecting systematic data on rebel groups' wartime organizational structures. The overarching challenge—as others have noted—is the difficulty of finding reliable data on clandestine organizations.[62] Potential problems in data collection stem from systematic sources of bias as well as incidental misrepresentation.

The systematic sources of bias are multifold and go in both directions. On the one hand, rebel groups have incentives to overrepresent noncombat activities—especially social service provisions—as a means of boosting their legitimacy.[63] And office-seeking groups may be even more prone to this tendency. On the other hand, government and some NGO accounts of rebel groups are likely to downplay or erase any political activities that may bolster the perception of rebels at home or abroad. A similar bias is likely evident in scholarship and media, albeit for different reasons. Due in part to the importance of documenting patterns of violence, and in part to the combat-centric organizational framework that shapes the literature, scholarship and news reports on rebel groups are liable to overdocument the actions and structure of the military to the exclusion of other divisions of the organization.[64]

Beyond the sources of systematic bias, data collection is also subject to incidental sources of error. Thinking back to the Salvadoran case, for example, the picture one paints of the FMLN's organization will look very different depending on whether the war is documented from Chalatenango, San Salvador, or Morazán.[65] While the FMLN exhibited more pronounced geographical distinctions in its local structures than other groups, this phenomenon is not unique either.

To be sure, the potential for missing data is high. Yet, the risk of associated bias is mitigated in two ways. First, while rebel groups are likely reticent about discussing ongoing military operations, they tend to be open—if not eager—to advertise the work of their political wings and their capacity to provide social services. Moreover, when it comes time to transition into politics, spotlighting their social and political experience during the war is a strategically beneficial way of mobilizing voters. However, their tendency to overrepresent proto-party structures is actually a double-edged sword. While it may lead to some biased accounts in documenting their wartime organization, the incentives to advertise the scope of their politically salient structures make it likely that absence of evidence for a given subdivision is actually evidence of absence.

Additional Variables

In addition to the proto-party index, I include a series of control variables capturing other salient organizational factors and alternative explanations: size, fragmentation, external sponsorship, rebel-to-party provisions, and postwar electoral institutions. I omit systemic correlates of rebel-to-party transition that do not contribute to our explanation of the phenomenon, such as the Cold War ending and whether the transformation took place on the African continent.[66] These variables predict civil war termination, which is correlated with rebel-to-party transformation, but do not explain it.

SIZE

Larger organizations are expected to exhibit greater diversification and possess more slack resources, both of which feed into an organization's resilience and capacity to adapt.[67] Moreover, large organizations during war potentially contribute to larger bases of political support at the ballot.[68] To the extent possible, the variable captures the estimated size of the organization at the end of the war (i.e., leading up to transition). Size estimates came from a variety of primary sources, secondary literature, and the Non-State Actor Data.[69] Where estimates diverged by more than a thousand members, I took the mean across estimates. All values are logged for the analysis.

> H2: Larger organizations are more likely to survive the end of war and transition into electoral politics.

FRACTURING

Staniland demonstrates that wartime resilience and adaptability are at least in part a function of organizational cohesion.[70] I draw on this argument to test whether the same features matter for resilience off the battlefield. I use organizational fracturing as an inverse proxy for cohesion. Fracturing is a count variable starting at 0 if the group exhibits no evidence of infighting. The variable is coded 0.5 if I find evidence of intraorganizational tensions, but no splits, and the count increases by 1 for every time the organization split over its lifetime. Drawing on the literature, I expect that high rates of fracture will detract from an organization's capacity to transition into a party by contributing to ideological and logistical gridlock as the organization negotiates their new tasks and their new role.

H3: Fracturing is negatively associated with transition.

ELECTORAL INSTITUTIONS

Another factor potentially influencing rebels' postconflict opportunity to launch a successful party are the country's electoral institutions. I include a binary control variable indicating whether the country's legislature is elected via proportional representation versus single-member districts. The rules governing postconflict elections may create an exogenous barrier to entry for new parties trying to break into electoral politics. Specifically, since single-member districts are more likely to foster two-party systems, former rebels otherwise well poised to succeed as a political party may face an institutional obstacle unrelated to their organizational advantages.[71] The variable *PR System* is coded 1 if at least half of the seats in the national legislature are allocated via proportional representation, and 0 otherwise. I anticipate that PR systems will make breaking into politics more likely, but will have little impact on longevity of the party.

> H4: Proportional representation systems facilitate early stages of transitioning (winning seats in the first postconflict elections), but do not have an effect on the longevity of rebel successor parties.

EXTERNAL SPONSORSHIP

According to Acosta's analysis, one of the most significant predictors of rebel-to-party transition is the extent to which the militant group has secured external sponsorship.[72] External sponsorship is a count variable documenting the rebels' number of state patrons. For the groups present in my data and his, I draw on REVMOD for the rebel group's number of sponsors; otherwise I adopt the same coding rule: the count increases for every country that provided the militants with funding, weapons, training, or sanctuary.[73] For a variety of reasons, I do not believe external sponsorship will predict transition, but I test the hypothesis from the literature. The first alternative hypothesis I test follows:

> A1: External sponsorship is positively associated with rebel-to-party success.

REBEL-TO-PARTY PROVISIONS

While scholarship is mixed on the effects of party transition clauses, I control for whether the conflict ended with a negotiated settlement that included explicit rebel-to-party provisions. Söderberg Kovacs and Hatz, for example, argue that "rebel-to-party provisions are likely to function as one mechanism among many that serve as a guarantee for the political and organizational survival of the rebel group."[74] *Rebel-to-party provisions* is a dichotomous variable coded 1 if the group signed an agreement with an explicit transition clause according to the UCDP Peace Agreement Dataset, and 0 otherwise. Similarly, the theoretical framework guiding this analysis leaves me with no priors on the efficacy of rebel-to-party provisions. I expect that in previous analyses, this variable captured the opportunity to transition, rather than a mechanism facilitating it.

> A2: Rebel-to-party provisions are positively associated with rebel-to-party success.

Empirical Analysis

This section examines whether rebels' wartime organizational structures predict electoral success. To test how proto-party structures perform in explaining rebel groups' transition into politics, I conduct a variety of statistical analyses on the ISO data. I turn to large-N analyses here to evaluate the extent to which the explanatory variables of the theory are observable across cases and to assess whether the theory travels beyond the Salvadoran context. After all, if proto-party structures were specific to the FMLN or even just the region, that fact would place an important scope condition on inference and call into question the contributions of this study.

First, I estimate a series of ordinal logistic regressions on the fully disaggregated outcome variable. Model 1 tests how organizational traits—proto-party structures, size, and fracturing—affect the likelihood and extent of transformation. Model 2 controls for the financial aspect of opportunity by estimating the impact of third-party sponsors. Model 3 controls for the institutional aspects of opportunity, adding in variables for rebel-to-party provisions in the settlement and whether the electoral system uses proportional representation. Finally, Model 4 presents a fully saturated model. Table 5.2 presents the results of the regression and table 5.3 report's a group's predicted probabilities of successful integration as its number of proto-party structures increases.

In addition to testing the model on the four-stage outcome variable, I also run the fully saturated model on three alternative codings of rebel-to-party transition, representing different levels of rebel successor party integration. Specifically, I recode *transition* as a series of dichotomous variables at three different cut points for success: nominal participation, seated participation, and long-term integration. Since the outcome is now dichotomous, I use logistic regression to estimate the model.[75]

TABLE 5.2. Ordinal models of rebel-to-party transition

| | DEPENDENT VARIABLE | | | |
| | REBEL-TO-PARTY TRANSITION | | | |
	(1)	(2)	(3)	(4)
Organizational traits				
Proto-party structures	0.594***	0.594***	0.667***	0.669
	(0.196)	(0.197)	(0.222)	(0.223)
ln (size)	0.728***	0.728***	0.767***	0.766***
	(0.217)	(0.219)	(0.234)	(0.234)
Fracturing	−0.396*	−0.396*	−0.299	−0.299
	(0.225)	(0.225)	(0.239)	(0.239)
Opportunity controls				
P.R. system			1.128*	1.123*
			(0.589)	(0.162)
External sponsors		0.002		0.010
		(0.151)		(0.162)
			0.459	0.474
			(0.671)	(0.715)
Observations	77	77	77	77

*p < 0.1; **p < 0.05; ***p < 0.01

TABLE 5.3. Predicted probabilities of transition for *X* proto-party structures

NO. OF PROTO-PARTY STRUCTURES:	5	4	3	2	1	0
No transition	0.006	0.013	0.028	0.059	0.120	0.231
Nominal participation	0.020	0.043	0.087	0.162	0.263	0.346
Short-term contender	0.042	0.083	0.146	0.215	0.246	0.211
Persistent contender	0.932	0.862	0.740	0.564	0.371	0.212

These analyses serve two main functions. First, by rerunning the analyses on a binary measure of nominal success, I can test whether the results of prior studies hold on their own turf, or whether they are driven more by inclusion criteria and omission of key organizational traits (as anticipated). Second, testing my hypotheses across a variety of cut points enables me to parse whether certain explanatory factors are more important for some stages of transition than others. The results of the analyses are depicted in figure 5.1a–d.

Results

The results from the main analyses on the four-stage outcome provide strong evidence in favor of H1: Rebel groups with more proto-party structures consistently experience higher levels of integration as their successor parties enter politics.

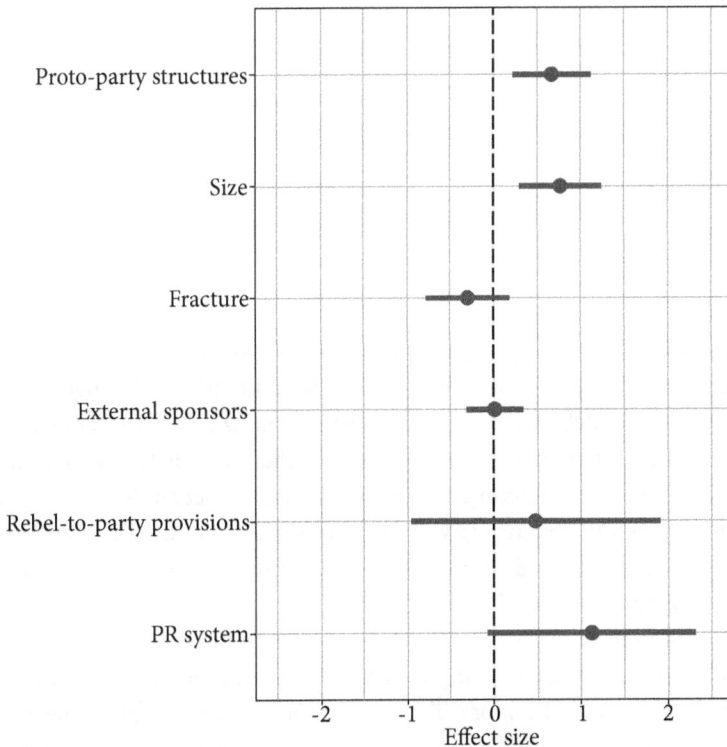

FIGURE 5.1A. Coefficient effect plots at different cut points for rebel-to-party success. Here, the cut point used is the full ordinal DV.

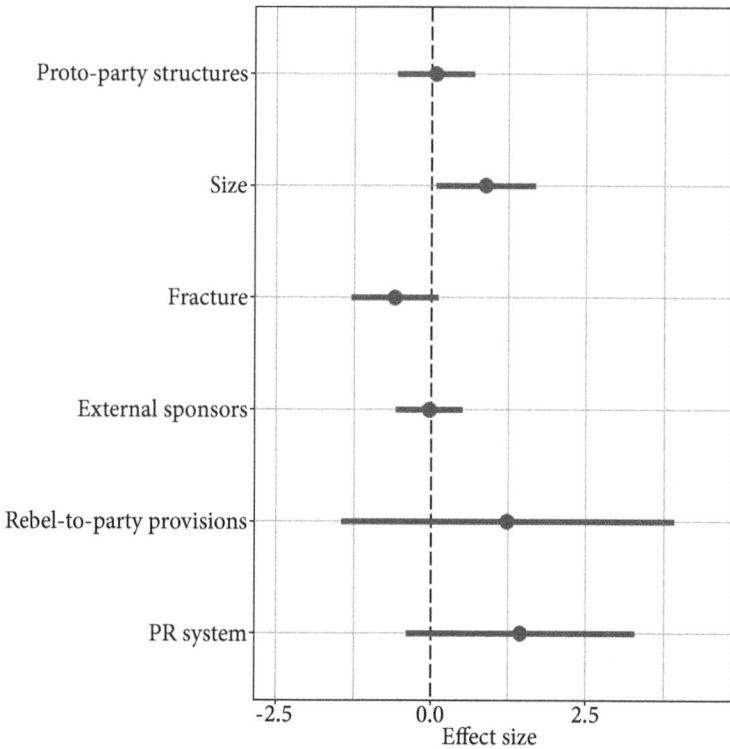

FIGURE 5.1B. Coefficient effect plots at different cut points for rebel-to-party success. Here, the cut point used is nominal participation.

The estimated size of the organization also consistently achieves significance, thus corroborating H2. Obviously, the mechanism for this result is not elucidated in a statistical model, though it is likely some combination of greater diversification and a larger base of potential voters.[76] Furthermore, as H3 predicts, higher rates of organizational fracturing are associated with lower levels of political integration. Though the fracturing variable loses significance as other variables are added, this outcome is likely a result of inflated standard errors penalizing the admittedly small sample.

Turning to the control variables that represent rebels' opportunity to transition, the results align with my expectations. Higher levels of rebel-to-party transition appear to be more likely under proportional representation systems than in single-member districts, which supports H4. The two alternative hypotheses that I test from the literature do not fare well. Regarding hypothesis A1, external sponsorship never achieves significance in any of the models. This

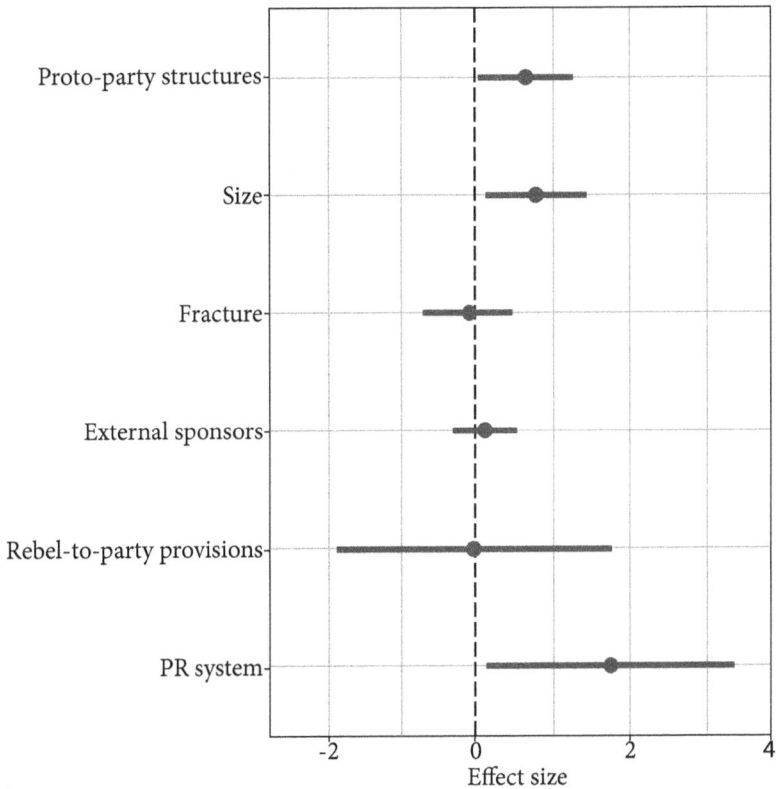

FIGURES 5.1C. Coefficient effect plots at different cut points for rebel-to-party success. Here, the cut point used is a single electoral victory.

result further substantiates the intuition I lay out in my 2024 article: statistically robust estimates of the effect of external sponsorship were likely driven by artifacts in the data used to estimate the model. Specifically, by including hundreds of small, less-viable contenders for rebel-to-party transition, this variable was likely sorting viable political aspirants from irrelevant failures. As such, third-party sponsorship was *associated* with transition in the dataset, but, in reality, it does little to parse groups that tried and failed from groups that tried and succeeded.

Furthermore, rebel-to-party provisions do not reliably predict transition success, thereby calling A2 into question. My hunch is that built-in provisions are likely good at parsing groups that had the opportunity to transition from those that did not, but since this dataset omits groups that lacked the opportunity to move into electoral politics, that feature is not captured.

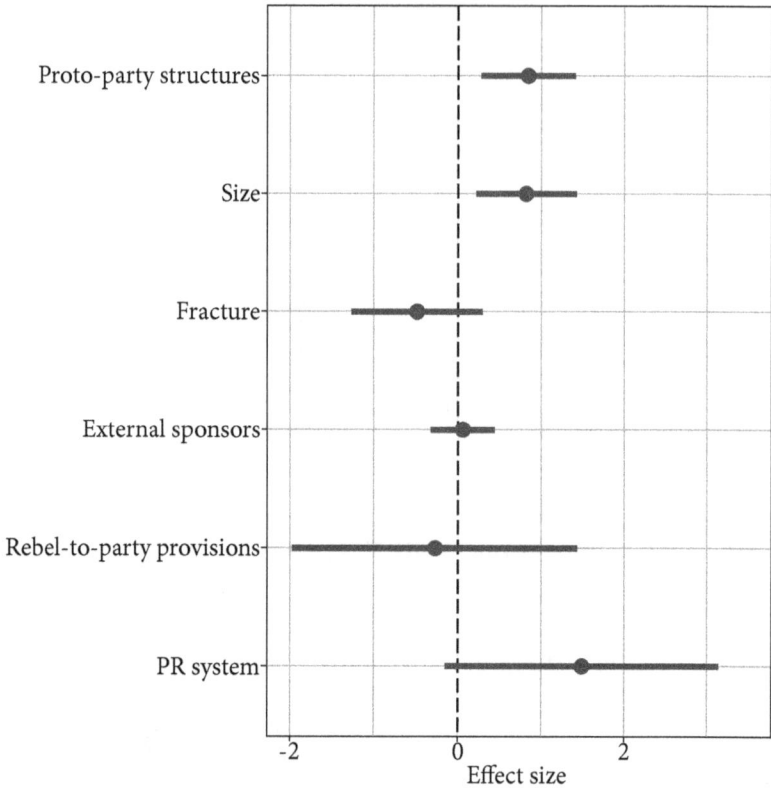

FIGURES 5.1D. Coefficient effect plots at different cut points for rebel-to-party success. Here, the cut point used is persistent contenders.

Running the saturated model on a variety of binary coding schemes proves useful for a few reasons. First, the results parse the point at which certain variables matter. Second, they reveal how sensitive rebel-to-party models are to how we operationalize the outcome.

Figure 5.1b reveals that slicing the dependent variable at a nominal conception of success causes almost every variable to lose significance. Indeed, this model specification is the only one in which proto-party structures fall out of significance. This result is unsurprising. Given the increasing rate at which rebel-to-party provisions are included in negotiated settlements, party registration is often an incidental result of merely implementing the negotiated settlement.[77] The factors that facilitate the actual organizational transformation, transition into electoral politics, and the party's long-term success are unlikely to predict settlement implementation.

Moreover, despite using the same coding for rebel-to-party success as previous analyses, expectations from the literature are not supported. The implications for the rebel-to-party literature are substantial. The results suggest that using "party registration" or "electoral participation" to demarcate transition is creating a heterogeneous success group comprising subpopulations that are systematically different on both the outcome and explanatory variables. The null results suggest that selection effects in dataset composition likely drove the results of prior models using this outcome.[78]

The results shift drastically when the outcome variable is coded to reflect a higher benchmark for success. Figure 5.1c depicts the coefficient estimates for a logit model in which rebel-to-party success is coded 1 if the group placed any candidates in office in at least one election, and 0 otherwise. At the point that winning seats is considered a defining feature of successful transition, proto-party structures become key to parsing success from failure. Additionally, PR systems become significant in this model, which corroborates the intuition that institutions affect groups' initial capacity to gain representation.

Finally, the last model, depicted in Figure 5.1d, codes a transition as success-ful only if the party occupies a lasting position in national or regional politics. The results of this model continue to align with the predictions of my theoretical framework, yet they differ from the previous model. Namely, electoral institu-tions are no longer a significant predictor of success. This result follows logically if we consider how electoral institutions should matter. Specifically, we should expect the institutional arrangement to affect whether a party can break into politics in the first place, but whether the party lasts once it is there is more a function of the party's political aptitude.

Proto-Party Structures and Municipal Election Results in El Salvador

The results just described provide compelling evidence that proto-party struc-tures built during war do a reasonable job of predicting rebel-to-party success. The hitch, of course, is that these models are based on aggregate data, which is less than ideal after I spent the preceding chapters demonstrating what we risk losing when we treat organizations exclusively at the aggregate level. The question these models leave unanswered is whether the organizations that build proto-party structures exhibit some other systematic difference that predicts rebel-to-party success, or whether these structures are really doing the heavy analytic lifting.

To ensure that proto-party structures are not merely capturing some corre-lated, aggregate trait of the groups, I dive into the FMLN case to test whether these dynamics are reflected at the local level. As demonstrated in chapters 3 and 4, proto-party structures were common throughout the FMLN, but not uniformly so. What makes the FMLN such an ideal case for testing rebel-to-party theories is that the suborganizational variation is geographically constrained. While the FPL, PRTC, PCS, and RN built robust political subdivisions during the conflict, the ERP's wartime structures functioned largely in service of its combat operations. Getting comprehensive and granular data about the presence (and absence) of particular structures built during the war would be a nearly insurmountable task for any country—even small ones. As such, I use the consistent presence of the respective OP-Ms as a proxy to represent whether proto-party subdivisions were present in a given municipality.

Drawing on hundreds of archival documents from the rebels, the US government, NGOs, and the Salvadoran government as well as secondary sources (scholarship and news reports), I create a municipal-level dataset accounting for different OP-M presence during the conflict, which I then merge with municipal-level electoral results from El Salvador's 1994 legislative elections. The dataset includes six binary variables: one for each of the five politico-military organizations, and a sixth denoting evidence of FMLN presence, but without clear indication of which OP-M occupied the territory (which occurred in only six instances).[79] In total, I find evidence of a strong FMLN presence in sixty-six municipalities (out of 262).

On average, the FMLN took 16 percent of the vote in a given municipality. In light of the new geopolitical data of FMLN presence, I slice the data in two ways and run analyses on each. First, I assess the average vote share in municipalities with a strong FMLN presence for each OP-M. Summary statistics are reported in table 5.4. I also collapse the proto-party OP-Ms into a single group to compare to the ERP. To test whether OP-M presence—and thus, a wartime legacy of proto-party structures—is associated with greater postconflict vote share, I run a series of two-tailed t-tests on the new data.

In line with my theory, I expect to find lower vote shares for the FMLN in ERP-dominant municipalities. Crucially, this is a difficult test for two reasons— one substantive, one methodological. First, as Leigh Binford notes, ERP-occupied areas (particularly in Morazán) comprised the strongest and most autonomous rearguard during the war.[80] Scholars have explicitly argued that strong bureaucracy and territorial control during war should translate into postconflict gains for rebel successor parties.[81] Additionally, Morazán saw a disproportionate amount of active fighting. As a result, the security provided by the ERP as well as the localized demobilization of former combatants may well act as a countervailing force in the FMLN's favor. Second, this test is difficult simply because of the relatively small number of cases.

TABLE 5.4. Summary of vote share in OP-M-dominant municipalities

OP-M (N)	MEAN	MIN	MAX
PCS (3)	46.1%	19.5%	85.7%
RN (2)	29.1%	25%	33.2%
FPL (30)	28.3%	3.2%	87.1%
PRTC (7)	26%	11.9%	42.1%
ERP (21*)	18.5%	0	44%

* This estimate omits the municipality of Meanguera, because the dynamics of returnee communities complicate the case.

Notwithstanding the analytic challenges, the results are clear. The municipalities occupied by OP-Ms that prioritized building diverse political and administrative subdivisions were considerably more likely to vote for the FMLN in the postconflict elections. To continue the ERP-FPL comparison, the average difference in FMLN vote share between ERP-dominant municipalities and FPL-dominant municipalities is nearly 10 percent. The results are nearly identical when the other OP-Ms are collapsed into a single group and compared to the ERP, though these estimates are significant at a higher level of confidence.[82] The results are illustrated in figures 5.2 and 5.3. For reference, I have also plotted the average vote share for the FMLN for every municipality and the average vote share for the FMLN in the municipalities occupied by any OP-M. The FMLN's vote share in the ERP zones is statistically indistinguishable from its countrywide average.

From a Thousand Proto-Party Structures to a Thousand Votes

The FMLN's overall showing in the 1994 elections was respectable for a multiparty system, but it was by no means breathtaking. However, a more complex story emerges when we disaggregate votes by municipality and compare them to the FMLN's local organizational structures. The results of the municipal-level analyses cast doubt on the optimistic quote that opened the chapter. Unfortunately for both Villalobos and the theories that propose the same, rebels need more than wartime collaborators—a thousand eyes—to guarantee postwar votes. To be sure, the ERP had a robust territorial stronghold, it exhibited a strong bureaucracy, and it rarely committed violence against local populations. Yet, these other wartime traits were insufficient to win it the votes it needed from the population on which it had come to rely. Rather, to win like a party, rebels actually have to look like one first.

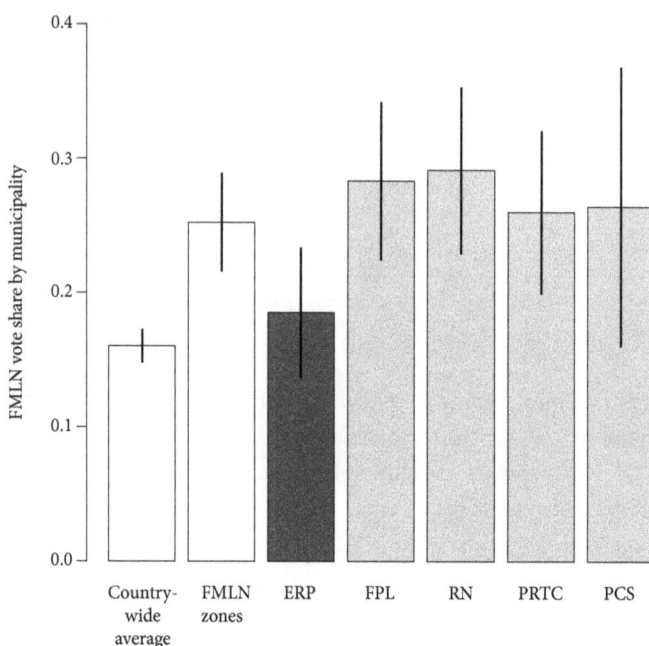

FIGURE 5.2. Vote share disaggregated by OP-M

Note: Each bar represents the FMLN's vote share (1) across the country as a whole (2) aggregated in all FMLN Zones (3) in ERP-controlled zones, (4) in FPL-controlled zones, etc. ERP = People's Revolutionary Army, FPL = Popular Liberation Forces, RN = National Resistance, PRTC = Central-American Workers Revolutionary Party, PCS = Communist Party of El Salvador.

Broadly, this chapter makes three core contributions. First, parsing transition from transformation lays the conceptual foundation to create more tailored theories and to more incisively sort the rebel-to-party literature. In light of this more explicit framework, one can more easily identify which scholars are focused on one versus the other and which factors are meant to explain which outcome. Moreover, the distinction paves the way for future explorations of the relationship between the two outcomes.

Crucially, this is not a matter of semantics. In Colombia's 2018 peace agreement with the Colombian Revolutionary Armed Forces (FARC), for example, one of the terms of the settlement affords the new FARC party a minimum quota of seats for the first two election cycles—irrespective of its vote share. The party's initial vote share would not have otherwise been sufficient to place it in office were it not for the quota. Since its initial integration into politics is not contingent on successful party formation or performance, we can now ask whether transition into politics begets transformation. Will the organization be more likely to

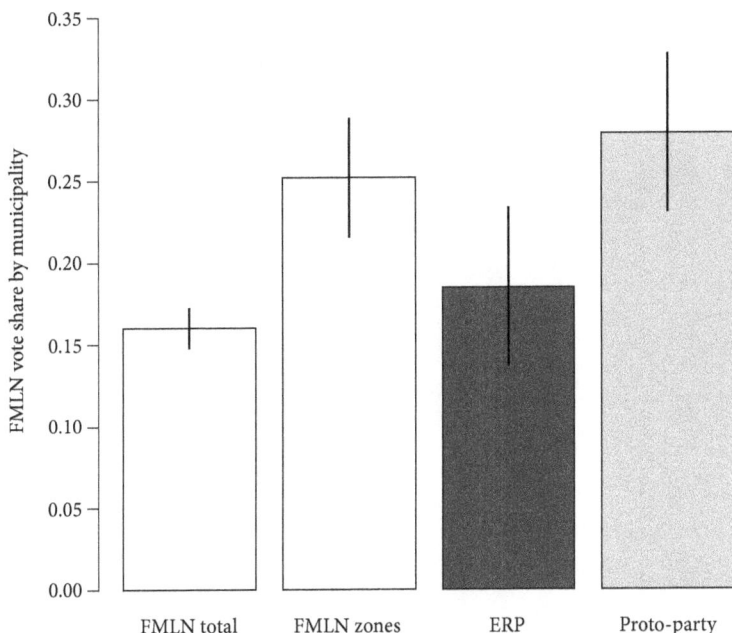

FIGURE 5.3. Comparing vote share under the ERP to proto-party OP-Ms

consolidate as a party given that it *has* to perform like one? In other words, can forced transition beget transformation? And will party consolidation help ensure its electoral longevity moving forward?

The second contribution is the introduction of the new dataset, which is specifically tailored in both its coding and composition to test theories of rebel-to-party transition. While others have conducted statistical analyses of transition in the past, previous attempts have expanded datasets that were originally curated for other purposes. As a result, ISO represents the first dataset that is constructed explicitly with rebel-to-party analyses in mind. The inclusion criteria are derived from the nuanced conceptual framework, which helps close an oft-ignored gap between composition, coding, and conceptualization.

Third, and most important for the book, the results of the analyses in this chapter provide strong evidence supporting the theory and its generalizability. While the previous chapters focused on demonstrating the mechanism by which wartime structures affect party formation, this chapter takes the critical step of demonstrating that these structures also affect party performance. As a result, not only does the new outcome variable capture political integration, but also the analyses demonstrate that proto-party structures built during war strongly improve the prospects for integration when the fighting stops.

Part III
EXTENDING THE TESTS
AND LOOKING AHEAD

POTENT PORTABLES

Organizational Transformation beyond El Salvador

None of us here are politicians nor have the political capacity to rule the country.

—Renamo leader Afonso Dhlakama, September 27, 1982

[I] have won democracy for the people. That is why we will contest the elections.

—Renamo leader Afonso Dhlakama, November 19, 1992

Arguably, the FMLN case was too good to be true, in every sense of the phrase. It is a perfect case for exploiting subnational variation. Its leaders left a paper trail most researchers could only dream of. The upper echelons of the organization were not only ideologically committed but also more highly educated than even the average university classroom. The FMLN was too good to be true from a moral standpoint as well. To wit, they committed an uncharacteristically low level of violence against noncombatants. They rarely engaged in coercive recruitment. Indeed, they are so "good" that Amelia Hoover Green leveraged the case to build her model of combatant restraint.[1] The organization and its postwar success may well be a function of a leadership that enforces restraint, spearheads wartime political engagement, and acts (during war) in such a way that mobilizing votes does not mean turning to the families whose children they stole. In short, was the FMLN's success more a function of its goodness than it was its organizational structures?

In this chapter I ask, how well does the theory travel beyond the unique borders of El Salvador? This chapter traces attempted rebel-to-party transformations in two cases: National Resistance of Mozambique (Renamo) in Mozambique and the Revolutionary United Front (RUF) in Sierra Leone. Renamo exhibits a successful transformation and transition into party politics; the RUF does not. After briefly discussing case selection, I use comparative process tracing to follow the groups' organizational trajectories. The case comparisons follow the analytic progression of the FMLN case. I begin with the sociopolitical backdrops to the wars and the process of organizational formation. Next, I trace their respective evolutions with a particular focus on critical organizational junctures and how their structures changed. Finally, I conclude with their divergent attempts to integrate into party politics.

Renamo and the RUF are ideal case comparisons (vis-à-vis each other and the FMLN) for individual, (marco-)structural, and organizational reasons. First, I wanted to move outside of Latin America to test the theory's portability. I chose two postcolonial cases in sub-Saharan Africa—the region with the most rebel-to-party transitions worldwide.[2] The RUF and Renamo exhibited similar recruitment profiles for much of the war (young males with little to no formal education), conducted similarly high levels of indiscriminate violence against local populations (unlike the FMLN), and faced almost identical power-sharing opportunities at the end of their respective conflicts.[3]

From an organizational standpoint, the two cases allow me to test alternative theories of wartime organizational structures. Politically diverse organizational structures are often attributed to communist influence.[4] Though chapter 2 demonstrated that the story is considerably more nuanced, the explanation may still be true at the aggregate level. After all, the FMLN was a communist movement, and it did build sophisticated proto-party structures during war. Renamo and the RUF allow me to get additional traction on testing this explanation. The RUF—like the FMLN—was born of exiled, radicalized students and professors of Sierra Leone's premier university. Influenced by Muammar Gaddafi's Green Book, Karl Marx, Frantz Fanon, Fidel Castro, and the like, the initial core of the RUF espoused an ideology that was at least communist-adjacent.[5] In contrast, Renamo arose in opposition to a communist regime. It advocated for free-market capitalism and religious freedom and was on the other side of the proxy wars that characterized the Cold War era. Thus, if the broad ideological bent is responsible for organizational form, we should expect proto-party structures to take root most comfortably in the RUF case.

I chose the RUF as a comparison case not because it was doomed to failure from the start, but—on the contrary—because the RUF was ostensibly poised for success. The initial organization had an educated and politically active core, a great deal of influence over disaffected men who could be recruited as foot soldiers, and nearly unobstructed access to rural populations with long-standing grievances against the All People's Congress (APC) government. Furthermore, before the RUF's first incursion into Sierra Leone, Muammar Gaddafi of Libya explicitly offered to fund the revolutionary movement on the sole condition that the RUF work toward transitioning into a political party. Thus, the RUF represents a good example of failure without falling into a straw-man problem.

Backdrops to Civil War

As with any rebellion, both Renamo's and the RUF's emergence and evolution are inseparable from the broader social, political, and economic contexts in which they coalesced. Here, I focus on the critical events and circumstances that directly influenced the rebellions.

The Mozambican Civil War

In the wake of Portuguese decolonization in 1974, the anticolonial rebel movement Mozambique Liberation Front (Frelimo) seized power and created a one-party communist state. Owing much to Soviet sponsorship and influence, Frelimo adopted a series of policies with three main pillars: the nationalization of the economy, the unification of Mozambican identity, and the modernization of society. All social services were nationalized immediately upon independence. Frelimo made it illegal for churches or private citizens to run schools, practice medicine or law, or even hold funerals.[6] The government pledged to bring health care to the whole of the country with a particular emphasis on rural areas, which it did with relative success in the early years of its rule.[7] The state also nationalized land and agriculture—forcing peasants onto large, state-owned cooperatives to farm cotton and other underproductive cash crops.[8] By 1977, Frelimo had fully nationalized industry as well. It adopted a zero-tolerance policy for political dissidents and sent anyone deemed *o inimigo interno* (the internal enemy) to reeducation camps.[9] As happens, however, these camps became hotbeds of resistance, and Renamo would later capitalize on Frelimo's convenient decision to house its opponents in concentrated areas.

In service of its second and third pillars, the government enacted draconian policies intended to unify Mozambican identity around the Communist Party. Under the guise of modernization, Frelimo went to massive lengths to dismantle traditional social structures—particularly in rural areas.[10] In a move that profoundly destabilized rural life, the government stripped tribal leaders of their power, uprooted communities, and forcibly relocated them to "communal villages" run by "dynamizing groups"—grassroots committees that were elected within the party and tasked with local administration.[11] Finally, one of the most consequential policies that would later play a key role in the civil war was Frelimo's codified ban on religion.

One cannot fully understand the emergence and development of Renamo without first understanding the geopolitical context of Mozambique vis-à-vis Rhodesia and South Africa (I use Rhodesia to refer to the country prior to its independence in 1980; thereafter, I use Zimbabwe. This usage allows for an easier distinction between Ian Smith's colonial regime and Robert Mugabe's post-independence regime). A long, yet narrow country situated along the southeastern coastline, Mozambique was the sole source of port access for its landlocked neighbors. Rhodesia, in particular, conducted 80 percent of its international trade through Mozambican ports. This economic relationship was stable when both Rhodesia and Mozambique had white colonial regimes at the helm, but devolved quickly when Frelimo took power and was no longer enthusiastic about being the economic hub of an oppressive power. This problem compounded because Mozambique quickly became a safe haven for groups fighting for Zimbabwean freedom. To mitigate its security concerns, Rhodesia began conducting cross-border raids into Mozambique.[12] In response, the Frelimo president Samora Michel closed the border, thereby cutting Rhodesia off from its main source of goods.

What were the implications of these policies and the geopolitical context in which they were enacted? The long answer is profound economic and social devastation that reverberated throughout the subcontinent. The short answer is, Renamo. Three factors worked in tandem to create fertile ground for a resistance movement in Mozambique. First, the social and economic policies enacted by the Frelimo government dismantled traditional structures of production and authority and replaced them with overly ambitious and underproductive state institutions aimed at exerting control over all aspects of daily life. These policies then coincided with both a massive economic crisis and one of the worst draughts the country had ever experienced. Together, these circumstances precipitated intense resentment among the population and concurrently exposed the state's administrative weaknesses, both of which Renamo would later make a career out of exploiting.

The Sierra Leonean Civil War

In the wake of independence, Sierra Leone faced auspicious political opportunities and dire economic challenges. On the one hand, decolonization was peaceful, the new government inherited a variety of institutions that poised the country for success, and Black Africans were well integrated into "the country's civil service and dominated white collar professions," even before decolonialization.[13] On the other hand, the economic climate left much to be desired. Diamond-producing areas in the east of the country were severely neglected. Infrastructure and public services including health care, education, and transportation were rapidly deteriorating, despite the government's continued reliance on diamond extraction and sales for the majority of its income.[14] People in the capital were benefiting handsomely from the wealth brought in by the mines in the east, while the people doing the labor in those areas saw none of the benefits. These widening economic disparities gave rise to deep-seated government resentment and ultimately tilled the soil for rebellion.

Even in light of the state's economic problems, the country was theirs to lose. That loss came with Siaka Stevens. Though democratically elected on the APC ticket, Stevens took swift and extreme measures to consolidate power and push the country toward one-party rule. Sierra Leone's political deterioration occurred on two dimensions: the intentional dismantling of democratic institutions and the gross mismanagement of the economy. Stevens abolished separation of powers, forced judges into retirement, vastly curtailed press freedom, and engaged in massive electoral fraud to ensure the party's staying power.[15] The APC stifled funding to the esteemed Fourah Bay College and sent undercover agents to monitor classrooms and union meetings.[16] Students were expelled, faculty were placed on watch lists, and demonstrations were violently repressed.

On the economic side, Stevens and other top APC officials engaged in a "massive looting of state resources," with minimal overhead cost. They lived lavishly in the capital and flaunted their money while much of the country fell into disrepair.[17] Kwesi Aning and Angela McIntyre note that "access to resources became virtually impossible for non-APC members, and membership of the APC became a necessary condition for access to jobs and state resources."[18] Rural areas became increasingly isolated as Stevens allowed public infrastructure outside of Freetown to decay. Anti-APC sentiment ran rampant both in the neglected hinterlands of the country and in the urban centers where highly educated citizens graduated college only to meet an unending bout of unemployment.

The final contextual detail central to the RUF's rise is the *potes*—periurban spaces on the outskirts of major cities that were initially home to wayward youngsters and petty criminals.[19] Once exclusively the purview of the lumpen youth, undereducated young men "who live by their wits and who have one foot in the underground economy," the *potes* became hotbeds of radical political socialization.[20] The combination of crackdowns at the university and dismal job prospects sent college graduates into the streets. There, they found disaffected youth who were enthusiastic to hear criticisms of the government and eager to fight.

A Tale of Two Organizations

The table was now set for Renamo and RUF. Exactly how each organization emerged will help forecast its organizational prospects for long-term success.

Renamo: Grassroots Rebellion or Geopolitical Puppet?

Since the Rhodesian government could no longer stage cross-border incursions without risking international condemnation, the director of the Central Intelligence Organisation (CIO) decided that in order to continue its mission in Mozambique, it needed a cover. And thus, Renamo was born. The CIO recruited Mozambican dissidents in service of a two-part project intended to destabilize the Frelimo government: (1) radio broadcasts of anti-Frelimo propaganda, and (2) armed force to conduct sabotage and reconnaissance. While some narratives of Renamo's origin make the group out to be little more than a tool of Rhodesia, Renamo was not a vapid puppet bending to the will of Ian Smith's government. The organization—and particularly, Orlando Cristina and other soon-to-be Renamo officials—understood the opportunity they had under Rhodesian sponsorship and exploited it to get a true Mozambican resistance force off the ground.

The CIO and the Rhodesian Broadcasting Company repurposed a military radio tower to make routine anti-Frelimo broadcasts in the hopes of riling opposition in Mozambique.[21] The early broadcasts, however, were relatively ineffectual—they were short and had a distinctly pro-colonial and pro-Smith bent. While discontent with Frelimo was rampant, few were especially nostalgic for their colonial past. The exiled Mozambican dissident Orlando Cristina saw these broadcasts as an ideal opportunity to lay the groundwork for the political opposition he had long envisioned, but he also knew he had to play the game, carefully toeing the line between his political aspirations and Rhodesia's interests.[22] It only took a few months for Cristina to take control of the station and pivot toward an explicitly Mozambican agenda. Thus, while the armed resistance was still a work in progress, the newly titled Voz da África Livre galvanized the people.

Rhodesian attempts to build an armed force did not go especially well. Its initial group comprised a large number of former members of the Portuguese military, who were never going to be welcomed into local communities with open arms.[23] The Frelimo defector André Matsangaissa came to Cristina and the CIO promising that he could successfully recruit Mozambican dissidents, which he did following a successful raid of one of Frelimo's reeducation camps. While the CIO went out of its way to keep Voz da África Livre "organizationally distinct" from the armed wing, this distinction did not hold in practice or in the perceptions of Mozambicans at home.[24] Once Matsangaissa convinced Cristina that his plan to recruit native Mozambicans was viable, Cristina began to explicitly discuss the movement in his radio broadcasts.

It is at this point that Renamo began coalescing into the organization that would shape its trajectory moving forward. In just over a year, Renamo went from a steady contingent of just under eighty members to an organization of well over a thousand.[25] As the CIO began losing its grip on the organization, Matsangaissa began scoping out locations and then building domestic bases among sympathetic populations in the north of the country. They distributed goods stolen from Frelimo's People's stores (state-run stores offering subsidized goods to local populations) and hosted large gatherings in which they would discuss the government's shortcomings.[26] Locals viewed Renamo as protecting them from Frelimo's policies. As one chief put it, "Frelimo never did anything in our areas—mambos could do rain ceremonies, n'angas could work, people could pray. . . . Renamo's presence was the reason why Frelimo could never establish secretaries or communal villages. We were happy because Renamo protected us from Frelimo."[27]

Though still heavily reliant on Rhodesian support, Renamo's leaders nevertheless managed get an authentic Mozambican resistance movement off the ground. They had established local bases; created a public relations team, which forged relations with both local populations and foreign correspondents; and assembled a dedicated telecommunications wing to maintain central control.[28] The telecom wing straddled the military and political-messaging divisions, thereby solidifying the ties between two aspects of the organization that Rhodesia had tried (in vain) to keep separate. Moreover, to leverage the power of local networks, Matsangaissa sought out *feitceiros* (witch doctors), whose power had been stripped by Frelimo.[29] By reinstating and validating the legitimacy of traditional local power structures, Renamo was then able to convert those networks to serve the organization.

The RUF: A Hopeful Emergence

Putting aside limitless access to physical resources, if we were to equip a rebel group with maximal organizational advantages at its inception, the RUF stacks up quite well. From the inside, the group had a great deal of promise; from the outside, it had a great number of opportunities. First, as noted, grievances against the APC pervaded every facet of Sierra Leonean society. Rural populations were exploited for cheap labor with no recompense in the way of development, the unemployment rate in the cities skyrocketed, and civil society groups were violently repressed. Moreover, the weakness of the Sierra Leone Army (SLA) and lack of reach of the government into the hinterlands of the country meant that rebellion had a good chance of taking hold of rural areas.

While the soil for rebellion had long since been tilled, the tipping point of the RUF's formation was a major government crackdown at Fourah Bay College in 1984. Violent repression of student demonstrations against the regime resulted in a three-month lockdown of the university and the permanent expulsion of forty-one students and three faculty members, who became the nucleus of the nascent RUF.[30] From an organizational standpoint, the integration of disaffected student activists into the lumpen youth culture represents an ideal foundation for a revolutionary political movement. The educated core of the movement was politically savvy, had well-articulated grievances, and had established relations with a group willing to take on a combat role. They sought a return to democratic rule and the implementation of fair and regulated mining practices to aid in Sierra Leone's development, which they argued would best be achieved by a prolonged revolutionary struggle. The lumpen youth—who were no strangers to organized violence—formed an ideal recruiting ground for the militant sect of the rebellion.[31]

Finally, to make matters even more auspicious, the expelled students and other radicals in Sierra Leone were recruited by Gaddafi for guerrilla and ideological training in Benghazi, Libya.[32] Gaddafi set out to fund groups that would stage "antiimperial rebellions" in accordance with his Green Book ideology. Crucially, Libya was not merely a wartime patron; Gaddafi's funding offer was contingent on the RUF converting itself into a political party.[33]

Taking Stock

Both organizations had fairly promising starts. They coalesced around a politically savvy core with clear visions for their countries' futures, they had patrons willing to train and sponsor the movements' growth, and they both faced local populations that harbored intense antigovernment sentiment. Renamo had more defined—and more diverse—organizational structures from the start, but fewer opportunities to fill them with skilled personnel; the RUF was a more inchoate organization, yet had a more educated pool from which to recruit.

However, early into their respective starts, both Renamo and the RUF experienced major organizational setbacks that disrupted their auspicious beginnings. For Renamo, 1979 was a comedy of errors. In the first place, the organization was growing faster than its disciplinary institutions could keep up. Though Matsangaissa envisioned an organization that was socially and politically embedded among local populations, opportunistic recruits began engaging in wanton and indiscriminate violence, undermining the organization's objectives.[34] But the organization's problems were not just at the bottom. Matsangaissa was soon assassinated, sparking a leadership crisis within the organization, which the CIO tried to exploit to keep Renamo firmly under Rhodesian control.[35] Finally, just as the new leader—Afonso Dhlakama—was trying to consolidate his tenuous power over the organization, Britain signed the Lancaster House Agreement, ceding control and granting independence to Rhodesia (now called Zimbabwe). Consequently, Renamo lost its sponsor overnight.

The RUF faltered even earlier. It lost its political footing as it consolidated around Foday Sankoh. The highly educated activists, who formed the initial nucleus, became disenchanted with the organization's direction as Sankoh pursued a more tight-knit relationship with Charles Taylor, the head of the NPFL in neighboring Liberia. They felt the RUF was liable to becoming a guise for wanton banditry, rather than the revolutionary political movement they intended. Prompted by these concerns, the majority of this early contingent defected from the RUF, choosing instead to continue their educations in Ghana.[36] Thus, to the extent that the nascent organization comprised politically active university students on the one hand, and galvanized lumpen youth on the other, the loss of the former made the organization susceptible to being overrun by the tendencies of the latter. In organizational terms, this early fracture had a homogenizing effect on the RUF from which it never recovered.

The question for both Renamo and the RUF was, what would their leaders do in the face of these shocks? While their demise was not necessarily imminent in either case, Renamo faced considerably more obstacles. It had a new leader, who, by all accounts, was "bookish" and far less charismatic than his predecessor. Their political-messaging wing was funded by a government that no longer existed, stationed in a country where they were no longer welcome, and they operated out of a radio tower that belonged to the now-defunct CIO. Thus, while a grassroots fight in Mozambique still seemed plausible, keeping the Renamo political-messaging division intact seemed almost impossible. In practice, this challenge could well have set Renamo on the same path as the RUF: becoming an organization whose educated, political core had been abscised.

Any way we turn it, the RUF had a clearer path forward. For one, although the early educated core was skeptical, Sankoh was not necessarily a harbinger of organizational deficiency. He grew up associated with lumpen culture; he joined the SLA, attaining the rank of corporal and specializing in radio and communications; and he later became a student activist.[37] In short, his experience had the potential to bridge social and logistical resources critical to the type of diversification that could have served the RUF throughout and beyond the war. Furthermore, the RUF had two external patrons willing to fund the rebellion, and it emerged among an aggrieved population ready to support and participate in an anti-APC movement.

Organizational Evolution: Resilience within Rebellion

Conveniently—at least from a narrative perspective—both conflicts divide naturally into three phases. For Renamo, those phases corresponded to its sponsors: its inception under Rhodesia, its transfer to South Africa, and finally, its break from regional sponsorship, resulting in its autonomous period. For the RUF, the phases are more idiosyncratic. The initial phase captures the first few years of the war, in which the RUF was making incursions from Liberia and quite effortlessly capturing territory along the east of the country. The second phase of the war was set off by augmented counterinsurgency efforts on the part of the SLA, which forced the RUF to reorganize and shift its tactics as it went on the defensive. Finally, the third phase of the war began in 1997, when the RUF and the SLA together staged a coup and took over the country until the war ended. For both groups, the onset of each phase represents a critical organizational juncture, in which leaders execute changes that shape the groups' trajectories moving forward. Each juncture was characterized by a range of possibilities with varying implications for the groups' development and rebel-to-party prospects. This section explores the most consequential decisions and their organizational consequences.

Renamo's Wartime Evolution

Broadly, Renamo's wartime evolution is characterized by impressive feats of organizational resilience in the face of an extreme dearth of resources. I trace the group's survival, adaptation, and evolution as it navigates new leadership, changing sponsorship, and a massive disparity between the leader's vision and his capacity to implement it. This case illustrates how a lack of financial, personnel, and material resources constrain the implementation of leaders' organizational ideology of rebellion—and their corresponding attempts to effect change at the margins.

RESILIENCE AND PROTO-PARTY DEVELOPMENT UNDER SOUTH AFRICAN SPONSORSHIP

As far as organizational resilience is concerned, Renamo made an impressive showing in 1980. As Zimbabwean independence became imminent—and, with it, the expiration on Renamo's welcome—leaders ramped up talks with South Africa in the hopes of negotiating a new sponsor and a safe location for Voz da África Livre.[38] The negotiations were swift and the transfers began immediately.[39] The deal with South Africa was a relief, but not a guarantee of organizational survival. All at once, Renamo was managing turnover in leadership, a change in sponsorship, and a major military setback after losing a military offensive at a newly established domestic base (Gorongosa) in the north of Mozambique. Thus, for Renamo, 1980 was a critical juncture if ever there were one. In service of both survival and the visions of the new leadership, Renamo undertook major organizational changes in this period, which would shape its future trajectory in important ways.

While organizational changes at the top can be particularly difficult, it was helpful that Dhlakama and his South African sponsors had a more aligned vision of Renamo's future than did Matsangaissa and the CIO. Indeed, while the CIO at best tolerated Renamo's political development, Renamo's South African sponsors prioritized it. From the jump, Dhlakama was determined to take Renamo in a more explicitly political direction. The corresponding proto-party development occurred along three dimensions. The first was the expansion and formal integration of the radio station (Voz da África Livre) into the organization. Beyond quickly relocating the radio station to South Africa, the radio staff was instructed to begin writing anticommunist literature, pamphlets, and posters to help spread Renamo's message more broadly.[40] Zooming out, the expansion of the size and scope of the Voz team is a prime example of organizational repurposing at the unit level.

The second dimension of Renamo's proto-party development in this period came in the push to develop a more sophisticated and cohesive political ideology. After all, if it wanted to expand its programming and literature, it needed substance with which to fill it. Here, we once again observe the convenient overlap in the organizational ideology of the leader and the preferences of the sponsor. Dhlakama believed that the only way to win the war was through meaningful political engagement with the people; the South African government wanted to shape Renamo into a viable political threat to Frelimo in the hopes of consolidating its own regional power.[41] Thus, in 1981, Renamo released its first Program and Manifest. This document represents the first consolidation of Renamo's political agenda. The manifesto calls for Mozambique to institute a multiparty democracy and an open-market economy, which by necessity also implies a cessation of Frelimo's communal villages and collective agriculture programs.

Finally, Renamo (and its sponsor) worked to build up a domestic and international contingent of political representatives. Dhlakama was trained in diplomatic tactics, and by late 1980, he was traveling around Europe to drum up support for the movement.[42] His diplomatic missions were quite successful, but constructing a domestic political-messaging front was considerably more difficult. Mozambique's dismal literacy rate (again, 92 percent of the country was functionally illiterate in this period) created both top-down and bottom-up problems. On one side of the coin, it was nearly impossible to find people who were capable of working as political commissars.[43] On the other side of the coin, Renamo faced a population that did not have the education to read—let alone understand—its message.

Though Dhlakama's early attempts to create a wing of political commissars failed, Renamo used religious networks and spiritual narratives to forge links with local communities and indirectly advance a political agenda. I argue that religious rhetoric was strategically used in place of *political* mobilization, but that its effects were the same: fostering an identity separate from that of Frelimo, mobilization on common grounds, and internal cohesion. For example, one of the most well-propagated myths was that Dhlakama and anyone else who participated in religious ceremonies would be impervious to "communist bullets." Here, we see an explicit fusion of religious and political concepts. Furthermore, by reinstating the power of tribal leaders—the authority structures that Frelimo tore down—Dhlakama evoked a clear image of an alternative and preferable organization of society under Renamo.

The sheer act of surviving both the leadership turnover and the South African hand-off constitutes a remarkable display of organizational resilience on the part of Renamo. And by all accounts, Renamo came back stronger.[44] Its capacity to weather the leadership turnover and simultaneous move to South African command contributed to what Debra Minkoff calls a "repertoire of flexibility."[45] In short, the more shocks an organization successfully endures, the better it becomes at adaptation and finding novel solutions to both new and old problems.

Cutting the Strings: Renamo's Transition to Autonomy

Renamo's wartime resilience was about to be put to the test a third time as the respective presidents of Mozambique and South Africa came to the negotiating table and signed the Nkomati Accord—an agreement to stop supporting violent coups. At the outset, the Nkomati Accord and consequent reduction in South African support was a huge blow to the organization. Renamo was heavily reliant on its patron for ammunition, radio supplies, food, and medical equipment. But, once again, Renamo's shocks seemed to come in twos: in addition to its loss of a sponsor and a foreign safe haven, Cristina (the head of the political-messaging division) had been recently assassinated. Renamo was essentially thrust into adulthood against its will, and these shocks had two important implications for the organization. First, with Cristina dead and no ability to reinstate the radio station inside Mozambique, Dhlakama made a major push to create a domestic political presence. Second—and often working against Dhlakama's political goal—Renamo now faced a resource crisis, and as a result, its relationships with local populations varied wildly from relative stability in some areas to unimaginably brutal and exploitative in others.

BUILDING DOMESTIC PROTO-PARTY STRUCTURES

According to top Renamo officials, the break from South Africa catalyzed Renamo to augment and consolidate the political core of the organization. Beginning in 1984, Renamo fundamentally shifted its recruitment tactics in service of this goal. Dhlakama (despite his previous failure in 1980) began a recruitment initiative aimed at creating divisions of "political-military commissars"—people tasked with communicating the political goals of the organization to the foot soldiers and to the local people inside Mozambique.[46]

As is common, the political-military commissars were combat-ready, but their role within the organization was purely about communication. Internally, they provided political education to recruits—explaining why they were fighting and why the organization should accept future negotiations with Frelimo.[47] The salience of this assignment cannot be understated. First, the aim of this unit represents the first real attempt to galvanize Renamo soldiers around a *political* message—as opposed to a religious one. Second, this message represents a clear push to soften members' intransigence toward the Frelimo government. To put it in perspective, by 1984, the Renamo leadership was already planting the seeds of working toward a negotiated solution—a full eight years before any such agreement would come to fruition.[48] By 1986, the political-military commissars were being deployed to engage civilian populations as well, which in turn helped the organization create "more credible liberated zones."[49] Renamo sought to install basic administrative structures and engage in political dialogue with the people under their control.

Renamo's shift toward political recruitment in this era was not just about adding more skills to the bottom of the organization. Instead, it contributed to a critical restructuring, the effects of which carried Renamo forward into its political negotiations with Frelimo and eventual transformation into a party. Every addition to Renamo's political structure from the bottom up requires a corresponding addition from the top down. For example creation of urban support networks (*nucleos*) also demanded a new set of roles and relations (in the form of an administrative and political-messaging staff) to be instituted at the top to manage those networks. This process is organizational diversification in practice. The top-down changes to correspond with its political recruitment were not limited to managing urban nucleos. Renamo's foreign minister, Evo Fernandez, described the structure of their National Council as follows:

> Renamo's political structure is like this. First, again, there is the President... then the Secretary-General... then the National Council, which is made up of chiefs, military people, civilians, and so on. Then we have

external and internal departments. The external departments include foreign relations, finances, information and studies . . . The internal departments include education, health, economy, and administration. Each department has a head who reports to the President.[50]

This account suggests a much greater level of organizational diversification than many conventional portrayals of Renamo include. While there is clear reason for Fernandez to exaggerate the breadth of Renamo's political sophistication, similar descriptions of the structure are corroborated by a variety of sources. See, for example, the organizational chart depicting civilian administrative structures compiled by Carrie Manning in collaboration with Renamo officials, which depicts fairly extensive proto-party structures.[51]

Crucially, while this phase of the war is characterized by a significant growth in the group's local administration and domestic political-messaging apparatus, locals' experiences of Renamo on the ground often departed violently from Dhlakama's vision. Mozambique's extreme poverty, famine, and unskilled population made it impossible to achieve regional structural consistency. As a result, some areas—where personnel and resources permitted—were characterized by relative stability in which Renamo bolstered social services, built schools, and created administrative structures by repurposing legacy institutions from the Catholic Church.[52] In other areas, however—particularly in the south of the country—Renamo's tactics became increasingly brutal.

The autonomous period was defining for Renamo along a number of dimensions. First, by weaning itself off of foreign support, Renamo was forced to become the truly Mozambican nationalist movement it painted itself as from the start. The organization once again displayed marked resilience to its changing conditions and managed to thrive after relocating entirely to Mozambique. Second, and relatedly, the political-messaging division now comprised networks of domestic opposition to Frelimo—as opposed to the more privileged expatriates, who previously staffed the radio station. The new administrative and messaging structures assembled in this period ultimately formed the core of the party organization, though there was still considerably more to be done.[53]

The RUF's Wartime Evolution

From a rebel-to-party perspective, the organizational evolution of the RUF is a tragedy of errors. Indeed, this case is a prime example of how early decisions can have deleterious and lasting organizational repercussions. Moreover, this cycle repeats itself throughout the war. At each major inflection point in the group's wartime life cycle, decisions from the top served only to isolate the organization and drive it further from its ideological roots. In short, while rebels do think about organizations as much as I expected, not all leaders are organizational savants.

PHASE 1: 1991–1993

The Sierra Leonean civil war began when RUF troops stationed across the border in Liberia began making incursions into the east of the country. Due to the government's severe neglect of both its armed forces and the eastern districts (those farthest from the capital), early incursions were swift and successful.[54] From an organizational standpoint, the first phase of the war was marked by countless invaluable opportunities to create an organization poised for electoral success and a population poised for political mobilization. The most fundamental opportunity was the astonishing lack of opposition the group faced: RUF forces moved freely throughout the east of the country encountering little to no resistance from the armed forces. Additionally, citizens in these areas harbored particularly acrimonious sentiments toward the government due to its unmitigated neglect of the region. Finally, while the initial core of the movement had long since broken away, numerous radical intellectuals in the east of the country willingly joined the RUF in the hopes of mounting a political revolution in Sierra Leone.[55] For example, Ibrahim Deen Jalloh—a political dissident and teacher at Bunumbu College—joined the movement along with his wife, who spearheaded the RUF's women's wing.[56] Former RUF members recount that he forged crucial links between the movement and other Bunumbu intellectuals and that together they helped shape the RUF's political message.[57]

The confluence of local support, the potential to reinvigorate the intellectual core, and the lack of pushback from government forces paved a smooth road for a relatively cohesive, diversified, and strongly embedded organization.[58] And the RUF went into the war with sanguine hopes of rallying enthusiastic support for its cause. The question was whether the leadership would exploit or spurn these opportunities. Two organizational issues stood in the way of building the organization envisaged at the RUF's outset: the first was the extent of its fragmentation, the second was Foday Sankoh.

In the first place, the RUF was decentralized and severely fragmented (characteristics that persisted throughout the war). This fragmentation existed on many dimensions: different area commanders had different approaches to waging conflict and engaging populations, leaders disagreed on the direction of the organization, and more generally, the RUF lacked institutions for communicating and enforcing codes of conduct. The consequence of this fragmentation was wide variation in the RUF's structures and its approaches toward interfacing with local populations.[59] In some areas, the RUF forged amicable ties, distributed supplies to communities, and implemented shadow governing institutions.[60] A chief from Kailahun district paints an almost unrecognizable picture of the RUF: "The RUF had this social agenda which made sense to the people. . . . [They] did not come with the 'face of war' but with promises."[61] Ultimately, however, the RUF's operations in Kailahun are more exemplary of the organization's inconsistencies than its holistic trajectory.

In many other areas, however, the RUF relied more on engaging and recruiting from lumpen populations in hinterland *potes* than on efforts to forge linkages with local communities. This tack left locals feeling "at best ambiguous" toward the organization, despite harboring "violent opposition to the regime."[62] Focusing its early efforts on lumpen recruitment had lasting organizational consequences. Rather than taking advantage of a willing population that agreed with the RUF's political message, it instead amassed a large group of undisciplined recruits, who exploited their affiliation with the RUF to extort and loot at will without regard to the organization's code of conduct.[63]

Disjunctures in the organization were evident at the top as well, which precipitated the second problem. Following a bout of internecine fighting among the leadership, Sankoh's priorities shifted toward consolidating his power over the RUF.[64] Sankoh's organizational decisions were guided by his fear of losing his place at the top. He perceived the Bunumbu College intellectuals as a direct threat to the loyalty that members had to him. According to former RUF fighters, Sankoh's distrust of the intellectual elite governed both recruitment and promotion choices within the organization: "Most commanders came from poor backgrounds and the movement upgraded them. Foday Sankoh promoted the semi-literate because these were more loyal to him and were less likely to take over the movement. He did not like the educated ones."[65]

Thus, Sankoh's attempt to marginalize rather than embrace the RUF's new political-messaging division meant that the ranks of the organization were swelling with the individuals who were least likely to have the skills needed to advance the RUF's political agenda.

In addition to quashing structures that could serve the organization's electoral future, Sankoh cracked down on anything he deemed a rival opinion. He executed popular commanders for challenging his decisions and effectively eliminated any institution (formal or informal) that would allow for bottom-up feedback to reach his ears.[66] As one former member recounts:

> The leadership of the RUF then changed to a five-man group and this changed our motto from "collective ideas and responsibility" to "five-man ideas and responsibility." We, the general body, had no power to talk about changes affecting the success of the movement, which all of

us, together with our late leader, had struggled for years to maintain. Anyone apart from the five-man team was considered an outsider. Now, most of [the outsiders] have either died or resigned from the party.[67]

Thinking back to the FMLN, Sankoh's absolute repudiation of conflicting advice represents a stark contrast to the Salvadorans' embrace of *autocrítico*. In the former case, the rebels actively sought critical feedback and interpretations of their progress to ensure they could learn from past errors. Here, loyalty was prized over aptitude—and the organization betrayed this deficiency at every turn.

PHASE 2: SHIFT TO A GUERRILLA MOVEMENT

The first major shock to the RUF came in the aftermath of a military coup in 1992. APC leaders were deposed and the National Provisional Ruling Council (NPRC) assumed power. The new government proposed a ceasefire and negotiated settlement to the rebels, which included full amnesty for RUF fighters. The RUF strategically signed the ceasefire—with the intention that it would use the downtime to rebuild some of its military capacity. Unbeknownst to the RUF leadership, however, the NPRC government was doing the same. The government took extreme measures between 1992 and 1993 to augment and train the national army. As such, when the RUF rejected the full settlement, believing that it could now handle a conventional military struggle against the SLA, it was caught off guard.[68] By the end of 1993, "eye witnesses describe a bedraggled RUF leadership contingent quitting Kailahun town . . . heading in the direction of the border forest reserves."[69]

Lacking the military and organizational strength to face off directly with the SLA, the RUF undertook its first major strategic overhaul in 1993, kicking off the second phase of the war.[70] This phase of the RUF's organizational development is marked by three key decisions that pushed the organization further from its proto-party potential: (1) a retreat to hidden bases in the jungle, (2) the group's official foray into illicit mining, and (3) its handling of the second round of negotiations.

The RUF leadership abandoned conventional military tactics in favor of retreating to the bush and adopting a more guerrilla-style strategy.[71] The external challenges the rebels faced from the state move in lockstep with what we observed in the FMLN case: the groups waged conventional wars for a few years before augmented counterinsurgency efforts forced the respective insurgencies to embrace guerrilla warfare. Once again, however, these external shocks were filtered through different organizational lenses. Even the same technology of war can look very different across cases. To wit, most RUF units abandoned towns they occupied to "adapt to life in a series of secure forest hide-aways," venturing out only to pillage for supplies.[72] However, a shift to guerrilla warfare does not necessitate a shift to isolationism. Thinking back to the FMLN, when leader Cayetano Carpio was asked whether the organization had the capacity to wage guerrilla war on flat terrain, Carpio responded, "The people are our mountains."[73]

While surviving this tactical transition and rebuilding its armed forces contributed broadly to the RUF's resilience, the way the organization executed this shift had negative consequences for its rebel-to-party prospects. To accommodate its isolation, leaders shifted from directly administering civilian enclaves to appointing "collaborators" (often young boys with "lumpen sympathies") to keep order and collect food and clothing for the RUF camps.[74] Though this approach was called the "ideology system," in practice it was little more than an institutionalized looting arrangement. Additionally, the RUF attenuated the scope of responsibilities for the ideological wing comprising the network of Bunumbu College intellectuals. Initially, this branch was assembled to disseminate the RUF's ideology and work in community outreach. After the retreat, it was limited to internal ideological training—which mostly amounted to justifying new members' forced conscription.[75] Ideological training was sporadic, at best, and the content of that ideology almost never made it beyond the boundaries of the organization.[76]

The second major organizational shift in this phase was Sankoh's decision to formally pursue diamond mining.[77] This pursuit had three organizational implications. First, the move into the mining sector piqued the generosity of Charles Taylor, who suddenly found the resources to "augment his support for the organization . . . and bolster these operations."[78] As a result, the RUF found itself even more beholden to Liberian interests.[79] Moreover, the RUF's involvement in mining only amplified its incentives to keep civilian populations at bay, thereby contributing to the organization's isolation.

Finally, this move altered the RUF's funding structure. After all, diamonds are of little use to rebels without a relatively efficient mechanism for extraction and sales. As such, the organization evolved to prioritize the structures associated with this goal. The roles and relations created to facilitate diamond sales became defining features of the RUF. At the lower levels of the organization, captives and children were put to work as miners. At the midand upper levels, the RUF forged links to buyers in Liberia and elsewhere.[80] Crucially, this restructuring represents a diversification move, just not a useful one where party transformation is concerned. Zooming out, this organizational change highlights why concepts like diversification are only useful alongside descriptors that specify the content of the new structures.

The third major organizational upset came in a surprising form: a negotiated settlement with a clause permitting the RUF to transition into legal politics.

Immediately, the agreement exacerbated an evergreen chasm in the organization between the sect committed to pursuing a peaceful, political solution, and another sect in favor of continued fighting.[81] The former comprised what few educated elites remained in the RUF, while the latter comprised mainly battalion commanders and lumpen recruits for whom fighting was a way of life with or without the RUF title. When it came to implementing the agreement, Sankoh acted as an obstructionist at every turn, which led directly to another flight of educated members in the upper echelons of the organization.[82]

However, this critical organizational juncture did not end with Sankoh's domestic intransigence. On March 6, 1997, Foday Sankoh was arrested in Lagos, Nigeria, on suspicion of carrying out an illegal arms deal. After discovering his identity, Nigerian authorities detained and jailed Sankoh for two years. In response, the four RUF members (including Deen Jalloh—one of the Bunumbu intellectuals recruited early in the war) on the Commission for the Consolidation of Peace staged a palace coup in an attempt to take over the organization and facilitate the path to peace. Yet, loyalty to Sankoh ran deeper than the four had realized. To combat what they saw as a hostile, government-sanctioned takeover of the RUF, Sankoh loyalists set up an elaborate ruse. They constructed what appeared to be a welcome party for the new RUF leaders—complete with music, dancers, and food. Yet, as the celebration was about to begin, a commander gave the signal, the dancers fled, and armed men leapt from the bush. The four men were kidnapped and detained by RUF commanders, who opted instead to nominate Sam Bockarie—a former diamond miner, professional dancer, and hairdresser—as the interim leader in Sankoh's absence.[83] Thus, in the wake of Sankoh's arrest, hopeful ideologues fighting for a peaceful political resolution to the war were replaced by "a group of embittered fatalists hell-bent on destroying those who had betrayed their leader."[84]

Negotiated settlements bookended the second phase of the civil war. In both cases, the RUF was offered amnesty. In the second agreement, it was offered the opportunity to transition into legal politics. In the face of these opportunities, Sankoh pushed the organization toward an evermore homogeneous structure—severing ties with the most educated and politically savvy members at every turn. These splits not only jeopardized organizational cohesion broadly—which diminished adaptive capacity—but also evinced conflict between the majority of the RUF and those few cadres most needed for successful political transformation. Finally, the RUF's control over mining areas incentivized recruits motivated to share in the spoils of war, rather than to contribute to the path to peace. Crucially, what we observe here is that when organizations are more structurally homogeneous, expectations from the literature hold.

PHASE 3: THE STRANGE(ST) BEDFELLOWS

Owing to an unpopular collaboration between the government and a grassroots civil defense force (the kamajors) following the 1996 elections, two groups inside Sierra Leone were left disenfranchised: the RUF and the SLA. The SLA was both resentful of the new president sidestepping the army in favor of the kamajors and notoriously corrupt—its members earning the nickname *sobels* (a portmanteau of "soldier" and "rebel"). In May of 1997, a group of junior SLA officers together with the RUF staged a coup ousting the new president and his party from Freetown.

Once again, the RUF faced an opportunity to make a play for legitimacy. With free rein over the capital, no military opposition, and nearly unbridled access to state resources, the RUF was ideally situated to make good on the egalitarian promises and democratic values on which the organization was supposedly built. Instead—and predictably—the RUF seized the opportunity to make major incursions into the mining areas in the east.[85] Ex-combatants recall getting their hands on luxuries that were unavailable in the bush, and the desire for more led to infighting fueled by greed.[86] As one former commander recounts, "From '97, when we joined with the AFRC [Armed Forces Revolutionary Concil], the infighting in the RUF started. Because then we saw what officers were entitled to, so everybody wanted to be a commander. And they did not take orders anymore."[87] After a year, the Economic Community of West African States removed the junta government and reinstated President Ahmad Tejan Kabbah. Shortly thereafter, Sankoh was extradited from Nigeria, convicted of treason, and sentenced to death. Despite its extrication from the capital, the RUF remained militarily strong.

What little political ideology was left in the organization was eradicated in this period. Where leaders once relied on internal ideological training and behavioral monitoring wings to keep troops in line, they now relied on drugs and patrimonial exchange relations.[88] Atrocities against civilians worsened during this era as the RUF fought tooth and nail to prove the government's ineffectiveness. Crucially, this analysis is not just a retrospective characterization of the RUF. Combatants with long-standing affiliations actually referred to post-1998 recruits by a different name to highlight the changing composition of the organization.[89] As one commander noted, "The ones who joined the RUF later on do not have the RUF ideology. We call them 'Junta II' because they joined after the junta period. These RUF combatants were not disciplined and were causing us a real headache. We feel that they betrayed and sabotaged the movement."[90]

TAKING STOCK OF THE ORGANIZATION

While the RUF was never far from roving banditry, the chain of events that ensued following the second failed settlement unraveled what little political clout the organization had left. According to Krijin Peters, the time that the RUF spent in the capital alongside the AFRC "not only emptied the minds of the ideological commitment generated in the bush, but also undermined the movement's organizational coherence."[91] This phase severely calls into question whether resource mobilization is sufficient for rebel successor party formation. The logic of these explanations is straightforward: with greater access to resources, the organization should be less prone to infighting and competition, since scarcity is mitigated. Indeed—particularly during the interregnum period—the RUF had access to state resources, the most consistent control of Sierra Leone's mines since the start of the war, and nearly free run of the capital. Yet, the RUF's sudden resource wealth served to divide rather than empower the organization. Again, this analysis does not mean to discredit the importance of resources entirely. Rather, it illustrates that resources alone are not only insufficient, but depending on the circumstances, can actually be inimical to the organization's functioning.

Rebel-to-Party Transformation(s)

As their respective conflicts were winding down, Renamo and the RUF faced nearly identical legal opportunities to transition into electoral politics. Both negotiated settlements granted amnesty to members. Both included explicit clauses allowing for party formation conditional on disarmament and demobilization. Both set a future date for competitive elections. The question is whether and to what extent successful party formation was possible given the organizational resources at their disposal. I demonstrate here that both organizations committed to transitioning into electoral politics, but only Renamo made a real attempt at *transformation*.

Renamo

Although Dhlakama had been pushing Renamo in a more explicitly politically engaged direction since the early 1980s, the group's First Party Congress in 1989 marked the true beginning of its transformation process. The goal was to discuss the future direction of the organization, and its content tracks directly with my expectations about the transformation process. Specifically, the First Congress served as an overt instance of the sort of organizational assessment I predicted in chapter 5. With an eye toward transformation, my theoretical framework predicts that leaders must conduct an organizational audit: taking note of what they have as well as what they need and creating a plan to implement those changes. Manning's analysis of the meeting strongly corroborates this expectation as she argues that "the real significance of the First Congress was that it consolidated the fundamental changes that had been in the works since the mid-1980s and were aimed at moving Renamo closer to something resembling a coherent opposition movement."[92] The leadership made explicit reference to two core needs: to bolster political engagement and administration of Renamo-controlled areas and to augment existing structures that managed Renamo's "political wing" in order to manage the transformation and take on postwar political roles.

Following the organizational assessment of the First Congress, Renamo embarked on its second major political recruitment effort. However, finding personnel who were even remotely qualified—to say nothing of willing—to take on high-ranking, party-relevant positions within Renamo was no easy task. Renamo's brutality was not lost on individuals in even the more well-off areas. Moreover, finding anyone with over a second-grade education in the country was difficult in its own right. Nonetheless, bribing students with false promises of education and scholarship abroad after the end of the war, Renamo recruited heavily from schools and universities. Dhlakama sought to surround himself and the National Council with "political people . . . [who could] give political education classes" to all the heads of Renamo's departments.[93] Dhlakama's objective—per his statements in the First Congress—was to ensure that existing administrative structures were poised to take on postwar roles. In short, this move is the organizational precursor to the structural repurposing my theory predicts.

The creation and trajectory of the Department of Political Affairs falls perfectly in line with my theoretical expectations. During the initial political recruitment drives in the mid-1980s, it was common for Renamo soldiers to forcibly recruit groups of people from a single area or a single school. In one instance, Anselmo Victor and some of his colleagues were kidnapped and placed into political-messaging roles. They were trained together and they worked and lived together at Renamo's national headquarters.[94] As I anticipate, the division was repurposed in its entirety to become the Department of Political Affairs under Victor's command.[95] This sort of reprioritization—retaining core structures with postwar relevance—mitigates the risks of organizational change.

Following the 1992 negotiated settlement, which granted Renamo a legal path to party formation, it held another Party Congress and enacted a two-pronged approach to transformation. In rural areas, Renamo worked to augment and legitimate its administrative capacity. It continued its wartime trends of relying largely on chiefs and local authorities to occupy administrative positions.[96] Evidence from the ground indicates that the areas with the strongest administrative capacities were the ones with wartime structural legacies.[97] In urban areas, Renamo worked to repurpose existing networks of clandestine support from the war into administrative and other party-relevant structures.[98] A prime example of this formalization comes from Sofala Province. In 1990, the anti-Frelimo activist and underground Renamo supporter Manuel Pereira was named Renamo's first provincial delegate.[99] Pereira, in turn, assisted Renamo in creating other provincial delegations throughout the center and north of the country.[100] At the war's end, Pereira became the official provincial representative of Sofala in the Mozambican government. Moreover, two of the other delegate heads created in 1990 went on to become members of Parliament.[101]

Of course, Renamo's transformation was not devoid of obstacles. While the organization made remarkable strides in augmenting divisions dedicated to governance and political messaging, it faced two major challenges to creating a functioning party. The first was a resource problem: Mozambique was in abject financial straits and could not afford even the most basic provisions for the party. Vincente Ululu, Renamo's secretary general, at one point said, "We don't need [political] training because Renamo during the war was a politico-military movement, so we have experienced personnel. We need money to create conditions to be able to function."[102] The scramble for basic supplies was so dire that at one point Dhlakama claimed, "Renamo's financial problems threaten democracy in Mozambique."[103] To be sure, material resources were not the only scarcity. Finding skilled individuals capable of filling in the organizational gaps was still a challenge in a country with the lowest literacy rate in the world.

The second impediment to Renamo's organizational transformation was its severe internal fragmentation. Having spent the last few years of the war prioritizing the recruitment of educated members for roles in administration, education, and political messaging, Dhlakama created a fissure in the organization. Although the new recruits benefited the organization by imbuing it with the relevant skill sets needed to operate in the political realm, they were nonetheless greeted with suspicion and resentment from foot soldiers who had been in the bush since Renamo's early days.[104] Wartime resentments grew into full-fledged internal conflicts as it became increasingly clear the new recruits would transition into the highest-ranking political positions and, thus, the highest-paying jobs. From an organizational standpoint, these tensions pose a very high risk of fracture; from a conflict standpoint, we might expect such rifts to manifest in the form of spoilers.

Ultimately, the "solution" to the second problem was a matter of bribery. High-ranking officers whose low levels of education disqualified them for government or military positions were trained in trades to be drivers or cooks. Foot soldiers accepted payoffs, sometimes from demobilization funds, other times from Frelimo, which bribed defectors to join its organization in exchange for jobs and information.[105] Despite—or perhaps because of—the longevity of the war, the general consensus is that demobilization was otherwise a relatively quick and easy process. Many foot soldiers on both sides (though more from Renamo than Frelimo) were redirected into the new, integrated Mozambican Army.[106] The concept of a job with pay largely compensated for the bitterness of not qualifying for a prestigious government post after the war.

1994 ELECTIONS AND RENAMO'S FUTURE

The loss of two leaders and two sponsors made Renamo no stranger to resilience under duress. In the lead-up to the 1994 elections, Renamo leaned heavily on the proto-party divisions it built during war. The organization was still in an understaffed and tenuous state, but crucially, so was Frelimo. Neither had ever campaigned for voluntary support without a gun in hand, and interviews with citizens suggest that many had no idea what to expect from either. Renamo incurred another sizable hiccup as both parties began campaigning. Having renounced communism, Frelimo began to steal much of Renamo's wartime rhetoric about free markets, free religious practice, and democratic institutions. This made the two parties even more undifferentiable in the eyes of the people. In the end, Renamo billed itself as a "coalition of the marginalized" in an attempt to appeal to those who Frelimo exploited during the war.[107] Frelimo made explicit attempts to remind people of Renamo's wartime atrocities.

The 1994 elections culminated in an executive win and legislative majority for Frelimo, but a sizable allocation of seats to Renamo.[108] As with the Salvadoran case, province-level vote share tells an even more nuanced story in direct support of my theory. The provinces with the most well-established proto-party structures (Sofala, Manica, Zambezia, Nampula, and Tete) also cast the most votes for Renamo. Out of the 112 seats they won in the 1994 elections, 98 were from these provinces alone. In essence, the people voted to repurpose wartime political structures into peacetime governance.

Attempted Transformation in the RUF

As the Sierra Leone civil war came to a close, the RUF, once again, found itself staring down opportunities it was unfit to exploit. Leveraging its military advantage, the 1999 Lomé Agreement granted the RUF a considerable amount of power in the transitional government. In addition to facilitating a path to transition into a political party to compete in elections set for 2001, the RUF won amnesty for Sankoh and a guaranteed post for him (as well as four additional cabinet posts) in the Transitional Government of National Unity.[109] The accord provided the right for the RUF to legally register as a party within thirty days of signing, set up an international trust fund to finance the transition, and explicitly provided "training for RUF membership in party organization and functions."[110]

Despite the massive concessions made in the RUF's favor, Sankoh, Bocka-rie, and other war-profiteering commanders managed to stonewall the accord's implementation. Commanders kept troops in the dark about the terms of the agreement, fearful that war-weary fighters would jump at the opportunity to take advantage of the reintegration packages.[111] Sankoh—aware that "the RUF would not fare well in national elections"—even mobilized a final incursion into Free-town in 2000 in the hopes of continuing the RUF's influence over the country by force.[112] The incursion failed and Sankoh was arrested, at which point Issa Sesay took charge of the RUF. He, unlike previous leaders, was committed to disarma-ment and pushed the RUF in the direction needed to implement the peace deal.[113]

After the two parties signed the final ceasefire agreement the previous May, the Sierra Leone civil war was officially declared over in January 2002. To finalize the Lomé Accord's implementation, the RUF needed to demobilize its rank-and-file combatants and transform what was left into a party in time to compete in the upcoming elections in May of that same year. Scholars acknowledging the RUF's eventual failure nonetheless argue that "the possibility of transition to democratic politics . . . cannot be ruled out *a priori*."[114] The authors cite Renamo as a coun-terexample—an insurgent group that was also a product of external sponsorship, frequently used as a proxy to fight regional conflicts, managed to transition into a party, so the RUF could (have) too. I argue, however, that key deficiencies in the RUF's organizational structure—identifiable a priori—made the RUF Party (RUFP) especially unfit for transformation.

An assessment of the RUF's structure at the end of the war reveals that the process of transforming into a party would require a ground-up construction of the party apparatus and a reorientation of the organization's priorities. As dem-onstrated earlier, the organization systematically marginalized and dismantled the structures most apposite to party formation. From the standpoint of organi-zational adaptation, these deficiencies make organizational change both difficult and highly risky.[115] The organizational and behavioral legacy of the RUF gave rise to three challenges that ultimately proved insurmountable for the fledgling party: (1) a small pool from which to draw willing and politically skilled recruits, (2) a high risk of resentment from "bush commanders" and other insiders who were passed over in favor of outside recruits, and (3) the challenge of mobilizing constituents from civilians who only interacted with the RUF in a violent capacity. First, the manner in which the RUF developed and dispersed its message made political recruitment a formidable task. Its linkages to politically active university affiliates were severed early on in the war, which left civilians largely unfamiliar with the political aims of the organization. Unable to rely on active supporters with ideological commitments to the organization, the RUF was forced to settle for educated opportunists to fill political posts.[116]

The second challenge the RUF faced was how to manage internal resentment as high-ranking yet illiterate commanders were passed over in favor of competent outsiders. For example, after the junta period, the university lecturer Paolo Bangura joined the RUF to help form a political-ideological wing.[117] During the 2002 elections, it was Bangura who ran for president on the RUFP ticket, despite being affiliated with the organization for only a few years. His short tenure, however, was characterized primarily by quarrels with Sankoh loyalists, and he resigned following the RUFP's electoral failure.[118] This endemic resentment on the part of the military wing mirrors Renamo's experience. I argue, however, that Renamo's successful transformation (and transition) highlights the organizational advantage of having even minimal proto-party structures as a legacy of wartime.

Finally, in addition to the scramble to patch together a functioning political party, the real obstacle was a matter of figuring out how to appeal to a country they themselves tore apart. The challenge of electoral mobilization existed on two dimensions. On the one hand, the RUF would have to find a way to convince the civilians—and, indeed, its own ex-combatants—that placing power in its hands would be wise. On the other hand, RUF leaders had to figure out what message they wanted to use to attempt to earn that trust in the first place. The junta period compounded this problem. Specifically, the RUF's brief time at the helm of Sierra Leone's government gave both citizens and low-ranking members unique insight into how the RUF leadership dealt with power. Those who were with the RUF from its early days noted that the AFRC collaboration and exposure to "city life" corrupted the leaders and desecrated the RUF ideology.[119] Consequently, the RUFP not only needed a substantive message, but it also had to convince voters that trusting the party with power would not just produce a redux of the junta period.

In the run-up to the elections, the RUFP tried and failed to rehash its bush ideology—painting itself as a party for socialism, agrarian self-sufficiency, and wiping out corruption in government and mining.[120] Put simply, from the moment of its inception, the RUFP was a company without a product—and it showed. Despite overcoming the severe personnel shortage to field 203 candidates in time for the May elections, the RUFP failed to win even a single seat.[121] In all, nine parties competed for 112 parliamentary seats in the election, yet only three parties—the Sierra Leone People's Party, the APC, and the Peace and Liberation Party—surpassed the 12.5 percent vote threshold needed to be awarded seats in the legislature. Adding insult to injury, the APC—the party in large part responsible for Sierra Leone's downfall into autocracy and civil war—garnered more votes than the RUFP by an order of magnitude in all but two provinces.

Epilogue: The Kailahun Exception

Beyond other cases, in which comparably brutal civil wars culminated in substantial electoral victories for the (former) perpetrators of violence, the most compelling evidence for the role of political diversification for the RUF's failure comes from Kailahun district. While the RUFP's electoral defeat was substantial, Table 6.1 reveals that the magnitude of its loss was not uniform. In this section, I explore the RUFP's most substantial electoral outliers: Kailahun district, in which the RUFP earned 7.8 percent of the vote share.

Nestled in the southeast corner of Sierra Leone, Kailahun district provides a fascinating shadow case that runs counter to the grim narrative characterizing most of the country. Kailahun was one of the first areas that the RUF settled in after its initial incursion into Sierra Leone. Yet, the group that set up shop in many areas of this district evolved very differently from the rest of the movement.[122] An RUF commander makes this point explicitly: "The life in the combat zone was different from the life in the rear. In the rear, nobody was forced to work on private farms. . . . Everything was for the betterment of the movement."[123] Indeed, the RUF's decentralization made for considerably more intraorganizational variation

TABLE 6.1. Percentage of vote share by party in the 2002 parliamentary elections

DISTRICT	SLPP	APC	PLP	RUFP*
West-West	46.3	25.1	15.8	1.1
West-East	45.5	34.2	7.6	2.2
Bombali	16.7	62.1	8.1	5.8
Port Loko	26.5	55.6	5.3	2.5
Kambia	56.0	28.3	4.6	2.3
Koinadugu	61.4	25.6	5.0	2.1
Tonkolili	16.5	63.0	2.4	5.9
Moyamba	89.4	6.0	0.6	0.3
Bo	93.9	4.2	0.5	0.4
Bonthe	98.5	0.3	–	0.3
Pujehun	99.1	0.1	0.2	0.2
Kenema	94.0	3.6	0.4	0.8
Kono	86.3	8.6	1.8	1.1
Kailahun	89.0	0.8	2.1	7.8

* Abbreviations in column heads stand for:
SLPP: Sierra Leone People's Party
APC: All People's Congress
PLP: Peace and Liberation Party
RUFP: Revolutionary United Front Party

than is typically recognized. Due in part to the local conditions and recruiting opportunities, select RUF cadres stationed throughout Kailahun evolved in a fundamentally different way than most others throughout the country. In stark contrast to the more forward camps (i.e., the westward bases approaching Freetown), the RUF established proper liberated zones characterized by relative stability and consistent interaction between the rebels and local populations.[124]

Away from the front lines of the war, the RUF was considerably more integrated into local communities. It built social service divisions that provided health care, education, and interest-free banking.[125] Various civilians also recall working on shared farms, the significance of which should not be understated. Not only did these farms help provide for the communities at a time when famine was rampant throughout the country, but, more importantly, the communal farms represent an instantiation of the RUF's agrarian ideology. According to Peters, the "rear" and more stable areas (such as Kailahun) also had more reliable and institutionalized mechanisms in place to help prevent civilian harassment. As such, the civilians in Kailahun saw a group not only rebelling against the state, but acting as an alternative.

> While in the RUF we made different types of farms: rice, yam, and swamp. We even made farms right inside Kailahun town. It was both the combatants and the civilians who made these farms. There is a big common farm which was aimed to promote unity among us. . . . The produce of the communal farm is for the betterment of the whole community.[126]
>
> We worked two times a week at the [RUF] farm in Pendembu, and sometimes we received food for work. Here in Pendembu there were free medicines, but not too much. There was also free primary education.[127]

Finally, RUF cadres in Kailahun had a higher retention of educated members due in large part to the contingent of recruits drawn from Bunumbu College. I argue that their retention of politically educated members, institutionalized liaisons with local communities, and lower propensity to engage in the wanton violence that came to characterize the RUF more broadly accounts for the significantly higher vote share for the RUFP from Kailahun as compared to the rest of the country.

Lessons from Renamo and the RUF

The divergent rebel-to-party experiences of Renamo and the RUF support my organizational theory of transformation on key dimensions. First and most broadly, these cases demonstrate that the theory travels outside of Latin America and can account as precisely for rebel-to-party failure as it can for success. Second, the analyses presented in this chapter provide additional tests of alternative explanations of rebel successor party formation. If ideology (particularly leftist ideology) were the driving force of both organizational structures and rebel-to-party success, we would have observed a robust proto-party legacy in the RUF. Similarly, if material wealth provided an independent advantage—rather than one mediated by the organizational structures through which it flows—the RUF still would have come out ahead.

Finally, both cases support the link between proto-party structures and postwar voter mobilization. While organizational structures do not necessarily translate into electoral appeal, the utility of proto-party structures transcends organizational boundaries. Beyond providing an anchor of stability in a volatile time, structures dedicated to governance, local administration, and social service provision enable the organization to forge the types of political linkages that are later conducive to political mobilization. The stark evidence of geographical distinctions in both Renamo's and the RUF's organizational development is telling. The capacity to convert wartime proto-party linkages to postwar party votes is as evident among successes as it is among failures.

ORGANIZATIONS WITHIN AND BEYOND REBELLIONS

This book set out to answer a single question: why are some rebel groups able to seamlessly transform into political parties while others falter?

The existing literature tells an intuitive story about how rebellions morph into parties. First, the fighting stops. Ceasefire agreements give way to negotiated settlements. More and more, settlements allow rebel groups to participate in electoral politics in the hopes of giving them incentives to drop their weapons for good. Finally, to continue their fight at the ballot box, rebel successor parties disarm, dismantle combat units, build party structures in their place, and mobilize voters to ensure their electoral success.[1]

This account, however, rests on two core assumptions about what militant organizations look like during war and what they can feasibly accomplish in its aftermath. An assumption of organizational homogeneity characterizes wartime structures as primarily combat-oriented, which, in turn, leads scholars look elsewhere for party-relevant skills. The next assumption—that transformation unfolds by building party structures from scratch—is the logical corollary to the previous one. Absent a usable legacy, scholars portray the preelection period as a scramble to dismember their organizations, hire skilled personnel, select candidates, and build party structures from the ground up.

Much like Italian cities, parties are not built in a day. Rebel-to-party transformation is a complex and protracted organizational process that unfolds over years and often begins long before the war ends. And the deeper we dig into the process, the more unanswered questions we find. How do rebels know what they need? What does the transformation process look like in practice? Once it starts the change, how does the organization survive it? Once it survives it, how does the party mobilize voters? When we consider rebel-to-party transformation for what it is—a massive organizational change—the questions are nearly endless, yet the answers are sparse.

My earliest attempts to get traction on these questions consistently led me back to the same insight: rebel-to-party transformation is an organizational phenomenon. Whether I was addressing the process of transformation, the group's transition into the electoral environment, its internal negotiations, or how it survived any of these outcomes in the first place, rebels' wartime organizational legacies always emerged in the answers.

This book took a novel approach to answering these questions by placing the militant organization at the center of the analysis. Beginning with a critical step back, I demonstrated that our existing organizational toolkit was ill equipped to even describe the groups at the heart of this phenomenon—let alone to theorize about how variation across rebellions affects postwar outcomes. I developed an organizational approach that forms the foundation of my theoretical and analytic framework. Taking an organizational approach yields a more accurate description of both militant organizations and the nature of the changes they must endure.

To make a convincing argument about the unique nature and effects of wartime structures, I began by accounting for their origins. The organizational approach first allowed me to predict and trace the origins of militant group structures. I expanded on the concept of organizational ideology to identify the distinct set of unified and consistent beliefs that govern militants' approach to rebellion. Resources, prewar networks, and doctrine are filtered through organizational frames, which in turn shape the structures rebels build.

Chapter 3's exploration of the FMLN's consolidation demonstrated that groups originating in the same doctrinal tradition can nonetheless exhibit vastly different organizational ideologies, which in turn give rise to fundamentally different organizational structures. This concept adds a new and critical dimension to existing frameworks accounting for other aspects of insurgent origins.

Building on these insights, I identified two variable features of militant groups that facilitate rebel-to-party transformation: one structural, one institutional. First, some groups construct proto-party structures: subdivisions built during war that mirror the core functions and forms of structures found in party organizations. Second, some groups develop traits that facilitate resilience: self-reflection, deference to expertise, and repertoires of flexibility. Proto-party structures imbue militant groups with relevant skills and routines needed to operate in legal politics. Resilience inoculates groups against the precarity of transformation. Together, these organizational features explain diverse outcomes in the face of equal opportunities.

Proto-party structures, in turn, beget a unique transformation strategy: repurposing analogous structures into the "new" party organization. This tack not only leads to a more efficient transformation but also mitigates the risks and challenges of building a party organization from scratch. I tested this hypothesis using within-case, comparative process tracing in three cases and further validated it with quantitative data. In the FMLN case, the subgroups with robust proto-party legacies exhibited a transformation process that tracks in lockstep with the repurposing hypothesis. The FPL, PCS, and PRTC not only directly place wartime subdivisions into related party roles but also made explicit reference to the postwar relevance of those subdivisions while they were still in the throes of conflict. Meanwhile, notwithstanding the ERP's size, influence, and military success throughout the war, its combat-centric structure proved to be its Achilles' heel when it came time to function as a party. Its process of party formation reflected the conventional portrayals of transformation in the rebel-to-party literature: hiring outside personnel and building new structures from scratch. Despite the formal arrangement decreeing that each group would have equal representation in the new party, I find that the ERP was marginalized to the point of separation, in large part because it had less to contribute to the organization's new objectives.

Finally, I demonstrated that proto-party structures also create distinct electoral advantages at the ballot stage. Specifically, groups with proto-party structures, by virtue of the diverse noncombat tasks they perform and their work beyond the conventionally understood boundaries of the organization, are able to forge politically salient linkages with local populations. While all militant organizations will have some relations with citizens, the nature of those relations can range from violent and extractive to symbiotic or even magnanimous. The organizational approach helps parse the nature—and implications—of different wartime relations with greater precision. I argue that linkages formed by providing governance, health care, education, and political messaging are especially conducive to political mobilization when it comes time for rebel successor parties to marshal votes. Both cross-national and subnational statistical tests provide support for this aspect of my theory. In the cross-national analysis, I demonstrated that proto-party structures more consistently predict successor parties' levels of integration than common explanations from the literature. The subnational tests leveraged municipal-level data on both the FMLN's different wartime strongholds and its postwar electoral performance. Crucially, I found comparable subnational evidence in both the RUF and the Renamo case. The results strongly support the mobilization hypothesis: municipalities occupied by

OP-Ms with robust proto-party structures during war voted for the rebel successor party at considerably higher rates than municipalities occupied by less politically diverse groups.

Together, the findings demonstrate that the formation and integration of rebel successor parties cannot be divorced from their wartime legacies. The organizational structures militant groups build during war vary considerably on unforeseen, yet crucial dimensions. Paying close attention to the variable diversity of roles and subdivisions within militant organizations adds color to a previously grayscale model.

Scholarly Implications

This book has several important implications for scholarship, all of which follow from the same question: What can we learn when we take organizations seriously? The answers to this question address and transcend our understanding of rebel-to-party transformation. This section identifies contributions and new avenues for research both within and beyond the conflict literature.

Rebel-to-Party Literature

At the most specific level, this book represents a number of important advancements in how we explain the formation, consolidation, and integration of rebel successor parties. Recasting the outcome as an organizational phenomenon reveals unforeseen challenges in the rebel-to-party process while simultaneously revealing the traits that enable some groups to overcome them. Future rebel-to-party studies—irrespective of their theoretical or analytic approaches—must account for the full scope of difficulty associated with transformation in order to provide a complete explanation of how it unfolds. Doing so forces us to look beyond conventional explanations, calling into question the plausibility of rebels timing their transformations to capitalize on military gains.

The book tests one of the central assumptions in the literature underlying the purported mechanism of transformation: that party building only begins once the war ends. In line with my theory, I demonstrate that this assumption, while sometimes valid, is highly variable. Only militant groups that did not build proto-party structures during war will take this approach to party formation. Parsing the different mechanisms of transformation—and the organizational roots of the respective mechanisms—lays an important foundation for future work aimed at further unpacking the power dynamics and internal negotiations of the different transformation processes. Furthermore, since party formation is only one type of organizational change militant groups undertake, this model of the transformation mechanism can shed light on a host of other outcomes that fall under the umbrella of "change." This framework lays the theoretical and analytic foundation for future work to explore the postwar formation of a wide variety of nongovernmental organizations as well as organized crime syndicates and joint policing forces.

Following from the previous contribution, the organizational approach provides more precise tools for specifying a mechanism of transformation. Rather than supplanting previous theories, this approach may illuminate previously unspecified mechanisms. Take, for example, the prewar party hypothesis: the theory that rebel groups born out of prewar political parties will be better equipped to reassemble parties at the war's end. Reevaluated under an organizational light, we might find that the salience of party legacies is less about an evergreen capacity to resurrect bygone party experience (which often occurred decades before the postconflict elections) and more about the types of organizations that former parties build when they transition to the battlefield.

Finally, building on an argument introduced in my 2024 article, the book elaborates on the distinction between transformation and transition. By distinguishing the internal organizational change and the environmental transition into electoral politics, future studies of rebel successor parties can more precisely identify the challenges and catalysts of the outcome they wish to engage. This distinction opens the door to asking new questions about the interplay between organizational change and electoral participation. The conceptual ambiguity is baked into the literature, but so too is the desire to better parse and measure the two outcomes. This need is no more clear than in the heading to Rachel M. Rudolph's conclusion to her discussion of Hamas's transition, which is titled, "A Successful Transition, but Will It Succeed?"[2] What at first glance looks like a tautology should instead be read as a call to distinguish between transformation, nominal transition, and long-term integration.

Taking these distinctions seriously allows us to ask important substantive questions as well. For example, if rebel successor parties are initially allotted seats by quota (as was the case of the new FARC party in Colombia), we can ask questions like, does this assisted transition into politics facilitate the organizational transformation(s) groups were ill equipped to make beforehand?[3] In short, does transition before transformation buy time or induce complacency? If indeed groups are better at consolidating party organizations once they are forced to govern, this result would suggest that negotiated settlements may better facilitate long-term stability by including early quota systems as part of the rebel-to-party provisions. However, the opposite may well be true. Introducing legislative quotas may disincentivize (or allow groups to procrastinate making) the type of radical changes needed to successfully participate in democratic processes.

Organizational Approaches to Conflict

Zooming out from the specific outcome at the heart of this book, I examine a few key areas of conflict research in which taking an organizational approach can shed new light on old questions. The scholarship dedicated to unpacking the microdynamics of civil war has a distinct behavioral focus: who chooses to join rebellions and why, when and under what conditions do rebellions forcibly recruit participants, how and when do rebels deploy different types of violence, and, more recently, how and when and why do they engage in behaviors beyond violence.[4] When do rebels govern, provide social services, or engage in international diplomacy? Important as these behaviors are, it is organization that makes both service provision and coordinated violence possible in the first place. The framework developed in this volume illuminates the organizational structures, institutions, and constraints undergirding the behaviors that characterize civil war. In so doing, it provides novel insights into the capacity for and variation in these behaviors and a newfound understanding of the sheer breadth of people whose behaviors we are trying to explain.

Outside of explaining rebel-to-party transformation, the book's most central contribution is a powerful set of tools for modeling rebel organizations and analyzing outcomes at the organizational level. The approach integrates disparate insights about rebel group behaviors into a unified framework for modeling rebels' organizational structures. Incorporating diversification and the types of subdivisions rebels build into our analyses of them allows scholars to gain new insight into groups' behaviors, recruitment profiles, and goals. In doing so, it reveals consequential dimensions along which groups differ from one another and opens the door to comparing and even categorizing militant organizations in new ways.

Moreover, the organizational approach has specific implications for how we use commonly invoked traits. Traits that describe the arrangement of roles or the nature of command-and-control institutions have been wielded in the absence of referents. Moving forward, the new framework forces us to specify the content of hierarchy, the locus of cohesion, and the dimension of capability, rather than applying those concepts to the organization as a whole without naming the structures or roles to which they refer. After all, it really only makes sense to discuss organizational capabilities in terms of the specific dimensions on which they are functioning. This approach, in turn, will yield more specific insights about variation both within and across groups. Finally, the Insurgent

Structures and Outcomes dataset lays the empirical groundwork to continue exploring both the causes and implications of varying wartime organizational structures among rebel groups.

One new avenue for research stems from one of the central questions in the rebel-to-party literature: How do violent rebels become good democrats? This question wrestles with the presumed gulf between those who participate in rebellion and those who staff party organizations. Conventional explanations of participation in rebellion tend toward broad-strokes dichotomies: the greedy or the aggrieved, the opportunists or the ideologues.[5] These motivations may be accurate, but they do little to bridge the participatory divide. However, when we consider participation in light of the diversity of rebels' organizational structures, the next logical step is to probe the diversity of people they recruit to staff them. What skills is a given group seeking? Are they looking for fighters or writers? The answer is more often the latter than previous work suggests. Yet, when we think about the participants who are recruited for their résumés— rather than their lethality—the gap between "rebel" and "politician" becomes imminently traversable.

Crucially, the motivating question is pertinent beyond the rebel-to-party inquiry. Armed with a more comprehensive understanding of how militant organizations vary, we can approach the study of recruitment and participation at a more nuanced level. As I demonstrated in both the FMLN case and the Renamo case, recruitment profiles are a function of both the organization into which members are being recruited and the broader political and socio-economic context in which the organization operates. In the case of the FMLN, a marginal opening of the political landscape led to some of the OP-Ms targeting participation from people who worked in industry or labor organizations. In the case of Renamo, we observed a shift toward high-skilled recruits (to the extent that was possible) when the group switched to an autonomous funding model. Moving forward, this framework can be leveraged to parse a broader range of recruitment profiles, which in turn may shed light on other important wartime dynamics.

Another natural extension of this project is to apply organizational approaches to the study of rebel governance. Specifically, examining rebel governance through an organizational lens allows us to take what is conventionally understood as a behavioral outcome and reframe it as an organizational one. After all, the routinized administration of local populations or provision of social services is impossible without dedicated subdivisions to support these activities. Of course, these frames are not mutually exclusive. Rebels who govern *do* behave differently than rebels who do not. However, understanding governance as an organizational outcome can provide insight into the types of structures rebels build to support governance activities, who they recruit into those structures, and how those structures are situated within the broader organization.

Related to its contributions to the rebel governance literature, the book raises important questions about the intersection of organizational structure and territorial control. In the FMLN case work, I revealed that the group with the strongest territorial stronghold was unable to convert its wartime capacity to administer territory into the type of postwar mobilization we are often led to expect.[6] Moving forward, careful specification of organizational subdivisions can provide scholars a more precise and direct indication of armed groups' governance capacity. In doing so, this approach would allow us to move away from proxies for governance (like territorial control) and toward a set of indicators that captures both the strength and nature of governance tasks. By divorcing governance from territorial control, scholars could move toward a broader typology of rebel governance strategies, including the variety of governance tasks that take place in urban areas.

Following from the application to rebel governance, the organizational approach developed in this volume can be used to bridge two emerging trends in civil war research: wartime orders and the local dynamics of rebellion. A wealth of recent scholarship has illuminated the variety of wartime political orders that characterize interactions between rebels, states, and civilians.[7] Noting that civil war is often characterized by a mix of violence, coordination, and cooperation, scholars in this tradition elucidate the wide scope of rebel-state (or rebel-civilian) interactions. In a related tradition, scholars like Ana Arjona and Séverine Autesserre have demonstrated the utility of taking subnational institutional dynamics of civil war into account.[8] A significant part of this manuscript is built on evidence of subnational geographical variation in wartime structures and the analytic tools for studying it. While the application here was limited to modeling structures conducive to rebel-to-party transformation, the approach can be extended to illuminate how different local structures give rise to different wartime orders. Alternately, we may find that the causal arrow is reversed, at which point we can ask whether the intention to build different wartime orders requires different organizational structures to manage them.

This line of research would provide both scholars and practitioners newfound insight into the local dynamics of civil war. Understanding how groups are structured differently across different regions can, in turn, shed light on both wartime and postwar phenomena. For example, scholars have established that patterns of violence against noncombatants often differ across space within the same rebellion. A nuanced understanding of local organizational structures may help elucidate how and why rebels organize violence differently in different regions. Insights on local organizational variation during war will likely have equally important implications for postwar dynamics as well. Different wartime organizational structures may explain why demobilization and reintegration are more difficult in some places than others, where the risks of remobilization and conflict resurgence are most salient, and why we see local variation in postconflict development.

The final contribution to the conflict literature is a revamped understanding of militant group ideology. Chapter 1 expounded on the concept of *organizational ideology* to capture the unified principles of conflict that arise when a broad ideology is filtered through an organizational body. In this book, I leveraged the concept of organizational ideology to explain how groups with similar doctrinal bents can harbor very different approaches to organization building and conflict. Specifically, organizational ideology helped parse unanswered questions about why groups with similar ideologies that emerged in the context of similar prewar networks with similar resource endowments nevertheless built very different organizational structures.

Combined with a more thorough understanding of militant organizational structures, organizational ideology can help scholars get newfound traction on the various ways ideology guides and manifests in rebel groups. Specifically, this concept can provide a template for understanding the structure, institutions, decision making, and goals of armed organizations. As such, organizational ideology builds a conceptual bridge between the tractable, yet often blunt, concept of ideology and the more comprehensive, yet elusive, concept of organizational culture.

Zooming out from conflict studies, an additional contribution of this research is that it brings the postconflict literature into more direct conversation with the party formation and democratization literatures. By centering preparty organizational structures, the book's core approach can answer elusive questions in both traditions. In the first place, patterns in rebel successor party formation can and should be integrated into the broader party formation literature. A lot of ink has been spilled on tracing extant party systems back to their origins in entrenched social cleavages, revolutionary groups, religious organizations, or labor and trade unions.[9] Yet, for every party traceable to a social movement or cleavage, we are left with dozens of movements that do *not* develop into parties—either because they never try, or because they try and fail. As Henry Hale astutely notes, "Many outstanding works on the formation of party systems tend to treat the 'pre-party period' as a shapeless transitional phase."[10] By identifying the pretransition structures that make the transformation from rebel group into party organization more likely, this book helps gives shape to the transitional phase and highlights new paths to party formation.

As a corollary, by getting traction on success and failure in party formation, this framework also has important implications for what we know about
democratic transition. Postconflict democratization is an especially high-stakes
outcome.[11] Despite the wide acceptance that democracy is untenable without
political parties—and more specifically, without *strong* parties—scholars of democratic transition rarely acknowledge that party failure in transitional periods
could result in a party system lacking in true competition. We can only learn so
much about postconflict democratization without accounting for the players in
the new political system.

The fact of the matter is that the lion's share of the party formation literature
was not written on (or for) postconflict societies. The insights derived in this
book have critical implications for postconflict democratic transition. Unsuc-
cessful rebel-to-party transition—that is, total failure or even becoming a party
in name only—can leave a group's competitor(s) with effective monopolies over
power in government, potentially giving rise to a de facto autocracy and even
re-creating the conditions that incited the conflict. Insights from this book can
help scholars get traction on where democracy is more or less likely to take root
across postconflict societies.

Finally, the organizational approach I propose lays the descriptive and analytic
foundation for studying political organizations beyond the battlefield. Organizations are the core of political order. Everything from the smallest social movements all the way up to states themselves function more reliably and predictably
to the extent that they develop "formalized roles and procedures for enforcing
their rules."[12] Any time collective action is routinized, organizational approaches
can help us get traction on its dynamics.

Until recently, however, political science has had a limited vocabulary of organizations and we have used that vocabulary in the absence of a syntax: the rules
for how different traits combine to give rise to different outcomes. The conceptual and analytic building blocks laid out in chapter 1 help fill in these linguistic
gaps: how to describe organizations, how to model organizational outcomes, how
the same trait can be helpful or harmful depending on what the group needs to
achieve. Additionally—as we saw with rebel-to-party transformation—organizational approaches can reveal new questions (and answers) when applied to
familiar problems at the core of our discipline.

For one among countless examples, consider regime change. In political science, at least, regime change is the organizational transformation par excellence:
an overhaul in leadership, institutions, operations, and goals. Yet, we rarely
describe or study it as such. The result is an intellectual divide between scholars
who take voluntaristic approaches—emphasizing the role of elite actors—and
scholars who focus on the role of macrostructural constraints.[13] However, a

state is no less an organization than a militant group—and regimes, therefore, are states' operational and organizing principles. Understanding regime transition in terms of organizational change can yield new insights about the internal microdynamics that govern and constrain change. This approach can add nuance to the work explaining where and why we observe institutional continuity.[14] It can explain the trends and implications of transitioning personnel from the *ancien regime* into new roles in the regime's successor. It can reveal new dynamics in our understanding of how party organizations change contemporaneously to accommodate regime overhauls.[15]

Policy Implications

Beyond its implications for past and future scholarship, the research presented here can provide key insights into some of the most pressing and intractable problems of global and regional security. Each academic contribution enumerated here has a corresponding implication for policy.

Armed with a framework capable of assessing rebels' prospects for successful transformation, policy makers can construct tailored negotiated settlements. For groups with promising postwar trajectories, settlements may be constructed with an eye toward facilitating the transformation and transition processes. Providing additional resources to the nascent successor party may help tip the balance toward party survival, thereby attenuating the risk of conflict recurrence or de facto one-party systems. Alternately, for groups lacking in key areas that make party formation and integration a likely outcome, settlements can be constructed to dedicate more resources to demobilization and other contingencies to reduce the likelihood of a return to conflict. For example, earmarking resources for job training, land allotments, resettlement, or education may help ensure that demobilized and disintegrated members have a tenable path to societal integration if political integration is outside the group's reach.

The second policy implication suggests a ground-up reimagining of disarmament, demobilization, and reintegration (DDR) programs. Although we can trace the origins of DDR programs back to the broader social, political, and economic vision of United Nations peace-building missions, DDR processes themselves have a narrow focus: disarming warring factions, decommissioning senior military personnel, and "breaking command and control" structures.[16] In short, DDR programs are aimed at removing soldiers from battlefields. Yet, in light of the organizational insights in the preceding pages, the question is, how do we square a policy aimed at soldiers with an organization that comprises so much more?

An artificially narrow view of militant organizations leads to a narrow understanding of who participates in them, which in turn gives rise to narrow policy directives for demobilizing those participants at the war's end. Ultimately, practitioners are not talking about what it means to demobilize or reintegrate members who occupy the host of noncombat roles that are just as essential to rebellion. As I have demonstrated, these individuals comprise wings that specialize in administration, communication, and outreach. Thus, when our postconflict policies treat all former rebels as though they are all former *soldiers*, these policies disregard the people who may retain the greatest capacity to remobilize former members after the war has ended.

If we think back to the FMLN—in which a significant number of leaders hailed from professional posts and their wartime roles transcended the military domain—it becomes clear that providing a path to integration into the state military or police forces would do little to incentivize DDR participation for people who still have university jobs. Understanding the variable diversification of militant organizations can illuminate new—and nuanced—policy options for postconflict reintegration. Looking ahead, reconstructed DDR policies should take into account wartime roles and not just wartime ranks.

When we consider this open policy problem in light of the established heterogeneity in local wartime dynamics, this insight may shed light on why demobilization and reintegration are more difficult in some places than others. Together, these insights may help policy makers identify areas where the risks of remobilization and conflict resurgence are most salient.

Furthermore, taking local organizational variation seriously can yield more nuanced counterinsurgency policy. Understanding the variation in wartime orders between rebels and local populations is critical if state forces are expecting to leverage civilian cooperation. Building on and applying the organizational and relational insights in this manuscript can help practitioners identify a priori where these strategies are more likely to succeed.

Finally, the book's descriptive insights about militant organizational diversity also have implications for how policy makers understand and address rebel groups' recruitment profiles. A central aim in counterinsurgency strategy is to cut off participation at its source. Conventional portrayals of militant organizations, however, lead practitioners to identify a narrow source of potential recruits. For example, it is common to see crackdowns on youth groups and radical student associations. Yet, structurally diverse militant groups will be recruiting for a wider array of roles. As such, understanding the scope of recruits (and skill sets) a given organization is seeking can yield a more nuanced approach to forestalling recruitment.

From Rebellions to Parties

This book offers a novel solution to a long-standing puzzle: how do violent rebels become good democrats? Parsing the question further revealed that it is not merely about accounting for the sequence by which rebel groups move from the battlefield to the ballot. After all, given the prevalence of electoral participation provisions, making a ballot appearance in the first postconflict election is not especially puzzling at all. As long as groups disarm and agree on a slate of candidates, much of the work is done for them. What I wanted to know instead was how a coalition of sometimes loosely bound militants becomes something so different from what they once were that political scientists rarely study the two types of actors in the same classroom.

The scale of change involved in rebel-to-party transformation would turn the heads of even the most optimistic organizational sociologists. Yet, they are the ones who bring a decades-long legacy of modeling organizational change, so I started my investigation with their tools. Taking an organizational approach led me to break from the conventional wisdom about what rebels do and how they are structured to do it. I showed that when we focus on the structures that produce violence to the exclusion of the structures that function in noncombat domains during war, we overlook important dynamics that affect both wartime and postwar outcomes.

Breaking from convention, however, is never costless. A colleague who read an early version of the manuscript said to me, "This is an interesting insight about rebel groups, but where's the violence?" It was one of those unfortunate deer-in-the-headlight moments that punctuate every research process. And I am certain that at the time I provided an unsatisfying answer. After all, violence is a (or *the*) defining feature of conflict studies, and the evidence in this book is skewed heavily to illustrate the diversity of structures that often—though not always—exist beyond the armed forces. So, if my civil war book wasn't about violence, was it even a civil war book? At the risk of indulging staircase wit, I conclude the book with the real answer.

Violence is neither absent from nor inconsequential to this narrative. Rather, the theory and findings demonstrate how much more we can learn when we stop focusing exclusively on how groups organize violence and begin focusing on how they organize, period. In doing so, we glean a more complete picture of how groups' technologies and repertoires of violence dovetail with their other decisions and activities. While breaking from convention may come at a price, the tools we get in exchange can push the field forward on many dimensions. We can learn about how groups justify and advertise violence in their propaganda; we can learn about how groups recruit and whether (or for which roles) recruitment itself is a violent or coercive act. We can learn about how rebel successor parties mobilize voters from communities beset by violence during wartime and the extent to which nonviolent relations with former rebels weighs more heavily in their electoral calculations. Violence remains central to civil war studies. What I have shown here is that we can get a more incisive understanding of the dynamics of violence if we understand how rebel groups are structured beyond that.

Notes

INTRODUCTION

1. Mitton 2008, 202.
2. This definition draws directly from Parkinson and Zaks 2018.
3. Kay Cohen 2013; Saul 2013; Gilligan, Samii, and Mvukiyehe 2012; Schwartz 2019; Stedman 1997; Fortna 2003; Collier, Hoeffler, and Söderbom 2008; Daly 2016.
4. Martin, Piccolino, and Speight 2022; Themnér 2015; Daly 2016.
5. Allison 2010; Marshall and Ishiyama 2016; Matanock 2017a.
6. Zaks 2024.
7. On dismantling combat units, see de Zeeuw 2008, 12, and Söderberg Kovacs and Hatz 2016. On reformulating decision-making structures, see Manning 2004, 2007; de Zeeuw 2008; and Sindre 2016b. On restructuring finances, see Manning 2007, 256. On recruiting candidates, see Manning 2004, 59. On building party structures, see de Zeeuw 2008, 13. On adapting to the postconflict environment, see Manning 2007, 255.
8. Close and Prevost 2007; de Zeeuw 2008.
9. According to Michael T. Hannan and John Freeman, "the process of dismantling one structure and building another" threatens internal legitimacy and destabilizes organizations (1984, 149, 159). Even scholars who are more optimistic about the prospects of organizational change would express skepticism when the new requirements depart sharply from existing skill sets (Haveman 1992, 1993a).
10. Hannan and Freeman 1984, 156. See also Amburgey, Kelly, and Barnett 1993.
11. Hannan and Freeman 1984.
12. For example, Gyda M. Sindre notes that "former rebel parties have to adjust to the procedural rules of multi-party democracy" (2016a, 196). Similarly, Manning asks, "What factors influence [rebel] parties' decisions to adapt to or subvert the rules?" (2007, 55). See also Acosta 2014.
13. Staniland 2014, 38.
14. As James G. March argues, organizations "rarely change in a way that fulfills the intention of a particular group of actors" (1981, 563). And when they try, we often observe "weak relations between intentions and outcomes" (Hannan and Freeman 1989, 22–23).
15. de Zeeuw 2008; Söderberg Kovacs and Hatz 2016; Acosta 2014; Matanock 2018.
16. Allison 2006; Manning and Smith 2019.
17. Allison 2006; Klapdor 2009.
18. Daly 2022.
19. On prewar party experience, see Wade 2008, 46; de Zeeuw 2008; and Manning and Smith 2016, 984. On centralization and cohesion in the organization, see Söderberg Kovacs 2007; Rudolph 2008; Klapdor 2009; Ishiyama and Batta 2011a; and Holland 2016. On convertible capabilities, see Dresden 2017. On wartime territorial control, see Allison 2010; Ishiyama and Widmeier 2013. On resource endowments, see Manning 2002, 108; Allison 2006; Wade 2008; Klapdor 2009.
20. Nelson and Winter 1982, 134.
21. As Scott Somers argues, while managers need control over their employees, "highly bureaucratized, command-and-control style structures impede creativity and adaptive behavior" (2009, 13).

22. Levitsky 2003, 28.

23. Allison 2010; Ishiyama and Widmeier 2013; Dresden 2017.

24. Hannan and Freeman 1989, 6.

25. Sarah Zukerman Daly (2016) observes similar problems with resources vis-à-vis conflict recurrence—namely, a group's latent mobilizational capacity mediates the effectiveness with which resources are leveraged should the group wish to reassemble.

26. For other examples of this approach, see Staniland 2014 and Parkinson 2016, 2022.

27. *Sobre los Problemas Mas Agudos en la Estructura de las MPL Según Apreciaciones de María del Organismo del PPL* (FPL, approx. 1984e).

28. Wantchekon and Neeman 2002.

29. Hannan and Freeman 1977, 957.

30. Panebianco 1988, 3; Parkinson and Zaks 2018.

31. For a review of the organizational trajectory in civil war research, see Parkinson and Zaks 2018.

32. On patterns of violence and restraint, see Hoover Green 2018. On wartime resilience, see Parkinson 2013, 2022. On fragmentation, see Bakke, Cunningham, and Seymour 2012. On conflict resurgence, see Daly 2012, 2016. On rebel-to-party transformation, see Lyons 2016; Ishiyama and Widmeier 2019.

33. The first three questions draw from Barnett and Carroll 1995.

34. Haveman 1993b.

35. On governing civilians, see Huang 2016b; Stewart 2021. On providing social services, see Heger and Jung 2016.

36. Parkinson 2013; Staniland 2014.

37. This distinction is first drawn explicitly in Zaks 2024.

38. Huang 2016b.

39. These propositions draw on Anna Grzymala-Busse's exploration of how the legacies of communist successor parties affect their post-democratization party structure (2002, 21).

40. Of course, some transnational groups may have local offshoots, whose aim is confined to a specific country. In these cases, the local offshoot would fall within the bounds of the theory.

41. This criterion may seem overly simplistic, yet at least two datasets with rebel-to-party variables omit this condition. As a result, groups like al-Qaeda Somalia are coded as rebel-to-party failures even though party formation was illegal in Somalia for the years the dataset covers (Matanock 2016).

42. Drawing on the Uppsala Conflict Data Program's definition of armed conflict, a civil war is "a contested incompatibility that concerns government and/or territory where the use of armed force between two parties, of which at least one is the government of a state, results in at least 25 battle-related deaths in one calendar year" (Gleditsch et al. 2002; Petterson 2023).

43. de Zeeuw 2008; Klapdor 2009; Söderberg Kovacs and Hatz 2016; Holland 2016.

44. Kenneth A. Bollen observes a similar problem with measures embedding "stability" in "democracy" (1980, 375).

45. Then, of course, there are groups on the margins, like the Sandinistas in Nicaragua. Here, the Sandinista National Liberation Front (FSLN) only briefly transitioned into a one-party state following a military victory. Soon thereafter, however, they opened up the political system and successfully competed in local and national elections.

46. This approach takes inspiration from what Amelia Hoover Green calls "institutional biographies," which focused on education and disciplinary institutions within the movement (2018, 19).

47. Parkinson 2021, 59. Parkinson develops this concept to refer to the disjuncture between how political scientists conceive of and ask about *ideology* and how people in militant organizations conceive of it outside of the simplified left-right spectrum.

48. Regarding who joins rebellions and why, see Berman et al. 2011; Humphreys and Weinstein 2008. Regarding forcibly recruiting participants, see Eck 2014. For how and when rebels deploy different forms of violence, see Weinstein 2007; Gutiérrez-Sanín and Wood 2014. On when and why rebels engage in behaviors beyond violence, see Mampilly 2011; Arjona 2016.

49. Huntington 1968; Panebianco 1988; Katz and Mair 1993; Grzymala-Busse 2002; Levitsky 2003; Weinstein 2007; Daly 2012.

1. AN ORGANIZATIONAL THEORY OF TRANSFORMATION

1. Parkinson and Zaks 2018.

2. de Zeeuw 2008, 13.

3. Gonzalez 2018, 4.

4. The PCS was banned from elections after the insurrection in 1932, and since political organizing was banned, the group was forced into a clandestine existence for nearly five decades (Montgomery 1995).

5. Bracamonte and Spencer 1995; Montgomery 1995, 52; Viterna 2013, 250.

6. *Veredas de la Audacia: Historia del FMLN* (Cienfuegos 1986). Emphasis added.

7. For accounts of the group's emergence and the political context surrounding it, see Pearce 1986; Bracamonte and Spencer 1995; Montgomery 1995; Byrne 1996; Binford 2004; Wood 2000, 2003; Hoover Green 2018; and Sprenkels 2018.

8. Bracamonte and Spencer 1995; de Zeeuw 2008, 9.

9. Hoover Green 2018, 59.

10. McClintock 1998, 90.

11. Montgomery 1995, 105; Binford 1997, 57.

12. Binford 1997, 57. In a document titled *Aproximación a la Historia del PRTC*, Nidia Díaz (2006), one of the founders of the PRTC, describes the organization in these terms. This was a turn of phrase she used both during and after the war to describe the FMLN leadership (Viterna 2013, 250).

13. Aldrich 1995.

14. Panebianco 1988, 6.

15. This definition draws on and modifies the Uppsala Conflict Data Program definition of "opposition organizations" (2021).

16. This condition does not exclude rebels who hold extralegal elections in captured territory. While rebel-held elections may indicate groups' willingness to *become* legal parties, these organizations are distinct from groups operating as militants and parties concurrently.

17. Sartori 1976, 54.

18. Shugart 1992, 122; de Zeeuw 2008, 5; Acosta 2014, 671; Manning and Smith 2016, 973; Söderberg Kovacs and Hatz 2016, 7; and Matanock 2016, Appendix, 2, all use this definition.

19. John Ishiyama and Anna Batta argue that "durable peace settlements require the active involvement and cooperative engagement of these political groups" (2011a, 369). Marshall and Ishiyama argue that "the inclusion and participation of former rebel parties in national government" is the mechanism by which transition fosters stability (2016, 1009). Manning and Smith ask "under what conditions are rebel groups successfully incorporated into democratic politics?" (2016, 972). Matanock notes the importance of "bringing armed actors into normal politics" (2018, 656).

20. On rebel groups, see Petersen 2001; Weinstein 2007; Pearlman 2011; Parkinson 2013; Balcells and Justino 2014; Staniland 2014. On parties, see Huntington 1968; Panebianco 1988; Katz and Mair 1993; Mair 1994; Grzymala-Busse 2002; Levitsky 2003.

21. Mampilly 2011, 6.

22. Díaz 1982–1984.

23. Wendy Pearlman, for example, argues that fragmented movements "lack leadership, institutions, and collective purpose," whereas cohesive movements "enjoy the organizational power to mobilize mass participation, enforce strategic discipline, and contain disruptive dissent" (2011, 2). See also Staniland 2012; Daly 2016, 16; and Balcells 2017, 64.

24. Ishiyama and Batta 2011a.

25. Hannan and Freeman 1984, 155; Haveman 1993b; Somers 2009.

26. Mintzberg 1979, 12.

27. Söderberg Kovacs 2007; Klapdor 2009; Ishiyama and Batta 2011a; Pearlman 2011; Bakke, Cunningham, and Seymour 2012; Staniland 2014.

28. Jeremy M. Weinstein, for example, asks "under what conditions rebel organizations will take on tasks of governance" (2007, 38). Additionally, Reyko Huang's theory of civilian mobilization argues that when rebels "depend heavily on civilian inputs" during the war, they "lay down extensive roots to draw on material and moral support," which results in popular mobilization and, eventually, democracy (2016b, 29). Even more directly, Cunningham, Huang, and Sawyer begin their article with the following: "Rebel actors engage in a number of behaviors beyond violent conflict, including social service provision, diplomacy, and establishing local governance" (2021, 81).

29. Zachariah Cherian Mampilly's definition of *governance system* is one of few that acknowledge the duality of organization and behavior. He defines rebel governance as "not only the structures that provide certain public goods but also the practices of rule insurgents adopt" (2011, 4).

30. Barnett and Carroll 1995.

31. de Zeeuw 2008.

32. Mintzberg 1979, 2.

33. A few notable exceptions are Petersen 2001, 2010; and Parkinson 2013. Roger D. Petersen observes that "a great deal of variation exists in the types of roles that individuals come to play during sustained rebellion" (2001, 8). Abdulkader H. Sinno, too, notes that "specialized subgroups within organizations" are one of the core components of structure (2010, 35). One of the core contributions of Parkinson's work is the compound insight that the variety of noncombat roles and relations present in rebel groups are not only more elaborate than what is typically acknowledged, but also that the subdivisions dedicated to logistical and support tasks often become the linchpin of organizational survival in times of crisis. Finally, as Ralph Sprenkels notes, "In-depth research demonstrates that insurgencies tend to covertly tie together multiple groups and individuals with an amalgam of roles, interweaving political, social, military, and economic aspects" (2018, 31).

34. Parkinson and Zaks 2018, 273.

35. I use *subdivisions* and *wings* interchangeably throughout the manuscript to refer to collective divisions within organizations. Though some do, I do not use *institution* as a synonym for *subdivisions*. I reserve the concept of institution to refer to the rules that structure relations and behavior within organizations.

36. Reyko Huang draws a crucial parallel distinction in her discussion of wartime extortion, arguing that "sporadic acts of extortion" should not be expected if rebels rely primarily on local populations for support (2016b, 32). Instead, we should expect them to build institutions "to regularize the process."

37. Parkinson and Zaks 2018, 274.

38. With few exceptions, the nature of these connections is neither specified nor questioned. The most notable counterexamples are Paul Staniland's work, which critically examines the role of prewar social networks in the formation of militant organizations (2014), and Sarah Parkinson's work, which finds that organizational resilience and other crucial outcomes are attributable to kinship relations, rumor networks, and other quotidian connections between individuals that tend to be overlooked in analyses of conflict (2013, 2016).

39. Wood (2003), Mampilly (2011), and Parkinson (2013) are some of the earlier examples of scholarship that go beyond such conventional portrayals. More recently, the rebel governance literature implicitly takes up questions of external relations. See Arjona 2016; Huang 2016a; Mampilly and Stewart 2021. On the production and type of violence between rebels and civilians, see Kalyvas 2006; Humphreys and Weinstein 2006; Weinstein 2007. On the lack thereof, see Hoover Green 2018.

40. See Parkinson 2013, 2016; Christia 2014; Staniland 2014; Huang 2016b; and Dresden 2017.

41. Horne and Orr 1998, 30; Sutcliffe and Vogus 2003.

42. Sewell 1992; Haveman 1993b; Sutcliffe and Vogus 2003.

43. Vogus and Sutcliffe 2007, 342; Somers 2009, 13; Minkoff 1999.

44. Katz and Mair 1993, 594–595.

45. Katz and Mair 1993, 596–597.

46. Scott and Davis 2007, 35.

47. Stinchcombe 1965.

48. Allison 2010; Ishiyama and Widmeier 2013; Dresden 2017.

49. To be clear, I make a distinction between the origins of rebels' organizational structures and the antecedents to civil war. I'm not asking why rebel groups emerge, I'm asking why they are structured the way they are—given that they have incentives to emerge. Of course, some of these might be related; and some scholars treat them as the same question. James Fearon and David Laitin (2003), for example, attribute both the mobilization of the insurgency and its wartime structure to the environmental and political conditions of the state in which it emerges.

50. Notable exceptions are Gates 2002; Weinstein 2007; Parkinson 2013; and Staniland 2014.

51. On ideology, see Selznick 1952; Huntington 1968; Eck 2007; Thaler 2012; Kalyvas 2015; Mampilly 2011; Stewart 2021. On state context, see Skocpol 1979. Theda Skocpol argues that state breakdowns are necessary conditions for peasant revolution. Revolutionaries and scholars alike argue that geological features are critical to sustaining rebellion (see, for example, Guevara [1961] 2006 and Gates 2002). Similarly, Fearon and Laitin argue that state characteristics shape "the political and military technology of the insurgency" (2003, 81). Indeed, FMLN leaders noted that some of their initial difficulty in securing funding was because no one believed a flat country like El Salvador could sustain a revolution. According to Fermán Cienfuegos, early negotiations always turned to the question, "Where are the mountains?" (Cienfuegos 1986). On resource endowments, see Weinstein 2007; Humphreys and Weinstein 2008; Lidow 2016. On prewar social networks, see Kaufman 1985. Herbert Kaufman notes the broad importance of social networks in shaping organizational structure (94). Doug McAdam, Sidney Tarrow, and Charles Tilly (2001) argue that mobilization is highly contingent on whether "would-be" activists are able to "socially appropriate" existing networks in service of organizational goals. See also Daly (2012, 474) and Staniland (2014, 23–33).

52. On patterns of violence, see Gutiérrez-Sanín and Wood 2014; Maynard 2019. On recruitment practices, see Gutiérrez-Sanín and Wood 2014; Wood and Thomas 2017.

On quotidian interactions and socialization, see Moro 2017; Parkinson 2021. On claim making, see Gutiérrez-Sanín and Wood 2014. On adopted institutions, see Schubiger and Zelina 2017.

53. Moro 2017, 945. The corollary, of course, is that early decisions have powerful and lasting impacts. See Pierson 2000, 253.

54. Staniland 2014, 23.

55. Consider, for example Newtonian mechanics. Newton's laws (and the variables constituting them) work well much of the time, but they break at both the subatomic level and as matter approaches the speed of light because the variables operate differently at these different levels.

56. Though used for more specific purposes, Suykens (2015, 139) advances a similar argument in his discussion of "governance ideology," which he defines as "how rebel groups understand the nature of their rebellion, their relations to the territory they operate in and to the civilians present in it." As such, Suykens is one of few who explicitly integrate local context with broad principles to explain how rebels organize.

57. Parkinson 2021, 52.

58. In the early days of the rebellion, the nascent movement "rallied a number of radical intellectuals with a Green Book background" (Richards and Vincent 2008, 83).

59. Interview quoted in Peters 2011, 93.

60. Abdullah and Muana 1998.

61. Staniland 2014.

62. Weinstein 2007, 37.

63. Mampilly 2011; Parkinson 2013.

2. ORGANIZATIONAL ORIGINS OF THE FMLN

1. This figure draws on "Veredas de la Audacia: Historia del FMLN" (Cienfuegos 1986) as well as Dunkerley 1982, 302–3; Montgomery 1995, 102; McClintock 1998; and Sprenkels 2018, 55.

2. On mass organizations, see Wood 2003, chap. 6. On OP-Ms, see Bracamonte and Spencer 1995; McClintock 1998, 52.

3. In an early PRTC document, *En Cerros de San Pedro*, the author (Ernesto Flores) describes an event in which the RN "conquered" some PRTC members and stole cattle and other supplies from their trade routes (Flores 1983).

4. The first move in this vein came in 1856 with a law mandating that two-thirds of all communal lands (both *tierras comunales* and *ejidos*) be planted with coffee; failure to comply would result in state seizure of the land (Montgomery 1995, 30). Then, in the early 1880s, the state outlawed *tierras comunales* and *ejidos* while simultaneously ramping up enforcement of vagrancy laws (Wood 2000, 28).

5. Wade 2018, 397; Paige 1997, 107.

6. Unsurprisingly, estimates vary widely. Wood (2001, 31) and others contend that the number is about seventeen thousand; Montgomery (1995, 37) puts the number closer to thirty thousand. The ten thousand to forty thousand range is cited in a number of journalistic and encyclopedic accounts, but without references.

7. Wood 2000, 31.

8. Wood 2000, 32. Moreover, between 1950 and 1960, the membership of the National Guard swelled at an estimated rate of 3,500 recruits per year, which amounts to 1 recruit for every 714 citizens (Walter and Williams 1993, 47). To put this number in context, the recruitment rate of the US armed forces amounts to 1 recruit for every 4,050 citizens.

9. Montgomery 1995, 39; Wood 2000, 32.

10. As of the mid-1960s, the PCS was estimated to have approximately two hundred members (Benjamin and Kautsky 1968, 122).

11. Staniland 2014, 21.

12. Hammond 1999, 70.

13. Montgomery 1995, 87.

14. Hammond 1999, 74.

15. Montgomery 1995, 89. *Campesino* is a self-referential term referring to El Salvador's rural poor. They often work in the agricultural sector, but as others have noted, the term itself does not translate well (Wood 2003, 5). As such, I use *campesino* throughout to refer to the people, and eventually, the collectives they built.

16. Hammond 1999, 74.

17. In 1975, 48.9 percent of men and 57.2 percent of women in rural areas were reported to be illiterate (*Statistical Abstract of Latin America* 1987).

18. Hammond 1999, 72.

19. According to Montgomery, more than fifteen thousand campesinos were trained as community leaders through church programs (1995, 89).

20. Bracamonte and Spencer 1995, 2.

21. Carpio's objective in coining this term was to highlight the balance between political and military work in what he called "a new type of Marxist-Leninist party." He wanted the balance between political and military engagement to be as explicit as possible (Harnecker 1983, 87).

22. Harnecker 1983, 84. Marcial was Carpio's nom de guerre. In the interview transcript, all leaders are referred to by their pseudonyms.

23. Bracamonte and Spencer 1995, 2.

24. Interview with the PCS leader Schafik Hándal (Harnecker 1983, 73).

25. Bracamonte and Spencer 1995; Montgomery 1995, 52.

26. Montgomery 1995, 110. The General Command—originally called the Unified Revolutionary Directorate—was the five-man decision-making body of the FMLN, which comprised the leaders of each OP-M.

27. Selznick 1952, 15; Huntington 1968, 336.

28. This fact gives rise to an additional and highly consequential problem. For groups that espouse other, less organizationally focused ideologies, mapping their belief systems onto structures will thus be a considerably more difficult task. Thus, even if it performs well here, ideology likely has heterogeneous utility for explaining organizational outcomes.

29. Gates 2002, 113; Fearon and Laitin 2003, 81; Arjona 2014; Wickham-Crowley 2015.

30. However, making more fine-grained predictions about suborganizational variation requires that we identify and define structural variation within state borders.

31. Horowitz, Perkoski, and Potter 2018, 141.

32. Weinstein 2007; Humphreys and Weinstein 2008.

33. Bracamonte and Spencer 1995, 16.

34. According to Bracamonte and Spencer (1995, 177), Farid Hándal (the brother of the PCS leader Shafik Hándal) went on "a world tour" securing funds from "the United States, the Soviet Union, Czechoslovakia, Bulgaria, East Germany, Algeria, Libya, Ethiopia, and Vietnam."

35. Sprenkels 2018, 366.

36. Hoover Green 2016, 26.

37. Chalatenango and Morazán are departments—roughly comparable to states—in El Salvador. Both are quite poor, both are dominated by agricultural labor, and both were primary targets of liberation theology in prior decades.

38. The organizational salience of the Christian base communities was as apparent to the rebels as it was to the scholars who studied them. Countless internal memoranda speak to the central role of religious sectors. In an FPL document detailing the growth and functioning of the movement, the author writes, "In the first place, Catholic groups are the sector to which we have the greatest access," and they go on to detail how (FPL 1984a).

39. Staniland 2014.

40. Staniland 2014, 25.

41. See Zaks (2017) on how relationships among "competing" explanations do not demand mutually exclusive relationships.

42. Once again, specifying the outcome in organizational terms sheds light on where existing explanations fall short. Namely, while each purports to account for organizational structure, they rely on different or incomplete notions of what structure entails. As a result, we encounter explanations of traits like cohesion without specification of what exactly is cohering.

43. Dunkerley 1982, 102.

44. Carpio 1982a.

45. Interview with Joaquín Villalobos (Comandancia General del FMLN 1985a). Emphasis added.

46. The Central Command (or Co-Cen) was a seven-person circle at the top of the FPL hierarchy (Carpio 1982b, 1).

47. FPL Central Command 1975.

48. McClintock 1998, 253.

49. Harnecker 1983, 352.

50. Roberto Roca, quoted in McClintock 1998, 57.

51. Bracamonte and Spencer 1995, 15. Carpio elaborates: "If we really want to promote revolution, it is necessary to build a Marxist-Leninist Party that looks after the interest of the working class, the poor peasantry, and the rest of the people. . . . Without the true Communist Party, any war will lead to partial results" (1981, 8).

52. Comisión Nacional de FPL 1981, 3.

53. On material provisions, see Tarrow 1998; Wood 2003; Mampilly 2011; Staniland 2014. On recruitment, see Kalyvas 2006. On discretion, see Wood 2003; Lewis 2020.

54. Carpio 1982b.

55. FPL, approx. 1972a; FPL 1972b; Carpio 1983.

56. Comisión Nacional de FPL 1981. Emphasis added.

57. Cienfuegos 1986.

58. Arnado 1972.

59. Arnado 1972; see also ERP, n.d.; and Villalobos 1989.

60. Montgomery 1995, 104. Foquismo theory hails primarily from the Cuban revolutionary Che Guevara, who argued that armed guerrilla cadres were necessary to foment a socialist revolution (Guevara [1961] 2006). Guevara further describes the approach as the logical application of Marxism-Leninism to the Latin American condition, which makes foquismo itself a prime example of organizational ideology.

61. Bracamonte and Spencer 1995, 14.

62. Bracamonte and Spencer 1995, 14.

63. Byrne 1996, 37.

64. Díaz 2006.

65. Dunkerley 1982, 102.

66. Díaz 2006. In his treatise *On War*, Carl Von Clausewitz famously quipped, "War is the continuation of politics by other means" (87).

67. In the document *Sobre el Plan de Contrainsurgencia*, more of their strategic principles focus on the importance of political and diplomatic work than the military work (PRTC early 1980s, 9).

68. Staniland 2014.

69. As Yvon Grenier argues, universities in El Salvador "offered distinct mobilizational resources" due to their "autonomy, the organizational configuration of the university community, and their specific disposition to act as society's vanguard" (1999, 103).

70. Due likely to the PRTC's modest size (five hundred to eight hundred members, compared to the three thousand to four thousand boasted by the FPL and ERP) and the fact that it did not hold anywhere near the same amount of territory throughout the war, information on the PRTC's social base beyond university students is sparse. Thus, I focus more extensively on the FPL and ERP for this discussion. However, because the FPL and ERP differ so considerably in their organizational ideologies, the countless similarities across their social bases is the more salient information here.

71. One of Jenny Pearce's interviewees called Chalatenango "the most punished zone" (1986, 178). Leigh Binford (1998) similarly documents horrific patterns of government repression in Morazán.

72. Pearce 1986; Montgomery 1995; Hammond 1999; Binford 2004.

73. Pearce 1986, 128, 202; Binford 1998; Consalvi 2010, xxviii.

74. Pearce likewise notes the ideological tension between Marxism and the role of the church in the revolution (1986, 128).

75. FPL Central Command 1975. Emphasis added.

76. Viterna 2013, 250.

77. Viterna 2013, 250. These estimates come from a declassified document from the Salvadoran military archives. They are likely biased downward, for a few reasons. Most notably, they are specifically estimates of the groups' armed factions. It is thus unlikely that they captured the full extent of participation, since a great deal of revolutionary work took place outside the combat realm.

78. Hoover Green 2018, 26.

79. Flores 1983.

80. Flores 1983.

81. Staniland 2014.

82. Staniland 2014, 25.

83. Weinstein 2007.

84. Prior to 1977, the ERP still exhibited divisiveness in its leadership, leading to the formation of the RN in 1974 and the PRTC in 1976. See Hoover Green (2018) on the effectiveness of disciplinary and control institutions across the FMLN.

85. Comisión Nacional de FPL 1981, 3.

86. Carpio 1982b. Yes, the FPL (as well as the PRTC) had a wing of its organization dedicated to organization.

87. FPL 1972b.

88. Carpio 1982b.

89. FPL, n.d.b.

90. Carpio 1982b.

91. The plans to create an organizational arm to accomplish this task are articulated in *Materiales Basicos de las FPL* (FPL 1972b), and both Montgomery (1995) and Wood (2000) confirm that the BPR functioned as intended.

92. Comandancia General del FMLN 1985a, 38. Emphasis added.

93. Carpio 1982b, 4. See also FPL 1984d.

94. Pearce 1986, 242, 294.

95. Pearce 1986; Hammond 1999.

96. ERP, n.d.

97. Dunkerley 1982, 95.

98. Vigil 1991, 141.

99. The ERP commander Joaquín Villalobos made frequent mention of this in early documents and interviews: "Communication," he argues, ". . . will become a fundamental part of our plans" (Harnecker 1983, 107).

100. Vigil 1991; Consalvi 2010, xxxiv.

101. *From Madness to Hope: The 12-Year War in El Salvador: Report of the Commission on the Truth for El Salvador* (1993).

102. See note 17 in this chapter.

103. Recall that Horowitz, Perkoski, and Potter (2018) touted the importance of state-centric factors for determining organizations, arguing that government repression would lead rebel organizations to be more tactically diverse

104. Vigil 1991, 3. Emphasis added.

105. Vigil 1991; Ching 2010, xxxviii.

106. I elaborate on their expansion in chapter 3.

107. Montgomery 1995, 151.

108. Interview with Joaquín Villalobos (Harnecker 1983, 113). Of course, propagandists always argue that their content is *the real story*, but in this case Villalobos was not stretching. In fact, it was well documented at the time that "even [the] enemies tuned in because its news reports were more reliable than the pro-government sources" (Consalvi 2010, xxxix).

109. Álvarez and Orero 2014, 678. Francisco Jovel would eventually leave the ERP to join the PRTC.

110. According to Leigh Binford, "Although the guerrillas functioned as a quasi-state and dominated through force when necessary, attainment of their strategic objectives was tied to the development of a modicum of hegemony over civilians, who served as a recruitment poll and supplied food, labor, information, and other forms of assistance crucial to the struggle" (1998, 4).

111. Interview with Joaquín Villalobos (Harnecker 1983, 98).

112. Resistencia Nacional 1975.

113. ERP, n.d. See also Montgomery 1995, 120; Binford 1998, 7.

114. Viterna 2013, 249.

115. Manning 2008a, 117.

116. Montgomery 1995, 107.

117. Montgomery 1995, 107.

118. ERP, n.d.; Montgomery 1995, 121.

119. Viterna 2013, 250.

120. This argument finds reasonable support among organizational sociologists (Blau 1970; Pugh 1973; Haveman 1993b; Minkoff 1999).

121. Kasfir 2015, 24.

122. Recall the complexity and diversity of the organizational diagram that motivated figure 1.1.

123. Díaz 2006.

124. Díaz 2006.

125. In the document *Sobre el Plan de Contrainsurgencia*, more of the group's "strategic principles" highlight the importance of political and diplomatic work than focus on militancy (PRTC early 1980s, 9).

126. This page is one of countless organizational depictions from the wartime diary of Nidia Díaz (1982–1984). Throughout her diary, the noncombat divisions take priority.

127. PRTC, n.d.a.

128. El Secretario Central de PRTC, n.d.

129. Pearce 1986, 133.

130. Resistencia Nacional 1975.

131. Resistencia Nacional 1975.

132. Montgomery 1995, 105; Ching 2010, xxx.

133. Montgomery 1995, 105; Bracamonte and Spencer 1995, 14.

134. Montgomery 1995, 107.

135. Montgomery 1995, 107.

136. Hándal interview (Harnecker 1983, 73).

137. Montgomery 1995, 105.

138. Hándal interview (Harnecker 1983, 73).

139. Bracamonte and Spencer 1995, 3.

140. On strength of disciplinary institutions, see Weinstein 2007. On ties to local populations, see Staniland 2014. On differences in tactical approaches, see Horowitz, Perkoski, and Potter 2018.

141. Recall that the ERP took years to build a mass front and once it did, its members viewed it more as a logistical support system than an autonomous source of revolutionary politics.

142. To be sure, the "most important" feature will change depending on the analysis.

143. Montgomery 1995, 107.

144. Weinstein 2007.

145. Bracamonte and Spencer 1995; Montgomery 1995; Viterna 2013.

146. Hoover Green 2018.

147. Wood 2003, 193.

148. Wood 2003, 193.

149. Moreover, Staniland's theory helps us get traction on an ostensible paradox within the FMLN. On the one hand, we observe severe fragmentation at the top of the organization. Yet, "fragmented" poorly describes the group, since we also observe strong cohesion and effective command-and-control structures within each OP-M. By differentiating among horizontal and vertical ties, Staniland's typology exemplifies the analytic purchase of specifying the different levels at which organizational traits apply to a given group.

150. Staniland 2014, 25.

151. Montgomery 1995, 109.

152. Bracamonte and Spencer 1995; Montgomery 1995, 52; Viterna 2013, 250.

153. Bracamonte and Spencer 1995, 16.

154. Bracamonte and Spencer 1995, 19.

155. Bracamonte and Spencer 1995, 18.

156. Although ¡Radio Venceremos! was transmitting, the signal at the time was too weak to reach enough of El Salvador for listeners to rely on that broadcast alone.

157. Montgomery 1995, 113.

158. Montgomery 1995, 113; Montgomery 1995, 113; Bracamonte and Spencer 1995, 19, 20.

3. WARTIME ORGANIZATIONAL LEGACIES

1. Weinstein 2002, 2; Kalyvas 2006; Humphreys and Weinstein 2008; Kalyvas and Balcells 2010; Horowitz, Perkoski, and Potter 2018.

2. On conflict strategies, see Kalyvas and Balcells 2010. On patterns of violence, see Gutiérrez-Sanín and Wood 2017.

3. de Zeeuw 2008, 8.

4. Manning 2004, 59.

5. Manning 2007, 57; de Zeeuw 2008, 13; Close and Prevost 2007, 7.

6. John Ishiyama (2019), for example, demonstrates that the majority of ex-rebel parties do not change their names significantly when they transform into parties, and that when they do, the name change has no discernible effect on their electoral performance. Furthermore, in a parallel exploration of party organizational change, Anna Grzymala-Busse (2002, 73) contends that one of "the first two tasks" communist successor parties faced at the end of the Cold War was to "break with the past decisively—by changing the party's name, program, symbols, and public representatives."

7. Manning and Smith 2016.

8. See, for example, Hannan and Freeman 1977, 1984, 1989; Haveman 1992, 1993b; Amburgey, Kelly, and Barnett 1993; Barnett and Carroll 1995; and Greve 1998. Of course, they focus on different traits and harbor varying levels of optimism (or pessimism) for the prospects of change in the face of upheaval. However, none denies the importance of looking at the structures and traits the organization has in place in the run-up to transformation.

9. Grzymała-Busse 2002, Levitsky 2003, and Parkinson 2013, 2022, are notable exceptions. Though they focus on different political organizations—communist successor parties, labor movements, and militant organizations, respectively—each masterfully demonstrates that organizational flexibility is key to adaptation and survival.

10. Hannan and Freeman 1984, 1989. Grzymała-Busse (2002, 23) echoes these challenges in her discussion of the organizational legacies of communist successor parties.

11. Haveman 1992.

12. Hannan and Freeman 1977, 1984; Haveman 1992, 1993b.

13. Barnett and Carroll 1995.

14. On rebel organizations, see Weinstein 2007; Pearlman 2011; Daly 2012; Parkinson 2013; Staniland 2014. On party organizations, see Janda 1983; Schonfeld 1983; Panebianco 1988; Levitsky 2003; Van Biezen 2005.

15. Panebianco 1988, 6–8.

16. Panebianco 1988; Levitsky 2003.

17. Key 1942; Huntington 1968; Janda 1983; Schonfeld 1983.

18. The quote is from Key 1942, 315. Similarly, Katz and Mair argue that aggregating traits to describe the party organization as a whole is problematic because "parties often have several separate bureaucracies" (1993, 595). Panebianco, too, characterizes parties as "mixed organizations" with multiple "bureaucratic elements, which are at times contradictory and at times harmonious" (1988, 201). Finally, Lars Svåsand (1994) identifies a similar set of structural elements in his exploration of Norwegian parties.

19. Key 1942, 377.

20. Katz and Mair 1993, 594–595.

21. Indeed, as Panebianco (1988, 20) notes, not only do subdivisions within the party have different goals, but those goals are sometimes incongruous with one another.

22. Katz and Mair 1993, 596–597.

23. Katz and Mair 1993, 596–597.

24. V. O. Key (1942, 316) makes a similar distinction in his disaggregation of party organizations.

25. Katz and Mair 1993, 598–599

26. Indeed, Katz and Mair (1993) disaggregate party subdivisions in the first place to demonstrate that parties are not in decline; rather, parties are de-emphasizing one subdivision in favor of dedicating more resources to another.

27. Katz and Mair (1993, 594) explicitly argue a full organizational analysis of a given party would require scholars to further disaggregate each "face" and specify the type and arrangement of its various components.

28. Manning 2004, 59; de Zeeuw 2008.

29. On governance, see Mampilly 2011; Arjona, Kasfir, and Mampilly 2015; Arjona 2016; Stewart 2021. On social services, see Flanigan 2008; Mampilly 2011; Heger and Jung 2016; Stewart 2018. On natural resources, see Humphreys 2005; Lujala 2010; Ohmura 2018. On political education, see Pearce 1986; Hoover Green 2016.

30. Arjona, Kasfir, and Mampilly (2015, 3) define *rebel governance* in terms of behavior, or actions.

31. Security and policing also fall under "governance," but I do not expect structures that redirect the coercive apparatus of war to the local level to have major implications for rebel-to-party transformation, as these tasks do not require the type of political or administrative skills associated with other governance activities. For excellent accounts on the origins, varieties, and implications of rebel governance, see Mampilly 2011; Arjona, Kasfir, and Mampilly 2015; Arjona 2016; and Stewart 2018.

32. Silverstein 2007; Flanigan 2008.

33. For perhaps the most extensive and impressive account of the PPLs, see Pearce (1986, 241–273).

34. Mampilly 2011, 62.

35. Katz and Mair 1993, 596.

36. Flanigan 2008, 505; Mampilly 2011, 63.

37. Monsma 1996; Chernov Hwang and Schulze 2018.

38. This assumption is most succinctly captured in the title of Humphreys and Weinstein's 2008 piece, "Who fights? The Determinants of Participation in Civil War," in which fighting and participation are treated as synonymous. For a more extensive account of how participation in rebellion varies, see Wood 2003.

39. Wood 2003; Parkinson 2013.

40. Amelia Hoover Green provides what is likely the most comprehensive account of internal political education in the FMLN. She notes that nearly all ex-combatants received formal political education and they can speak at length about the reasoning underlying the war (2018, 90–91).

41. Hannan and Freeman 1984.

42. Ramzipoor 2015.

43. Manning 2007, 2008a; de Zeeuw 2008.

44. Manning argues, "Electoral politics require a different set of skills than those demanded during wartime" (2004, 59).

45. Close and Prevost 2007, 7.

46. Katz and Mair 1993, 597.

47. Mampilly 2011; Arjona 2016; Stewart 2021.

48. Minkoff 1999, 1671.

49. As Kaufman (1985, 46) argues, organizational change "entails reasoned assessments" of both the environment and the organization.

50. Tan 2020, 80.

51. Zachariah Cherian Mampilly briefly remarks on the importance of organizational "feedback mechanisms" in explaining rebel governance outcomes (2011, 17). For his theory, the feedback mechanisms relate specifically to fostering civilian participation, yet we would do well to think more broadly about how this trait manifests and varies from one organization to the next.

52. Padgett and Powell 2012. For an example of this dynamic during war, see Parkinson's analysis of organizational plasticity in the Palestine Liberation Organization (2013, 2022).

53. Minkoff 1999, 1671

54. Close and Prevost 2007, 9.

55. Parkinson 2013, 422. Emphasis added.

56. Grzymala-Busse 2002.

57. Grzymala-Busse 2002, 29.

58. Reno, n.d., 265.

59. More broadly, the lack of coordination among FMLN factions—though rooted ideologically—was made worse by its limited capacity for communication. The movement had not yet established the radio communications system it would come to rely on later in the war. As a result, even the cadres that *did* participate failed to coordinate the simultaneous attacks that the original plan called for (Bracamonte and Spencer 1995, 19).

60. Moreover, knowing that they lacked the military strength to overthrow the regime themselves, the ERP leaders believed success was contingent on mass mobilization in the form of a national strike. That facet of the plan, however, was built on an assumption that revolutionary fervor was stirring throughout all sectors of the population. Dominated largely by the ERP's reasoning that conspicuous shows of force would ignite these grievances, sending people flooding into the streets in solidarity with the insurrection, the FMLN "felt no need to prepare for this event" (Bracamonte and Spencer 1995, 19).

61. Bracamonte and Spencer 1995, 19.

62. This argument comes directly from Cynthia McClintock's analysis (1998, 90). Bracamonte and Spencer 1995, Montgomery 1995, and Manning 2008a corroborate this point, arguing that the FMLN's internecine rivalries were a greater obstacle to success than the Salvadoran state.

63. Bracamonte and Spencer 1995, 116.

64. Bracamonte and Spencer 1995, 116.

65. Bracamonte and Spencer 1995, 116.

66. Bracamonte and Spencer 1995, 21.

67. The ERP leader Villalobos considered the insurrection less a failure than some of the others, which comports with the ERP's guiding principles. He writes, "The fact that most analyses [of the insurrection] started from a political vantage, they reached the conclusion that since we did not fully seize power, January 10th could be considered a failure. This situation did not allow others to evaluate the event as a momentous change in the development in the war and the quality of our military forces" (Villalobos 1981, 88).

68. Bonasso and Gómez Leyva 1992, 35.

69. Villalobos 1986, 8.

70. Dweck and Sorich 1999.

71. In the FPL document *Cuadernos de Formación No. 3* the authors recount shifting their approach to organizational development in response to a series of misguided approaches ("*un serie de enfoques equivocados*") (Carpio 1982b, 2). A collection of early ERP documents is rife with explicit references to how they shifted organizational tactics on the basis of *autocrítico* (ERP 1977). The founding document of the RN is itself called *Balance Auto-Crítico* (Resistencia Nacional 1975). Throughout her diaries, Nidia Díaz routinely scheduled "*reunions de autocrítico*"—meetings for self-critique (Díaz 1982–1984). Finally, in multiple interviews, Schafik Hándal of the PCS routinely highlighted the importance of *autocrítico* for the FMLN to move forward (Harnecker 1983, 1988).

72. For example, see ¡*Revolución o Muerte: El Pueblo Armado Vencera!* (Carpio 1983, 21) and *Con el Tiempo a Nuestro Favor* (Comandancia General del FMLN 1985a, 35; among many others).

73. On paper, the FMLN General Command officially operated according to the Leninist principle of democratic centralism, which required consensus from all five leaders (Cienfuegos 1986).

74. Bracamonte and Spencer 1995, 8.
75. Bracamonte and Spencer 1995, 116.
76. Harnecker 1983, 95.
77. Ching 2010, xxxii.
78. Harnecker 1983, 95.
79. Dunkerley 1982.
80. Binford 1997, 61; Ching 2010, xxxii. Villalobos describes the training conditions in the aftermath of the retreat: "The offensive put the army on the defensive . . . which gave us a few months of peace and allowed us to create seven strategic fronts. [Quickly], however, the enemy's offensives ramped up and became a combat-preparation school. We were forced to solve the problem of tactical and combat training in real time, by facing the enemy" (Harnecker 1983, 95).
81. In an interview with Marta Harnecker, Villalobos wavers at the term "liberated zone" because the ERP "was not fully self-sufficient" (Harnecker 1988).
82. Binford 1997, 61.
83. According to these arguments territorial control provides the opportunity to build proto-party structures. For example, John Ishiyama and Michael Widmeier argue, "Rebels that control territory are more likely to establish order and set up 'bush bureaucracies'" (2013, 533). Similarly, Paul Staniland argues that "vertical ties [to local populations] make it possible for leaders to quickly establish institutions for local control . . . [and] . . . share their ideology with the people at the local level, facilitating political education" (2014, 27).
84. Huang 2016b, 39.
85. Ventura 1990, 8.
86. As Leigh Binford recounts, "Within the areas in which it exercised nominal day-to-day control . . . attainment of [the ERP's] strategic objectives was tied to . . . civilians, who served as a recruitment pool and supplied food, labor, information, and other forms of crucial assistance to the struggle" (1998, 4).
87. Harnecker 1983, 98.
88. Binford 1997, 62.
89. Harnecker 1983.
90. Binford 1997, 61.
91. Montgomery 1995, 173; Wood 2003, 157.
92. Montgomery 1995, 173; Wood 2003, 157.
93. Montgomery 1995, 120.
94. Bracamonte and Spencer 1995, 15.
95. Ching 2010, xxxii.
96. Comisión Nacional de FPL 1981, 3; Carpio 1982a, 1982b.
97. Pearce 1986, 242.
98. Comandancia 1981.
99. Comandancia 1981, 1.
100. Pearce 1986, 242.
101. *Linea de Masas—FPL* was written in March of 1981, just a few weeks after the January 10 offensive.
102. Comisión Nacional de FPL 1981, 3.
103. For a detailed description and analysis of PPLs, see chapter 8 in Pearce 1986.
104. Pearce 1986, 242. In *Linea de Masas*, the first objective for rural territories is "to participate actively in the construction, development, and consolidation of 'far-abundista' popular power" (Comisión Nacional de FPL 1981, 5). Jenny Pearce confirms the FPL's guiding hand in her analysis of the structures, describing them as playing an "orienting role" and shaping the political priorities of the PPLs throughout their growth (1986, 248).

105. FPL, n.d., 1; FPL 1984c, 1.

106. Pearce goes on to describe the structure in detail:

> "Each PPL was elected by and responsible to 400–500 people . . . a 'locality.' The entire area of Chalatenango under guerrilla control was divided into three sub-zones[;] . . . sub-zone one had seven PPLs and a sub-regional government. The highest power in each locality was the popular assembly, a general meeting of the whole population. Between popular assemblies, power rested with the junta or council of the PPL, made up of a president, a vice president, and secretaries for production and popular economy, for social affairs (health and education), for legal affairs, for political education, and for defense. . . . Every eight days there would be a meeting of the general secretaries of the mass organizations in the locality who represented the *consejo* of the PPL and whose task was to mobilize the population behind the decision of the PPL." (1986, 243–244).

107. Pearce 1986, 250.

108. Pearce 1986; Binford 1997.

109. Pearce 1986, 242. Emphasis added.

110. Cienfuegos 1986, 84. Emphasis added.

111. PPL member, quoted in Pearce 1986, 244.

112. While official estimates place illiteracy rates at 43 percent at the time, Hammond and Portillo argue that the true figure is closer to 70 percent (1991, 91–92).

113. In an analysis of "popular education" in El Salvador, Hammond and Portillo argue that education is "viewed as a political act and an obligation of both the teacher and the learner" (1991, 91).

114. As Jenny Pearce observed, "Learning to read and write was one of [the population's] expectations of the revolution, a way to 'break our silence'" (1986, 261). In another interview, a former teacher describes an "anxiety to learn" among adults in the community (Pearce 1986, 261).

115. Pearce 1986, 261.

116. ANDES (the National Association of Salvadoran Educators) was a progressive teachers' union that came under increasingly heavy scrutiny and oppression in the early 1980s (Hammond and Portillo 1991, 93). While many members fled the country and taught literacy programs in the refugee camps, many others stayed behind and joined sects of the FMLN. For example, the FPL's second-in-command, Mélinda Anaya Montes (a.k.a. Ana María), held a PhD from the University of El Salvador and was one of the founders of ANDES (McClintock 1998, 256). The FPL's use of its international wing in service of its educational subdivision also sheds important and interesting new light on the nature of international patronage. While we normally think about rebel state sponsors as supplying money, guns, and training to insurgents, the FPL implored its donors to send notebooks and pencils for its students (Pearce 1986, 267).

117. Interview excerpt from Pearce 1986, 266–267.

118. Freire 1970.

119. FPL 1984b, 1, 2, 5.

120. FMLN 1980s.

121. CONEPI 1984, 2–4.

122. CONEPI 1984, 4.

123. Wood 2003, 28.

124. The US aid to the Salvadoran military was not exactly an enforcement of human rights. In response to Senator Edward Kennedy's request for an impact statement on US military assistance to El Salvador, Joseph E. Kelley of the National Security and Affairs

division of the General Accounting Office prepared a report that includes the following details. US advisers to El Salvador told the government to "do what you need to stop the commies, just don't get caught" (Kelley 1991, 138). More horrific, a former US intelligence officer suggested that the death squads needed to leave less visual evidence of human rights violations. Specifically, they should "stop dumping bodies on the side of the road" because "they have an ocean and they ought to use it" (Kelley 1991, 139).

125. Cynthia McClintock (1998, 118) reports that the number of civilians abducted by government and paramilitary forces dropped from 535 to 53 over the course of a year.

126. Montgomery 1995, 185.

127. Viterna 2013, 63.

128. Viterna 2013, 63.

129. Schwartz 2019.

130. Bracamonte and Spencer 1995, 23.

131. José Angel Moroni Bracamonte and David E. Spencer argue that the FMLN's early embrace of tactical diversity imbued the organization with "a flexibility rarely seen in previous guerrilla groups . . . allowing them to pick and choose between what worked and what didn't" (1995, 8).

132. Byrne 1996, 98. According to Bracamonte and Spencer (1995, 23), the General Command's new directive pushed the organization to "adopt a new strategy loosely based on that of the FPL, with elements of the RN and ERP lines of thought incorporated."

133. FMLN 1987, 23.

134. Byrne 1996, 132; McClintock 1998, 83.

135. Montgomery 1995, 198.

136. Montgomery 1995, 198.

137. According to Sarah Miles and Bob Ostertag, organizing politically "became the centre of the rebel plan during this period" (1991, 222).

138. The General Command explicitly acknowledged the importance of these early structures when it wrote, "The experience that has been accumulated in some areas of the Eastern Front is very positive and [moving forward] we must generalize that approach" (Comandancia General del FMLN 1986, 9–10).

139. Wood 2000, 49.

140. FMLN 1987, 26.

141. Comandancia General del FMLN 1986, 9–10. See also Binford 1997, 13.

142. For a rich analysis of the FMLN's internal political education structures, see Hoover Green 2018. For example, documents from the FPL (dated February 1984) explicitly address the need for evaluation, training, augmentation, and specialization of its cadres (FPL 1984d).

143. Díaz 1982–1984.

144. Secretariado Central del PRTC, n.d., 4.

145. The General Command representative of the RN Fermán Cienfuegos addresses the issue directly: "We have a repopulation process in which the refugees return to their place of residence, *raising a new organizational challenge that we must face and resolve*" (Cienfuegos 1986, 86–7; emphasis added).

146. FPL 1983; FPL 1984f.

147. FMLN 1987, 26; *Documentos Propuestas y Projectos a Reunión CG (Junio / 84)*, Nidia Díaz Papers, box 1, folder 1, Hoover Institution Library & Archives.

148. In one internal document, for example, the authors write, "Recruitment campaigns should be launched for personnel who can use typewriters, for professors, radio operators, draughtsmen (people trained in technical drawing), theater artists, and auto and bank mechanics. . . . Yet, it is politically and strategically fundamental that they all come from the working class" (PRTC, n.d.c, 1).

149. Wood 2000, 49; 2003, 166–167.
150. Binford 1998.
151. Wood 2003, 167.
152. Binford 1998, 30. The disparate evolution of the ERP and other OP-Ms further highlights the importance of distinguishing between organizational outcomes and behavioral ones.
153. Binford 1998, 29.
154. Orero 2016.
155. Regarding the PRTC's health provisions, Ilja Luciak notes that four cadres were "sent to Mexico to receive training in basic dental care" (2001, 104). This expedition is helpful context for understanding a common joke among the PRTC leadership: "The best way for Salvadoran security forces to identify FMLN collaborators in the countryside would have been to look for the peasants with the cleanest teeth" (Luciak 2001, 104).
156. Comandancia General del FMLN 1985a, 36.
157. Viterna 2013, 118. Emphasis added.
158. Huang 2016b, 39.

4. PATHWAY(S) TO POLITICS

This chapter draws extensively on Zaks 2025.
1. Manning 2007; de Zeeuw 2008; Klapdor 2009; Söderberg Kovacs and Hatz 2016.
2. Across the rebel-to-party literature, Klapdor makes this distinction most explicit, arguing that "transformation is both an outcome and a process" (2009, 13).
3. The quote is from Klapdor 2009, 13. Jereon de Zeeuw specifies two attitudinal changes: the "democratization of decision making" and the "adaptation of strategies and goals" in service of their "new political tactics." The two structural changes he proposes are the demilitarization of combat structures and the "development of a party organization" (2008, 13–15.). On internal elite negotiations, see Manning 2007.
4. Hannan and Freeman 1977, 1984, 1989; Cummings and Huse 1985; Greve 1998.
5. Scott and Davis 2007, 35.
6. The quotes, in order, are from de Zeeuw 2008, 13; Manning 2007, 57; and Close and Prevost 2007, 4.
7. Fligstein and Dauber 1989, 84–85.
8. Hannan, Pólos, and Carroll 2003.
9. Hannan and Freeman 1977, 957.
10. Wantchekon and Neeman 2002, 439. Emphasis added.
11. To be sure, characterizing the new environment as tumultuous should not raise too many eyebrows. Volatility among new democracies is well known and multidimensional. From a domestic vantage, scholars note the significantly increased risk of regime collapse and authoritarian reversals (Svolik 2008). From an international vantage, scholars also observe that new democracies are more prone to interstate conflict (Mansfield and Snyder 1995). Ralph Sprenkels echoes this critique, arguing that "what democratic transition theory tends to interpret as highly positive steps in the process—the demobilization of guerrilla troops, for example—raised for many of those directly involved complex and uncomfortable questions about the future of their movement" (2018, 2).
12. Kaufman 1985, 46.
13. Panebianco 1988.
14. As Rebecca M. Henderson and Kim B. Clark (1990, 118) argue, major organizational change is difficult because the "knowledge of the organization—particularly its communication channels, information filters, and problem-solving strategies" are deeply embedded. Consequently, organizations have a hard time imagining or correcting for their own obsolescence. On this point, also see Scott 2003, 287.

15. Levitsky 2001a.

16. Wildavsky 1988.

17. Specifically, *adaptation* is defined as a specific type of organizational change that "reduces the distance [or increases congruence] between the organization and its institutional environment" (Sarta, Durand, and Vergne 2021).

18. Sutcliffe and Vogus 2003.

19. Dresden 2017; Ishiyama and Widmeier 2019.

20. In his exploration of party adaptation, Steven Levitsky (2001a) takes a similar tack. Namely, he identifies that it was specifically weak institutionalization that enabled the Partido Judicialista to adapt—flouting conventional assumptions that strong institutionalization was a uniformly beneficial trait associated with party longevity.

21. Amburgey, Kelly, and Barnett 1993, 52. Emphasis added.

22. Minkoff 1999; Sewell 1992; Haveman 1993a; Sutcliffe and Vogus 2003.

23. Hannan and Freeman 1989, 8.

24. Hamel and Välikangas 2003, 12–3.

25. Haveman 1992, 48.

26. Manning and Smith 2016.

27. Hamel and Välikangas 2003, 5

28. Levitsky (2001b, 33–34) elaborates on this assumption and the implications for studying the evolution of party organizations.

29. Gerlach and Hine 1970, 34.

30. Jets are equipped with a tailhook to catch the high-tensile arresting wires, which absorb the shock of landing and allow the aircraft to come to a stop in the space allotted.

31. Rochlin, La Porte, and Roberts 1987, 78.

32. (ibid.) P. Rochlin, La Porte, and Roberts 1987, 83.

33. Rochlin, La Porte, and Roberts 1987, 83.

34. Sutcliffe and Vogus 2003, 10; Wruck and Jensen 1994.

35. Often, though not always, this moment occurs at the negotiating table. After the dance of luring other parties into negotiations, a now-common item on the agenda is whether a settlement will include electoral participation provisions (Matanock 2018). In other cases, the two sides do not engage in direct negotiations, but as the fighting subsides, militant groups decide to exploit existing openings in the political system and undertake party formation in the absence of formal provisions. I do not differentiate among these options. In addition, who makes the decision to exploit that opportunity varies by organization. In some cases, the decision is spearheaded by a single leader; in others (and more often) it's made in consultation with a broader set of top leaders and commanders in the group.

36. Manning 2007; Close and Prevost 2007; de Zeeuw 2008; Ishiyama and Batta 2011b.

37. To be sure, routine assessments occur throughout the group's life cycle. Usually, the needs are small and the corresponding changes are incremental: more weapons, different smuggling networks, more recruits for a given unit, or altered combat strategies, to name just a few. With demobilization and elections on the horizon, however, this task is infinitely more complex.

38. As Herbert Kaufman argues, organizational changes demand "reasoned assessments of the relevant conditions and of the changes considered most likely to achieve the desired ends" (1985, 46).

39. When this internal assessment is addressed, it is most commonly portrayed as a black box of internal negotiations (Manning 2007). To be sure, this depiction is not entirely inaccurate, just—by the author's own admission—incomplete.

40. Grzymala-Busse 2002, 21.

41. Elsewhere throughout the organizational literature, these paths to organizational change are known as "exploration" and "exploitation" (March 1991, 71). They refer to an organization's decision to expand into new markets either by building structures to explore new territory or by exploiting and refining existing structures to take advantage of a related opportunity.

42. Evolutionary-learning theories of party formation hold that without quickly adapting during the trial-and-error periods of early party formation, parties will face extinction (Kitschelt 1989, 44).

43. Hannan and Freeman 1984, 159.

44. Hannan and Freeman 1984, 156.

45. Many people who are hired in the party-building stage are either total outsiders to the organization or were part-time affiliates during the war (Manning 2008b), and these outsiders are often confronted with intense resentment on the part of long-standing members.

46. Dresden 2017; Ishiyama and Widmeier 2013; Manning and Smith 2016.

47. Stinchcombe 1965, 148.

48. As Stinchcombe goes on to note, creating new structures "relies heavily on social relations among strangers" where "trust is precarious" (1965, 149).

49. Padgett and Powell 2012; Parkinson 2013.

50. Sewell 1992.

51. Vines 1991; Manning 2002; Manning 2008b.

52. Internal documents as well as secondary sources reveal that the OP-Ms were more likely to work together in this period—carrying out joint operations, meeting at lower levels (below the General Command), and even meeting up socially (Díaz 1982–1984). Moreover, in a diary entry dated September 20, 1984, Díaz (1982–1984) pens a to-do list ahead of a joint-command meeting, including the need to "work on propaganda at the FMLN-level" (as opposed to the level of the PRTC, of which she was a commander). Cienfuegos 1986; FPL approx. 1984e.

53. For example, if rebel-to-party transformation unfolded by massive hiring initiatives, the ex-rebel party's ability to recruit skilled personnel would likely be a function of two core factors. The first factor is the group's repertoires of violence against local populations during war (which, if high, would disincentivize joining). The second factor is the structural composition of the labor market (availability of skilled workers, literacy rates, etc.).

54. Bracamonte and Spencer 1995, 35.

55. Wade 2008, 38.

56. UNSC 1992, 38.

57. Pearce 1986, 282.

58. Union leader interview, quoted in Pearce 1986, 242.

59. Union leader interview, quoted in Pearce 1986, 242.

60. Wood 2003, 167.

61. Comandancia General del FMLN 1985b.

62. Hoover Green 2018, 119.

63. Bracamonte and Spencer 1995, 116.

64. Bracamonte and Spencer explicitly attribute the failed strike to the injudicious repurposing of political cadres into militant roles (1995, 116).

65. Comandancia General del FMLN 1985a, 36, 76.

66. PCS 1993.

67. de Zeeuw 2008, 13–15.

68. Díaz 1982–1984.

69. FMLN-FDR, n.d.

70. FPL, n.d.c.

71. Partial document (PRTC, n.d.b, 4).

72. FPL 1984d.

73. In another example, Díaz wrote a formal document criticizing the organization for adopting a "circular" promotion strategy—that is, promoting people into command positions based on personal friendship networks, rather than expertise.

74. Political memorandum (FMLN-FDR 1991). Emphasis added.

75. FPL, n.d.a. Emphasis added.

76. PCS 1991. Emphasis added.

77. PRTC 1992. Emphasis added.

78. ERP, n.d.b. Emphasis added.

79. Villalobos 1993. Emphasis added.

80. ERP, n.d.b, 5. While other OP-Ms also sought to integrate grassroots leaders further into the party, the difference is that for the FPL and PRTC, those structures were not new—nor were their political relations with grassroots leaders.

81. Wade 2008, 40.

82. Luciak 2001, 98, 99.

83. Spence 1997, 18. Emphasis added.

84. Final three quotes in the paragraph are from Montgomery 1995, 254; Sprenkels 2018, 115; and PCS 1993.

85. FMLN 1992, 2; ERP, n.d.; see also Luciak 2001, 99.

86. FMLN 1992, 4.

87. Sprenkels 2018, 88.

88. The PCS also recounts similar dynamics in its account of the organizational direction ahead of party formation (PCS 1991).

89. FMLN-FDR, n.d. Emphasis added.

90. As Sprenkels notes, "The socioeconomic strategy laid out in the internal documents of the FPL essentially consisted of reconverting the civil-political front into a channel for development projects to benefit the historical OP-M constituents" (2018, 115).

91. Wood 2003, 178.

92. Land reform was one of the FMLN's central priorities in the negotiating process. As Wood documents, "Insurgent cooperatives and the FMLN forced a transfer of approximately eight percent of the nation's farmland" (2003, 182).

93. PRTC 1992.

94. Montgomery 1995, 249

95. Tommie Sue Montgomery further observes that the UN "had to flatter, cajole, and bully the commission to do the job it was created to do" (1995, 247–251).

96. Montgomery 1995, 232; May, Schneider, and Arana 2018.

97. May, Schneider, and Arana 2018, 59.

98. Viterna 2013.

99. *Equipo Maiz, Cuaderno No. 4: Los Acuerdos de Paz*, 1992.

100. Sprenkels 2018, 116.

101. Luciak 2001, 78.

102. Vigil 1991, 231.

103. Sprenkels 2018, 125.

104. Leonhard 1999, 30–32.

105. Allison 2006, 145.

106. Díaz 2006.

107. Sprenkels (2018, 135–136), for example, observes that "many former insurgents relied on interpersonal ties developed during the war to survive in peacetime. Their ability to do so [however] depended on the particular skills they had developed during their

revolutionary career, some of which allowed for peacetime reconversion more easily than others. All OP-Ms formally dissolved as organic entities, but this did not mean that they also disappeared as relevant interpersonal networks."

108. FPL 2009; FPL 2007.

109. Ramos, López, and Quinteros 2015, 12.

110. Ishiyama and Widmeier 2019, 130; Sprenkels 2018, 123.

111. Huang 2016b.

112. Luciak (2001, 98) and Montgomery (1995, 254) clearly document the ERP's political lag in this period and how that lag shifted the balance of power.

113. Wood 2003, 174.

114. Sprenkels 2018, 122.

115. Sprenkels 2018, 122.

116. Spence 1997, 14; Close and Prevost 2007, 4.

5. "FROM A THOUSAND EYES TO A THOUSAND VOTES"

1. Comandancia General del FMLN 1985a. Yes, a thousand eyes should really only translate into five hundred votes, but good math doesn't always make for pithy quotes.

2. Allison 2006; de Zeeuw 2008; Ishiyama and Batta 2011b; Sindre 2016b.

3. Söderberg Kovacs and Hatz 2016; Manning and Smith 2016.

4. Barnett and Carroll 1995.

5. Zaks 2024.

6. According to Ishiyama and Batta, transition into electoral competition may beget transformation of the party organization (2011b, 372). See also Söderström 2016, 215, and Sindre 2018, 23.

7. Of seventeen articles and books, only seven stick with one term; among those, many conflate indicators, which makes it difficult to even recognize the few works that employ consistent usage, such as de Zeeuw 2008; Sindre 2016a, 2016b; and Söderström 2016.

8. This section draws considerably on Zaks 2024.

9. Lyons 2005; Norris 2008; Hartzell and Hoodie 2015; Marshall and Ishiyama 2016; Matanock 2017b.

10. Hannan and Freeman 1989.

11. Olson 1998; Levitsky 2003; Levitsky, Loxton, and Van Dyck 2016.

12. For example, see Shugart 1992; Acosta 2014; Manning and Smith 2016; Söderberg Kovacs and Hatz 2016; Matanock 2016; Ishiyama 2019; Acosta and Rogers 2020. In contrast, de Zeeuw (2008) and a few of his contemporaries (e.g., Klapdor 2009) consistently use "transformation" to describe the outcome of their analyses, and their definitions focus largely on internal structural changes, which are outside the scope of this discussion.

13. According to Robert Adcock and David Collier (2001), conceptual frameworks must capture the "broad constellation of meanings" associated with the concept we wish to pin down.

14. On party registration, see, for example, Acosta 2014; Manning and Smith 2016; Acosta 2019. On ballot appearance, see, for example, Matanock 2016; Söderberg Kovacs and Hatz 2016.

15. Acosta 2014; Manning and Smith 2016; Söderberg Kovacs and Hatz 2016; Matanock 2016; Ishiyama 2019; and Acosta 2019 rely on a binary outcome variable. Relying solely on registration to demarcate transition creates a set of positive cases that does not differentiate between groups that registered but never even ran in elections and rebel successor parties with long-standing careers in political office. See Zaks 2024 for a deeper theoretical and methodological elaboration of this problem.

16. Shugart 1992.

17. Sartori 1970; Goertz 2006.

18. Acosta (2014, 2019) and Matanock (2016) take this approach in the analyses that accompany their respective datasets. Similarly, Manning and Smith (2016) and Söderberg Kovacs and Hatz (2016) add a rebel-to-party variable to different UCDP datasets.

19. The Legion of Doom is a now-defunct group of hackers that operated out of Boston in the 1980s. The Animal Liberation Front is a transnational organization dedicated to freeing animals from scientific and cosmetic testing facilities. Their recent communiques include "17 Chickens Liberated (Midlands, UK)" and "Shoplifters Liberate 51 Lobsters (USA)" (Animal Liberation Front, 2022). Neither have expressed the desire to take political control of a specified country.

20. On the distinction between disarmament and party formation, see Matanock 2016; Matanock and Staniland 2018. On disarmament and transformation, see de Zeeuw 2008; Klapdor 2009. On disarmament and transition, see Söderberg Kovacs and Hatz 2016.

21. Söderberg Kovacs and Hatz 2016.

22. Of course, some settlements mandate demobilization as a prerequisite to party registration, but that constraint is itself a separate variable.

23. This logic echoes E. E. Schattschneider'sadage that "democracy is not to be found in the parties, but between the parties" (1942, 60).

24. Kenneth A. Bollen (1980, 375) observes a similar problem with measures embedding "stability" in definitions of *democracy*.

25. ORDEN stands for Organización Democrática Nacionalista.

26. Shugart 1992, 122; de Zeeuw 2008, 5; Acosta 2014, 671; Manning and Smith 2016, 973; Söderberg Kovacs and Hatz 2016, 7; and Matanock 2016, appendix p. 2, all use this definition.

27. Sartori 1976, 54.

28. Sartori 1970, 62.

29. Sartori 1970; Adcock and Collier 2001; Goertz 2006.

30. Sartori 1970, 58. I use failed transitions because it is an intuitive shorthand for identifying the zeroes. However, *success* and *failure* are loaded terms, the definitions of which can change depending on the question, so I also use *nontransition*.

31. They may have reverted to violence, disintegrated, or transitioned into another sector.

32. Allison 2006.

33. Ishiyama and Widmeier (2019) make this argument directly. Huang (2016b, 39) similarly argues, "Where rebels tap into civilians as a significant war-making resource, the latter become politically mobilized." Elements of the argument are also evident in Wickham-Crowley 1987.

34. Manning and Smith 2016, 2019. Additionally, while de Zeeuw (2008) primarily engages rebels' postconflict transformation, he echoes this logic in his discussion of postconflict success.

35. Even in the most straightforward case—the mobilization of ex-combatants—demobilized members do not always come through as loyal voters, as Michael E. Allison posits. He argues that the size of insurgent groups predicts electoral performance because rebel successor parties can rely on ex-combatants to mobilize on election day (2006, 153). Yet, in Sierra Leone, the newly formed RUFP (successor party to the Revolutionary United Front) not only failed to win more than 2 percent of the popular vote, but more damningly, notoriously failed to mobilize even its former members (Mitton 2008, 202).

36. Shefter 1977; Lawson 1980; Kitschelt 2000; Levitsky 2003; Roberts 2016.

37. Of course, some might argue that the party, new as it is, has simply not had time to create linkages. But the previous two chapters demonstrate that this argument would vastly oversimplify the plurality of rebel-citizen relations forged during war.

38. Mampilly 2011, 6.

39. Duverger 1951.

40. Matanock 2017b.

41. The four datasets are Acosta's 2014 and 2019 Revolutionary and Militant Organizations Dataset (REVMOD); Söderberg Kovacs and Hatz's 2016 expansion of the Uppsala Conflict Data Program (UCDP) Peace Agreement Data (hereafter cited as SK&H); Manning and Smith's 2016 expansion of the UCDP Conflict Termination data (hereafter cited as M&S), and Matanock's Militant Group Electoral Participation (MGEP).

42. As Zaks 2024 further notes, the number of rebel-to-party transitions ranges from 33 to 91, and the number of rebel-to-party failures ranges from 60 to 660. Yet, the datasets all cover roughly the same years.

43. See the empirical discussion and appendix in Zaks 2024 for comprehensive documentation of the disparities and the problems that follow.

44. In contrast, both Manning and Smith (2016) and Söderberg Kovacs and Hatz (2016) expand datasets from the UCDP to conduct rebel-to-party analyses. Manning and Smith add a rebel-to-party variable to the conflict termination data, for which observations are conflict centric. Söderberg Kovacs and Hatz expand the peace agreement data, in which the observations are all peace agreements signed to conclude a conflict.

45. Conventionally, civil war is defined as "a contested incompatibility that concerns government and/or territory where the use of armed force between two parties, of which at least one is the government of a state, results in at least 25 battle-related deaths in one calendar year" (UCDP 2021).

46. The UCDP, for example, differentiates among conflicts over "political" versus "territorial" claims. However, in light of the stakes of rebel-to-party transition, I choose to include both—especially since we observe transition in both kinds of cases. For example, the FMLN made purely revolutionary claims on the Salvadoran government. In contrast, territorial autonomy was a core issue for both the Provisional Irish Republican Army (and its successor party, Sinn Fein) as well as groups that lay claim to occupied Palestinian territory, such as Fatah, Hamas, the Democratic Front for the Liberation of Palestine (DFLP) and the Popular Front for the Liberation of Palestine (PFLP).

47. Most of the groups omitted on this basis express no desire to participate in politics. They tend to view the system itself as the problem and expressly prefer to operate outside of legal bounds. For example, anarchist groups like Black Star (Mavro Astari) in Greece, whose actions are focused on the violent dismantling of the system itself. Black Star opposes what it sees as worldwide US imperialism and it most often fights US presence by throwing Molotov cocktails at diplomats' cars.

48. See, for example, Acosta 2014. Of course, al-Qaeda's local offshoots may be viable contenders. Relatedly, transnational groups are different from rebels with a base in a neighboring country but who are making specific political claims on a target government.

49. Matanock 2018, 657.

50. As I demonstrated in the 2022 article, MGEP includes al-Qaeda Somalia and codes it as "not having participated" in elections, yet party formation was not legal in Somalia during the scope of its inclusion in the dataset. Conversely, Söderberg Kovacs and Hatz (2016) rely on electoral provisions in negotiated settlements as a scope condition, when party formation is often legal outside these bounds.

51. Matanock 2016, 846; Acosta 2019. Though Acosta uses this criterion as well, he assembles the universe of cases ($N = 2,322$) then selects a random sample ($N = 536$), of which 457 are assigned values for rebel-to-party transition (Acosta 2019, appendix).

52. Matanock 2012, 87; 2016, 847.

53. King and Zeng 2001; Zaks 2024.

54. Söderström (2013), Marshall (2019), and Manning and Smith (2019) also speak to the theoretical relevance of distinguishing short-term and long-term contenders in the electoral system.

55. Analogously, Suazo (2013) argues that existing conceptions of "inclusive peace processes" miss key implications for security by omitting the duration of inclusiveness.

56. This number is empirically derived: parties tend to either fail after the third election or persist indefinitely.

57. LeBas 2011, 26.

58. LeBas 2011.

59. While health care structures are not directly translatable into party structures, health services rank highly among the critical needs of populations in war-torn areas. As such, I consider maintaining a health division as part of the local infrastructure that falls under the governance umbrella.

60. I use the name requirement as a proxy for consistency. The goal is to separate episodic round-ups of students for the sake of recruitment from lasting engagement with civilian communities.

61. To further ensure that one of the domains was not driving the results, I created a series of attenuated indices, which systematically omitted each of the components, and reran all of the tests. The differences between the results with the full index and the attenuated ones are insignificant.

62. See similar discussions from Huang 2016b, 61; Heger and Jung 2016; Stewart 2018; Albert 2022, 626.

63. Albert (2022, 626) notes this concern as well.

64. Huang 2016b, 61.

65. The divergent accounts between Pearce (1986) and Binford (1998) illustrate the potential problems that could arise from aggregating based on a geographical snapshot.

66. Matanock 2018; Söderberg Kovacs and Hatz 2016.

67. Haveman 1993b; Minkoff 1999.

68. Allison 2006.

69. Cunningham, Gleditsch, and Salehyan 2009.

70. Staniland 2014.

71. Duverger 1951; Lijphart 1994.

72. Acosta 2014.

73. While Acosta's dataset is significantly larger, it also exhibits a high rate of missing data. Due presumably to the random selection, REVMOD is missing a substantial number of groups from transition-heavy states and regions: Afghanistan (missing six groups), Bosnia and Herzegovina (missing two groups), Burundi (missing all four groups), Cambodia (missing both major parties), Central African Republic (missing two groups), Chad (missing five groups), Congo (Brazzaville) (missing four groups), Democratic Republic of Congo (missing three groups), Djibouti (missing two groups), Ethiopia (missing three groups), Liberia (missing two groups), Sri Lanka (missing three groups) Uganda (missing two groups). Of these cases, twenty-nine successor parties have won seats in at least one postconflict election, twenty-two of those have won seats in three or more elections, and fourteen have achieved nominal participation.

74. Söderberg Kovacs and Hatz 2016, 5; see also de Zeeuw 2008, 19–20.

75. Nominal participation aligns with the coding used in Acosta 2014; Manning and Smith 2016; Söderberg Kovacs and Hatz 2016; Matanock 2016. That said, Söderberg Kovacs and Hatz (2016) also include disarmament as a necessary condition for success, which would exclude a few groups from consideration here.

76. An alternative explanation for the significance of size is actually a bias in the measure itself. It is possible that estimating the size of rebellions is easier for groups with higher levels of cohesion. As such, higher estimates on group size may actually be reflecting something important about the organization itself.

77. Matanock 2018.

78. This result further corroborates the propositions and conclusions laid out in Zaks 2024.

79. The municipalities with evidence of FMLN presence but without clear evidence of which OP-M was in charge are Zacatecoluca, Guatajiagua, Sensembra, San Gerardo, Berlin, and Nueva Granada.

80. Binford 1997.

81. Ishiyama and Widmeier 2013, 2020.

82. In the first analysis, the p-value on the results is 0.059; in the second analysis the p-value is 0.047.

6. POTENT PORTABLES

1. Hoover Green 2016.

2. Söderberg Kovacs and Hatz 2016.

3. Weinstein 2007.

4. Staniland 2014; Stewart 2021.

5. Abdullah 1998, 209.

6. Hanlon 1990, 46.

7. Manning 2002, 51.

8. Morgan 1990, 610.

9. Vines 1991, 5.

10. Funada-Classen 2013, 382.

11. Cabrita 2001, 116; Manning 2002, 51.

12. Hanlon 1990, 51; Emerson 2014, loc. 485.

13. Sesay and Ukeje 2009, 27. According to Kwesi Aning and Angela McIntyre (2004, 27, 67), Sierra Leone had a well-functioning Westminster-style parliament, already established political parties, and the "promise of a budding democracy."

14. Sesay and Ukeje 2009, 27.

15. Sesay and Ukeje 2009, 8–9, 30.

16. Sesay and Ukeje 2009, 30.

17. Aning and McIntyre 2004, 68.

18. Sesay and Ukeje 2009, 30.

19. Abdullah 1998, 208.

20. Rashid 1997; Savage and Rahall 2003, 49. The quote is from Abdullah 1998, 208. The terminology "lumpen youth" derives from *lumpenproletariat*.

21. Fauvet 1984, 115.

22. Cabrita 2001, 139–40.

23. Cabrita 2001, 146.

24. Fauvet and Gomes 1982, 114.

25. Cabrita 2001, 157.

26. Alexander 1995, 9.

27. Quoted in Alexander 1995, 9.

28. Cabrita 2001, 140.

29. Hanlon 1990, 228–9.

30. Abdullah 1998.

31. Aning 2010, 286.

32. Abdullah and Muana 1998.

33. Hazen 2013, 83.

34. Fauvet and Gomes 1982, 12.

35. Specifically, the CIO suggested that Renamo be split under two commands, one under each potential replacement: Afonso Dhlakama and Lucas M'lhanga (Fauvet and Gomes 1982).

36. Abdullah and Muana 1998, 177.

37. Denov 2010, 62. Given the critical role that experienced radio operators have played in both the FMLN and Renamo, having a communications specialist in a leadership role should have been advantageous for the centralization and cohesion of the RUF.

38. South Africa had two primary motivations for sponsoring Renamo and using the group to continue a war against the Machel regime in Mozambique. The first interest was security related. Frelimo tacitly supported the African National Congress, which made frequent incursions into South Africa from its bases in the south of Mozambique. South Africa's second interest was economic. Any extent to which Mozambican ports or railways were out of commission was the extent to which South Africa retained a monopoly on regional port access. Understanding South Africa's motivations behind its sponsorship helps to contextualize Renamo's actions under its leadership.

39. Martin and Johnson 1986; Cabrita 2001; Emerson 2014.

40. Emerson 2014, loc. 1226, 1890.

41. Emerson 2014, loc. 1226.

42. Fauvet and Gomes 1982, 15; Fauvet 1984, 117.

43. For example, in 1980, Dhlakama appointed Renamo's first "political commissar," Henrique Sitoe. Sitoe's role would be to help communicate the political goals of the organization to the foot soldiers and the local people inside Mozambique. This early venture into establishing a contingent of political commissars failed, as Sitoe admitted to having no knowledge of politics and defected shortly thereafter (Fauvet and Gomes 1982, 12).

44. Emerson 2014.

45. Minkoff 1999, 1677.

46. Manning 2008a, 61.

47. Manning 2008a, 61.

48. Carrie Manning corroborates this interpretation when she argues that "the establishment of formal political activities and structures within Mozambique began as a direct outgrowth of attempts to negotiate an end to the conflict beginning in 1984" (1998, 177).

49. Manning 2008a, 61.

50. Evo Fernandez, quoted in Hall 1990.

51. Chart in Manning 1998, 164. For additional evidence on this point, see Vines 1991. This source is especially compelling since Vines's work focuses almost exclusively on the humanitarian atrocities committed at the hands of Renamo soldiers. His account seems otherwise committed to painting Renamo as little more than well-organized bandits, and indeed, the subtitle of the book is "Terrorism in Mozambique." Additionally, see issue 10 of the newsletter *Africa Confidential*.

52. Alexander 1995, 29.

53. Manning 2002.

54. Sesay and Ukeje 2009; Denov 2010.

55. Richards and Vincent 2008, 83

56. Richards and Vincent 2008, 83.

57. As Paul Richards and James Vincent (2008, 92) note, he infused the otherwise hollow rhetoric of "emancipation" with grounded tenets of the Bunumbu curriculum, including "rural self-reliance and cooperative empowerment."

58. Cohesion was always going to be difficult since the RUF included the Special Forces contingent of Liberian soldiers, who had fewer direct stakes in a political revolution in Sierra Leone.

59. Peters 2011, 127.

60. Richards and Vincent 2008, 88.

61. Peters 2011, 83.

62. Abdullah and Muana 1998, 178.

63. Peters 2011, 144.

64. Richards and Vincent 2008; Hazen 2013.

65. Interview with a former RUF combatant, quoted in Peters 2011, 93.

66. Abdullah 1998, 226.

67. Michael Ganawa, the public relations officer of the RUFP, and two former commanders, Edward Kamara and David Vandi, quoted in Richards and Vincent 2008, 93.

68. As Jennifer M. Hazen notes, the SLA's military offensive successfully ejected the RUF from mining areas and cornered the group along and over the Liberian border (2013, 91).

69. Abdullah and Muana 1998, 183.

70. Abdullah and Muana 1998, 183.

71. Hazen 2013, 92.

72. Abdullah and Muana 1998, 183.

73. Harnecker 1983, 84.

74. Abdullah and Muana 1998, 191.

75. Peters 2011, 85.

76. One ex-RUF commander estimates that across the whole organization (which numbered around twenty thousand at its peak), approximately forty people were in charge of ideological training (Peters 2011, 130).

77. While many rank-and-file members were involved in illicit mining, the RUF's official policy was to stay out of this sector until Sankoh shifted his stance.

78. Hazen 2013, 79–80.

79. This situation is in some ways comparable to the patronage structures under which Renamo emerged. While Renamo had its own agenda, we consistently observe the organization being forced to bend to the will of its Rhodesian sponsors and, later, to that of its South African sponsors.

80. Reno 2004; Hazen 2013.

81. Abdullah 1998, 227–228.

82. Abdullah 1998, 229.

83. Two of the men, Fayia Musa and Ibrahim Deen Jalloh, were held in RUF captivity for over two years before being released in November of 1999; the fate and whereabouts of the other two remain unknown (Hirsch 2000, 56).

84. Richards and Vincent 2008, 90.

85. Hazen 2013, 84.

86. Peters 2011, 151.

87. Former RUF commander, quoted in Peters 2011, 151.

88. Peters 2011, 153–159.

89. Peters 2006, 79.

90. Former RUF commander, quoted in Peters 2006, 79.

91. Peters 2011, 152.

92. Manning 2002, 92.

93. Manning 2002, 94.

94. Manning 2002, 94.

95. Manning 2002, 94.
96. Alexander 1997, 14.
97. Alexander 1997, 14.
98. Manning 2008c, 188.
99. Manning 2002.
100. Specifically, he oversaw the appointment of delegates in Zambezia, Tete, Manica, and Nampula provinces (Manning 2002, 96).
101. Manning 2002, 96.
102. Vincente Ululu in 1994 addressing potential international donors in the run-up to elections (Manning 2002, 105–6).
103. Afonso Dhlakama, quoted in the Waterhouse and Lauriciano 1993.
104. Manning 2002, 114.
105. Manning 2002, 114.
106. Manning 2002, 111.
107. Manning 2008b, 55.
108. Frelimo won 129 seats in the assembly with 44.33 percent of the vote, and Renamo won 112 seats with 37.78 percent of the vote (Africa Elections Database).
109. Governance provisions for the RUF are detailed in Articles III, IV, and V of the Lomé Peace Accord (UNSC 1999).
110. UNSC 1999, 7.
111. The demobilization packages entailed counseling, a small "reinsertion allowance," and relocation to a community in which the ex-combatants would receive vocational training in any of a variety of fields (Humphreys and Weinstein 2007, 539).
112. Mitton 2008, 200.
113. Keen 2005.
114. The quote is from Richards and Vincent 2008, 88. As I discuss in the introduction, a number of recent works code this transition as a success because the RUFP appeared on the ballot in the 2002 national elections (Acosta 2014; Söderberg Kovacs and Hatz 2016; Manning and Smith 2016), and thus "participated in competitive electoral politics" (Acosta 2014, 671). This argument is largely a response to others who claim that the RUF was either fighting solely to control diamonds (Collier 2000), or that it was little more than a proxy force against ECOMOG troops run by Charles Taylor of Liberia (Gberie 2005).
115. Hannan and Freeman 1984.
116. Richards and Vincent 2008, 93.
117. Richards and Vincent 2008, 93.
118. Richards and Vincent 2008, 102.
119. Peters 2011, 151.
120. Mitton 2008, 202.
121. Mitton 2008, 202.
122. Interviews with RUF commanders reveal not only the nature of the differences but also the fact that higher-ranking members of the organization knew to some extent how distinct Kailahun's sect was from RUF units elsewhere. One commander recalls, "In Kailahun . . . there were no food-finding missions, because the people were producing it themselves" (Peters 2011, 170).
123. Peters 2011, 170.
124. Peters 2011, 106.
125. Peters 2011, 170.
126. Peters 2006, 82.
127. Peters 2006, 169.

CONCLUSION

1. Söderberg Kovacs and Hatz 2016; Allison 2006, 2010; Manning and Smith 2019.
2. Rudolph 2008, 92.
3. Starting in 2018, the FARC party was allocated five seats in the House of Representatives and five in the Senate, irrespective of vote share. This quota is set to remain in place until 2026.
4. On who joins rebellions and why, see Gurr 1970; Gates 2002; Humphreys and Weinstein 2008. On how and when rebels deploy types of violence, see Weinstein 2007, Gutiérrez-Saním and Wood 2017. On how, when, and why rebels engage in behaviors beyond violence, see Mampilly 2011; Arjona, Kasfir, and Mampilly 2015; Arjona 2016; Kasfir, Frerks, and Terpstra 2018; Stewart 2021.
5. Collier and Hoeffler 2004; Humphreys 2006; Weinstein 2007.
6. Dresden 2017; Ishiyama and Widmeier 2020.
7. Staniland 2012; Arjona 2016; Staniland 2021; Mampilly and Stewart 2021.
8. Autesserre 2009; Arjona 2016.
9. On revolutionary groups, see Lipset and Rokkan 1967; Kitschelt 1994; Zielinski 2002. On religious organizations, see Kalyvas 1996. On labor and trade unions, see Collier and Collier 1991.
10. Hale 2006, 8.
11. Huang 2016b.
12. Hannan and Freeman 1989, 3.
13. O'Donnell and Schmitter 1986; Huntington 1991; Karl 1990.
14. Bratton and Van de Walle 194.
15. Grzymala-Busse 2002.
16. Knight 2008; Muggan and O'Donnell 2015.

References

Abdullah, Ibrahim. 1998. "Bush Path to Destruction: The Origin and Character of the Revolutionary United Front/Sierra Leone." *Journal of Modern African Studies* 36 (2): 202–235.

Abdullah, Ibrahim, and Patrick Muana. 1998. "The Revolutionary United Front of Sierra Leone: A Revolt of the Lumpenproletariat." In *African Guerrillas*, edited by Christopher Clapham. Oxford: James Currey Ltd.

Acosta, Benjamin. 2014. "From Bombs to Ballots: When Militant Organizations Transition to Political Parties." *Journal of Politics* 76 (3): 666–683.

Acosta, Benjamin. 2019. "Reconceptualizing Resistance Organizations and Outcomes: Introducing the Revolutionary and Militant Organization Dataset (REVMOD)." *Journal of Peace Research* 56 (5): 724–734.

Acosta, Benjamin, and Melissa Ziegler Rogers. 2020. "When Militant Organizations Lose Militarily but Win Politically." *Cooperation and Conflict* 55 (3): 365–387.

Adcock, Robert, and David Collier. 2001. "Measurement Validity: A Shared Standard for Qualitative and Quantitative Research." *American Political Science Review* 95 (3): 529–546.

Albert, Karen E. 2022. "What Is Rebel Governance? Introducing a New Dataset on Rebel Institutions, 1945–2012." *Journal of Peace Research* 59 (4): 622–630.

Aldrich, John H. 1995. *Why Parties? The Origin and Transformation of Political Parties in America*. Chicago: University of Chicago Press.

Alexander, Jocelyn. 1995. *Political Change in Manica Province, Mozambique: Implications for the Decentralization of Power*. Technical report. Friedrich Ebert Foundation, Maputo, Mozambique.

Alexander, Jocelyn. 1997. "The Local State in Post-War Mozambique: Political Practice and Ideas about Authority." *Africa: Journal of the International African Institute* 67 (1): 1–26.

Allison, Michael E. 2006. "The Transition from Armed Opposition to Electoral Opposition in Central America." *Latin American Politics and Society* 48 (4): 137–162.

Allison, Michael E. 2010. "The Legacy of Violence on Post-Civil War Elections: The Case of El Salvador." *Studies in Comparative International Development* 45 (1): 104–124.

Álvarez, Alberto Martín, and Eudald Cortina Orero. 2014. "The Genesis and Internal Dynamics of El Salvador's People's Revolutionary Army (1970–1976)." *Journal of Latin American Studies* 46:663–689.

Álvarez, Alberto Martín. 2010. *From Revolutionary War to Democratic Revolution: The Farabundo Martí National Liberation Front (FMLN) in El Salvador*. Berghof Transitions Series. Edited by Véronique Dudouet and Hans J. Giessman. Berlin: Berghoff Conflict Research.

Ama, Jose Feliciano. 1972. *Comunicado No. 1 Del Ejercito Revolucionario del Pueblo— ERP—*. Technical report. Centro de Información, Documentación, y Apoyo a la Investigación, San Salvador, El Salvador.

Amburgey, Terry L., Dawn Kelly, and William P. Barnett. 1993. "Resetting the Clock: The Dynamics of Organizational Change and Failure." *Administrative Science Quarterly* 38:51–73.

Animal Liberation Front. 2022. "Shoplifters Liberate 51 Lobsters (USA)." https://animalliberationpressoffice.org/NAALPO/2022/06/03/shopliftersliberate-51-lobsters-usa-2/.

Aning, Kwensi. 2010. "Understanding the Character and Politics of the Revolutionary United Front in Sierra Leone." In *Violent Non-State Actors in World Politics*, edited by Klejda Mulaj, chap. 13. London: Hurst.

Aning, Kwesi, and Angela McIntyre. 2004. "From Youth Rebellion to Child Abduction: The Anatomy of Recruitment in Sierra Leone." In *Invisible Stakeholders: The Impact of Children on War*, edited by Angela McIntyre. Pretoria: Institute for Security Studies.

Arjona, Ana. 2014. "Wartime Institutions: A Research Agenda." *Journal of Conflict Resolution* 58 (8): 1360–1389.

Arjona, Ana. 2016. *Rebelocracy: Social Order in the Colombian Civil War*. Cambridge Studies in Comparative Politics. New York: Cambridge University Press.

Arjona, Ana, Nelson Kasfir, and Zachariah Cherian Mampilly. 2015. *Rebel Governance in Civil War*. New York: Cambridge University Press.

Autesserre, Séverine. 2009. "Hobbes and the Congo: Frames, Local Violence, and International Intervention." *International Organization* 63 (2): 249–280.

Bakke, Kristin M., Kathleen Gallagher Cunningham, and Lee J. M. Seymour. 2012. "A Plague of Initials: Fragmentation, Cohesion, and Infighting in Civil Wars." *Perspectives on Politics* 10 (2): 265–283.

Balcells, Laia. 2017. *Rivalry and Revenge: The Politics of Violence during Civil War*. New York: Cambridge University Press.

Balcells, Laia, and Patricia Justino. 2014. "Bridging Micro and Macro Approaches on Civil Wars and Political Violence: Issues, Challenges, and the Way Forward." *Journal of Conflict Resolution* 58 (8): 1343–1359.

Barnett, W. P., and G. R. Carroll. 1995. "Modeling Internal Organizational Change." *Annual Review of Sociology* 21:217–236.

Berman, Elie, Michael Callen, Joseph H. Felter, and Jacob N. Shapiro. 2011. "Do Working Men Rebel? Insurgency and Unemployment in Afghanistan, Iraq, and the Philippines." *Journal of Conflict Resolution* 55 (4): 496–528

Benjamin, Roger W., and John H. Kautsky. 1968. "Communism and Economic Development." *American Political Science Review* 62 (1): 110–123.

Binford, Leigh. 1997. "Grassroots Development in Conflict Zones of Northeastern El Salvador." *Latin American Perspectives* 24 (2): 56–79.

Binford, Leigh. 1998. "Hegemony in the Interior of the Salvadoran Revolution: The ERP in Northern Morazan." *Journal of Latin American Anthropology* 4 (1): 2–45.

Binford, Leigh. 2004. "Peasants, Catechists, Revolutionaries: Organic Intellectuals in the Salvadoran Revolution, 1980–1992." In *Landscpaes of Struggle: Politics, Society, and Community in El Salvador*, edited by Aldo Lauria-Santiago and Leigh Binford, 105–125. Pittsburgh: University of Pittsburgh Press.

Blau, Peter M. 1970. "A Formal Theory of Differentiation in Organizations." *American Sociological Review* 35 (2): 201–218.

Bollen, Kenneth A. 1980. "Issues in the Comparative Measurement of Political Democracy." *American Sociological Review* 45 (3): 370–390.

Bonasso, Miguel, and Ciro Gómez Leyva. 1992. *Cuatro Minutos para las Doce: Conversaciones con el Comandante Shafik Hándal*. Puebla, Mexico: Magno Graf.

Bracamonte, José Angel Moroni, and David E. Spencer. 1995. *Strategy and Tactics of the Salvadoran FMLN Guerrillas*. Westport, CT: Praeger.

Bratton, Michael, and Nicolas Van de Walle. 1994. "Neopatrimonial Regimes and Political Transitions in Africa." *World Politics* 46 (4): 453–489.

Byrne, Hugh. 1996. *El Salvador's Civil War: A Study of Revolution*. Boulder, CO: Lynne Rienner.

Cabrita, Joao M. 2001. *Mozambique: The Tortuous Road to Democracy*. Gordonsville, VA: Palgrave Macmillan.

Carpio, Salvador Cayetano "Marcial." 1981. *Cuaderno No. 1: Sobre Algunos Problemas de Organización que Considero el Comando Central*. Technical report. Centro de Documentación de los Movimientos Armados, Valencia, Spain.

Carpio, Salvador Cayetano "Marcial." 1982a. *Cuaderno No. 2: Nuestros Esfuerzos por Compartir Nuestras Obligaciones con Otros Sectores Que Se Califican Marxistas*. Technical report. Centro de Documentación de los Movimientos Armados, Valencia, Spain.

Carpio, Salvador Cayetano "Marcial." 1982b. *Cuaderno No. 3: Como se ha Desarrollado Nuestra Organización*. Technical report. Centro de Documentacion de los Movimientos Armados, Valencia, Spain.

Carpio, Salvador Cayetano "Marcial." 1983. *¡Revolucion o Muerte! ¡El Pueblo Armado Vencera! Testamento Politico de Salvador Cayetano Carpio (Comandante Marcial)*. Sistema de Comunicacion Farabundo Martí.

Chernov Hwang, Julie, and Kirsten E. Schulze. 2018. "Why They Join: Pathways into Indonesian Jihadist Organizations." *Terrorism and Political Violence* 30 (6): 911–932.

Ching, Erik. 2010. "Introduction: Peasant Insurgency and Guerrilla Radio in Northern Morazan, El Salvador." In *Peasant Insurgency and Guerrilla Radio in Northern Morazán, El Salvador*, edited by Carlos Henriquez "Santiago" Consalvi. Austin: University of Texas Press.

Christia, Fotini. 2014. *Alliance Formation in Civil Wars*. Cambridge: Cambridge University Press.

Cienfuegos, Fermán. 1986. "Veredas de la Audacia: Historia del FMLN." David Spencer Collection, box 1, folder 3, Hoover Institution Library & Archives: Ediciones Roque Dalton.

Close, David, and Gary Prevost. 2007. "Introduction: Transitioning from Revolutionary Movements to Political Parties and Making the Revolution 'Stick.'" In *From Revolutionary Movements to Political Parties: Cases from Latin America and Africa*, edited by Kalowatie Deonandan, David Close, and Gary Prevost, 1–16. New York: Palgrave Macmillan.

Collier, Paul. 2000. "Rebellion as a Quasi-Criminal Activity." *Journal of Conflict Resolution* 44 (6): 839–853.

Collier, Paul, and Anke Hoeffler. 2004. "Greed and Grievance in Civil War." *Oxford Economic Papers* 56 (4): 563–595.

Collier, Paul, Anke Hoeffler, and Måns Söderbom. 2008. "Post-Conflict Risks." *Journal of Peace Research* 45 (4): 461–478.

Collier, Ruth Berins, and David Collier. 1991. *Shaping the Political Arena: Critical Junctures, the Labor Movement, and Regime Dynamics in Latin America*. Notre Dame Kellogg Institute of International Studies. South Bend, IN: University of Notre Dame Press.

Comandancia, D.R.U. 1981. *Orden de Perparar Segunda Ofensiva*. Technical report. David Spencer Collection, box 5, folder 4.5. Hoover Institution Library & Archives, Palo Alto, CA.

Comandancia General del FMLN. 1984. *Fundamentación Politica y Metodo de la Realización de las Campañas de Reclutamiento Patriotico por la Defensa de la (—) Nacional*. Internal documentation. Nidia Díaz Papers, box 1, folder 1. Hoover Institution Library & Archives, Palo Alto, CA.

Comandancia General del FMLN. 1985a. "Con el Tiempo a Nuestro Favor" [With Time on Our Side]. Ediciones Sistema Radio Venceremos, Morazán, El Salvador.

Comandancia General del FMLN. 1985b. *Los 15 Principios del Combatiente Guerrillero*. Mimeograph. Museo de la Palabra y la Imagen, San Salvador, El Salvador.

Comandancia General del FMLN. 1986. *Línea de Accion de Masas FMLN: Fase Preperatoria de la Contraofensiva Estratégica*. Communiqué. David Spencer Collection, box 4, folder 4.6. Hoover Institution Library & Archives, Palo Alto, CA.

Comisión Nacional de FPL; 1981. *Linea de Masas*. Technical report. David Spencer Collection, box 5, folder 4.5, Hoover Institution Library & Archives, Palo Alto, CA.

CONEPI (Comisión Nacional de Educación Politco-Ideologica del Comite Central de FPL). 1984. *Valoracion del Trabajo Politico-Militar del FAS en Las Zonas de Disputa*. Internal documentation. Chana Collection, box 3, folder 617, Museo de la Palabra y la Imagen, San Salvador, El Salvador.

Consalvi, Carlos Henriquez "Santiago." 2010. *Peasant Insurgency and Guerrilla Radio in Northern Morazán, El Salvador*. Austin: University of Texas Press.

Coutu, Diane L. 2002. "How Resilience Works." *Harvard Business Review*, May, 1–8.

Cummings, Thomas G., and Edgar F. Huse. 1985. *Organization Development and Change*. St. Paul, MN: West Publishing.

Cunningham, David E., Kristian Skrede Gleditsch, and Idean Salehyan. 2009. "Non-State Actor Data, version 3.4." Available from http://ksgleditsch.com/eacd.html.

Cunningham, Kathleen Gallagher, Reyko Huang, and Katherine M. Sawyer. 2021. "Voting for Militants: Rebel Elections in Civil War." *Journal of Conflict Resolution* 65 (1): 81–107.

Daly, Sarah Zukerman. 2012. "Organizational Legacies of Violence: Conditions Favoring Insurgency Onset in Colombia, 1964–1984." *Journal of Peace Research* 49 (3): 473–491.

Daly, Sarah Zukerman. 2016. *Organized Violence after Civil War: The Geography of Recruitment in Latin America*. New York: Cambridge University Press.

Daly, Sarah Zukerman. 2022. *Violent Victors: Why Bloodstained Parties Win Postwar Elections*. Princeton, NJ: Princeton University Press.

de Zeeuw, Jeroen. 2008. "Understanding the Political Transformation of Rebel Movements." In *From Soldiers to Politicians: Transforming Rebel Movements after Civil War*, edited by Jereon de Zeeuw, 1–32. Boulder, CO: Lynne Rienner

Denov, Myriam S. 2010. *Child Soldiers: Sierra Leone's Revolutionary United Front*. New York: Cambridge University Press.

Díaz, Nidia. 1982–1984. "Diary." Nidia Díaz Papers, box 1, folder 6, Hoover Institution Library & Archives, Palo Alto, CA.

Díaz, Nidia. 2006. *Aproximación a la Historia del PRTC*. Communiqué archivo digital. Centro de Documentación de los Movimientos Armados, Valencia, Spain.

Doctor, Austin C., and John D. Willingham. 2020. "Foreign Fighters, Rebel Command Structure, and Civilian Targeting in Civil War." *Terrorism and Political Violence*. 34 (6): 1125–1143.

Dresden, Jennifer Raymond. 2017. "From Combatants to Candidates: Electoral Competition and the Legacy of Armed Conflict." *Conflict Management and Peace Science* 34 (3): 240–263.

Dunkerley, James. 1982. *The Long War: Dictatorship and Revolution in El Salvador*. London: Junction Books.

Duverger, Maurice. 1951. *Political Parties: Their Organization and Activity in the Modern State*. New York: Wiley.

Dweck, Carol S., and Lisa A. Sorich. 1999. "Mastery-Oriented Thinking." In *Coping: The Psychology of What Works*, edited by C. R. Snyder, chap. 11. Oxford: Oxford University Press.

Eck, Kristine. 2007. "Recruiting Rebels: Indoctrination and Political Education in Nepal." In *The Maoist Insurgency in Nepal: Revolution in the Twenty-First Century*, edited by Mahendra Lawoti and Anup K. Pahari, 33–51. New York: Routledge.

Eck, Kristine. 2014. "Coercion in Rebel Recruitment." *Security Studies* 23 (2): 364–398.

Emerson, Stephen A. 2014. *The Battle for Mozambique: The Frelimo-Renamo Struggle, 1977–1992*. Kindle edition. West Midlands, UK: Helion.

Equipo Maiz, Cuaderno No. 4: Los Acuerdos de Paz. 1992. David Spencer Collection, box 7, folder 7.15, Hoover Institution Library & Archives, Palo Alto, CA.

ERP. 1977. *"Prensa Comunista: 6 Años de Organizar Combatir y Luchar."* Salvadoran Subject Collection, box 1, folder 1.1. Hoover Institution Library & Archives, Palo Alto, CA.

ERP. n.d.a. *Origen y Desarrollo del Ejército Revolucionario del Pueblo*. Technical report. Centro de Documentacion de los Movimientos Armados, Valencia, Spain.

ERP. n.d.b. "La Estrategia Organizativa Del Partido" [The Organizing Strategy of the Party]. David Spencer Collection, box 4, folder 4.4. Hoover Institution Library & Archives, Palo Alto, CA.

Fauvet, Paul. 1984. "Roots of Counter-Revolution: The 'Mozambique National Resistance.'" *Review of African Political Economy* 11 (29): 108–121.

Fauvet, Paul, and Alves Gomes. 1982. "South Africa's Marionettes of Destabilisation." *Ufahamu, A Journal of African Studies* 12 (1): 8–18.

Fearon, James D., and David D. Laitin. 2003. "Ethnicity, Insurgency, and Civil War." *American Political Science Review* 97 (1): 75–90.

Flanigan, Shawn Teresa. 2008. "Nonprofit Service Provision by Insurgent Organizations: The Cases of Hizballah and the Tamil Tigers." *Studies in Conflict & Terrorism* 31 (6): 499–519.

Fligstein, Neil, and Kenneth Dauber. 1989. "Structural Change in Corporate Organization." *Annual Review of Sociology* 15:73–96.

Flores, Ernesto. 1983. *En Cerros de San Pedro*. Technical report. Nidia Díaz Papers, box 1. Hoover Institution Library & Archives, Palo Alto, CA.

FMLN. 1980s. *Unidad de Cine y T.V. El Salvador C.A.* Technical report. Salvadoran Subject Collection, box 3, folder 1, Hoover Institution Library & Archives, Palo Alto, CA.

FMLN. 1987. *El Poder Popular de Doble Cara*. San Salvador: Publicaciones FMLN

FMLN. 1992. *Organizando al Frente: Criterios Básicos para el Trabajo de Organización*. Internal documentation item 8610. Archivo Personal de Tino Brugos, San Salvador, El Salvador.

FMLN-FDR. n.d. *Documento Sobre Situación Organica*. Internal communique. David Spencer Collection, box 4, folder 4.4. Hoover Institution Library & Archives, Palo Alto, CA.

FMLN-FDR, Comisión Seminario. 1991. Memorandum. Documento politico. David Spencer Collection, box 4, folder 4.9. Hoover Institution Library & Archives, Palo Alto, CA.

Fortna, Virginia Page. 2003. "Scraps of Paper? Agreements and the Durability of Peace." *International Organization* 57 (2): 337–372.

FPL. Approx. 1972a. *Los Grupos de Apoyo*. Internal documentation. Centro de Documentación de los Movimientos Armados, Valencia, Spain.

FPL. 1972b. *Materiales Basicos de las FPL*. Internal documentation. Centro de Documentación de los Movimientos Armados, Valencia, Spain.

FPL. 1983. *Plan de Repoblación*. Internal documentation. Chana Collection, box 2, folder 536. Museo de la Palabra y la Imagen, San Salvador, El Salvador.

FPL. 1984a. *Informe de la Pega*. Internal communique. Escaneos de Baja Resolucion, Embutido Chana del 501. folder 534. Museo de la Palabra y la Imagen, San Salvador, El Salvador.

FPL. 1984b. *Informe de Trabajo de Masas*. Comunicado. Museo de la Palabra y la Imagen, San Salvador, El Salvador.

FPL. 1984c. *Lineamiento para el Impulso del Accionar Politco-Militar en la Coyuntura Elecciones*. Internal documentation. Chana Collection, box 3, folder 618. Museo de la Palabra y la Imagen, San Salvador, El Salvador.

FPL. 1984d. *Lineamientos para Impulsar la Politica de Cuadros en Nuestro Partido*. Comunicado. Chana Collection, box 2, folder 522. Museo de la Palabra y la Imagen, San Salvador, El Salvador.

FPL. Approx. 1984e. *Sobre los Problemas Mas Agudos en la Estructura de las MPL Según Apreciaciones de María del Organismo del PPL*. Internal documentation. Chana Collection, box 3, folder 530. Museo de la Palabra y la Imagen, San Salvador, El Salvador.

FPL. 1984f. *Texto Sobre Reubicación y Repoblación de Refugiados*. Internal documentation. Chana Collection, box 2, folder 535. Museo de la Palabra y la Imagen, San Salvador, El Salvador.

FPL. 2007. "A 37 Años: La Lucha Continúa." Centro de Documentación de los Movimientos Armados. Valencia, España.

FPL. 2009. "Hace 39 Años." Centro de Documentación de los Movimientos Armados. Valencia, España.

FPL. n.d.a. *Estrategia Parcial de las FPL Para el Periodo de la Post-Guerra*. Internal documentation. David Spencer Collection, box 4, folder 4.10. Hoover Institution Library & Archives, Palo Alto, CA.

FPL. n.d.b. *Ficha de Militancia*. Internal documentation. Chana Collection, box 3, folder 644. Museo de la Palabra y la Imagen, San Salvador, El Salvador.

FPL. n.d.c. *Relación de ANDES con el Partido PPL*. Memorandum. David Spencer Collection, box 4, folder 4.3. Hoover Institution Library & Archives, Palo Alto, CA.

FPL. n.d.e. *Propuesta: Sobre el Código de Justicia Popular*. Chana Collection, box 2, folder 518. Museo de la Palabra y la Imagen, San Salvador, El Salvador.

FPL Central Command. 1975. *Estrella Roja 2*. Technical report. Marxist Internet Archive.

Freire, Paulo. 1970. *Pedagogy of the Oppressed*. New York: Herder & Herder.

From Madness to Hope: The 12-Year War in El Salvador: Report of the Commission on the Truth for El Salvador. 1993. Number S/25500, 5–8. UN Security Council, Annex.

Funada-Classen, Sayaka. 2013. *Origins of War in Mozambique: A History of Unity and Division*. Somerset West, South Africa: African Minds.

Gates, Scott. 2002. "Recruitment and Allegiance: The Microfoundations of Rebellion." *Journal of Conflict Resolution* 46 (1): 111–130.

Gberie, Lansana. 2005. *A Dirty War in West Africa: The RUF and the Destruction of Sierra Leone*. Bloomington: Indiana University Press.

Gerlach, Luther P., and Virginia H. Hine. 1970. *People, Power, Change: Movements of Social Transformation*. New York: Bobbs-Merril.

Gilligan, Michael, Cyrus Samii, and Eric Mvukiyehe. 2012. "Reintegrating Rebels into Civilian Life: Quasi-Experimental Evidence from Burundi." *SSRN* 57 (4): 598–626.

Gleditsch, Nils Petter, Peter Wallensteen, Mikael Eriksson, Margareta Sollenberg, and Håvard Strand. 2002. "Armed Conflict 1946–2001: A New Dataset." *Journal of Peace Research* 39 (5): 617–631.

Goertz, Gary. 2006. *Social Science Concepts: A User's Guide.* Princeton, NJ: Princeton University Press.

Gonzalez, Antonio. 2018. "Can you come to DC . . . right now? Mobilizing SuVoto 94 in El Salvador." *Tales from Central America,* vignette 6.

Grenier, Yvon. 1999. *The Emergence of Insurgency in El Salvador: Ideology and Political Will.* Pittsburgh: University of Pittsburgh Press.

Greve, Henrich R. 1998. "Performance, Aspirations, and Risky Organizational Change." *Administrative Science Quarterly* 43 (1): 58–86.

Grzymala-Busse, Anna. 2002. *Redeeming the Communist Past: The Regeneration of Communist Parties in East Central Europe.* Cambridge: Cambridge University Press.

Guevara, Che. (1961) 2006. *Guerrilla Warfare.* New York: Ocean Books.

Gurr, Ted Robert. 1970. *Why Men Rebel.* New York: Routledge.

Gutiérrez-Sanín, Francisco, and Elisabeth Jean Wood. 2014. "Ideology in Civil War: Instrumental Adoption and Beyond." *Journal of Peace Research* 51 (2): 213–226.

Gutiérrez-Sanín, Francisco, and Elisabeth Jean Wood. 2017. "What Should We Mean by 'Pattern of Political Violence'? Repertoire, Targeting, Frequency, and Technique." *Perspectives on Politics* 15 (1): 20–41.

Hale, Henry E. 2006. *Why Not Parties in Russia? Democracy, Federalism, and the State.* New York: Cambridge University Press.

Hall, Margaret. 1990. "The Mozambican National Resistance Movement (Renamo): A Study in the Destruction of an African Country." *Africa: Journal of the International African Institute* 60 (1): 39–68.

Hamel, Gary, and Liisa Välikangas. 2003. "The Quest for Resilience." *Harvard Business Review.* September.

Hammond, John L. 1999. "Popular Education as Community Organizing in El Salvador." *Latin American Perspectives* 26 (4): 69–94.

Hammond, John L., and Julio Portillo. 1991. "Popular Education in the Midst of Guerrilla War: An Interview with Julio Portillo." *Journal of Education* 173 (1): 91–106.

Hanlon, Joseph. 1990. *Mozambique: The Revolution under Fire.* London: Zed Books.

Hannan, Michael T., and John Freeman. 1977. "The Population Ecology of Organizations." *American Journal of Sociology* 82 (5): 929–964.

Hannan, Michael T., and John Freeman. 1984. "Structural Inertia and Organizational Change." *American Sociological Review* 49 (2): 149–164.

Hannan, Michael T., and John Freeman. 1989. *Organizational Ecology.* Cambridge, MA: Harvard University Press.

Hannan, Michael T., László Pólos, and Glenn R. Carroll. 2003. "The Fog of Change: Opacity and Asperity in Organizations." *Administrative Science Quarterly* 48 (3): 399–432.

Harnecker, Marta. 1983. *Pueblos en Armas: Entrevistas a los Principales Comandantes Guerrilleros de Nicaragua, El Salvador, Guatemala.* Mexico: Universidad Autónoma de Guerrero.

Harnecker, Marta. 1988. *El Salvador, Partido Comunista y Guerra Revolucionaria: Entrevista a Schafik Jorge Hándal (1985–1988).* Havana, Cuba: Biblioteca Popular.

Hartzell, Caroline A., and Matthew Hoodie. 2015. "The Art of the Possible: Power Sharing and Post–Civil War Democracy." *World Politics* 67 (1): 37–71.

Haveman, Heather A. 1992. "Between a Rock and a Hard Place: Organizational Change and Performance under Conditions of Fundamental Environmental Transformation." *Administrative Science Quarterly* 37 (1): 48–75.

Haveman, Heather A. 1993a. "Follow the Leader: Mimetic Isomorphism and Entry into New Markets." *Administrative Science Quarterly* 38 (4): 593–627.

Haveman, Heather A. 1993b. "Organizational Size and Change: Diversification in the Savings and Loan Industry after Deregulation." *Administrative Science Quarterly* 38 (1): 20–50.

Hazen, Jennifer M. 2013. *What Rebels Want: Resources and Supply Networks in Wartime.* Ithaca, NY: Cornell University Press.

Heger, Lindsay L., and Danielle F. Jung. 2016. "Negotiating with Rebels: The Effect of Rebel Service Provision on Conflict Negotiations." *Journal of Conflict Resolution* 61 (6): 1203–1229.

Henderson, Rebecca M., and Kim B. Clark. 1990. "Architectural Innovation: The Reconfiguration of Existing Product Technologies and the Failure of Established Firms." *Administrative Science Quarterly* 35 (1): 9–30.

Hirsch, John L. 2000. *Sierra Leone: Diamonds and the Struggle for Democracy.* International Peace Academy Occasional Paper Series. Boulder, CO: Lynne Rienner.

Holland, Alisha C. 2016. "Insurgent Successor Parties: Scaling Down to Build a Party after War." In *Challenges of Party-Building in Latin America*, edited by Steven Levitsky, James Loxton, Brandon Van Dyck, and Jorge I. Domínguez, chap. 10. New York: Cambridge University Press.

Hoover Green, Amelia. 2016. "The Commander's Dilemma: Creating and Controlling Armed Group Violence." *Journal of Peace Research* 53 (5): 619–632.

Hoover Green, Amelia. 2018. *The Commander's Dilemma: Violence and Restraint in Wartime.* Ithaca, NY: Cornell University Press.

Horne, John F., III, and John E. Orr. 1998. "Assessing Behaviors That Create Resilient Organizations." *Employment Relations Today* (Winter):29–39.

Horowitz, Michael C., Evan Perkoski, and Philip B. K. Potter. 2018. "Tactical Diversity in Militant Violence." *International Organization* 72 (1): 139–171.

Huang, Reyko. 2016a. "Rebel Diplomacy in Civil War." *International Security* 40 (4): 89–126.

Huang, Reyko. 2016b. *The Wartime Origins of Democratization: Civil War, Rebel Governance, and Political Regimes.* Problems of International Politics. New York: Cambridge University Press.

Humphreys, Macartan. 2005. "Natural Resources, Conflict, and Conflict Resolution." *Journal of Conflict Resolution* 49 (4): 508–537.

Humphreys, Macartan, and Jeremy M. Weinstein. 2006. "Handling and Manhandling Civilians in Civil War." *American Political Science Review* 100 (3): 429–447.

Humphreys, Macartan, and Jeremy M. Weinstein. 2007. "Demobilization and Reintegration." *Journal of Conflict Resolution* 51 (4): 531–567.

Humphreys, Macartan, and Jeremy M. Weinstein. 2008. "Who Fights? The Determinants of Participation in Civil War." *American Journal of Political Science* 52 (2): 436–455.

Huntington, Samuel P. 1968. *Political Order in Changing Societies.* New Haven, CT: Yale University Press.

Huntington, Samuel P. 1991. *The Third Wave: Democratization in the Late Twentieth Century.* Norman: University of Oklahoma Press.

Ishiyama, John. 2019. "Identity Change and Rebel Party Political Success." *Government and Opposition* 54 (3): 454–484.

Ishiyama, John, and Anna Batta. 2011a. "Rebel Organizations and Conflict Management in Post-Conflict Societies, 1990–2009." *Civil Wars* 13 (4): 437–457.

Ishiyama, John, and Anna Batta. 2011b. "Swords into Plowshares: The Organizational Transformation of Rebel Groups into Political Parties." *Communist and Post-Communist Studies* 44 (4): 369–379.

Ishiyama, John, and Michael Widmeier. 2013. "Territorial Control, Levels of Violence, and the Electoral Performance of Former Rebel Political Parties after Civil Wars." *Civil Wars* 15 (4): 531–550.

Ishiyama, John, and Michael Widmeier. 2019. "From "Bush Bureaucracies" to Electoral Competition: What Explains the Political Success of Rebel Parties after Civil Wars?" *Journal of Elections, Public Opinion, and Parties* 30 (1): 42–63.

Janda, Kenneth. 1983. "Cross-National Measures of Party Organizations and Organizational Theory." *European Journal of Political Research* 11:319–332.

Kalyvas, Stathis N. 1996. *The Rise of Christian Democracy in Europe*. Ithaca, NY: Cornell University Press.

Kalyvas, Stathis N. 2006. *The Logic of Violence in Civil War*. New York: Cambridge University Press.

Kalyvas, Stathis N. 2015. Rebel Governance during the Greek Civil War, 1942–1949. In *Rebel Governance in Civil War*, edited by Ana Arjona, Nelson Kasfir, and Zachariah Cherian Mampilly, chap. 6. New York: Cambridge University Press.

Kalyvas, Stathis N., and Laia Balcells. 2010. "International System and Technologies of Rebellion: How the End of the Cold War Shaped Internal Conflict." *American Political Science Review* 104 (03): 415–429.

Karl, Terry Lynn. 1990. "Dilemmas of Democratization in Latin America." *Comparative Politics* 23 (1): 1–21.

Kasfir, Nelson. 2015. "Rebel Governance—Constructing a Field of Inquiry: Definitions, Scope, Patterns, Order, Causes." In *Rebel Governance in Civil War*, edited by Ana Arjona, Nelson Kasfir, and Zachariah Mampilly, 21–46. New York: Cambridge University Press

Kasfir, Nelson, Georg Frerks, and Niels Terpstra. 2018. "Introduction: Armed Groups and Multi-layered Governance." *Civil Wars* 19 (3): 1–22.

Katz, Richard S., and Peter Mair. 1993. "The Evolution of Party Organizations in Europe: The Three Faces of Party Organization." *American Review of Politics* 14:593–617.

Kaufman, Herbert. 1985. *Time, Chance, and Organizations: Natural Selection in a Perilous Environment*. Chatham, NJ: Chatham House.

Kay Cohen, Dara. 2013. "Explaining Rape during Civil War: Cross-National Evidence (1980–2009)." *American Political Science Review* 107 (3): 461–477.

Keen, David. 2005. *Conflict and Collusion in Sierra Leone*. New York: Palgrave Macmillan.

Kelley, Joseph E. 1991. *El Salvador: Military Assistance Has Helped Counter but Not Overcome the Insurgency*. Report (declassified). GAO/NSIAD-91-166. General Accounting Office, National Security International Affairs Division, Washington, DC.

Kenny, Paul. 2010. "Structural Integrity and Cohesion in Insurgent Organizations: Evidence from Protracted Conflicts in Ireland and Burma." *International Studies Review* 12:533–555.

Key, V. O. 1942. *Politics, Parties, & Pressure Groups*. New York: Thomas Y. Crowell Company.

King, Gary, and Langche Zeng. 2001. "Explaining Rare Events in International Relations." *International Organization* 55 (3): 693–715.

Kitschelt, Herbert. 1989. *The Logics of Party Formation: Ecological Parties in Belgium and West Germany*. Ithaca, NY: Cornell University Press.

Kitschelt, Herbert. 1994. *The Transformation of European Social Democracy*. Cambridge: Cambridge University Press.

Kitschelt, Herbert. 2000. "Linkages between Citizens and Politicians in Democratic Polities." *Comparative Political Studies* 33 (6–7): 845–879.

Klapdor, Dominik. 2009. "From Rebels to Politicians: Explaining Rebel to Party Transformations after Civil War: The Case of Nepal." Phd diss. Development Studies Institute at London School of Economics.

Knight, W. Andy. 2008. "Disarmament, Demobilization, and Reintegration and Post-Conflict Peacebuilding in Africa: An Overview." *African Security* 1 (1): 24–52.

Lawson, Kay. 1980. *Political Parties and Linkage: A Comparative Perspective*. New Haven, CT: Yale University Press.

LeBas, Adrienne. 2011. *From Protests to Parties*. Oxford: Oxford University Press.

Leonhard, Ralf. 1999. *Ondas Rebeldes, Ondas Conformes*. San Salvador, El Salvador: Ediciones Heinrich Böll.

Levitsky, Steven. 2001a. "Organization and Labor-Based Party Adaptation: The Transformation of Agentine Peronism in Comparative Perspective." *World Politics* 54 (1): 27–56.

Levitsky, Steven. 2001b. "An Organized Disorganization: Informal Structures and the Persistence of Mass Organization in Argentine Peronism." *Journal of Latin American Studies* 33:29–65.

Levitsky, Steven. 2003. *Transforming Labor-Based Parties in Latin America: Argentine Peronism in Comparative Perspective*. New York: Cambridge University Press.

Levitsky, Steven, James Loxton, and Brandon Van Dyck. 2016. "Introduction: Challenges of Party-Building in Latin America." In *Challenges of Party-Building in Latin America*, edited by Steven Levitsky, James Loxton, Brandon Van Dyck, and Jorge I. Domínguez. New York: Cambridge University Press.

Lewis, Janet I. 2020. *How Insurgency Begins: Rebel Group Formation in Uganda and Beyond*. Cambridge: Cambridge University Press.

Lidow, Nicholai Hart. 2016. *Violent Order: Understanding Rebel Governance through Liberia's Civil War*. New York: Cambridge University Press.

Lijphart, Arend. 1994. *Electoral Systems and Party Systems: A Study of Twenty-Seven Democracies, 1945–1990*. Oxford: Oxford University Press.

Lipset, Seymour Martin, and Stein Rokkan. 1967. *Party Systems and Voter Alignments: Cross-National Perspectives*. New York: Free Press.

Los Acuerdos de Paz. 1992. David Spencer Collection, box 7, folder 7.15. Hoover Institution Library & Archives, Palo Alto, CA.

Luciak, Ilja A. 2001. *After the Revolution: Gender and Democracy in El Salvador, Nicaragua, and Guatemala*. Baltimore: Johns Hopkins University Press.

Lujala, Päivi. 2010. "The Spoils of Nature: Armed Civil Conflict and Rebel Access to Natural Resources." *Journal of Peace Research* 47 (1): 15–28.

Lyons, Terrence. 2005. *Demilitarizing Politics: Elections on the Uncertain Road to Peace*. Boulder, CO: Lynne Rienner.

Lyons, Terrence. 2016. "Victorious Rebels and Postwar Politics." *Civil Wars* 18 (2): 160–174.

Mair, Peter. 1994. "Party Organizations: From Civil Society to the State." In *How Parties Organize: Change and Adaptation in Party Organizations in Western Democracies*, edited by Richard S. Katz and Peter Mair, 1–21. Thousand Oaks, CA: Sage.

Mampilly, Zachariah Cherian. 2011. *Rebel Rulers: Insurgent Governance and Civilian Life during War*. Ithaca, NY: Cornell University Press.

Mampilly, Zachariah Cherian, and Megan A. Stewart. 2021. "A Typology of Rebel Political Institutional Arrangements." *Journal of Conflict Resolution* 65 (1): 15–45.

Manning, Carrie. 1998. "Constructing Opposition in Mozambique: Renamo as Political Party." *Journal of Southern African Studies* 24 (1): 161–189.

Manning, Carrie. 2002. *The Politics of Peace in Mozambique*. Westport, CT: Praeger Publishers.

Manning, Carrie. 2004. "Armed Opposition Groups into Political Parties: Comparing Bosnia, Kosovo, and Mozambique." *Studies in Comparative International Development* 39 (1): 54–76.

Manning, Carrie. 2007. "Party-building on the Heels of War: El Salvador, Bosnia, Kosovo and Mozambique." *Democratization* 14 (2): 253–272.

Manning, Carrie. 2008a. *The Making of Democrats*. New York: Palgrave Macmillan.

Manning, Carrie. 2008b. "Mozambique: RENAMO's Electoral Success." In *From Soldiers to Politicians: Transforming Rebel Movements after Civil War*, edited by Jeroen de Zeeuw, chap. 3. Boulder, CO: Lynne Rienner.

Manning, Carrie. 2008c. "Revolutionaries to Politicians: The Case of Mozambique." In *From Revolutionary Movements to Political Parties: Cases from Latin America and Africa*, edited by Kalowatie Deonandan, David Close, and Gary Prevost. New York: Palgrave Macmillan.

Manning, Carrie, and Ian Smith. 2016. "Political Party Formation by Former Armed Opposition Groups after Civil War." *Democratization* 23 (6): 972–989.

Manning, Carrie, and Ian Smith. 2019. "Electoral Performance by Post-Rebel Parties." *Government and Opposition* 54 (3): 415–453.

Mansfield, Edward D., and Jack Snyder. 1995. "Democratization and the Danger of War." *International Security* 20 (1): 5–38.

March, James G. 1981. "Footnotes to Organizational Change." *Administrative Science Quarterly* 26 (4): 563–577.

March, James G. 1991. "Exploration and Exploitation in Organizational Learning." *Organization Science* 2 (1): 71–87.

Marshall, Michael Christopher. 2019. "Foreign Rebel Sponsorship: A Patron-Client Analysis of Party Viability in Elections Following Negotiated Settlements." *Journal of Conflict Resolution* 63 (2): 555–584.

Marshall, Michael Christopher, and John Ishiyama. 2016. "Does Political Inclusion of Rebel Parties Promote Peace after Conflict?" *Democratization* 23 (6): 1009–1025.

Martin, David, and Phyllis Johnson. 1986. "Mozambique: To Nkomati and Beyond." In *Destructive Engagement: Southern Africa at War*, edited by Phyllis Johnson and David Martin, chap. 1. Harare: Zimbabwe Publishing House.

Martin, Philip A., Giulia Piccolino, and Jeremy S. Speight. 2022. "The Political Legacies of Rebel Rule: Evidence from a Natural Experiment in Cote d'Ivoire." *Comparative Political Studies* 55 (9): 1439–1470.

Matanock, Aila. 2012. "International Insurance: Why Militant Groups and Governments Compete with Ballots Instead of Bullets." PhD diss. Stanford University, Palo Alto, CA.

Matanock, Aila. 2016. "Using Violence, Seeking Votes: Introducing the Militant Group Electoral Participation (MGEP) Dataset." *Journal of Peace Research* 53 (6): 845–863.

Matanock, Aila. 2017a. "Bullets for Ballots: Electoral Participation Provisions and Enduring Peace after Civil Conflict." *International Security* 41 (4): 93–132.

Matanock, Aila. 2017b. *Electing Peace: From Civil Conflict to Political Participation*. Cambridge: Cambridge University Press.

Matanock, Aila. 2018. "External Engagement: Explaining the Spread of Electoral Participation Provisions in Civil Conflict Settlements." *International Studies Quarterly* 62 (3): 656–670.

Matanock, Aila, and Paul Staniland. 2018. "How and Why Armed Groups Participate in Elections." *Perspectives on Politics* 16 (3): 710–727.

May, Rachel A., Alejandro Schneider, and Roberto González Arana. 2018. *Caribbean Revolutions: Cold War Armed Movements*. New York: Cambridge University Press.

Maynard, Jonathan Leader. 2019. "Ideology and Armed Conflict." *Journal of Peace Research* 56 (5): 635–649.

McAdam, Doug, Sidney Tarrow, and Charles Tilly. 2001. *Dynamics of Contention*. Cambridge Studies in Contentious Politcs. New York: Cambridge University Press.

McClintock, Cynthia. 1998. *Revolutionary Movements in Latin America: El Salvador's FMLN & Peru's Shining Path*. Washington, DC: United States Institute of Peace Press.

Miles, Sarah, and Bob Ostertag. 1991. "The FMLN: New Thinking." In *A Decade of War: El Salvador Confronts the United States*, edited by Anjali Sundaram and George Gelber, 216–246. New York: Monthly Review.

Minkoff, Debra C. 1999. "Bending with the Wind: Strategic Change and Adaptation by Women's and Racial Minority Organizations." *American Journal of Sociology* 104 (6): 1666–1703.

Mintzberg, Henry. 1979. *The Structuring of Organizations*. New York: Pearson.

Mitton, Kieran. 2008. "Engaging Disengagement: The Political Reintegration of Sierra Leone's Revolutionary United Front: Analysis." *Conflict, Security & Development* 8 (2): 193–222.

Monsma, S. V. 1996. *When Sacred and Secular Mix: Religious Nonprofit Organizations and Public Money*. Lanham, MD: Rowman and Littlefield.

Montgomery, Tommie Sue. 1995. *Revolution in El Salvador: From Civil Strife to Civil Peace*. 2nd ed. Boulder, CO: Westview Press.

Morgan, Glenda. 1990. "Violence in Mozambique: Towards an Understanding of Renamo." *Journal of Modern African Studies* 28 (4): 603–619.

Moro, Francesco N. 2017. "Organizing Emotions and Ideology in Collective Armed Mobilization." *PS: Political Science and Politics* 50 (4): 944–947.

Muggah, Robert, and Chris O'Donnell. 2015. "Next Generation Disarmament, Demobilization and Reintegration." *Stability* 4 (1): 1–12.

Nelson, Richard R., and Sidney G. Winter. 1982. *An Evolutionary Theory of Economic Change*. Cambridge, MA: Harvard University Press.

Norris, Pippa. 2008. *Driving Democracy: Do Power-Sharing Institutions Work?* Cambridge: Cambridge University Press.

O'Donnell, Guillermo A., and Philippe C. Schmitter. 1986. *Transitions from Authoritarian Rule: Tentative Conclusions about Uncertain Democracies*. Baltimore: Johns Hopkins University Press.

Ohmura, Hirotaka. 2018. "Natural Resources and the Dynamics of Civil War Duration and Outcome." *Asian Journal of Comparative Politics* 3 (2): 133–148.

Olson, David M. 1998. "Party Formation and Party System Consolidation in the New Democracies of Central Europe." *Political Studies* (XLVI):432–464.

Orero, Eudald Cortina. 2016. "Redes Militantes y Solidaridad con El Salvador: Una Aproximación desde la Comunicacion Insurgente." *Nuevo Mundo Mundos Nuevos*, October 10. http://journals.openedition.org/nuevomundo/69645.

Padgett, John, and Walter Powell. 2012. "The Problem of Emergence." In *The Emergence of Organizations and Markets*, 1–30. Princeton, NJ: Princeton University Press.

Paige, Jeffrey M. 1997. *Coffee and Power: Revolution and the Rise of Democracy in Central America*. Cambridge, MA: Harvard University Press.

Palmer-Rubin, Brian. 2019. "Evading the Patronage Trap: Organizational Capacity and Demand Making in Mexico." *Comparative Political Studies* 52 (13–14): 2097–2134.

Panebianco, Angelo. 1988. *Political Parties: Organization and Power*. Cambridge: Cambridge University Press.

Parkinson, Sarah E. 2013. "Organizing Rebellion: Rethinking High-Risk Mobilization and Social Networks in War." *American Political Science Review* 107 (3): 418–432.

Parkinson, Sarah E. 2016. "Money Talks: Discourse, Networks, and Structure in Militant Organizations." *Perspectives on Politics* 14 (4): 976–994.

Parkinson, Sarah E. 2021. "Practical Ideology in Militant Organizations." *World Politics* 73 (1): 52–81.

Parkinson, Sarah E. 2022. *Beyond the Lines: Social Networks and Palestinian Militant Organizations in Wartime Lebanon*. Ithaca, NY: Cornell University Press.

Parkinson, Sarah E., and Sherry Zaks. 2018. "Militant and Rebel Organization(s)." *Comparative Politics* 50 (2): 271–293.

PCS. 1991. *Resoluciones Núcleo con CP*. Memorandum. David Spencer Collection, box 4, folder 4.9. Hoover Institution Library & Archives, Palo Alto, CA.

PCS. 1993. *Informe del CC al VIII Congreso del PCS*. Comunicado Item 3819. Centro de Documentación de los Movimientos Armados, Valencia, Spain.

Pearce, Jenny. 1986. *Promised Land: Peasant Rebellion in Chalatenango, El Salvador*. London: Latin America Bureau.

Pearlman, Wendy. 2011. *Violence, Nonviolence, and the Palestinian National Movement*. New York: Cambridge University Press.

Peters, Krijn. 2006. "Footpaths to Reintegration: Armed Conflict, Youth and the Rural Crisis in Sierra Leone." PhD diss. Wageningen University, Wageningen, Netherlands.

Peters, Krijn. 2011. *War and the Crisis of Youth in Sierra Leone*. New York: Cambridge University Press.

Petersen, Roger D. 2001. *Resistance and Rebellion: Lessons from Eastern Europe*. Cambridge: Cambridge University Press.

Petterson, Therese. 2023. UCDP/PRIO Armed Conflict Dataset Codebook v 23.1. Codebook Uppsala Conflict Data Program. Centre for the Study of Civil Wars, Oslo, Norway.

Pierson, Paul. 2000. "Increasing Returns, Path Dependence, and the Study of Politics." *APSR* 94:251–268.

PRTC. 1992. *Entrevista a Oscar Miranda, de la Comisión Política del PRTC*. Interview Item 4792. Centro de Documentacion de los Movimientos Armados, Valencia, Spain.

PRTC. n.d. (early 1980s). "Sobre el Plan de Contrainsurgencia." Nidia Díaz Papers, box 1. Hoover Institution Library & Archives, Palo Alto, CA.

PRTC. n.d.a. *Ficha de Control de Militares y Candidatos del PRTC*. Technical report. Nidia Díaz Papers, box 1, folder 1, Hoover Institution Library & Archives, Palo Alto, CA.

PRTC. n.d.b. *Incomplete Document: Section "Principios Basicos."* Technical report. Nidia Díaz Papers, box 1, folder 2. Hoover Institution Library & Archives, Palo Alto, CA.

PRTC. n.d.c. *Sugerencias a la Estructura y Funcionamiento del Partido en Región M*. Internal documentation. Nidia Díaz Papers, box 1, folder 3, Hoover Institution Library & Archives, Palo Alto, CA.

Pugh, D. S. 1973. "The Measurement of Organization Structures: Does Context Determine Form?" *Organizational Dynamics* 1 (4): 19–34.

Ramos, Carlos Guillermo, Roberto Oswaldo López, and Aída Carolina Quinteros. 2015. *The FMLN and Post-War Politics in El Salvador: From Included to Inclusive Actor?* Technical Report 14. Berlin: Berghoff Conflict Research.

Ramzipoor, Evan Roxanna. 2015. "Pressing the Attack: The Strategic Function of Underground Literature." Master's thesis, University of California, Berkeley.

Rashid, Ishmail. 1997. "Subaltern Reactions: Lumpens, Students, and the Left." *Africa Development* 22 (3/4): 19–43.

Reno, Paul, and James Vincent. 2008. "Sierra Leone: Marginilization of the RUF." In *From Soldiers to Politicians: Transforming Rebel Movements ater Civil War*, edited by Jeroen de Zeeuw, chap. 4. Boulder, CO: Lynne Rienner.

Reno, William. 2004. "The Collapse of Sierra Leone and the Emergence of Multiple States Within States." In *States Within States: Incipient Political Entities in the Post-Cold War Era*, edited by Paul Kingston and Ias Spears, chap. 3. Gordonsville, VA: Palgrave Macmillan.

Reno, William. n.d. "Predatory Rebellions and Governance: The National Patriotic Front of Liberia, 1989–1992." In *Rebel Governance in Civil War*, edited by Ana Arjona, Nelson Kasfir, and Zachariah Cherian Mampilly, chap. 13. New York: Cambridge University Press.

Resistencia Nacional. 1975. *Balance Auto-Crítico 1975–1976: Resistencia Nacional (R.N.)*. Comunicado Centro de Información, Documentación, y Apoyo a la Investigación: Biblioteca Florentino Idoate de la UCA, San Salvador, El Salvador.

Roberts, Kenneth M. 2016. "Historical Timing, Political Cleavages, and Party-Building in Latin America." In *Challenges of Party-Building in Latin America*, edited by Steven Levitsky, James Loxton, Brandon Van Dyck, and Jorge I. Domínguez, chap. 2. New York: Cambridge University Press.

Rochlin, Gene I., Todd R. La Porte, and Karlene H. Roberts. 1987. "The Self-Designing High-Reliability Organization: Aircraft Carrier Flight Operations at Sea." *U.S. Naval War College Review* 40, no. 4 (Autumn): 76–92.

Rudolph, Rachael M. 2008. "The Islamic Resistance Movement in Palestine (Hamas): A Successful Transition, but Will It Survive?" In *From Terrorism to Politics*, edited by Anisseh Van Engeland and Rachael M. Rudolph, chap. 5. Abingdon, UK: Ashgate.

Sarta, Andrew, Rodolphe Durand, and Jean-Philippe Vergne. 2021. "Organizational Adaptation." *Journal of Management* 47 (1): 43–75.

Sartori, Giovanni. 1970. "Concept Misformation in Comparative Politics." *American Political Science Review* 64 (4): 1033–1053.

Sartori, Giovanni. 1976. *Parties and Party Systems: A Framework for Analysis*. New York: Cambridge University Press.

Saul, Jack. 2013. *Collective Trauma, Collective Healing: Promoting Community Resilience in the Aftermath of Disaster*. New York: Routledge.

Savage, Tyrone, and Joseph Rahall. 2003. "Sierra Leone: History Hidden by Horror." In *Through Fire with Water: The Roots of Division and the Potential for Reconciliation in Africa*, edited by Erik Doxtader and Charles Villa-Vicencio, chap. 2. Capetown, South Africa: Africa World Press.

Schattschneider, E. E. 1942. *Party Government*. New York: Farrar & Rinehart.

Schonfeld, William R. 1983. "Review: Political Parties: The Functional Approach and Structural Alternative." *Comparative Politics* 15 (4): 477–499.

Schubiger, Livia Isabella, and Matthew Zelina. 2017. "Ideology in Armed Groups." *PS: Political Science and Politics* 50 (4): 948–952.

Schwartz, Stephanie. 2019. "Home, Again: Refugee Return and Post-Conflict Violence in Burundi." *International Security* 44 (2): 110–145.

Scott, W. Richard. 2003. *Organizations: Rational, Natural, and Open Systems*. 5th ed. New York: Pearson College Division.

Scott, W. Richard, and Gerald F. Davis. 2007. *Organizations and Organizing Rational, Natural, and Open Systems Perspectives*. New York: Routledge.

Secretario Central de PRTC. n.d. *Linea de Trabajo Politico de Expanción*. Internal communique for the commission on organization. Nidia Díaz Papers. Hoover Institution Library & Archives, Palo Alto, CA.

Selznick, Philip. 1952. *The Organizational Weapon: A Study of Bolshevik Strategy and Tactics*. New York: McGraw-Hill.

Sesay, Amadu, and Charles Ukeje. 2009. *Post-War Regimes and State Reconstructure in Liberia and Sierra Leone*. Dakar, Senegal: Codesria.

Sewell, William H. 1992. "A Theory of Structure: Duality, Agency, and Transformation." *American Journal of Sociology* 98 (1): 1–29.

Shefter, Martin. 1977. "Party and Patronage: Germay, England, and Italy." *Politics and Society* 7 (4): 403–451.

Shugart, Matthew Soberg. 1992. "Guerrillas and Elections: An Institutionalist Perspective on the Costs of Conflict and Competition." *International Studies Quarterly* 36 (2): 121–151.

Silverstein, Ken. 2007. "Parties of God: The Bush Doctrine and the Rise of Islamic Democracy." *Harper's Magazine* (March):33–44.

Sindre, Gyda M. 2016a. "In Whose Interests? Former Rebel Parties and Ex-Combatant Interest Group Mobilisation in Aceh and East Timor." *Civil Wars* 18 (2): 192–213.

Sindre, Gyda M. 2016b. "Internal Party Democracy in Former Rebel Parties." *Party Politics* 22 (4): 501–511.

Sindre, Gyda M. 2018. "From Secessionism to Regionalism: Intra-Organizational Change and Ideological Moderation within Armed Secessionist Movements." *Political Geography* 64:23–32.

Sinno, Abdulkader H. 2010. *Organizations at War in Afghanistan and Beyond*. Ithaca, NY: Cornell University Press.

Skocpol, Theda. 1979. *States and Social Revolutions: A Comparative Analysis of France, Russia and China*. Cambridge, MA: Cambridge University Press.

Söderberg Kovacs, Mimmi. 2007. "From Rebellion to Politics: The Transformation of Rebel Groups to Political Parties in Civil War Peace Processes." PhD diss. Uppsala University, Uppsala, Sweden.

Söderberg Kovacs, Mimmi, and Sophia Hatz. 2016. "Rebel-to-Party Transformations in Civil War Peace Processes, 1975–2011." *Democratization* 23 (6): 990–1008.

Söderström, Johanna. 2013. "Second Time Around: Ex-Combatants at the Polls in Liberia." *Journal of Modern African Studies* 51 (3): 409–433.

Söderström, Johanna. 2016. "The Resilient, the Remobilized and the Removed: Party Mobilization among Former M19 Combatants." *Civil Wars* 18 (2): 214–233.

Somers, Scott. 2009. "Measuring Resilience Potential: An Adaptive Strategy for Organizational Crisis Planning." *Journal of Contingencies and Crisis Management* 17 (1): 12–23.

Spence, Jack. 1997. *Post-War Transitions: Elections and Political Parties in El Salvador and Nicaragua*. Guadalajara, Mexico: Latin American Studies Association Congress.

Sprenkels, Ralph. 2018. *After Insurgency: Revolution and Electoral Politics in El Salvador*. Notre Dame, IN: Notre Dame Press.

Staniland, Paul. 2012. "Between a Rock and a Hard Place: Insurgent Fratricide, Ethnic Defection, and the Rise of Pro-State Paramilitaries." *Journal of Conflict Resolution* 56 (1): 16–40.

Staniland, Paul. 2014. *Networks of Rebellion: Explaining Insurgent Cohesion and Collapse*. Cornell Studies in Security Affairs. Ithaca, NY: Cornell University Press.

Staniland, Paul. 2021. *Ordering Violence: Explaining Armed Group-State Relations from Conflict to Cooperation*. Ithaca, NY: Cornell University Press.

Statistical Abstract of Latin America. 1987. Technical report. Los Angeles, CA: UCLA Center for Latin American Studies.

Stedman, Stephen John. 1997. "Spoiler Problems in Peace Processes." *International Security* 22 (2): 5–53.

Stewart, Megan A. 2018. "Civil War as State-Making: Strategic Governance in Civil War." *International Organization* 72 (1): 205–226.

Stewart, Megan A. 2021. *Governing for Revolution: Social Transformation in Civil War*. Cambridge: Cambridge University Press.

Stinchcombe, Arthur L. (1965) 2013. "Social Structure and Organizations." In *Handbook of Organizations*, edited by James G. March, 142–193. New York: Routledge.

Suazo, Adan E. 2013. "Tools of Change: Long-Term Inclusion in Peace Processes." *PRAXIS: The Fletcher Journal of Human Security* 28:5–27.

Sutcliffe, Kathleen M., and Timothy J. Vogus. 2003. "Organizing for Resilience." In *Positive Organizational Scholarship*, edited by J. E. Dutton and D. M. Quinn, 94–110. San Francisco: Berrett Koehler.

Suykens, Bert. 2015. "Comparing Rebel Rule through Revolution and Naturalization: Ideologies of Governance in Naxalite and Naga India." In *Rebel Governance in Civil War*, edited by Ana Arjona, Nelson Kasfir, and Zachariah Cherian Mampilly. New York: Cambridge University Press.

Svolik, Milan. 2008. "Authoritarian Reversals and Democratic Consolidation." *American Political Science Review* 102 (2): 1–16.

Svåsand, Lars. 1994. "Change and Adaptation in Norwegian Party Organizations." In *How Parties Organize: Change and Adaptation in Party Organizations in Western Democracies*, edited by Richard S. Katz and Peter Mair, 304–331. Thousand Oaks, CA: Sage.

Tan, Vaughn. 2020. *The Uncertainty Mindset: Innovation Insights from the Frontiers of Food*. New York: Columbia University Press.

Tarrow, Sidney. 1998. *Power in Movement: Social Movements and Contentious Politics*. New York: Cambridge University Press.

Thaler, Kai M. 2012. "Ideology and Violence in Civil Wars: Theory and Evidence from Mozambique and Angola." *Civil Wars* 14 (4): 546–567.

Themnér, Anders. 2015. "Former Military Networks and the Micro-Politics of Violence and Statebuilding in Liberia." *Comparative Politics* 47 (3): 334–353.

UNSC (United Nations Security Council). 1992. *Chapúltepec Peace Agreement*. Number A/46/864. Mexico City: United Nations. https://peaceaccords.nd.edu/wp-content/accords/Chapultepec_Peace_Agreement_16_January_1992.pdf.

UNSC (United Nations Security Coucil), ed. 1999. *Peace Agreement between the Government of the Republic of Sierra Leone and the Revolutionary United Front of Sierra Leone*. Number S/1999/777. Lomé: United Nations.

Uppsala Conflict Data Program. UCD Definitions. https://www.uu.se/en/department/peace-and-conflict-research/research/ucdp/ucdp-definitions. Accessed November 21, 2024.

Van Biezen, Ingrid. 2005. "On the Theory and Practice of Party Formation and Adaptation in New Democracies." *European Journal of Political Research* 44:147–174.

Ventura, Miguel. 1990. "El Salvador: The Church of the Poor and the Revolution." *Challenge* 1 (2): 8–11.

Vigil, José Ignacio López. 1991. *Rebel Radio: The Story of El Salvador's Radio Venceremos*. Translated by Mark Fried. Willimantic, CT: Curbstone Press.

Villalobos, Joaquín. 1981. "Acerca de la Situacion Militar en El Salvador." In *Cuadernos Politicos,* no. 30 (October–December): 85–101.

Villalobos, Joaquín. 1986. *El Estado Actual de la Guerra y Sus Perspectivas.* Madrid: Textos Breves.

Villalobos, Joaquín. 1989. *El Salvador Ingovernable: Entrevista a Joaquín Villalobos.* El Salvador: Editorial Sistema Venceremos.

Villalobos, Joaquín. 1993. "Discurso de Joaquín Villalobos en el Acto de Cierre del Primer Congreso del PRS-ERP." FMLN San Salvador, El Salvador.

Vines, Alex. 1991. *Renamo: Terrorism in Mozambique.* Bloomington: Indiana University Press.

Viterna, Jocelyn. 2013. *Women in War: The Micro-processes of Mobilization in El Salvador.* New York: Oxford University Press.

Vogus, Timothy J., and Kathleen M. Sutcliffe. 2007. "Organizational Resilience: Towards a Theory and Research Agenda." In *IEEE International Conference on Systems, Man and Cybernetics,* 3418–3422. IEEE.

Von Clausewitz, Carl. (1832) 1976. *On War.* Princeton, NJ: Princeton University Press.

Wade, Christine. 2008. "El Salvador: The Success of the FMLN." In *From Soldiers to Politicians: Transforming Rebel Movements after Civil War,* edited by Jeroen de Zeeuw, chap. 2. Boulder, CO: Lynne Rienner.

Wade, Christine J. 2018. "El Salvador: Civil War to Uncivil Peace" In *Latin American Politics and Development,* edited by Harvey E. Kline, Christine J. Wade, and Howard J. Wiarda, chap 22. 9th ed. New York: Routledge

Walter, Knut, and Philip J. Williams. 1993. "The Military and Democratization in El Salvador." *Journal of Interamerican Studies and World Affairs* 35 (1): 39–88.

Wantchekon, Leonard, and Zvika Neeman. 2002. "A Theory of Post–Civil War Democratization." *Journal of Theoretical Politics* 4 (14): 439–464.

Waterhouse, Rachel, and Gil Lauriciano. 1993. "Mozambique Peace Process Bulletin." *European Parliamentarians for Southern Africa,* no. 3 (June).

Weinstein, Jeremy M. 2002. *The Structure of Rebel Organizations: Implications for Post-Conflict Reconstruction.* Technical Report 4. Washington, DC: World Bank.

Weinstein, Jeremy M. 2007. *Inside Rebellion: The Politics of Insurgent Violence.* New York: Cambridge University Press.

Wickham-Crowley, Timothy P. 1987. "The Rise (and Sometimes Fall) of Guerrilla Governments in Latin America." *Sociological Forum* 2 (3): 473–499.

Wickham-Crowley, Timothy P. 2015. "Del Gobierno de Abajo al Gobierdo de Arriba . . . and back: Transitions to and from Rebel Governance in Latin America, 1956–1990." In *Rebel Governance in Civil War,* edited by Ana Arjona, Nelson Kasfir, and Zachariah Cherian Mampilly, chap. 3. New York: Cambridge University Press.

Wildavsky, Aaron. 1988. *Searching for Safety.* New Brunswick, NJ: Transaction Publishers.

Wood, Elisabeth Jean. 2000. *Forging Democracy from Below: Insurgent Transitions in South Africa and El Salvador.* Cambridge: Cambridge University Press.

Wood, Elisabeth Jean. 2001. *Forging Democracy from Below: Insurgent Transitions in South Africa and El Salvador.* Cambridge: Cambridge University Press.

Wood, Elisabeth Jean. 2003. *Insurgent Collective Action and Civil War in El Salvador.* Cambridge: Cambridge University Press.

Wood, Reed M., and Jakana L. Thomas. 2017. "Women on the Frontline." *Journal of Peace Research* 54 (1): 31–46.

Wruck, Karen Hopper, and Michael Jensen. 1994. "Science, Specific Knowledge, and Total Quality Management." *Journal of Accounting and Economics* 18 (3): 247–287.

Zaks, Sherry. 2017. "Relationships among Rivals (RAR): A Framework for Analyzing Contending Hypotheses in Process-Tracing." *Political Analysis* 25 (3): 344–362.

Zaks, Sherry. 2024. "Do We Know It When We See It? (Re)-Conceptualizing Rebel-to-Party Transformation." *Journal of Peace Research* 61 (2): 246–262.

Zaks, Sherry. 2025. "Repurposing Rebellion: Building Rebel Successor Parties on the Heels of War?" *European Journal of International Relations* (forthcoming).

Zielinski, Jakub. 2002. "Translating Social Cleavages into Party Systems." *World Politics* 54:184–211.

Index